JANE AUSTEN AND THE MORALITY OF CONVERSATION

Anthem Nineteenth Century Studies

Series Editor: Robert Douglas-Fairhurst

JANE AUSTEN AND THE MORALITY OF CONVERSATION

Bharat Tandon

Anthem Press

This edition first published by Anthem Press 2003

Anthem Press is an imprint of
Wimbledon Publishing Comapny
75–76 Blackfriars Road
London SE1 0HX

British Library Cataloguing in Publication Data
Data available

Library of Congress Cataloging in Publication Data
A catalog record has been applied for

1 3 5 7 9 10 8 6 4 2

ISBN 1 84331 101 1 (hbk)
ISBN 1 84331 102 X (pbk)

Typeset by Regent Typesetting, London

For Max and Leela

and in memory of

KRISHNA KUMAR TANDON
1931–1978

and

WILBUR SANDERS
1936–2002

Great consequences, like great folks, are generally attended and even *made* great by small causes, and little incidents.

Samuel Richardson, *Clarissa*

The same words (e.g. a man says to his wife: 'I love you') can be commonplace or extraordinary according to the manner in which they are spoken. And this manner depends on the depth of the region in a man's being from which they proceed without the will being able to do anything.

Simone Weil, *Gravity and Grace*

No metaphysical Iron Curtain exists compelling us to be for ever absolute strangers to one another, though ordinary circumstances, along with some deliberate management, serve to maintain a reasonable aloofness. Similarly no metaphysical looking-glass exists compelling us to be for ever completely disclosed and explained to ourselves, though from the everyday conduct of our sociable and unsociable lives we learn to be reasonably conversant with ourselves.

Gilbert Ryle, *The Concept of Mind*

CONTENTS

LIST OF PLATES

LIST OF FIGURES

ACKNOWLEDGEMENTS

This book has been a long time in the making, and I have, in the course of its writing, racked up many debts, intellectual, financial and emotional. Under these circumstances, I hope readers will forgive a list of acknowledgements of a length only seen elsewhere in tearful Oscar-acceptance speeches. However, my gratitude to those named below is, I hope, unfeigned.

I am indebted to the Masters and Fellows of Trinity and Selwyn, the two Cambridge Colleges in which this book was conceived, and of Emmanuel, where it was completed. The Cambridge English Faculty offered me the chance to give a course of lectures on Jane Austen, which contributed signally to the development of this book; more recently, Mary Jacobus invited me to give a lecture on space in *Persuasion*, the traces of which can be found in Chapter 4. This chapter also borrows from my essay 'Singing the Sofa: *Mansfield Park* and William Cowper', in Fiona L Price and Scott Masson, eds, *Silence, Sublimity, and Suppression in the Romantic Period* (Lewiston, Queenston & Lampeter: Mellen Press, 2002). I owe a great debt of gratitude to the editorial staff of *The Times Literary Supplement* past and present, in particular to Lindsay Duguid, Ferdinand Mount and Peter Stothard, for the books (many of them on Austen) which they have asked me to review for them over the last decade.

Many people have been generous with advice, criticism, help and support during and after my doctoral research, and during the preparation of this book. I should like to extend my especial thanks to the following: Eleanor Babb, Mazzi Binaisa, Gila and Luke Boucher, Andrea Brady, Joe Bray, Pat Byrne, Owen and Trish Cameron, David Chirico, Cyrus and Jean Chothia, Philip Connell, Tom Cornford, Natalie Davies, Sandra Davies, Akane and Paul Davis, Robert Douglas-Fairhurst, Kendal Gaw, Katherine Gerson, Karen Glossop, Nigel Green, Chris Greenwood, Eric Griffiths, Miriam Handley, Margaret Hay, Anne Henry, Tim Holmes, Simon James, Freya Johnston, Ewan Jones, Siân Jones, Tom Jones, Liz Kalton, David Knight, Claudia Levi, Robert Macfarlane, Mark Manning, the late Jeremy Maule, Lizzie Muller, Stella Pendrous, Adrian Poole, Peter Poole-Wilson, Fiona

Price, Angela Rafferty, Sophie Ratcliffe, Katie Ray, Antonia Robinson, Natasha Rulyova, Corinna Russell, Jenny Sanders, Mike Sewell, Darren Sharma, Adam Smith, David Smith, John and Patricia Stead, Keith Stretten, John Sutherland, Keston Sutherland, Mini Tandon, Kate Thornton, James Thraves, Michael Tilby, and Philip West.

Tom Penn, Noel McPherson and all at Anthem Press have been accommodating, encouraging and patient while I prepared the final version of this book; I thank them for their faith.

I have also been lucky enough to supervise some excellent student dissertations on Jane Austen, which have in turn enriched my own appreciation of the novels; in particular, those by Saskia Burrowes, Fiona Challacombe, Stephanie Cross, Katie Halsey, Barney Harkins and Jenni Hibbert.

My greatest debts are to my research supervisor, Susan Fitzmaurice, and to my mother, Dr Asha Tandon.

PREFACE

This book is a study of different ways in which people behave in Jane Austen's fiction, and of different ways in which Austen's fictional language behaves towards them, and towards its readers. To that end, it centres on a close analysis of the resources, techniques and effects of that language, and it is to that extent an exercise in 'literary stylistics'. However, one aim with which I set out was to show ways in which stylistics and narratology are beholden to larger cultural and historical considerations, and, conversely, ways in which close attention to the pragmatics of narrative language is essential for a nuanced understanding of the textures of linguistic and social history.[1] As Hugh Sykes Davies has argued:

> There is no incompatibility, in my view, between linguistic studies and literary criticism. They are, or ought to be, different phases of the same analytic process – complementary, not hostile. For some purposes the one is more effective, for other purposes, the other. There is no good reason why studies which begin with linguistic analysis should not pass into literary criticism, and none why literary criticism should not pass into linguistics. Indeed they should do so. Linguistic studies, especially of texts of great literary quality, cannot afford to stop short of that deeper analysis of thought and feeling which the words themselves serve to convey. And literary critics cannot afford to be ignorant of all that linguistic study can tell them about the words themselves.[2]

Austen is often considered to be a 'comedian of manners'; I have tried to explore some less familiar implications of this apparent truism. My central argument in this book is that Austen's fiction goes beyond simply portraying or reflecting the *moeurs* of Regency England, and engages its readers in experiences of perception, judgement and puzzlement which are in turn measured critically against the good and bad manners displayed by the characters within the stories. In order to explore this topic, I have made use of a variety of sources. The concern, in the eighteenth and early nineteenth centuries, with conversation as a socially cohesive activity, has led me to works on rhetoric and polite conduct; Austen's emphasis on conversation as a complex social performance has made her work fertile ground for the application of the language-use philosophy of Wittgenstein, Austin and Grice; and the 'linguistic turn' in twentieth-century philosophy has in turn nourished a growth of similar interest in the work of historians such as Quentin Skinner and JGA Pocock[3] – the latter of whom has paid much attention to eighteenth-century manners himself. I have also found Geoffrey Hill's borrowing of the term 'contexture' from Hobbes[4] particularly thought-provoking, since it comprehends both the 'context' which literary works breathe and the distinctive 'texture' through which they work upon those circumstances.[5] Since it is one of my aims to suggest potentially fertile over-laps of methodology between these various approaches, I have tried to pitch the critical idiom of the book in such interstices.

Although it begins roughly at the beginning of Austen's career and ends roughly with her late works, this book does not offer a strictly chronological survey of the fiction. I have organized the chapters more around particular concerns addressed by the novels, with the result that the individual works are not all treated at equal length; my apologies to admirers of *Sense and Sensibility*, in particular.

Many serious artists are comedians, a fact frequently registered without amazement by readers; critics can, however, sometimes forget, or feel obliged to ignore, that many artists' 'seriousness' is achieved *in* their comedy, not in spite of it. If nothing else, I hope that this book remembers how funny Jane Austen is.

TEXTUAL NOTE

The long 's' has been silently modernized wherever it occurs. All ellipses, unless enclosed thus in square brackets ('[...]'), are those in the original texts. All references to the *Oxford English Dictionary* (*OED*) are to the two-volume edition (Oxford: Oxford University Press, 1971).

1

THE MORALITY OF
CONVERSATION

The Vortex of Eloquence

> Why, she was a little old maid 'oo'd written 'alf a dozen books about
> a hundred years ago [...] But, as I was sayin', what beat me was
> there was nothin' *to* 'em nor *in* 'em. Nothin' at all, believe me.
>   Humberstall in Rudyard Kipling, 'The Janeites'[1]

Edmund Burke, imperious in his silences, still found it necessary to shout.
One of his most articulate and sympathetic recent defenders, Conor Cruise
O'Brien, has suggested that silences are 'the dark side of the Burkean moon'[2]
– a metaphor in tune with Burke's enduring image as not only eloquent
but magniloquent. Burke might have even been flattered by the felicity of
O'Brien's conceit: as a teenage astronomer, he had enthused about 'System
running into System! and worlds bordering on worlds!'[3] and his mature vision
of an hereditary social cohesion, realized most fully in *Reflections on the
Revolution in France*, gains some of its strength from metaphors of an ordered or
disordered universe. One famous example is Burke's memory of Marie
Antoinette: 'It is now sixteen or seventeen years since I saw the queen of
France, then the dauphiness, at Versailles; and surely never lighted on this
orb, which she hardly seemed to touch, a more delightful vision. I saw her just
above the horizon, decorating and cheering the elevated sphere she just
began to move in, — glittering like the morning-star, full of life, and splendor,
and joy.'[4] When speaking in public, however, Burke was capable of being
elemental in other ways. Fanny Burney watched him at work in the impeachment of Warren Hastings, and found herself almost convinced: 'Yet, at times I
confess, with all that I felt, wished, and thought concerning Mr Hastings, the
whirlwind of his eloquence nearly drew me into its vortex.'[5]

Burney's diary entry registers the impact of Burke's speech in its incongruous but strangely appropriate phrasing. Her attempt to make 'eloquence'
consort with 'whirlwind' and 'vortex' responds to a conjunction of rhetorical
aptitude and gale-force. However, if Burney was almost drawn in by Burke,

Jane Austen's cousin Phila Walter was almost blown away. According to the family records, she certainly heard the proceedings of the impeachment differently:

> They went to the trial one day "and sat from ten till four, complete-
> ly tired; but I had the satisfaction of hearing the celebrated orators -
> Sheridan, Burke, and Fox. The first was so low we could not hear
> him, the second so hot and hasty we could not understand, the third
> was highly superior to either, as we could distinguish every word,
> though not to our satisfaction [...]"[6]

Likewise, RB Sheridan noted of Burke's defence of the parliamentary *status quo*, that he 'attacked W. Pitt in a scream of Passion, and swore Parliament was and always has been precisely what it ought to be.'[7] As many commenta-tors on Burke have remarked, the fact that his writings and speeches 'are on occasion not above theatricality'[8] is itself a part of their design, one which any critic needs to take on board. 'The very strength of his feelings,' notes JT Boulton, is a salient feature of the case he is arguing [...] his emotive prose is the embodiment of the fundamental nature of his thought.'[9] Other distinctive textures of Burkean thinking, such as his scepticism about the self-sufficiency of abstract reason, combine with this emotive force to create the flexible alloy of principles for which he is celebrated.

Even with his eye for the political and aesthetic 'long view', though, Burke could not wholly have foreseen that the *Reflections on the Revolution in France* were to usher in one of the most vituperative slanging-matches in English political history, and that he would be indirectly responsible for works which ranged from the epoch-making to the flimsy – such works as Mary Wollstonecraft's *Vindication of the Rights of Men*, Thomas Paine's *Rights of Man*, and the anony-mous *Wonderful Flights of Edmund the Rhapsodist into the Sublime and Beautiful regions of Fancy, Fiction, Extravagance, and Absurdity, exposed and laughed at.*[10] And inevitably, the tone of the 1790s controversy became steadily more shrill. If Wollstonecraft, writing within a month of Burke's publishing the *Reflections*, could still claim to be reasoning with him as she took him to task:

> It is, Sir, *possible* to render the poor happier in this world, without
> depriving them of the consolation which you gratuitously grant
> them in the next.[11]

such claims of reason themselves came to shrink into formal clearings of the throat, the stock preludes to less restrained forms of invective. The young radical John Thelwall was one of protégés of the linguist John Horne Tooke, that thorn in the establishment's side, and his own political imprisonment no doubt sharpened his animus; in his reply to Burke's *Letter to a Noble Lord*, six years after the *Reflections*, Thelwall claims the '*Sober*' high ground against his '*Seditious and Inflammatory*' opponent; he questions the tendency of political opponents to think 'that there can be nothing virtuous or liberal in the character of any man who is of an opposite principle to themselves,'[12] while still reserving the right to paint Burke as a 'political maniac'.[13] For Burke, too, there came points at which silence was the less honourable course, as when – realising that his unwavering commitment had alienated him even from his own party – he rounded upon the Whigs in a directly theatrical mode, as the embattled King Lear: 'The little dogs and all, Tray, Blanche, and Sweetheart, see, they bark at me!'[14] Theatrical gesture also embellished his silence in the speech of 21 December 1792, described by Cobbett's *Parliamentary History* with a fine eye for the melodramatic stage-direction: '[Here Mr. Burke drew out a dagger which he had kept concealed, and with much vehemence of action threw it to the floor].'[15] One major meeting-place between the languages of literature and political rhetoric at this time was within the vocabularies of outrage and panic; Ian Christie, for example, has remarked on the prevalence of 'myth' in the conduct of late eighteenth-century politics,[16] and Chris Baldick has pointed out that the monster-metaphors so popular in the 1790s pamphlet wars bequeathed in turn a resonant vocabulary to the likes of Mary Shelley.[17]

Placed next to such vituperation and histrionics, exchanges marked by 'much vehemence of action', Austen's comedies of manners can seem to be little more than a case of looking after the pennies and leaving the pounds to look after themselves. Indeed, the novels are not only short on 'vehemence of action', but it could be argued that they are comparatively short on action of any kind (a fact which has not deterred film and television directors).[18] It is against the background of these contextures and constraints that I shall explore the central role played in Jane Austen's art by her creative ear for familiar and familial conversation. In her novels, conversation is not simply a vehicle for abstract content, nor is it just 'an appropriate morally objective ground against which character can be judged'.[19] Fittingly for a writer so attuned to pitch and attitude, conversation is in Austen less a technique than a constitutive atmosphere of her work. Growing up at the end of a century in which much had been hoped for and feared from the practices of talk and manners, Austen bore personal and aesthetic witness to a culture of 'polite' conversation which was increasingly feeling the weight of linguistic and social diffusion, and which could no longer take much for granted about what that conversation might represent or achieve. But this potential for confusion is where her writing takes its cue, and finds its voice.

The Reformation of Manners

At the end of Chapter V of *Northanger Abbey*, Austen's knowing narrator looks back to earlier writers as she[20] mounts her defence of novels:

> there seems almost a general wish of decrying the capacity and undervaluing the labour of the novelist, and of slighting the performances which have only genius, wit, and taste to recommend them. "I am no novel reader – I seldom look into novels – Do not imagine that *I* often read novels – It is really very well for a novel." – Such is the common cant.— "And what are you reading, Miss — — ?" "Oh! it is only a novel!" replies the young lady; while she lays down her book with affected indifference, or momentary shame.— "It is only Cecilia, or Camilla, or Belinda;' or, in short, only some work in which the greatest powers of the mind are displayed, in which the most thorough knowledge of human nature, the happiest delineation of its varieties, the liveliest effusions of wit and humour are conveyed to the world in the best chosen language. Now, had the same young lady been engaged with a volume of the Spectator, instead of such a work, how proudly would she have produced the book, and told its name; though the chances must be against her being occupied by any part of that voluminous publication, of which either the matter or manner would not disgust a young person of taste: the substance of its papers so often consisting in the statement of improbable circumstances, unnatural characters, and topics of conversation, which no longer concern any one living; and their language, too, frequently so coarse as to give no very favourable idea of the age that could endure it.[21]

The passage is full of jokes, at the expense of those both under- and over-impressed with fiction; but its deepest ironies may not even be intentional ones. One of the joys (and definitions) of being young is that one can readily take earlier generations to task for being coarser and less sophisticated than oneself, without having to bother about one's eventual destiny as a target for someone still younger – this would have added resonance in a novel which 'leave[s] it to be settled by whomsoever it may concern, whether the tendency of this work be altogether to recommend parental tyranny, or reward filial disobedience.'[22] The narrator's defence of fiction, likewise, leaves it to be settled by the reader whether Austen is knowingly pastiching a distinctive feature of *The Tatler* and *The Spectator*, or whether she is unwittingly visiting on Addison and Steele a nineteenth-century version of their own reaction to Restoration manners. Compare, for example, Steele's account of Wycherley's *The Country Wife*, in which 'The Character of *Horner*, and the Design of it, is a good Representation of the Age in which that Comedy was written; at which Time Love and Wenching were the Business of Life, and the Gallant Manner of pursuing Women was the best Recommendation at Court.'[23] That Austen's narrator could talk of *The Spectator* in tones uncannily similar to those in which Addison and Steele once berated their predecessors points to more than the inevitable cycles and displacements of literary history, that process of cultural weathering which Johnson detected in his comment that 'all works which describe manners, require notes in sixty or seventy years';[24] it shows what had happened to a distinctive cluster of ideas and linguistic practices in their transit through the contingencies of a century. A culture of polite conversation, which authors like Shaftesbury, Addison and Steele had hoped to nurture, and in part to create through their writings, is looked back upon in *Northanger Abbey* as something of a relic, a world whose voice is only imperfectly heard and sustained.

Edward and Lillian Bloom have commented on one of *The Spectator*'s central values: 'In an age when conversation was regarded as a refinement of class, not divorced from the ethical, Addison and Steele more successfully than any preceding English writers translated the tone of civilized oral exchange into print. The easy flow of written speech became not only their literary signature but their avowal of communal identity.'[25] This 'communal identity' carried greater weight in the context of the painful histories against which early eighteenth-century polite conversation came to define itself, and the more congenial and cohesive practices with which it sought to replace them. A writer at the beginning of the eighteenth century would have felt the pressure of the two major schisms that had divided English politics and culture in the previous century: the Civil War, and much more recently, the Exclusion Crisis, and the Revolution Settlement of 1688, whose after-effects were still palpable as the literary careers of Addison and Steele began. In such conditions, there would have been a particular appeal in a new mode of 'politeness' and gentlemanly civilization, a discourse of conduct which might replace the perceived factiousness of the past. In *Spectator* 125, for example, Addison has Sir Roger de Coverley, genial relic of the old Tory squires, recall his distant youth:

> My worthy Friend Sir ROGER, when we are talking of the Malice of Parties, very frequently tells us an Accident that happened to him when he was a School-boy, which was at the Time when the Feuds ran high between the Round-heads and Cavaliers. This worthy Knight being then but a Stripling, had Occasion to enquire which

was the Way to St. *Ann*'s Lane, upon which the Person whom he spoke to, instead of answering his Question, called him a young Popish Cur, and asked him who had made *Ann* a Saint? The Boy being in some Confusion, enquired of the next he met, which was the Way to *Ann*'s Lane; but was called a Prick-eared Curr for his Pains; and instead of being shewn the Way was told, that she had been a Saint before he was born, and would be one after he was hang'd. Upon this, says Sir ROGER, I did not think fit to repeat the former Question, but going into every Lane of the Neighbourhood, asked what they called the Name of that Lane. By which ingenious Artifice he found out the Place he enquired after, without giving Offence to any Party.[26]

Sir Roger's age ('now in his Fifty sixth year'[27]), which elsewhere in *The Spectator* serves to mark him as both an ageing man and as one of the 'Old Men' whom the Whig ascendancy and the Protestant succession had come to replace, here offers Addison another advantage: the chance implicitly to connect the two major conflicts of the previous century, as part of his larger argument against that divisiveness which, he suggests, gave rise to them. The excesses of political partisanship may manifest themselves as absurd social prejudice, forcing the young Sir Roger to go 'into every Lane of the Neighbourhood' in order to find one street, but within Addison's sketch, and within his Whig ideology, they tend towards more dangerous conclusions. Musing on Sir Roger's experience, Mr Spectator remarks: 'There cannot be a greater Judgment befall a Country than such a dreadful Spirit of Division as rends a Government into two distinct People, and makes them greater Strangers and more averse to one another, than if they were actually two different Nations [...] A furious Party Spirit, when it rages in its full Violence, exerts it self in Civil War and Blood-shed; and when it is under its greatest Restraints naturally breaks out in Falshood, Detraction, Calumny, and a partial Administration of Justice. In a Word, It fills a Nation with Spleen and Rancour, and extinguishes all the Seeds of Good-nature, Compassion and Humanity'.[28]

'Falshood, Detraction, Calumny [...] Spleen and Rancour' contrasted with 'Good-Nature, Compassion and Humanity': Addison could be drawing up a table of the cardinal virtues and vices of the eighteenth-century mentality for which he and Richard Steele were among the earliest literary spokesmen. In place of the straitened manners and mutually uncomprehending rhetorics which Addison perceived in Restoration England, the new ideal of gentlemanly benevolence offered what Lawrence E Klein has called 'a centripetal rather than centrifugal force';[29] the culture of politeness aimed to transcend old enmities by creating an easy-mannered, clubbable morality, which would

in turn foster intellectual and social progress (these Whig writers thus prac-
tised what is now known as the 'Whig interpretation of history'). Central to
these aims was 'conversation' in its broadest senses – a term whose application, in this period, often blends, or hovers between, the social practices of talk
and the larger '[m]anner of conducting oneself in the world or in society'. Put
simply, conversation was, for Whig writers, not just a descriptive vehicle for
the new culture's civilizing process, but could itself enact that process by
bringing its participants together in the ideal conditions for mutual benefit. As
Pocock observes, 'in the *Spectator* essays, politeness becomes an active civilizing
agent. By observation, conversation, and cultivation, men and women are
brought to an awareness of the needs and responses of others and of how they
appear in the eyes of others; this is not only the point at which politeness
becomes a highly serious practical morality [...] It is also the point at which
Addison begins to comment on the structure of English society and the reconciliation of its diverse "interests".'[30] For Addison, however, this could not be
achieved without some re-mapping of the field in which the morality of conversation could operate, and the terms in which he describes the desired shift
carry particular charges. If, in an increasingly legalistic society, 'manners' had
come to be a deliberately narrowed-down version of the classical virtues,
more fitted to the demands of a modern version of 'civic humanism', much
depended on how one defined these manners, and the particular range of
interests with which one could identify them.

In *Spectator* 119, Addison contrasts manners in the town (since urban and
urbane spaces were becoming identified with Whig commerce) to those in the
country, the natural habitat of Sir Roger and the Tory interest. 'By Manners,'
Mr Spectator claims, 'I do not mean Morals, but behaviour and Good
Breeding, as they shew themselves in the Town and in the Country';[31] he continues with one of the most comprehensive statements of Addison's position
on the aesthetic and ideological values of polite conversation:

> [...] I must observe a very great Revolution that has happened in
> this Article of Good Breeding. Several obliging Deferencies,
> Condescensions and Submissions, with many outward Forms and
> Ceremonies that accompany them, were first of all brought up
> among the politer Part of Mankind who lived in Courts and Cities,
> and distinguished themselves from the Rustick part of the Species
> (who on all Occasions acted bluntly and naturally) by such a mutual
> Complaisance and Intercourse of Civilities. These Forms of Con-
> versation by degrees multiplied and grew troublesome; the Modish
> World found too great a Constraint in them, and have therefore
> thrown most of them aside. Conversation, like the *Romish* Religion,

was so encumbered with Show and Ceremony, that it stood in need of a Reformation to retrench its Superfluities, and restore it to its natural good Sense and Beauty. At present therefore an unconstrained Carriage, and a certain Openness of Behaviour are the height of Good Breeding. The Fashionable World is grown free and easie; our Manners, sit more loose upon us: Nothing is so modish as an agreeable Negligence. In a word, Good Breeding shows it self most, where to an ordinary Eye it appears the least.[32]

One need not dig too deep into Addison's suggestive employment of 'a very great Revolution' and 'a Reformation' to recognize the ends to which he turns the language of politeness; indeed, his implication is so direct that it can hardly be described as a 'subtext'. For Addison, the culture of conversation both embodies and legitimizes the Revolution Settlement of 1688, and its associated Protestant succession, substituting 'an unconstrained Carriage, and a certain Openness of Behaviour' for that 'Show and Ceremony' which he sees at work in the time of James II; in addition, this political allegiance is implicitly naturalized by association with 'natural good Sense and Beauty', a point made even sharper by the fact that after Harley's rise to power in August 1710, Addison and Steele were now distanced from the centres of influence.[33] The naturalization of Whig aesthetics and politics renders into a more practical, less philosophically aristocratic idiom the ideas which run consistently through Shaftesbury's *Characteristics*, first published in their collected form in 1711, the year in which *The Spectator* began. In 'Soliloquy, or Advice to an Author', for example, Shaftesbury strikes a fundamental note in the philosophy of polite Whiggism when he asserts that 'in our nation, upon the foot things stand and as they are likely to continue, it is not difficult to foresee that improvements will be made in every art and science';[34] 'An Inquiry Concerning Virtue or Merit' predicates its analysis of natural benevolence on an organic metaphor ('[n]or will anyone deny that this affection of a creature towards the good of the species or common nature is as proper and natural to him as it is to any organ, part, or member of an animal body, or mere vegetable, to work in its known course and regular way of growth'[35]); likewise, in 'Sensus Communis', Shaftesbury praises the Classical dialogue as a model for polite ease, which might offer much to modern thinkers ('It is not to be imagined what advantage the reader has when he can thus cope with his author, who is willing to come on a fair stage with him and exchange the tragic buskin for an easier and more natural gait and habit'[36]). Polite conversation is seen in Shaftesbury as both socially cohesive and politically performative, but the 'ease' which the philosopher recommends is still socially circumscribed, confined to a primarily aristocratic sphere; as Klein notes, '[a]ssuming that post-1688 politics ought to be those of a gentlemanly oligarchy, he proceeded to propose an appropriate culture to support it'.[37]

Addison and Steele, in contrast, make it their business to widen the franchise of polite Whig ideals; indeed, as Johnson remarked, '[b]efore the *Tatler* and *Spectator*, if the writers for the theatre are excepted, England had no masters of common life'.[38] The length, tone, format and price of the *Spectator* numbers enabled them to reach not only gentlemanly Whig oligarchs but the emerging mercantile class on whom the post-1688 ascendancy relied, an opportunity which was not lost on Addison, and which he worked into the fabric and purpose of the introductory essays. *Spectator* 10 promises 'to enliven Morality with Wit, and to temper Wit with Morality',[39] and offers a prospectus for the periodical: 'It was said of *Socrates*, that he brought Philosophy down from Heaven, to inhabit among Men; and I shall be ambitious to have it said of me, that I have brought Philosophy out of Closets and Libraries, Schools and Colleges, to dwell in Clubs and Assemblies, at Tea-Tables, and in Coffee-Houses'.[40] Writing at this particular point in the history of print and readership, Addison and Steele were presented with a felicitous opportunity – the chance at least partly to write their own audience into existence; by pitching *The Spectator* in such a manner as to appeal to 'all well regulated Families', 'the Fraternity of Spectators who live in the World without having any thing to do in it', 'the Blanks of Society', and 'the female World',[41] they managed to create a stage on which the ethics of politeness could be seen, but which also reflected back upon its readers, in that reading *The Spectator* could become not only a literary depiction of polite manners but part of their active practice. The spirit of tolerance to which Addison lays claim evidently suggests the make-up of Mr Spectator's club, which includes the Tory Sir Roger alongside the Whig man of commerce Sir Andrew Freeport, the representative of the 'New Men' who have come to supplant the country squires; the socially and politically ecumenical range of the Club finds an even more persuasive parallel in the conversational geniality of Addison's style.

'His prose,' Johnson wrote of Addison, 'is a model of the middle style; on grave subjects not formal, on light occasions not grovelling; pure without scrupulosity, and exact without apparent elaboration; always equable, and always easy, without glowing words or pointed sentences.'[42] One advantage of a 'middle style', at least in theory, is that since it bears fewer of the inflections of any one class, group or faction, it might seek to navigate the middle ground in the fields of action which it describes; Mr Spectator, himself a wanderer between different social scenes and strata, embodies reconciliation, recommending that 'we should not any longer regard our Fellow-Subjects as Whigs or Tories, but should make the Man of Merit our Friend, and the Villain our Enemy'.[43] Indeed, Addison's later writings make this appeal even more explicit, as when, in *Freeholder* XXXI, he charges his friend, the Tory cleric Francis Atterbury, with having 'omitted the middle Way of Proceeding between these two Extreams':[44] an eighteenth-century precedent for what has now come to be known – not wholly coincidentally – as the rhetoric of 'The Third Way'.[45] Usefully for a writer aiming to convey moral instruction in the form of periodical entertainment, Addison's 'middle style' allows him to embellish general observations on contemporary manners with an eye for humorous and pathetic particulars, a quality which, in the decades following *The Spectator*, came to be identified with the emerging genre of the novel. Aptly enough, this often manifests itself when Addison depicts the comical extremes of party zeal, as in Mr Spectator's recollection of the 'Popish Plot' of 1679–80:

> I remember when Dr. *Titus Oates* was in all his Glory, I accompan-ied my Friend WILL. HONEYCOMB in a Visit to a Lady of his Acquaintance: We were no sooner sat down, but upon casting my Eyes about the Room, I found in almost every Corner of it a Print that represented the Doctor in all Magnitudes and Dimensions. A little after, as the Lady was discoursing my Friend, and held her Snuff-Box in her Hand, who should I see in the Lid of it but the Doctor. It was not long after this, when she had occasion for her Handkerchief, which upon the first opening discovered among the Plaites of it the Figure of the Doctor. Upon this my Friend WILL. who loves Raillery, told her, That if he was in Mr. *Truelove*'s Place (for that was the Name of her Husband) he should be made as uneasie by a Handkerchief as ever *Othello* was. *I am afraid*, said she, *Mr.* HONEYCOMB, *you are a Tory; tell me truly, are you a Friend to the Doctor or not?* WILL. instead of making her a Reply, smiled in her Face (for indeed she was very pretty) and told her that one of her Patches was dropping off. She immediately adjusted it, and looking a little seriously, *Well*, says she, *I'll be hang'd if you and your silent Friend there are not against the Doctor in your Hearts, I suspected as much by his say-ing nothing.* Upon this she took her Fan into her Hand, and upon the opening of it again display'd to us the Figure of the Doctor, who was placed with great Gravity among the Sticks of it.[46]

A memory of a more formal, divided age is rendered by Addison in his easier eighteenth-century mode, measuring one style against another so as to regis-ter the differences: the rigidity of Mrs Truelove's High Church obsession sounds in the repeated references to 'the Doctor', which Addison times in order to make them sound as incongruous in his own sentences as Titus Oates's image is among the woman's domestic furnishings ('placed with great

Gravity among the Sticks'). Excessive zeal is not overtly excoriated, but made instead to look silly, nudged gently in the ribs in the hope of another 'reformation'. However, the genial wit, in which Addison's 'middle style' deals so readily at such moments, also ironically highlights a deeper potential unease within the theory and practice of conversational politeness.

Shaftesbury's defence of the 'Freedom of Wit and Humour' in 'Sensus Communis' is not absolute and unconditional: raillery is useful only when it operates as 'a more lenitive remedy against vice, and a kind of specific against superstition and melancholy delusion'.[47] This idea of humour as in some way therapeutic is characteristic of the language of Whig politeness, and occurs repeatedly in Addison's *Spectator* papers on the aesthetics of wit, and in his later writings ('Raillery is Useless when it has no Moral under it'.[48]) Good wit, for Addison, acts a corollary to polite conversation, and it is one of the duties of Mr Spectator's readers to learn how to distinguish cohesive, progressive humour from its destructive counterfeit: 'I would desire my Readers, when they meet with this Pretender, to look into his Parentage, and to examine him strictly, whether or no he be remotely allied to TRUTH, and lineally descended from GOOD SENSE? if not, they may conclude him a Counter-feit'.[49] Addison's politically loaded definition of true wit (defined in opposition to the 'Pretender' of wasteful humour) bears comparison with Shaftesbury's even more explicit assimilating of humorous 'Freedom' to a Whig order ('wit is its own remedy. Liberty and commerce bring it to its true standard [...] The same thing happens here as in the case of trade. Impositions and restrictions reduce it to a low ebb. Nothing is so advantageous to it as a free port'[50]). In practice, these definitions present a number of problems; if human psychology corresponds to an organic complex of benevolent motives, and wit is only 'true' if it tends to the advancement and progress of those motives, then the scope of wit is confined to what is at best a genial raillery, and at worst a harmless, overly cleanly 'joshing'. Moreover, the demands of polite decency may make demands of a writer which the pressure of circumstances renders untenable – for instance, the imperative of equanimity can leave one straining to sit on a fence which is no longer really there, as Addison discovered when he responded to the Jacobite rebellion of 1715 in *The Freeholder*. One of the sobering fascinations of this later periodical is that it is stylistically close enough to be instantly recognizable as a successor of *The Spectator*, yet far enough removed for a reader to trace back what the earlier work's polite surfaces have clearly only just been keeping in check. 'By the time he wrote the *Freeholder*,' argue Edward and Lillian Bloom, '[...] sensibility and literary elegance had yielded to propagandistic hyperbole'.[51] This is something of an understatement: in *The Freeholder*, a reader has the chance to see Mr Spectator with his gloves off. Addison's treatment of the old order in *The Spectator* is primarily one of tolerant absorption, crystallized in the image of Sir Roger's kindness to his domestic animals – which acts in turn as a metaphor for the way the squire is being treated by his author ('a grey Pad that is kept in the Stable with great Care and Tenderness out of regard to his past Services, tho' he has been useless for several Years'[52]). By the time of *The Freeholder*, however, Addison feels he can no longer extend such courtesy to his opponents, substituting for the kindly rural Tory the coarse, barely literate figure of the Fox-hunter, who 'had learned a great deal of Politicks, but not one Word of Religion, from the Parson of his Parish; and, indeed, that he had scarce any other Notion of Religion, but that it consisted in Hating Presbyterians'.[53] The gently mocking portrait of Mrs Truelove's obsession with Titus Oates is recast in a more vituperative mode, in which party rage is even imagined deforming women's features; Whig ladies 'are much more expert in the Use of their Airs and Graces than their female Antagonists',[54] the strength of whose allegiances, unlike the 'very pretty' Mrs Truelove, seems to turn them ugly: 'The finest Woman, in a Transport of Fury, loses the Use of her Face'.[55] In the light of *The Freeholder*, the claim of *The Spectator* to disinterestedness ('I never espoused any Party with Violence, and am resolved to preserve an exact Neutrality between the Whigs and Tories'[56]) comes to look like an interested manoeuvre itself, as the disavowal of ideology can be one of ideology's smartest moves; an ethics of 'centripetal' conversation is seen straining to accommodate the harsher demands of actual circumstance.

Whatever its attendant problems, however, that vision of conversation as a cohesive activity, which not only displayed but materially advanced the refinement of civilization, had a great tenacity in eighteenth-century writing on the subject, not least within the genre of guides to conversational conduct – works often written in the form of dialogues themselves. In particular, that shift which Addison identifies in *Spectator* 119, from 'outward Forms and Ceremonies' to 'an unconstrained Carriage, and a certain Openness of Behaviour', underpins many writers' recommendations. In *The Conversation of Gentlemen Considered* (1738), for instance, the characters Cleander and Eudoxus find it 'incredible, that nothing should be more practiced, and yet scarce any thing so ill managed as *Conversation*',[57] and, in order to rectify this state of affairs, praise naturalness and ease at the expense of 'superficial and in-digested Notions':[58]

> But alas! the interrupting and contradicting Gentleman, of whom I was speaking, is quite a Stranger to such soft and insinuating ways of leading People into his Opinions. He fancies himself a great Master at Reasoning well, and at Speaking handsomely. He thinks, that his *German* Schemes of Rhetorical Figures, have formed him to

persuasive Eloquence, and his Tables of *Predicables* and *Predicaments*, to close reasoning.[59]

Nearly twenty years later, comparable sentiments are still alive and well in *The Art of Conversation; or, The Polite Entertainer* (1757), in which studied ease ('It is the most difficult Thing in the World to be easy'[60]) is contrasted with the pre-fabricated manners of the dandyish Mr Forward ('There is something more disgustful even than this in his Conversation. You always know what he is going to say before he speaks it'[61]), and the Addisonian 'Third Way' is explicitly endorsed once more ('Changes are frequently made from one Extream to the other: But this will serve to remind you both of stopping in the Midway, and it is there Politeness lies'[62]). In both these instances, however, the writers' disapproval of overly formulaic conversation may also reveal the fear that they, too, might be contributing to it – a possibility implicit in the existence of the writing itself. Peter Burke comments on this paradox, noting that the conversation guides cannot always be taken wholly on their own terms: 'the references to spontaneity of speech [...] are contradicted by the very existence of the treatises as well as their advice to study in order to improve conversational performance. A reading of the texts suggests that a truly general theory of conversation should discuss the tension and the balance between the competitive and cooperative principles, between equality and hierarchy, between inclusion and exclusion, and between spontaneity and study, rather than placing all the weight on the first item in each of these pairs'.[63]

Addison and Steele's former friend and literary collaborator Jonathan Swift would have had particular cause to feel the paradox of politeness when he published *Polite Conversation* in 1738. If, as Alasdair MacIntyre argues, 'the costs of consensus are paid by those excluded from it',[64] Swift stands as a prime example of what the loaded consensus of *The Spectator*'s aesthetic had excluded. As is clear from his *Hints towards an Essay on Conversation* (c.1710), Swift set great store by the power of conversational manners: [t]he two chief Ends of Conversation,' he writes, 'are to entertain and improve those we are among, or to receive those Benefits ourselves [...] when any Man speaketh in Company, it is to be supposed he doth it for his Hearer's Sake, and not his own; so that common Discretion will teach us not to force their Attention, if they are not willing to lend it; nor on the other Side, to interrupt him who is in Possession, because that is in the grossest Manner to give the Preference to our own good Sense'.[65] However, by the time he finally collected and published *Polite Conversation*, the awkward circumstantial ironies of his position meant that he could not wholeheartedly endorse the prevailing views. The primary obstacle in his way was the fact that, as Klein puts it, 'the language of "politeness" had been seized to legitimize those very institutions that Swift thought worked against true politeness';[66] a Tory who believed in the value of polite manners had, therefore, to face an unpalatable possibility – that even his dissent from Whig aesthetics might now have to be couched in the terms which his opponents had made their own. If there is no getting out of this double-bind, however, *Polite Conversation* shows Swift as more than capable of working through it; and this ability to engage creatively with one's own inescapable conditions is one which, as I shall go on to explore in later chapters, is also central to Austen's comic methods. Swift's outstanding comic achievement in *Polite Conversation* is only partly attributable to the actual dialogues, for all their value as what the twentieth-century Swiftian Flann O'Brien came to call a 'Catechism of Cliché':[67]

> *Lady Ans*[werall]. Consider, Mr. *Neverout*, four bare Legs in a Bed; and you are a younger Brother.
> *Col*[onel Atwit]. Well, Madam, the younger Brother is the better Gentleman. However, *Tom*, I would advise you to look before you leap.
> *Lord Sp*[arkish]. The Colonel says true: Besides, you can't expect to wive and thrive in the same Year.
> *Miss* [Notable]. [*Shuddering.*] Lord, there's some Body walking over my Grave.[68]

Where Swift really bites is in his creation of Simon Wagstaff's introduction to the treatise, which patrols the same grey areas, between public-spirited 'projecting' and egotistical smugness, more famously explored in *A Modest Proposal*. In *Spectator* 10, Addison has Mr Spectator recommend his work for general consumption and public utility, as part of a ritual of less metaphorical 'consumption': 'I would therefore in a very particular Manner recommend these my Speculations to all well regulated Families, that set apart an Hour every Morning for Tea and Bread and Butter; and would earnestly advise them for their Good to order this Paper to be punctually served up, and to be looked upon as a Part of the Tea Equipage';[69] *Polite Conversation* teases out the implications of this image and pushes them to their ludicrously logical conclusion. Wagstaff typifies what Swift saw as the Whig appropriation of polite culture's languages and channels; the fictional projector, serenely confident that he is part – perhaps even the most important part – of a civilization which has reached the pinnacle of sophisticated politeness (I have, in Justice to my Country, allowed the Genius of our People to excel that of any other Nation upon Earth'[70]), offers his 'Complete Collection' as a conversational vade mecum for every conceivable situation. But what in *The Spectator* sounds like genteel progressivism is worked by Swift into a scheme of poker-faced absurdity, which could almost come from the Grand Academy of Lagado in *Gulliver's Travels*:

> BUT, before this elaborate Treatise can become of universal Use and Ornament to my native Country, two Points that will require Time and much Application, are absolutely necessary. For first, whatever Person would aspire to be compleatly Witty, Smart, Humorous, and Polite; must by hard Labour be able to retain in his Memory every single Sentence contained in this Work; so as never to be once at a Loss in applying the right Answers, Questions, Repartees, and the like immediately, and without Study or Hesitation.[71]

Conversational wit, figured in Shaftesbury and Addison as a therapeutic, unifying force, is worn down in Wagstaff's project into an cheap cure-all, a box of coarse tricks which can be applied with little or no thought or effort; indeed, it seems at times that one of the purposes of the treatise is precisely to turn wit into a matter of reflex, or of automatism. 'When this happy Art of polite conversing, shall be thoroughly improved,' reasons Wagstaff, 'good Company will be no longer pestered with dull dry tedious Story-tellers, or brangling Disputers. For, a right Scholar of either Sex, in our Science, will perpetually interrupt them with some sudden surprising Piece of Wit, that shall engage all the Company in a loud Laugh; and if, after a Pause, the grave Companion resumes his Thread, in the following Manner; well; but, to go on with my Story; new Interruptions come from the Left and Right, until he be forced to give over.'[72] Within the texture of Swift's comedy, 'projecting' begins to blur into something uncomfortably like prophecy, as Wagstaff, with a suspicious, alliterative fluency ('dull dry', 'sudden surprising'), looks forward to a future so certain, and so predictable, that even spontaneity can be timed in advance ('a right Scholar [...] will perpetually interrupt them with some sudden surprizing Piece of Wit'). If Swift can no longer find a 'polite' vocabulary that has not been commandeered by his opponents, he can in turn take on that language's confidence in such a way as does not inspire confidence in its larger goals; Wagstaff, his cultural snake-oil salesman, exposes, at the level of satire, the thought which shadows other more earnest real-life manuals for conversation: that the manners on which their vision of society depends cannot wholly be insulated from self-defeating mannerism.

Austen, one of the early nineteenth century's most rigorous explorers of morality and conversation, came into the world in 1775, a year later than one of the eighteenth century's most notorious exposures of conversation and its vexed relationship to morality – a work which also looks askance at the identification of manners with artlessness. Addison had set 'Openness of Behaviour' against 'outward Forms and Ceremonies'; by 1756, Chesterfield was already seeking to redefine the terms, and thereby to redraw the social contracts which they described:

> We are accused by the French, and perhaps but too justly, of having no word in our language which answers to their word *police*, which therefore we have been obliged to adopt, not having, as they say, the thing.
> It does not occur to me that we have any one word in our language (I hope not from the same reason) to express the ideas which they comprehend under their word *"les mœurs."* Manners are too little, *morals* too much. I should define it thus; *a general exterior decency, fitness and propriety of conduct in the common intercourse of life.*[73]

Rather than ease, careful and artful management of social surface (*'general exterior decency'*) is the repeated keynote for conduct in Chesterfield's *Letters to His Son*, published in their collected form in 1774. Chesterfield cannot now be wholly separated from Johnson's condemnation of the *Letters* ('they teach the morals of a whore, and the manners of a dancing master'[74]) and from Boswell's qualified concurrence with his judgment ('[t]hat collection of letters cannot be vindicated from the serious charge of [...] recommending, with disproportionate anxiety, a perpetual attention to external elegance of manners'[75]); but the fact that these and other writers were so clearly vexed by the *Letters* and their implications suggests something of Chesterfield's ability to get under the skin of polite morals. Within the Shaftesburian and Addisonian ideals, as I have discussed, genteel conversation polishes rough edges, and ease of manner tends to the participants' mutual benefit; the characteristic mode of Chesterfield is, in contrast, one of *'volto sciolto* and *pensieri stretti*; that is, a frank, open, and ingenuous exterior, with a prudent and reserved interior'.[76] Time and again in advising his natural son, Chesterfield emphasizes that to preserve virtuous appearance is the highest imperative – even when that might seem to conflict with conventional notions of morality:

> I have seldom or never written to you upon the subject of religion and morality; your own reason, I am persuaded, has given you true notions of both; they speak best for themselves; but if they wanted assistance, you have Mr. Harte at hand, both for precept and example; to your own reason, therefore, and to Mr. Harte, shall I refer you, for the reality of both, and confine myself [...] to the decency, the utility, and the necessity of scrupulously preserving the appearances of both.[77]

In a vocabulary thick with references to appearance and viewing ('[c]onsider what lustre and *éclat* it will give you',[78] 'I have Arguses, with an hundred eyes each, who will watch you narrowly'[79]), Chesterfield portrays a world of 'manners' in which to be all things to all men ('*omnis homo, l'homme universel*[80]) is the accomplishment which makes all others workable and pertinent. The charge of immorality is an easy one to level ('[t]ake out the immorality, and it should be put into the hands of every young gentleman,' said Johnson[81]), and it is not wholly unjustified; but it is not one which Chesterfield would have accepted unconditionally. Rather, the *Letters* witness his accommodation to the facts of a world not of his making, which he feels powerless to change: 'The world is taken with the outside of things,' he writes, 'and we must take the world as it is; you and I cannot set it right'.[82] It is under these circumstances that he recommends his son's course of action: 'A man of the world must, like the Cameleon, be able to take every different hue; which is by no means a criminal or abject, but a necessary complaisance; for it relates to manners, and not to morals'.[83] This last distinction may be where Chesterfield is most troubling to the eighteenth-century 'morality of conversation'; in contrast to the likes of Shaftesbury, for whom manners express a 'just disposition or proportionable affection [...] towards the moral objects of right and wrong',[84] and Francis Hutcheson, who assimilates social virtue to a natural '*moral sense*',[85] he challenges the natural, organic basis of those connections. Most worryingly, Chesterfield may be not so much a perversion of polite conversation's hopes, but the logical conclusion of possibilities implicit within the original model; in this, his relationship to his times has parallels with that of Machiavelli to Renaissance Florence – particularly, the perception that while practical tactics 'may sometimes overlap with the conventional virtues, the idea of any necessary or even approximate equivalence between *virtù* and the virtues is a disastrous mistake'.[86]

Austen, with her conservative temperament, had also, in some ways, to 'take the world as it is', in that however irksome she may have found so many of the practices and conventions with which she was surrounded, she was not (unlike Godwin or Shelley) in the business of imagining wholesale alternatives to them; however, much of the rest of this book will be devoted to studying the numerous ways in which her imaginative facing-up to the unavoidable results in works that are creatively exploratory, even at times experimental, rather than quiescent or complacent. If she had to take the world as it was, that did not stop her remaking it in an art which consistently gets the better of situations of which there is no getting rid: as she writes of Henry VI in 'The History Of England' (c.1791), '[i]t was in this reign that Joan of Arc lived & made such a *row* among the English. They should not have burnt her—but they did'.[87] Emma Woodhouse's embarrassed outburst about the significantly named Frank Churchill ('What right had he to come among us with affection and faith engaged, and with manners so *very* disengaged?'[88]) and Knightley's distinction between English 'amiability' and its French counterpart,[89] suggest that Austen may not have looked with approval on Chesterfieldian 'manners', but her fiction recognizes their existence as part of the world with which it has to deal; indeed, one of Chesterfield's letters from 1752 may provide an even earlier source of *Pride and Prejudice*'s title than Burney's *Cecilia*.[90] What is certain is that by the time she began to write fiction in the late 1780s, Austen could not rely on conversational manners as naturally virtuous, binding forces, even as she made dialogue one of her major stylistic and ethical techniques. In between the time of *The Spectator* and that of *Northanger Abbey*, not only had the 'culture of politeness' become more disparate and threatened, bearing diverse and often perverse fruits, but many ideas of how language worked in and upon the world had also changed; therefore, before turning to how Austen began to treat 'the world as it is', I shall trace briefly some shifts in how eighteenth-century writers did things with words.

Words in Action

> Horne Tooke had called his book *Epea Pteroenta*, 'winged words.' In Coleridge's judgment it might have been much more fitly called *Verba Viventia*, or 'living words,' for words are the living products of the living mind and could not be a due medium between the thing and the mind unless they partook of both. The word was not to convey merely what a certain thing is, but the very passion and all the circumstances which were perceived as constituting the perception of the thing by the person who used the word.
>
> Coleridge, 'Lectures on Shakespeare and Milton', 5 (1811),
> Tomalin report[91]

James Beattie voiced one of the major concerns of British linguistics in the latter part of the eighteenth century, when he declared in 'The Theory of Language' (1783): 'The faculty of Speech is Active, because we act, while we make use of it'.[92] Moving away from ideas of innate speech and 'Adamic' language – the 'vulgar notion, that a person brought up from infancy without hearing any language would of himself speak Hebrew'[93] – Beattie offers instead an analysis beginning from the assumption that 'words derive their meaning from the consent and practice of those who use them'.[94] That emphasis on the function of language in use, rather than simply as a means of identifying objects and ideas, typifies one way in which eighteenth-century linguistics had changed focus; to adopt Saussure's modern terms, grammarians were growing increasingly interested in the various relationships between *langue* (the full range of possible usages in a language) and *parole* (the actual selections made in any particular written or spoken utterance).[95] Similarly, while it would be easy to read too much into the proximity of 'Speech' and 'act' in Beattie's definition, eighteenth-century language study undoubtedly bears witness to some early formulations of what, after JL Austin, we have come to call 'speech-act theory'; as I shall be suggesting repeatedly in this book, this is a circumstance which renders a qualified application of ideas of speech-acts particularly appropriate for writers such as Austen. Murray Cohen has traced a gradual movement in linguistics away from the practices of the seventeenth century, which he characterizes as being based around descriptive correspondence:

> Seventeenth-century linguists self-consciously discovered language not only as an object of scientific study but also as an instrument of knowledge. For everyone concerned with language in the middle of the seventeenth century, it seemed possible to organize, recover, or invent a language that represented the order of things in the world. The varieties of their interests led to visual grammars, shorthand systems, theories of signs, and universal languages. In all these efforts, the goal was not simply to analyze the elements of language but to show how these reflect the structure of nature itself.[96]

The evidence of seventeenth-century empiricism and its intellectual milieu, for instance, bears this out as a broad description, since many writers desired (or at least laid claim to the desire for) a language as free as possible from complex contingencies, a language fine-tuned to the purposes of intellectual utility; it is not so certain, however, whether 'everyone' was equally confident about their ability practically to 'organize, recover, or invent' that language. In *Leviathan*, Hobbes contended that '[t]he light of humane minds is Perspicuous Words, but by exact definitions first snuffed, and purged from ambiguity; *Reason* is the *pace*; Encrease of *Science*, the *way*; and the Benefit of man-kind, the *end*. And on the contrary, Metaphors, and senslesse and ambiguous words, are like *ignes fatui*; and reasoning upon them, is wandering among innumerable absurdities; and their end, contention, and sedition, or contempt';[97] this view of language bears upon the purposes and occasions which he allows to the poetic voice. While his account of the ideal circumstances for poetic language starts as an ideal of decent leisure or '*otium*' ('to please and delight our selves, and others, by playing with our words, for pleasure or ornament, innocently'[98]), it soon also comes to sound like a veiled threat to possible poetic 'Indiscretion':

> In a good *Poem*, whether it be *Epique*, or *Dramatique*; as also in *Sonnets*, *Epigrams*, and other Pieces, both Judgement and Fancy are required; But the Fancy must be more eminent; because they please for the Extravagancy; but ought not to displease by Indiscretion.[99]

Locke, too, remarked 'it is easy to perceive, what imperfection there is in Language, and how the very nature of Words, makes it almost unavoidable, for many of them to be doubtful and uncertain in their significations',[100] and Berkeley noted with dry frustration in his common-place book: 'The impossibility of defining or discoursing clearly of most things proceeds from the fault & scantiness of language, as much, perhaps, as from obscurity & confusion of thought'.[101] That said, to recognize something as a problem does not make it disappear; and Hobbes, who could write of language 'snuffed, and purged of ambiguity', could not but be aware of the insistent and unavoidable pressure of both 'Metaphors' and similes ('like *ignes fatui*'). *Leviathan*'s prose recoils ironically upon itself here, as the wish for an ideally expressive language runs up against the knotty reality of the language in which that desire might be expressed; as Geoffrey Hill has commented of Locke and Berkeley, these philosophical styles can reveal 'a briskly nuanced play', which goes further than 'the empiricist desideratum that words should excite only the "proper sentiments"'.[102]

While the nature of language – as shown by the example of Hobbes and Locke – meant that any progression or refinement was never going to be smooth or complete, seventeenth-century thought on language frequently regretted that fact: complexities and ambiguities could be regarded as occupational hazards, into which the more important business of empirical plain-dealing was perhaps doomed to fall. Within the history of English prose, this was not the first time writers had been troubled by these contingencies; the problematic force of complexity was a cause for worry whose roots stretched at least as far back as the English Reformation in the early sixteenth century, when early Protestants like William Tyndale had hoped to remove Biblical English from the earshot of clerical Latin ('Shrift in the ear is verily a work of Satan'[103]). Over time, the focus of linguistic study changed: 'the basic linguistic unit', according to Cohen, moved from being the 'letter, sound, syllable or word' to the 'syntactic function'.[104] As a result, many treatises of the mid-eighteenth century sought to depict correspondences, not between words and the world, but between particular grammatical functions, thereby shifting the focus from 'semantics' to 'pragmatics', from description to performance – the 'analogy of the function of speech to the operations of the mind'.[105] The most influential of these works was James Harris's *Hermes; or a Philosophical Inquiry Concerning Universal Grammar* (1751), a work so influential that its traces are clearly detectable in Beattie, amongst others. Harris's grammatical claims are founded on the idea that 'ALL MINDS, that are, are SIMILAR and CONGENIAL: and so too are *their ideas*, or *intelligible Forms*'[106] – an idea which gains an additional layer of irony when one considers later writers' ability to lift whole ideas from him:

> WHY the FURIES were made *female*, is not so easy to explain, unless it be that female Passions of all kinds were considered as susceptible of greater excess, than male Passions; and that the *Furies* were to be represented, as Things superlatively outrageous. (Harris)[107]

> The antients made females of the Furies; those dreadful beings, who were supposed to haunt the guilty in this world, and torment them in hell. (Beattie)[108]

The particular achievement of *Hermes* lies in its clearly registering the function of language as a transactional, as well as simply descriptive, force; admitting that '*there never was a Language, nor indeed can possibly be framed one, to express the Properties and real Essences of things, as a Mirrour exhibits their Figures and their Colours*',[109] Harris tries to provide an overview of grammatical functions, and their rhetorical applications. His basic point is that if primitive humans were confined to naming objects ('the *first words* of Men, like their *first Ideas*, had an immediate reference to *sensible Objects*'[110]), they have now reached the stage where 'they took those Words, which they found *already* made, and Transferred them by metaphor to *intellectual* Conceptions';[111] one major practical consequence of this can be seen clearly in that parallel but related history which runs alongside grammar and linguistics in the eighteenth century – the growth of the novel as an expressive form. Since language was now studied less in terms of its correspondence to objects than its description and performance of various mental functions, fictional language in turn could offer a mode of expressive psychological analysis, dramatizing not just sequences of events but the complex and sometimes conflicting modal relationships in which characters and narrators stood to those events: an analysis which, according to John A Dussinger, characteristically 'represents the paradox of self as the object caught in the momentary flux of consciousness and as the subject, freed from time, viewing discriminately past experience'.[112]

Harris and the grammarians who followed him were, therefore, especially interested in plotting grammar as form of mental map: in 1773, Lord Monboddo argued '[b]y language I mean *the expression of the conceptions of the mind by articulate sounds*',[113] and Beattie went further, noting that '[i]n speaking, we not only convey our thoughts to others, but also give intimation of those peculiar affections, or mental energies, by which we are determined to think or speak'.[114] It was, however, a map that could not fully represent the extra dimensions through which language sometimes moves in order to achieve meaning – or to have meaning thrust upon it. The eighteenth-century universal grammarians, for all their attention to words in action, sought to find a common grammatical 'deep structure' ('*conceptions of the mind*', or 'mental energies') to cover all usages in all languages: 'How few then must be those,' Harris wondered, 'who know GRAMMAR UNIVERSAL; *that Grammar, which without regarding the several Idioms of particular Languages, only respects those Principles, that are essential to them all?*'[115] As a result, universal grammar was primarily concerned with illustrating the larger common principles underlying all language, rather than the local applications and problems with which fiction habitually dealt; it could exhaustively categorize how words do things, but was less well equipped for 'how to do things with words'. Stephen K Land has described Harris's tendency 'to see language in terms of human action [...] The unit of speech, the utterance or speech act, may be defined in Harris's theory not only grammatically [...] but also in terms of powers. A speech is the product of a single exercise of one of the powers of perception or volition'.[116] One difficulty, though, opened up by Harris's position, is that to confine every function of speech to 'a single exercise of one of the powers of perception or volition' may restrict its ability fully to account for 'human action'. If each grammatical performance is the working out of a single tendency within the framework of language, then any utterance must be explicable in terms of strict categorical logic, rather than with reference to its particular, contingent circumstances. There are moments in *Hermes* when Harris's logic shows the strain of this attempt, as when he tries to give interjections a grammatical class of their own, as 'adventitious Sounds; certain VOICES of NATURE, rather than Voices of *Art*, expressing those Passions and natural Emotions, which spontaneously arise in the human Soul'.[117] In the twentieth century, JL Austin famously distinguished between 'locutionary' and 'illocutionary' acts ('an "illocutionary" act, i.e. performance of an act *in* saying something as opposed to performance of an act *of* saying something'[118]); universal grammar, by insisting on language's reflection of a deep mental script, privileges the 'locutionary' at the expense of the 'illocutionary' – one result of this is that Harris's account undervalues one of the most important factors in how language is understood in day-to-day communication, and in the act of reading historical and literary texts: context. Austin emphasizes 'the circumstances of the utterance':

> Thus we may say "coming from *him*, I took it as an order, not as a
> request"; similarly the context of the words "I shall die some day",

"I shall leave you my watch", in particular the health of the speaker, make a difference in how we shall understand them.[119]

In practice, whether in immediate speech or in the more distanced and mediated interpretative processes of reading, neither dictionary definitions nor grammatical functions are enough to determine completely how one 'takes things'; what people mean, or are taken to mean, can play off context, or be confined and compromised by it. This murky circumambience can only partly be represented in a universal grammar, which would, for example, be logically bound to explain why 'He's standing in the garden' is a statement, while 'You're standing on my foot' usually operates as a less decorous prompt. In this respect, the taxonomies of the universal grammarians share a quality with so many treatises on polite conversation: they concentrate on language's points of origin, without sufficiently considering how it might be refracted by the medium through which it has to pass.

The discussion of language in terms of mental grammar or rhetorical functions did not convince everyone in the eighteenth century, notably John Horne Tooke, whose *ΕΠΕΑ ΠΤΕΡΟΕΝΤΑ*, or, *The Diversions of Purley*, made its first appearance in 1786: 'I say that a little more reflection and a great deal less reading,' he claims, 'a little more attention to common sense, and less blind prejudice for his Greek commentators, would have made Mr. Harris a much better Grammarian, if not perhaps a Philosopher'.[120] For Horne Tooke, the universal grammarians are guilty of philosophical error and excess, both mistaking words' nature and function, and larding that mistake with too many scholastic verbal distinctions of their own. The *Diversions* nod approvingly in passing at Tyndale, and traces of the zeal with which the English reformer attacked Latin ('First they nosel them in sophistry, and in *benefundatum*'[121]) echo through Horne Tooke's disdain for the sophistry of Harris's grammatical divisions ('And these *Prepositive* conjunctions, once separated from the others, soon gave birth to another subdivision; and Grammarians were not ashamed to have a class of *Postpositive Prepositives*'[122]). Instead of ascribing grammatical functions to capacities of the mind, he tries to get back to the fundamentals of syntax in operation, the noun and the verb, illustrated with examples which, as often as possible, attack the conservative consensus at the same time ('I have avoided AYE and NO, because they are two of the most mercenary and mischievous words in the language, the degraded instruments of the meanest and dirtiest traffic in the land'[123]). Olivia Smith has usefully summarized the significance of Horne Tooke's project:

His etymologies ignore many of the fundamental points of conservative theorists: the distinction between refined and vulgar language, the alleged limitations of primitive language, and the vernacular's lack of intellectual potential. Horne Tooke's tracing of all parts of speech to nouns and verbs disregards the prevalent assumption that two distinct vocabularies exist for the learned and the vulgar, one which was pure and the other corrupt or barbaric. His method does away with the concept of a refined language by demonstrating that all words originate in the material, transitory world.[124]

Sensitive as she is to Horne Tooke's cultural and political importance, Smith has less to say about the complications and dangers which his appeal to etymological primitivism may court. Given Horne Tooke's radicalism, and the arbitrary humiliations which he suffered for it, after his internments for treason in 1793–4, the motives for his appeal to Anglo-Saxon (the language of the time before the 'Norman Yoke') are easier to understand, if no easier to apply. Taking the fact of a word's original Anglo-Saxon etymology, and telescoping that into its current usage, lead Horne Tooke into such views of philology as '*Prepositions* also are the names of *real objects*'[125]:

> If to one of our modern grammarians, I should say, "*A House*, JOIN;"—He would ask me—"JOIN *what?*" [...] If, instead of JOIN, I should say to him,—"*A House* WITH;"—he would still ask the question, "WITH *what?*" [...] yet it would be evident by his question, that he felt it had a meaning of its own; which is indeed the same as JOIN.[126]

While this may avoid the over-elaborations of universal grammar, and focus attention back productively on to linguistic transactions, rather than mental capacities, Horne Tooke's appeal to Anglo-Saxon as an historical ideal of clarity (and as a weapon against 'the inveterate prejudices which [...] for two thousand years have universally passed for learning'[127]) risks erasing the cumulative traces and scars which the language of his time bears from usage; as Thomas Hardy later divined in the abstract ideal of Victorian 'church restoration', such endeavours can ignore 'the actual process of organic nature herself, which is one continuous substitution'.[128] Recording his imprisonment in the margins (and in the manner) of a copy of *The Diversions of Purley*, Horne Tooke managed at times to turn the unsavoury facts of his confinement, under constant surveillance by government agents, into grim comic defiance ('That I might give Kinghorn something to carry for his listening, I told Vaughan in the broadest terms – that the ministry might kiss my arse'[129]). His dramatic pause at the dash catches finely his playing up to a listener who is writing down his words as evidence against him – black comedy indeed, since it is the comedian, rather than his audience, who is captive. But in his prison diary, the '*real objects*' of prepositions sound differently: 'I shall certainly die With the principles which I have always professed; and I am very willing to dye For them'.[130] While Horne Tooke's allusions to his own style in the marginalia defiantly insist on the identity between the free man who wrote the printed words and the prisoner who reads and annotates them, his prepositions also have a sadder irony, witnessing his failure, like the universal grammarians before him, to tackle what JL Austin grittily described as 'the innumerable and unforeseeable demands of the world upon language'.[131]

Jane Austen's writing faces these demands head-on as a matter of course; admittedly, she had an advantage over the likes of Harris and Horne Tooke, in that she was not trying to provide an exhaustive explanation for the mental or social workings of language, but, as I shall explore at length in this book, her fiction not only acknowledges the inability of polite conversation and universal grammar to provide a complete explanation of experience, but often treats with detachment or scepticism the claims of fiction to furnish its own explanatory frameworks or moral instruction. 'The comic part of the Character I might be equal to,' she wrote when requested to create a modern clergyman, 'but not the Good, the Enthusiastic, the Literary.'[132] A moralist suspicious of moralizing, surrounded by various forms of literary didacticism, Austen discovers her own ethical texture amid slips, misunderstandings, and the sundry other ways in which people may get things wrong, and embodies it in what her narratives invite from their readers. Roland Barthes notably suggested that 'the birth of the reader must be at the cost of the death of the author':[133] Austen's morality of conversation imagines author and reader, not as master and slave (or vice versa), nor as connate twins, with their proverbial clarity of mutual understanding, but as related, however distantly and awkwardly – and both at least partly alive.

Dull Elves and Gilded Pills: Austen and the Morality of Reading (1)

Alberto Manguel has commented on the Austen family's reading out loud to one another at Steventon Rectory and elsewhere:

> Because reading out loud is not a private act, the choice of reading material must be socially acceptable to both the reader and the audience [...] Being read to for the purpose of purifying the body, being read to for pleasure, being read to for instruction or to grant the sounds supremacy over the sense, both enrich and diminish the

act of reading. Allowing someone else to speak the words on a page for us is an experience far less personal than holding the book and following the text with our own eyes. Surrendering to the reader's voice – except when the listener's personality is overwhelming – removes our ability to establish a certain pace for the book, a tone, an intonation that is unique to each person [...] At the same time, the act of reading out loud to an attentive listener often forces the reader to become more punctilious, to read without skipping or going back to a previous passage, fixing the text by means of a certain ritual formality [...] The ceremony of being read to no doubt deprives the listener of some of the freedom inherent in the act of reading – choosing a tone, stressing a point, returning to a best-loved passage – but it also gives the versatile text a respectable identity, a sense of unity in time and an existence in space that it seldom has in the capricious hands of a solitary reader.[134]

When the matter for reading aloud came to be Austen's own first two novels, works which were respectively a 'sucking child'[135] and a 'darling Child'[136] to their author, the distancing effect of hearing one's words spoken by another would have had further resonances, reminding Austen that once children make their way into the world at large, they sound different enough from their parents to be embarrassing, but not different enough to be comfortably distanced (I discuss this at greater length in Chapter 2).[137] Manguel describes, lyrically and painstakingly, part of the matter, but some of his contrasts are less absolute than he makes out. In particular, the evidence of Austen's fiction suggests that it is not only reading aloud which lends a text 'a sense of unity in time and an existence in space'; *Northanger Abbey*, for example, very deliberately draws attention to its existence 'in space' and in its readers' hands, when the narrator jokingly remarks: 'The anxiety, which in this state of their attachment must be the portion of Henry and Catherine, and of all who loved either, as to its final event, can hardly extend, I fear, to the bosom of my readers, who will see in the tell-tale compression of the pages before them, that we are all hastening together to perfect felicity'.[138] Nor are the hands of a silent individual reader necessarily any more 'capricious' than the voice which reads aloud to others, giving the words on the page a specific contour of intonation which forecloses (for that particular reading at least) the many possible illocutions that may be jostling for attention in the lines of type. Austen was writing at a time when, as her letters record, reading fiction aloud to small circles was still a common practice, as it continued to be in certain quarters until well into the twentieth century. (Nowadays, only the audiences of novelists' promotional tours, and the members of fiction workshops and creative writing classes, regularly hear fiction read to an audience – radio adaptations and 'audiobooks' have a different relationship to their listeners.) Alongside the culture of audible *coterie* or hearthside performance, however, early nineteenth-century reading also, increasingly, implied a silent communion of reader with text, in which the act of voicing was not abandoned but internalized – enabling writers to compose into the comparatively stable medium of print questions, for example, as to what it was possible or impossible, decent or indecent, to say out loud. Eric Griffiths has plotted the shape of this 'printed voice' with care, noting in particular what it cannot hope to plot itself: 'No page displays a voice's pace, its dips and rises, how some words come readily to it and others only with reluctance, the ever-varying timbres of allegiance, longing, shyness, or disdain which colour utterance and give character to a voice, voice to a character [...] Print does not give conclusive evidence of a voice; this raises doubts about what we hear in writing but it also gives an essential pleasure of reading, for as we meet the demand a text makes on us for our voices, we are engaged in an activity of imagination which is delicately and thoroughly reciprocal'.[139] This double appeal that texts can make – at once inviting the re-imagination of speech, and reminding the reader of what that speech may be lacking, of thoughts which may simultaneously be running against the grain of its voice – offered Austen the opportunity to compose conversation as a vital part of the social encounters depicted in her plots, whilst also creating narratives which go behind and beyond these exchanges, and engaging in trickier and more distanced conversations with her readers. Such a style was of particular value at a time when Austen was surrounded with forms of writing – sentimental fiction and conduct literature, for example – which imagined and advocated more direct, morally didactic relationships between writer and reader.

'There is a Time of Life', wrote Samuel Richardson in 1741 to the physician George Cheyne, 'in which the Passions will predominate; and Ladies, any more than Men, will not be kept in Ignorance; and if we can properly mingle Instruction with Entertainment, so as to make the latter *seemingly* the View, while the former is *really* the End, I imagine it will be doing a great deal. For when the Mind *begins* to be attach'd to Virtue, it will improve itself, and outstretch the poor Scenes which I intend only for a *first Attractive*'.[140] Richardson's description of his ethical manifesto for *Pamela* (the term is not too strong in this instance) finds sympathetic echoes not only in his own subsequent career, but throughout the fictional genre of which he was the most notable mid-century exponent; for instance, he still holds to this view of instructive purpose when writing to Lady Echlin, one of his favoured circle of female readers, in 1755: 'Instruction without Entertainment (were I capable of giving the best) would have but few readers. Instruction, Madam, is the Pill;

Amusement is the Gilding. Writings that do not touch the Passions of the Light and Airy, will hardly ever reach the Heart'.[141] As I shall discuss at greater length in Chapter 3, for a novelist who set such store by emotional sincerity to be discussing his own work in terms of deliberate subterfuge and disguise ('Amusement is the Gilding') has its own ironies; that said, Richardson was not the first novelist in the eighteenth century to feel the need to employ the tactics of the Trojan Horse. Indeed, at the beginning of the century, one of the means by which the whole inchoate and morally questionable genre of fiction rendered itself legitimate and popular was by purporting not to be fictional at all. JL Austin, rather mysteriously, classifies 'the sub-heading "A Novel..."' as an 'explicit performative', i.e. a linguistic formula which indicates directly its illocutionary force;[142] following a similar logic, many early-eighteenth century fictions traded on the idea of being, whether explicitly or implicitly, 'Not a Novel', presenting themselves as found documents, spiritual autobiographies, true histories, and the like.[143] Even in *Pamela* and *Clarissa*, Richardson's general praise of sentimental authenticity is underpinned and validated by the naturalistic apparatus with which it is larded: 'having the umbrage of the editor's character to screen myself behind',[144] as he described it in 1741, he can present the main epistolary bodies of his novels as genuine documents, offered to the reader without the modalities and biases of authorial invention:

> Confident therefore of the favourable reception which he ventures to bespeak for this little Work, he thinks any *apology* for it unnecessary: and the rather for two reasons: 1st, Because he can appeal from his *own* passions, (which have been uncommonly *moved* in perusing it) to the passions of *every one* who shall read with attention: and, in the next place, because an *Editor* can judge with an impartiality which is rarely to be found in an *Author*.[145]

In the connection plotted between the fictional editor's 'passions' and the 'passions of *every one* who shall read with attention', Richardson also sketches a model of how he wishes his 'Instruction' to be transmitted, and his gilded pill to be swallowed. This is the practice to which Johnson was alluding when he told Boswell: 'Why, Sir, if you were to read Richardson for the story, your impatience would be so much fretted that you would hang yourself. But you must read him for the sentiment, and consider the story as only giving occasion to the sentiment'.[146] Richardson's hope was that by a process of sympathetic identification, not so much with the characters themselves but with the virtuous sentiments which they espouse and express, the practice of virtue might translate directly from reading to living – an influence as direct and beneficial as that of Pamela upon Mr B, under which he turns from importunate rake ("'D—n you!", said he [...] "for a little witch; I have no patience with you'"[147]) to ideal husband ('How does this excellent man indulge me in every thing!'[148]). For all the success of this dualistic, didactic vision, which prompted Richardson to publish a separate compendium of his novels' *Moral and Instructive Sentiments* in 1755,[149] the contingencies of fiction, and in particular of its reading, did not always lend themselves so readily to the transmission of virtue, along the sympathetic channels of sentimental response. Richardson may have written to Hester Mulso in 1754 that perfection

> if attainable, ought not to be aimed at in stories, any more than in characters, designed to display life and manners: the whole piece [*Sir Charles Grandison*] abounds, and was intended to abound, with situations that should give occasion for debate, or different ways of thinking. And it is but fair that every one should choose his or her party.[150]

Nevertheless, the freedom which he grants is circumscribed, not only by the parliamentary cast of his metaphor ('debate' and 'party' only provide a finite number of sides with which one can be aligned), but by his habit of policing the interpretation of his texts by revisions and 'editorial' interventions, designed to forestall ambiguity; as John Mullan argues in his study of sentimentalism, '[t]he need to clarify and re-propose speaks of a doubt inherent in "Instruction"'.[151] That doubt was one which other writers were not slow in picking up; if Richardson presents the tremblings of Pamela's pen as indices of sentimental authenticity, and as potential cues for comparable reactions by readers ('How crooked and trembling the lines! Why should the guiltless tremble so, when the guilty can possess their minds in peace?'[152]), Fielding's *Shamela*, for one, exposes a less comfortable truth – that the bodily vibrations that take place near books are not always virtuous. *Shamela*'s main narrative is replete with alternative readings of Richardsonian sentiment ('because you have taken a servant-maid, forsooth! you are jealous if she but looks (and then I began to water) at a poor p-a-a-rson in his p-u-u-lpit, and then out burst a flood of tears'[153]); in addition, the dialogues between Oliver and the ominously-named Tickletext, which bracket Shamela's story, highlight the salacious ends to which a reading of *Pamela* might be susceptible, savaging in the process the innocence of 'right' response: 'Oh!', writes Tickletext, 'I feel an emotion even while I am relating this: methinks I see Pamela at this instant, with all the pride of ornament cast off'.[154] And while Sterne's *Tristram Shandy* features its fair share of sentimental tableaux, notably the scene of Le Fever's death:

> The blood and spirits of Le Fever, which were waxing cold and slow within him, and were retreating to their last citadel, the heart,—rallied back,—the film forsook his eyes for a moment,—he looked up wishfully in my uncle Toby's face,—then cast a look upon his boy,—and that *ligament*, fine as it was,—was never broken.—Nature instantly ebbed again,—the film returned to its place,—the pulse fluttered—stopped—went on—throbbed—stopped again—moved —stopped—shall I go on?—No.[155]

Sterne's novel invites a version of camaraderie in which these sentiments are not cleanly separable from the numerous sexual innuendoes in which a clubbable reader is invited to collaborate, as he (or 'she' as Tristram often imagines his reader) detects the words beneath the decently indecent asterisks on the page:

> The chamber-maid had left no ******* *** under the bed:—Cannot you contrive, master, quoth Susannah, lifting up the sash with one hand, as she spoke, and helping me up into the window-seat with the other,—cannot you manage, my dear, for a single time, to **** *** ** *** ******?
>
> I was five years old.—Susannah did not consider that nothing was well hung in our family,—so slap came the sash down like lightning upon us […][156]

Despite sentimentalism's increasing tendency to patrol its own limitations, to such an extent that, as Mullan notes, novels began to portray 'the protagonist who relies on feeling […] as one who is a species only by being an exception',[157] one aspect of Richardson's model still had some life in it by Austen's time: the dualistic view of instruction as the pill gilded by entertainment. If, in the age of *The Spectator*, manners had been figured as the medium and the stage for social virtue, they were largely presented, by the end of the century, in the form at which Swift's *Polite Conversation* had hinted darkly: as collections of *a priori* rules and prohibitions. This was especially true of guides to correct usage and manuals for female conduct. The anonymous *Address to a Young Lady, on Her Entrance into the World* (1796) voices some sentiments which might have found favour with Austen ('[t]rue piety is in every respect opposite to gloomy dejection, and sour severity'[158]), but even these are delivered in tones which do not square with the novelist's methods, as the treatise bemoans 'the contagious levity diffused by modern manners over every rank of the community'.[159] Works of conservative moralism like Jane West's *Letters to a Young Lady* (1806) are more explicit and prescriptive: not only are women's roles tied morally to the domestic sphere ('the impropriety of our engaging in public concerns becomes evident, from the consequent unavoidable neglect of our immediate affairs'[160]), but the fall of the French *ancien régime* is ascribed directly to 'the dissipated indelicate behaviour and loose morals of its women'.[161]

Nor was this prescriptive tone confined to conduct literature; language study could also shade into social demarcation, as for example in the case of 'synonymies', which hoped to control manners by keeping undesirable words away from refined usage. Hester Lynch Piozzi, friend and correspondent of Johnson, published a notable example of this genre in *British Synonymy; or, an Attempt at Regulating the Choice of Words in Familiar Conversation* (1794) – a work anxious to maintain the boundaries of polite, refined speech, desirous vigilantly to keep 'the confines of conversation free from all touch of vicinity with ordinary people, who are known to be such *here*, the moment they open their mouths'.[162] Mrs Piozzi's larger argument against vulgarisms of language admits the thought that if conversation is an index of social status, improving one's speech might advance that standing: 'nothing is so offensive to English men and women *in general*,' she argues, '[...] as to be rated among the LOW PEOPLE or the VULGAR, conscious that every native of our happy country may die a gentleman if he will but learn to live like one'.[163] However, the pathological fear underpinning her own choice of words suggests otherwise: the proximity of 'touch of vicinity' to 'open their mouths' raises the possibility that vulgarisms might issue infectiously from the mouths of the poor, like germs or bad breath, and *British Synonymy* repeatedly attempts to keep the objects of its disapproval at least at arm's length. 'Brawl' is reproved, not only for its coarseness, but seemingly for its etymology, 'from the obsolete French *brauler*, or the modern *se brouiller*, and it is devoutly to be wished that all the synonymy belonging to it may for ever keep in Paris, and among her *poissardes*';[164] Piozzi even engages the performative resources of her book, in order emphatically (and literally) to draw the line between the acceptable and the unacceptable:

how, if decent times in Europe ever should return, how would their conduct contribute

---

TO BRAND OR STIGMATIZE
Men so unfeeling to their country's danger [...] For this word glides most naturally into a verb [...][165]

Manners, once viewed as socially binding, become, in writings like Piozzi's, an anxious means of self-defence; therefore, it is not surprising that 'manners' should have become prime targets for writers of Radical sympathies from the

1790s onwards. Indeed, it was at the very beginning of the nineteenth century that the words 'mannered' and 'mannerism' came to be used as terms of disapproval: the artist Henry Fuseli, once the object of Wollstonecraft's desire, berated the 'mannered and feeble etchings of Theodore van Tulden'[166] in 1801, and in 1803 the *Edinburgh Review* praised 'character without mannerism'.[167] Within the classic polemics of the 1790s, the older notion of manners comes repeatedly to stand for a much larger complex of obfuscating or stultifying 'prejudice', layers of accreted practice which stand in the way of individual freedoms. For instance, William Godwin's attack on social superstition in the *Enquiry Concerning Political Justice* rounds on conversational manners:

> There is at present in the world a cold reserve that keeps man at a distance from man. There is an art in the practice of which individuals communicate for ever, without anyone telling his neighbour what estimate he forms of his attainments and character, how they ought to be employed, and how to be improved. There is a sort of domestic tactics, the object of which is to elude curiosity, and keep up the tenour of conversation, without the disclosure either of our feelings or opinions. The friend of justice will have no object more deeply at heart than the annihilation of this duplicity.[168]

Similarly, in the *Vindication of the Rights of Woman*, his future wife deals sarcastically with the conventional prescriptions of female 'accomplishment' – 'those pretty feminine phrases, which the men condescendingly use to soften our slavish dependence [...] that weak elegancy of mind, exquisite sensibility, and sweet docility of manners, supposed to be the sexual characteristics of the weaker vessel'.[169] But this unease with the thoughtless adherence to 'mannerism' was not confined to politically radical writers, as the example of Austen abundantly proves. Whether detailing the real-life social accoutrements of Mrs Blount at the Hurstbourne ball ('She appeared exactly as she did in September, with the same broad face, diamond bandeau, white shoes, pink husband, & fat neck'[170]), or the unproductive accomplishments of Maria and Julia Bertram in *Mansfield Park* ('They could not but hold her cheap on finding that she had but two sashes, and had never learned French [...] they adjourned to whatever might be the holiday sport of the moment, making artificial flowers or wasting gold paper'[171]), Austen shows herself to be as aware as her Tory predecessor Swift of the means by which socially constitutive manners can become self-defeating, settling into so many tics and reflexes. Unlike writers such as Godwin and Wollstonecraft, however, she did not seek to overturn the social institutions which gave rise to those frequently insufferable conditions; rather, she sought in her art to clear an imaginative space, however fragile, amid a variety of circumstances which she could not remove or ignore – to outflank what she could not wholly avoid. Geoffrey Hill has argued, in relation to the nuances of Swift's satire, that he 'is especially vulnerable to those distortions of interpretation which occur when ideas are extracted from the texture of language', and that his distinctive comic awareness 'can be fully realized only in the medium of language itself, the true marriage, in words, or wit and feeling';[172] Austen, in her own way, is vulnerable to similar 'distortions', and her writing composes her predicament into a style which asks of its readers something distinct from the direct sympathetic identifications imagined in Richardson's models, figuring 'in the medium of language itself' a means of bearing the unbearable. In this, she is assisted by the larger changes in the phenomenology of reading which took place between *The Spectator* and *Northanger Abbey's* memory of it – changes intimately bound up with the relations between vocal and silent reading, between the Steventon family performances and the reception afforded, by a less identifiable and predictable public, to 'SENSE AND SENSIBILITY: A NOVEL. / IN THREE VOLUMES / BY A LADY'.[173]

Meditating in January 1810 on the possibilities and difficulties faced by his periodical *The Friend*, Coleridge measured his situation against that of Addison (a predecessor and, in part, a model for his own work), and found a number of significant differences that had opened up in the space of a century. He wrote to Thomas Poole:

> We will take for granted, that the Friend can be continued. On this supposition, I have lately *studied* the Spectator—& with increasing pleasure & admiration. Yet it must be evident to you, that there is a class of Thoughts & Feelings, and these too the most important, even practicably, which it would be impossible to convey in the manner of Addison: and which if Addison had possessed, he would not have been Addison [...] Consider too the very different Objects of the Friend & of the Spectator: & above all, do not forget, that these are AWEFUL TIMES!—that the love of Reading, as a refined pleasure weaning the mind from grosser enjoyments, which it was one of the Spectator's chief Objects to awaken, has by that work, & those that followed (Connoisseur, World, Mirror &c) but still more, by Newspapers, Magazines, and Novels, been carried into excess: and the Spectator itself has innocently contributed to the general taste for unconnected writing—just as if 'Reading made easy' should act to give men an aversion to words of more than two syllables, instead of drawing them *thro'* those words into the power of reading Books in general.[174]

Coleridge's distaste for the current state of affairs, in which *The Friend* may be met with incomprehension or indifference out in the reading world, manifests the anxiety about 'general taste' which leads him in the 1820s towards his coinage of 'Clerisy', an intelligentsia which might hope to arbitrate taste;[175] but the elision of cause and effect in his account of *The Spectator* also points to another occupational hazard – the fear that the 'AWEFUL TIMES' in which he finds himself writing have partly been brought into being by the unforeseen results of a work aiming for the opposite effect ('weaning the mind from grosser enjoyments, which it was one of the Spectator's chief objects to awaken'). If, however, one reason why Coleridge was perhaps doomed to be misunderstood in his own time was 'the general taste for unconnected writing', that may have been because of the greater unconnectedness of those doing the reading. Addison and Steele did not have a ready-made readership, but that readership's relatively small size, combined with the metropolitan focus of *The Tatler* and *The Spectator*, meant that they could, as I have discussed, at least partly write their audience into being, with a reasonable assurance that they would achieve their desired response. Whether or not Coleridge's account pinpoints the right causes, it is undeniable that someone writing in 1810 could not take anything like as much for granted about the social make-up of his or her audience, or the spirit in which his or her words might be read. As Martin Nystrand observes, towards the end of the eighteenth century, the spread of literacy, and the concomitant emphasis on written texts as transmitters of knowledge, led to a decentralization of reading practice, and '[a] major effect of this shift was an abstraction of audience'.[176] As a result, a writer's works would not only have to speak to audiences whose identities could only dimly be guessed, but might also have to speak to more than one audience at the same time, and in the same words; if this is a predicament which Coleridge's criticism and letters sometimes bemoan, it is one which his poetry faces more soberly as an inevitable constraint.

This predicament is also the basic condition and nourishment for Austen's work: having seen what had happened to the hopes of 'polite conversation', and witnessed the sentimental novel's growing awareness that direct emotional mappings might be the exception rather than the rule, her fiction, for all its sometimes embarrassing psychological intimacies, does not invite attempts at empathetic identification; nor is it given to the detachable, didactic *sententiae* of which many of her contemporaries were fond. Rather, one of her enduring achievements is her ability to make reticence speak, to make what might otherwise seem like slight, arch withdrawals and withholdings work as hermeneutic puzzles – and this is achieved in the novels' simultaneous invitations to vocal performance, and their appeals to the multiple possibilities of silent reading. Modern readers are familiar with the idea that the experience of a text is to some extent interactive, whether expressed in Barthes' strong claims for readerly liberation from the 'Author-God'[177], or in Wolfgang Iser's more equitable view, where 'convergence of text and reader brings the literary work into existence, and this convergence can never be precisely pin-pointed, but must always remain virtual, as it is not to be identified either with the reality of the text or with the individual disposition of the reader'.[178] However, as the evidence of eighteenth-century fiction proves, this is not only a modern wisdom; even so, the conditions of 'implied readership' at the turn of the nineteenth century were undergoing changes. In *The Enquirer* (1797), Godwin suggested that 'the impression we derive from a book, depends much less upon its real contents, than upon the temper of mind and preparation with which we read it';[179] while Austen would not have phrased the contrast so strongly, her fiction's interpretative wrinkles and ambiguities embody, within the texture of her narrative, invitations for disparate and successive readers to exercise their 'temper of mind'.

In this light, the analytical distinctions made by Russian Formalist critics and their French structuralist successors provide some useful perspectives; of particular relevance is the distinction between the French terms *histoire* and *récit*, the former denoting the events of a story, considered in isolation, the latter the full narrative language in which those events are arranged, rearranged, timed and modalized. In this book, I shall follow the contrast between 'story' and 'narrative' expounded by the most penetrating French analyst of narrative time, Gérard Genette:

> I propose, without insisting on the obvious reasons for my choice of terms, to use the word *story* for the signified or narrative content (even if this content turns out, in a given case, to be low in dramatic intensity or fullness of incident), to use the word *narrative* for the signifier, statement, discourse or narrative text itself, and to use the word *narrating* for the producing narrative action and, by extension, the whole of the real or fictional situation in which that action takes place.[180]

One only has to attempt a written summary of the basic *story* of a novel like *Mansfield Park* (unlike Maria and Julia Bertram, the *précis* would not waste much paper), to see that sheer weight of event is not what drives Austen's fiction; similarly, the accurate reproduction of story in Austen adaptations does not automatically translate into fidelity to the novels – which may be why Amy Heckerling's brilliant *Clueless* (1995) seems to understand *Emma* better than Douglas McGrath's direct cinematic translation from the following year. These novels do not display the eventfulness which animates the political thriller plot of Godwin's classic *Caleb Williams*, or the didactic melodramas of Mary Brunton's *Self-Control*, whose qualities Austen summarized pithily in 1813: 'I am looking over Self Control again, & my opinion is confirmed of its' being an excellently-meant, elegantly-written Work, without anything of Nature or Probability in it. I declare I do not know whether Laura's passage down the American River, is not the most natural, possible, every-day thing she ever does'.[181] While Austen's works may be comparatively sparse in terms of story, they more than make up for this in the comic unpredictability and the analytical rigour of their narratives: characters wonder what others, and often they themselves, might be up to, and Austen finds a corollary for these situations, by activating her readers' capacities to piece matters out, and to get things wrong; to imagine how conversations sound, and to realize, thanks to the silent inscrutability of her texts, that they may mean something else altogether. Her narrative can provide the reassurances of shape and design, and the prickings of risk and contingency; the novels are thus not only the records of fictional conversations, but points at which new conversations begin. As she wrote to her sister Cassandra about *Pride and Prejudice*, '"I do not write for such dull Elves"/ "As have not a great deal of Ingenuity themselves."'[182]

Process and Product: Austen and the Morality of Reading (2)

Austen was parodying the sixth Canto of Walter Scott's *Marmion* ('I do not rhyme to that dull elf/ Who cannot image to himself'[183]), and Scott was one of the first major commentators to note that Austen's novels were, on the face of it, quieter than the public rhetoric of her times, as for example in his now legendary praise of her in 1826:

> That young lady had a talent for describing the involvement and feelings of ordinary life which is to me the most wonderful I ever met with. The Big Bow-wow strain I can do myself like any now going, but the exquisite touch which renders ordinary common-place things and characters interesting from the truth of the description and sentiment is denied to me.[184]

Scott's prose also registers a subtle but significant movement in fictional ethics away from some eighteenth-century readings: 'description and sentiment' are given an equally weighted zeugmatic link to 'truth', rendering them less easily separable than they would have seemed to Richardson and Johnson. Although Scott was, in practice, more fond of the 'Big Bow-wow strain' than his comic terms might suggest, his remark magnanimously acknowledges what separates the two writers. Much can be learned – and not just about the history of Austen's critical reception – from examining what her readers from 1811 onwards have made of her alleged restraint, her refusal to sound that 'Big Bow-wow strain'. Of course, any particular act of reading, whether recorded on paper or lodged evanescently in a human memory, is historically contingent and conditioned, but that fact need not seal it off completely, either from the work to which it is responding, or from other readings; therefore, taking the contextual caveats into account, a history of readings can also yield a series of responses to something that the original text might be argued to have been doing. Pocock has addressed this issue, with reference to Stanley Fish's famous argument that meanings are predominantly produced by the values of interpreters, rather than anything intrinsic to the texts themselves:

> The historian will not challenge this as a normative proposition; interpreters may legitimately behave in the way it presupposes, and the historian will not be at all surprised to find them so behaving in history. But he will be no more surprised to find – indeed he thinks he knows already – that human communities in history have sometimes ascribed extraordinary and even divine authority to certain texts, have maintained them in stable textual forms for centuries and even millennia, and have discussed the various ways in which they may be established and discussed subject to the premise that they possess the authority ascribed to them. When this has happened, there is a text in the historian's class, in the sense that he observes the persistence of a literary artifact of a certain authority and *durée*, and he sets out to investigate the historical occurrences that have accompanied its persistence. There is an obvious contextual sense in which no application or interpretation of an authoritative text is exactly like any other, because it is performed by a specific set of actors in (and on) a specific set of contingencies or circumstances; but this will not persuade the historian that the text has disappeared.[185]

Kelvin Everest has applied comparable arguments to more specifically literary-critical instances, in particular, the status and authority of poetic texts:

> A poem always means something particular in a particular context of textual production and reception; but the poem is not temporally confined by the parameters of this event, but persists in basically the same recognisable form through many such events. Poems are not existent in time in the same way as for example human beings, or material objects, or institutions; indeed, this difference in temporal

existence is something in respect of which poetry is often implicitly
or explicitly self-conscious. Any reading of a poem involves an effort
to bring it back into relationship with a specific temporality, but the
relationship is characterised by its intersection of this specific temporality with a meaning which is by no means specifically confined
by that temporality.[186]

In other words, the very grammar of critical response implies a history of
partly discrete acts of reading, each one contingent upon specific situations,
but also predicated on the existence of an object to which readers are
responding. Therefore, the history of different reactions to Austen's perceived
quietness may help bring into focus important properties of the novels
themselves – not least their capacity to invite such reactions; Barthes' 'multi-
dimensional space in which a variety of writings, none of them original, blend
and clash'[187] may be proof not of the death of this author but of Austen's
continued imaginative life.

'The predominant image of Shakespeare in the eighteenth century', writes
Jonathan Bate, 'was that of Milton in "L'Allegro": he was "fancy's child",
warbling "his native wood-notes wild". In other words, he was a natural
genius, the great poet of imagination'.[188] Bate's remark captures nicely the
equivocation in 'natural genius', since to be a 'natural' genius in Shakespearean English could well mean being an idiot savant.[189] And a prevalent
image of Jane Austen throughout the nineteenth century, common to
Archbishop Whately, Macaulay, GH Lewes and Tennyson, figured her as a
'Shakespearean' dramatist in prose. Whately praised 'a regard to character
hardly exceeded even by Shakspeare himself';[190] for Macaulay, she
'approached nearest to the manner of the great master';[191] for Lewes, she was
a 'prose Shakspeare';[192] and Tennyson claimed that the 'realism and life-
likeness of Miss Austen's Dramatis Personæ come nearest to those of Shakespeare.[193] These views merit serious consideration, not only because they
were held by such famous people, but because they touch (with differing
degrees of success) on the ways in which Austen's imaginative prompts might
work. However, to take the Victorian, 'Shakespearean' Austen seriously, one
needs also to recognize that alongside the insightful readings lie many pieces
of well-intentioned fluff: Austen the artless observer of social detail could
sometimes stand in the same kind of relationship to the nineteenth century as
Shakespeare the untutored 'natural' genius did to the eighteenth.

In Rudyard Kipling's 'The Janeites', the soldiers ponder the thought of
Austen's offspring: "'Pa-hardon me, gents,' Macklin says, "but this *is* a matter
on which I *do* 'appen to be moderately well-informed. She *did* leave lawful
issue in the shape o' one son; an' 'is name was 'Enery James.'"[194] Be that as it

may, James was one of the first to tackle the excesses of the Janeite myth directly; but, sceptical as he was of the cult of 'their "dear", our dear, everybody's dear, Jane',[195] he still (perhaps as an act of 'filial disobedience') fought shy of according to Austen anything approaching conscious poetic intelligence. On the contrary, the keyword for his appraisals of her work is 'unconscious'. He remarked in 1883 on her 'narrow unconscious perfection of form';[196] and in his 1905 lecture on Balzac, he both satirized Macaulay, 'her first slightly ponderous amoroso', and took his own views further:

> The key to Jane Austen's fortune with posterity has been in part the extraordinary grace of her facility, in fact of her unconsciousness: as if, at the most, for difficulty, for embarrassment, she sometimes, over her work-basket, her tapestry flowers, in the spare, cool drawing-room of other days, fell a-musing, lapsed too metaphorically, as one may say, into wool-gathering, and her dropped stitches, of those pardonable, those precious moments, were afterwards picked up as little touches of human truth, little glimpses of steady vision, little master-strokes of imagination.[197]

As with those of Scott before him, James's opinions tell us much about their author as well as about Jane Austen. When he says of Austen's heroines that they 'had undoubtedly small and second-rate minds and were perfect little she-Philistines',[198] he is in effect lamenting the failure of Elizabeth Bennet and Emma Woodhouse to be as sophisticated as his own creations Isabel Archer or Maggie Verver – and it cannot be denied that Elizabeth and Emma would seem out of place 'in one of the many rooms of an ancient villa crowning an olive-muffled hill outside of the Roman gate of Florence'.[199] However, the irony of James's criticism, one that shows up his literary lineage despite himself, is that his acute observations on Isabel Archer in the New York preface to *The Portrait of a Lady* might serve equally well to account for Austen's imagination at work on her subjects: 'Without her sense of them, her sense *for* them, as one may say, they are next to nothing at all; but isn't the beauty and the difficulty just in showing their mystic conversion by that sense, conversion into the stuff of drama or, even more delightful word still, of "story"?'[200] James's small yet crucial distinction between 'of' and '*for*' demonstrates the engagement of mind which it praises; I shall be spending much of this book trying to elucidate Austen's own 'sense *for*' things in language – although I would dissent from James's assessment of how 'unconscious' that sense is. However low James's prose, with its *cadenza* of 'fell [...] lapsed [...] drooped', might esteem the action, I shall address Austen's 'little master-strokes of imagination', in the belief that there is much ground between unconsciousness and disingenuousness. James's discomfort with Janeite legend, and the more cloying forms which it took, is understandable; the force of his sarcasm exposes clearly the tendency of some Victorian Janeites to shrink Austen into a touchstone for harmless gentility, or into England's first 'heritage novelist', truly Shakespearean only in being used as a cultural property or commodity. For example, the *Englishwoman's Domestic Magazine* for 1866 traded on the novels' escapism, and their presentation of a certain notion of English femininity:

> One of the greatest charms to us of Miss Austen's novels is the complete change of scene they afford: we are transferred at once to an old world which we can scarcely believe was England only half-a-century ago [...] To conclude, and for a moment leave the consideration of Miss Austen's genius in itself, to judge it by a larger standard. We must admit that its principle [*sic*] characteristic is moderation. She has been called "the most ladylike of artists," an expression which in itself conveys a sense of moderation.[201]

Not that such readings died with Queen Victoria; Percy Fitzgerald, writing in 1912 (when James was already nearly seventy), remarked: 'Jane Austen has now been before the public – an expression her delicately sensitive nature would have shrunk from – for nearly a whole century'.[202] Fitzgerald misrepresents Austen's reticence by confusing subtlety of imagination with a delicate constitution ('her delicately sensitive nature'), and by conflating the flesh-and-blood woman completely with her distinctive textual traits; he is neither the first nor the last person to do this. His flinching parenthesis would have been more applicable to a writer like Fanny Burney, who nudged *Evelina* anonymously into the public domain with words of similar hesitancy:

> *The following letters are presented to the public - for such, by novel writers, novel readers will be called - with a very singular mixture of timidity and confidence, resulting from the peculiar situation of the editor; who, though trembling for their success from a consciousness of their imperfections, yet fears not being involved in their disgrace, while happily wrapped up in a mantle of impenetrable obscurity.*[203]

Henry James was wise enough to see that Austen's friends could do her at least as much damage as her enemies; indeed, the dissent of a reader like Charlotte Brontë is more precise about Austen's distinctive qualities than many more positive nineteenth-century responses. Writing to WS Williams in 1850, she complained of Austen that 'the Passions are perfectly unknown to her; she rejects even a speaking acquaintance with that stormy Sisterhood

[...] Her business is not half so much with the human heart as with the human eyes, mouth, hands and feet; what sees keenly, speaks aptly, moves flexibly, it suits her to study, but what throbs fast and full, though hidden, what the blood rushed through, what is the unseen seat of Life and the sentient target of Death—*this* Miss Austen ignores; she no more, with her mind's eye, beholds the heart of her race than each man, with bodily vision sees the heart in his heaving breast'.[204] This is a perceptive reading, if not necessarily a convincing dismissal, of Austen; Brontë is right to notice that Austen's points of focus are not confined to the heart which 'throbs' at the centre of the Richardsonian novel, but this fact need not imply the conclusions she draws from it. Firstly, Brontë's contrast suggests 'the human heart' and 'the human eyes, mouth, hands and feet' as antithetical points; given that her reservations about Austen are predicated on a greater intimacy with the physiology of desire ('what the blood rushed through'), it might seem odd that she does not mention how 'the human eyes, mouth, hands and feet' can, in context, be the most direct signs of 'the human heart' and its workings, rather than, as Brontë implies, its distant relations. Gilbert Ryle argues, as he debates the existence of internal 'volitions' in human minds: 'Novelists describe the actions, remarks, gestures, and grimaces, the deliberations, qualms, and embarrassments of their characters; but they never mention their volitions. They would not know what to say about them'.[205] But, as Ryle maintains, this does not imply that they are missing something; according to him, they are in fact recording the perceptible operations of the mind or the 'heart'. 'Boswell,' he suggests, 'described Johnson's mind when he described how he wrote, talked, ate, fidgeted, and fumed.'[206] Moreover, Brontë dismisses the fact that Austen 'no more, with her mind's eye, beholds the heart of her race than each man, with bodily vision sees the heart in his heaving breast' as a shortcoming, when, as I shall be exploring in Chapter 3, it may simply indicate Austen's suspicions of absolute emotional transparency, a doubt about whether writing ever could or should fully 'behold the heart'. For all its loaded argument, Brontë's criticism, though, does not patronize Austen, unlike some of Austen's admirers – and unlike James himself. Even as he lampoons the excesses of the Victorian Janeites, James's references to 'tapestry flowers' and 'dropped stitches' are not that far removed from Fitzgerald's image of Austen and her 'delicately sensitive nature', conspiring to leave 'dear aunt Jane' much where he found her, 'in the spare, cool drawing-room'.

One of the salutary effects of the enormous and varied body of Austen criticism which appeared in the twentieth century is that the novelist has often been successfully brought out of that drawing-room (and, in some readings, out of other small domestic spaces); critics have also illuminatingly sketched the larger physical, ideological and economic environments that cluster around the room. However, one element of so many nineteenth-century readings, whether at the level of tone or of subject, has slipped down the list of priorities: affection. Given the excesses of uncritical admiration which some Victorian and Edwardian Janeites could voice, this is understandable. Nineteenth-century commentators unashamedly wrote of Austen's popularity with her 'admirers' (a word with its own suggestions of courtship) in terms of love: the 'Eminent Women Series' noted that '[t]hose who do appreciate her novels will think no praise too high for them, while those who do not, will marvel at the infatuation of her admirers',[207] while RH Hutton mentioned 'many statesmen and thinkers, and [...] many humorous women who love Miss Austen's books'.[208] 'Janeolatry' could often elide affection for the novels into an imagined affection for 'dear Jane' their author, a blurring witnessed in Hutton's move from those 'who love Miss Austen's books' to 'the true charm of Miss Austen to those who love her'.[209] That more recent Austen criticism does not simply reproduce such uncritical warmth, or such slides from literary to personal affection, is probably a good thing; but to approach Austen with complete sangfroid may be to retreat too far from an imaginative invitation which the Janeites seized too indulgently. As I shall discuss in detail in the following chapters, one of the perennially disturbing pleasures of Austen's fiction is that, while it disavows some earlier mappings of emotion between literary sentiment and readers' responses, it still appeals, albeit less immediately, to readers' understanding of affection, their feeling for feeling; Barbara Everett has suggested that there exists 'a Janeite in every reader, even the most technically sophisticated, an aspect of the mind that reads the deft and light symbolism of feeling; for this reason we respond to the simple romance of Jane Austen's novels'.[210] Whether or not this inner Janeite is quite as ubiquitous as Everett claims, the claims made on readers' sympathies by 'simple romance' come deliberately and unavoidably to bear upon how they are asked to react to the novels' 'most technically sophisticated' effects.

In moving away from many of the exemplary and didactic modes of her predecessors, and in pitching her style at the realities of an increasingly diffuse readership, Austen also becomes part of a larger remoulding of what it might mean to be a literary moralist – another aspect of her fiction with which twentieth-century readings have not always been in tune. To analyse in detail the varieties of modern 'ethical criticism' would require a book in itself; for the present purpose, I shall confine myself to two writers, separated by time, geography and professional discipline, but whose various claims for the 'moral' value of literary works sometimes overlap, even as neither quite encompasses how fiction such as Austen's works – FR Leavis and Martha C Nussbaum.

✳

Value, evaluation and 'revaluation' are everywhere in Leavis's criticism, from large claims such as the famous opening of *The Great Tradition* ('The great English novelists are Jane Austen, George Eliot, Henry James, and Joseph Conrad – to stop for the moment at that comparatively safe point in history'[211]) to the smaller implicit judgements and 'compacted doctrines'[212] with which his prose abounds. In an attempt to fence literature off from what he sees as damaging alternative modes of assessment – the modern kinds of cost-benefit analysis which he dismisses under the heading of the 'technologico-Benthamite'[213] – he emphasizes intrinsic value and hierarchies of taste. However, this also leads him insistently towards a poetics of linguistic triumphalism, where works of art can be graded according to the number of successful illocutions they perform; one danger in this view is that it may become simply a matter of counting the number of poetic hoops through which they jump. This is especially evident when he holds up his own idea of 'the Shakespearean use of English', with its telling definite article, as the yard-stick for poetic value. In his influential criticisms of Milton in *Revaluation* (1936), Leavis explains what he finds missing in *Paradise Lost*:

> So complete, and so mechanically habitual, is Milton's departure from the English order, structure, and accentuation that he often produces passages that have to be read through several times before one can see how they go, though the Miltonic mind has nothing to offer that could justify obscurity – no obscurity was intended: it is merely that Milton has forgotten the English language. There is, however, a much more important point to be made: it is that, culti-vating so complete and systematic a callousness to the intrinsic nature of English, Milton forfeits all possibility of subtle or delicate life in his verse.[214]

He goes on to cite Donne's third 'Satyre' as a counter-example:

> On a huge hill,
> Cragged and steep, Truth stands, and hee that will
> Reach her, about must, and about must goe;
> And what the hills suddenness resists, winne so;
> Yet strive so, that before age, deaths twilight,
> Thy Soule rest, for none can worke in that night.

This is the Shakespearean use of English; one might say that it is the English use – the use, in the essential spirit of the language, of its characteristic resources. The words seem to do what they say; a

very obvious example of what, in more or less subtle forms, is pervasive being given in the image of reaching that the reader has to
enact when he passes from the second to the third line.[215]

These two passages from *Revaluation* contain between much that is central to
Leavis's critical thought. Recurring shapes and titles can be a form of author-
ial 'branding'; as shown by writers from Fanny Burney (*Evelina*, *Cecilia*,
Camilla) to Robert Ludlum (*The Bourne Identity*, *The Osterman Weekend*), titles can
give readers an idea of what to expect. One trademark in Leavis's titles is the
formula of 'definite article-adjective-abstract noun', employed in *The Great
Tradition*, *The Common Pursuit* (although the phrase is originally TS Eliot's), and
The Living Principle: English as a Discipline of Thought. In *Revaluation*, likewise, the
definite article is a reliable index of what is of most value to Leavis. 'Milton's
departure from the English order, structure, and accentuation', 'the Miltonic
mind', 'the English language', 'the intrinsic nature of English', 'the
Shakespearean use of English', 'the English use', 'the essential spirit of the
language': Leavis's critical prose converges towards intensive nodes of argument at those points at which he is most worked up about divergence.
Revaluation itself opens with a chapter on 'The Line of Wit', and phrases such
as 'intrinsic nature' and 'essential spirit', with their semantic insistence on
what is inward, presuppose a standard of fidelity to a particular 'Line' or
'spirit'; the most obvious casualty of this standard in *Revaluation* is Milton, for
his offences against 'the intrinsic nature of English'.

It is a simple enough matter to see what Leavis is getting at in these judgements: measured against a particular idea of English as she was and is spoken,
Milton's language is indeed, as Leavis remarks in passing, 'in the spirit of
Spenser – incantatory, remote from speech.'[216] The issue only becomes con-
tentious when Leavis draws from this undeniable fact, the debatable conclusion that Spenser and Milton must therefore run against the grain of 'English'
per se. He is conflating an abstention from the essence of speech-rhythm with
an apostasy from the language itself, with the result that, on these terms, a
poetic utterance can only be judged truly successful if it displays 'close and
delicate organic wholeness',[217] or if its attitudes are 'concretely embodied'.[218]
This criterion, however, raises several potential objections. Firstly, and most
obviously, there is the question of whether there is just one 'English' that
people speak; *spoken* English can exhibit wide variations at any particular time.
And geographical distance is not the only contributing factor; within a single
region, even within a single city, the idiolectal pressures of particular occupa-
tions, allegiances and creeds produce nuances of great complexity between
speakers. Neither should one ignore Austin's 'coming from *him*, I took it is
an order, not as a request.' Personal knowledge (or the lack of it) bears

significantly on how we understand or misunderstand each other's words. So for Milton, as for the likes of Austen and Dickens after him, part of the task is to compose the varieties of pitch, stress and incomprehension by which any particular poetic voice is surrounded, and within which it must hold its own.

A fidelity to the rhythms of spoken English, and a rightness of mimetic fit ('The words seem to do what they say'): these may be defensible criteria for assessing poetic performance, but they are not incontrovertible ones. Leavis's arguments, on the other hand, often present these standards as necessary ontological predicates of 'English', with the result that we have to assent to them in order to be understanding Leavis (or English) at all. John Casey has spotted such sleight-of-hand at work. Leavis writes of Lawrence: 'And this genius here we see as a penetrating human intelligence, something indistinguishable from a complete and irresistibly impersonal disinterestedness that, without condescension, overbearingness, self-blinding or indulgence on his part, enables him to be on sympathetic terms of person to person, or human life to human life, with the other'.[219] Casey comments:

> It is not that one could not make sense of this passage (except for the 'irresistibly' – who might offer the resistance?) but that one objects to the irresistibly interested equation of terms. 'This' genius may or may not deserve Leavis's description, but whether it does so is a matter of fact not of logic. 'Genius', on any normal understanding of the word, may well go without several of the intellectual qualities ascribed to Lawrence, and such intellectual qualities may well go without some or most of the moral qualities. Whether they do is a matter of fact which has to be shown – it does not all follow from the definition of 'genius'. The passage commits a typical philosophical confusion, in that it both suggests that it follows as a matter of principle ('genius ... indistinguishable from ...') and at the same time guarantees that it *shall* follow by establishing it as a matter of fact ('*This* genius ...') If Lawrence's genius involves all these qualities, that is because it is *Lawrence's* genius, not because it is Lawrence's *Genius*. Of course this does follow from Leavis's usage of the terms 'genius', 'intelligence', and so on (one could say 'from his redefinition'), but it is just this usage, or redefinition, that one might wish to quarrel with.[220]

What he pinpoints here is Leavis's capacity, in his zeal for the 'essential' and authentic, to present 'qualities which are criteriologically related as if they were deductively related'.[221] Kant distinguished in the *Critique of Pure Reason* between two types of proposition:

Analytical judgments (affirmative) are therefore those in which the connection of the predicate with the subject is cogitated through identity; those in which this connection is cogitated without identity, are called synthetical judgments.[222]

What one often finds in Leavis's ideas on 'the Shakespearean use of English' and Lawrence's 'genius' are synthetical judgments offered as if they were analytical judgements. These 'compacted doctrines' can be tendentious enough when taken singly, but the value which Leavis attaches to 'organic wholeness' can lead him to build them into chains, as when he says of George Eliot's *The Mill on the Floss*: 'The intensity of Maggie's naïve vision is rendered with the convincing truth of genius; but the rendering brings in the intelligence that goes with the genius and is *of* it, and the force of the whole effect is the product of understanding. This is an obvious enough point.'[223] Once again, the definite articles focus the argument; but in addition, Leavis implies a deeper connectedness in his series of possessives ('The intensity of Maggie's naïve vision [...] the convincing truth of genius [...] with the genius and is *of* it [...] the force of the whole effect [...] the product of understanding.') Such connections might have appealed to a critic who so appreciated Hopkins' 'The Wreck of the Deutschland' ('Our héarts' charity's héarth's fire, our thóughts' chivalry's thróng's Lórd');[224] but where Hopkins' poem bears theological witness to the final dependence upon, and enfolding within, the 'Lord' who governs the possessives, Leavis tries to make a number of judgments with different catchment-areas nest neatly within each other, as if each step were logically predicated upon the previous one.

Similar problems arise with 'the Shakespearean use of English', where Leavis turns aspects of Shakespeare's poetic practice into exclusively defining characteristics. His standards of speech-rhythm and performative mimesis refuse to countenance examples where the fulfilment of a poet's responsibility might consist in turning against speech rhythm, or in refusing to map form on to content; in short, Leavis's 'Shakespearean' finds no room for much that can be found in Shakespeare himself. For example, in *The Great Tradition*, Leavis praises 'a vital capacity for experience, a kind of reverent openness before life, and a marked moral intensity'.[225] What he does not admit is that the force of his words cuts both ways; within the argument he is trying to make, 'vital capacity', 'experience', 'openness', 'life' and 'intensity' are all offered as qualities to be reckoned on a positive scale, as possessions which guarantee aesthetic seriousness. But the supreme irony here is that all these abstracts have a duplicity about them which turns Leavis's assertion, ironically, into a more comprehensively 'Shakespearean use of English': a 'vital capacity for experience' can bring home the wearying finitude of that experience; as 'openness before life' can leave one vulnerable to 'The Heart-ake, and the thousand Naturall shockes | That Flesh is heyre too'.[226] Leavis's catchwords of plenitude point equally surely to the gravity, whether of tragic weight or comic bathos, that runs through 'Shakespearean' works such as *Troilus and Cressida*:

> This is the monstruositie in loue Lady, that the will is infinite and the execution confin'd; that the desire is boundlesse, and the act a slaue to limit.[227]

The sanguine, positive sense in which Leavis understands 'Shakespearean' does not allow for the fact that the sheer difficulty of expression is one thing that poets might legitimately express. Neither does he envisage that poets can make creative use of the gap between their sense of their own works and others' expectations of them, composing in their language not only the implied 'ideal reader' but the reader who gets things wrong. (Indeed, one could argue that Austen's ideal reader *is* one who initially gets things wrong – making 'rereading' a less distinctively modern practice than Barthes suggests.[228])

One reason why Leavis excludes such practice from 'the intrinsic nature of English' appears as early as the first chapter of *New Bearings in English Poetry*. 'Poetry matters because of the kind of poet who is more alive than other people, more alive in his own age. He is, as it were, at the most conscious point of the race at the time.'[229] When Leavis first describes significant poets as 'more alive', one might be forgiven for thinking that he is speaking figuratively, that he means something like 'more alert, more on the qui vive'. It is reasonable to imagine talented poets as more perceptive, more alive to their times than others; but this is not what Leavis means. To him, the great writer is genuinely more alive '*in* his time', which raises more troubling questions. The positive charge which he attaches to 'the essential spirit of the language' comes close to suggesting that poets are not just more perceptive, but actually a higher order of mortals. TS Eliot wrote of Matthew Arnold that, in his criticism, 'literature, or Culture, tended [...] to usurp the place of Religion';[230] within Leavis's development of Arnold's ideas, not only does the literary critic assume a prophetic role with respect to his or her culture, but, despite Leavis's disavowal of the thought that 'Poetry will save us',[231] literature itself takes on a quantifiably moral, if not salvific force. For Leavis, Austen is 'the inaugurator of the great tradition of the English novel – and by "great tradition" I mean the tradition to which what is great in English fiction belongs'.[232] This is literary criticism as prophecy – at least, as self-fulfilling prophecy; the circularity of Leavis's definition renders it almost invulnerable to falsification, although the defining quality of that 'great tradition' is less certain. For all Leavis's professed dedication to 'the basic human need that the technologico-Benthamite age denies',[233] 'life', the quality by which suitability for the tradition is measured, becomes so worn by repetition in different contexts that it begins to sounds perversely like what it is supposed to resist – a product, an object.

More recently, the American philosopher and classicist Martha C Nussbaum has offered a sharper interpretation of the ethics of literary form, with particular attention to the novel; where Leavis's criticism concentrates primarily on the complexity and moral seriousness of literary texts themselves, Nussbaum sees them as models of perception whose ethical value consists in their analogical relationship to their readers' perceptions. Taking as her founding documents Aristotle's *Nichomachean Ethics* and James's prefaces to the New York edition of his works, she argues that

> novels can play an important role in the articulation of an Aristotelian morality. For novels, as a genre, direct us to attend to the concrete; they display before us a wealth of richly realized detail, presented as relevant for choice. And yet they speak to us: they ask us to imagine possible relations between our own situations and those of the protagonists, to identify with the characters and/or the situation, thereby perceiving those similarities and differences. In this way their structure suggests, as well, that much of moral relevance is universalizable: learning about Maggie Verver's situation [in James's *The Golden Bowl*] helps us understand our own.[234]

This view has much to recommend it, not least the emphasis placed by Nussbaum on 'the concrete' and 'detail', which militates against those broad, dualistic reading practices which sometimes produce phrases such as 'Austen's treatment of the theme of Marriage'. Similarly, the importance which she gives to the faculty of noticing can be illuminating. Her essay on the repeated narrative motif of Steerforth's arm in *David Copperfield* is a case in point; 'Steerforth's gesture,' she argues, '[…] signifies nothing publicly communicable. Its only meaning is that he is there. It is mysteriously, sensuously his, his beyond explanations and reasons. Its power to haunt comes not from the public world of reason-giving (in fact, it distracts David from that world, making moral judgment upon Steerforth's actions impossible), but from the private world of personal emotion and personal memory. It is irreducibly particular, characteristic of him and no other. It is what David recognizes him by.'[235] Nussbaum here responds acutely to an important element in the psychology of Dickens's narrative. His fiction often repeats irreducible, personal quirks (distinctive gestures, catch-phrases, speech-rhythms, or physical characteristics); in his long, serially published fictions, this has a practical, mnemonic function, in that a recognizable textual signature or character-motif can help remind readers of a character who has been out of the story for many weeks and hundreds of pages. This structural convenience is more than just a matter of technique for Dickens, since it offers a parallel in narrative for that capacity to retain irreducible memories which he so admires in childhood, and ideally in healthy adulthood: 'There are real people and places that we have never outgrown,' he wrote in 1853, 'though they themselves may have passed away long since: which we always regard with the eye and mind of childhood.'[236]

Picking up on James's lead in his prefaces, Nussbaum offers what might be called a morality of perception; indeed, 'perception(s)' and 'particular(s)' form the keynotes of her literary ethics. 'Obtuseness and refusal of vision,' she argues with reference to James, 'are our besetting vices. Responsible lucidity can be wrested from that darkness only by painful, vigilant effort, the intense scrutiny of particulars.'[237] She is responding here to cues such as James's remark, in the New York preface to *The Princess Casamassima*, that characters like Isabel Archer are 'so far as their other passions permit, intense *perceivers*, all, of their respective predicaments'.[238] What James sees in the possibilities of his art is redescribed by Nussbaum in terms which are themselves noticeably Jamesian – a manoeuvre which has the benefits of sympathy, but can sometimes elide or occlude critical distance. 'Moral knowledge,' for Nussbaum, '[…] is not simply intellectual grasp of propositions; it is not even simply intellectual grasp of particular facts; it is perception.'[239] This thought leads her to a much larger claim:

> In the war against moral obtuseness, the artist is our fellow fighter, frequently our guide. We can develop, here, the analogy with our sensory powers that the term *perception* already suggests. In seeing and hearing we are, I believe, seeing not the world as it is in itself, apart from human beings and human conceptual schemes, but a world already interpreted and humanized by our faculties and our concepts. And yet, who could deny that there are some among us whose visual or auditory acuity is greater than that of others; some who have developed their faculties more finely, who can make discriminations of color and shape (of pitch and timbre) that are unavailable to the rest of us? who miss less, therefore, of what is to be heard or seen in a landscape, a symphony, a painting? Jamesian

moral perception is, I think, like this: a fine development of our human capabilities to see and feel and judge; an ability to miss less, to be responsible to more.[240]

This is less problematic than Leavis's account of the sensitivity of artists in their time (which it superficially resembles), since Nussbaum does not equate the possession of greater aesthetic 'acuity' with being quantitatively 'more alive' than others. However, the cumulative effect of her post-Jamesian terms begins to turn her central value, 'perception', into an entity as all-encompassing and beneficial as 'life' in Leavis's criticism. One particular idea which crops up repeatedly in James, and which Nussbaum quotes approvingly herself on several occasions, pertains to the artistic virtues of being a person 'on whom nothing is lost'; the most famous instance of the phrase occurs in James's 1884 essay 'The Art of Fiction', in which he offers advice to potential novelists ('if I should certainly say to a novice, "Write from experience and experience only," I should feel that this was rather a tantalizing monition if I were not careful immediately to add, "Try to be one of the people on whom nothing is lost!"'[241]). Given the aggregate force of Nussbaum's terms in the extract quoted above ('*perception*', 'acuity', 'developed their faculties', 'make discriminations', 'moral perception, 'fine development', 'responsible'), the appeal of James's exhortation is clear. But the optative undertone of '*Try* to be one of those' (italics mine), complicates matters, as James tacitly admits that such clarity of perception and retention may be a hope rather than an achievement. Neither is it clear, either in James or in Nussbaum's re-formulations of him, why 'to be one of those on whom nothing is lost' is always an advantage. For example, Dickens's dark Christmas fable *The Haunted Man* imagines a ghostly gift, oblivion of the world's cares, turning into a dehumanizing curse, since within Dickens's aesthetics, this oblivion also dissolves the ties which make life worthwhile – leading the misanthrope Redlaw to beg for his memory back.[242] Against this, though, one could set a tradition of poetic enquiry into when one might decently wish to have done with things, taking in the youthful Byron ('Love, Hope, and Joy, alike adieu!— / Would I could add Remembrance too!'[243]) and the mature Beckett ('Oh all to end'[244]). James and Nussbaum do not countenance the possibility that 'to be one of those on whom nothing is lost' could itself be a version of hell: 'wealth of richness and detail' can become unbearably synaesthetic, perception and responsiveness turning into a pathological hypersensitivity to every stimulus, like having a fly buzzing inside one's head for all eternity. Moreover, the form of fictional narrative, which James and Nussbaum both rightly champion, sometimes depends less on nothing's being lost than on a dialectic of forgetting and remembering, as readers are reminded of what they may have missed before.

Another major thread of Nussbaum's criticism concerns the possible parallels between the perceptive sensitivity shown by an artist like James, in creating situated examples of human choice, and the sense for particulars which reading James might inculcate; as she argues, 'learning about Maggie Verver's situation helps us understand our own'. Nussbaum helpfully points to one possibility of fiction, which I shall be considering at length in what follows: at the level of *récit*, novelists can involve their readers in interpretative processes, existential puzzles and comic routines which are, in turn, contingent on questions and events treated within the *histoire*. For example, in Chapter 2, I explore how the narrative of *Pride and Prejudice* offers a performative, critical reflection on some of the social dilemmas which it depicts. Nussbaum, however, suggests not only parallels but ethical causalities; in reading the likes of James right, she claims, we too become more sensitive perceivers: 'this conception of moral attention implies that the moral/aesthetic analogy is also more than analogy. For [...] our own attention to [James's] characters will itself, if we read well, be a high case of moral attention'.[245] In this context, 'if we read well' is a big 'if', since the only accessible criterion for whether we are reading well or not, seems to be whether or not we are reading in a Jamesian manner. In Nussbaum's work, analogies between readerly and artistic perception frequently become less tenable, direct mappings. Her review of Wayne C Booth's *The Company We Keep: An Ethics of Fiction* is entitled 'Reading for Life', and in it, she writes of 'David Copperfield's "reading for life"';[246] but, as shown in the quotation from *David Copperfield* with which she begins the review, this is (oddly, for a critic who so values 'scrutiny of particulars') not exactly what Dickens wrote:

> My father had left a small collection of books in a little room upstairs, to which I had access (for it adjoined my own) and which nobody else in our house ever troubled. From that blessed little room, Roderick Random, Peregrine Pickle, Humphrey Clinker, Tom Jones, the Vicar of Wakefield, Don Quixote, Gil Blas, and Robinson Crusoe, came out, a glorious host, to keep me company. They kept alive my fancy, and my hope of something beyond that place and time—they, and the *Arabian Nights*, and the *Tales of the Genii*,—and did me no harm [...] This was my only and my constant comfort. When I think of it, the picture always rises in my mind, of a summer evening, the boys at play in the churchyard, and I sitting on my bed, reading as if for life [...] The reader now understands, as well as I do, what I was when I came to that point of my youthful history to which I am now coming again.[247]

Dickens's narrative evokes sharply what narrative itself might offer to young David: a generosity of 'fancy' which will not be constrained by his otherwise dour new life under Murdstone's rule; but he is not 'reading for life', but 'reading as if for life'. For all Dickens's approval of fiction's imaginative licence (a freedom which he defends vehemently in his journalism[248]), David's 'as if' decently senses the limits of the potential crossover; in addition, the phrase 'reading as if for life' is haunted subliminally by the thought that it may be an expedient, as a shipwrecked sailor might 'hang on for dear life' to a piece of flotsam – an early indication of that fear, never wholly articulated or dispelled in David's narration, that his living with creatures of the imagination may have alienated him from some other forms of human companionship. For Nussbaum, however, the need to make situated fictional choices 'exemplary' elides the distance between reading and life;[249] in her recent work, this emphasis has taken even stronger forms, as she has expanded this aesthetic of 'perceptive' literary response into a jurisprudential application: 'novel-reading will not give us the whole story about social justice, but it can be a bridge both to a vision of justice and to the social enactment of that vision'.[250] Where Leavis railed against 'technologico-Benthamism', Nussbaum's *bête noire* is post-structuralism ('[a]fter reading Derrida, and not Derrida alone, I feel a certain hunger for blood; for, that is, writing about literature that talks of human lives and choices as if they matter to us all'[251]). In her attempts to make perceptions 'matter to us all', though, Nussbaum's criticism, despite the many valuable insights it affords, can also portray that perception as less an ethical capacity than a transferable skill.

In this light, 'The Janeites' may get closer to the heart of how Austen's fiction works than either Leavis's insistence on exemplary linguistic fullness, or Nussbaum's comparable 'wealth of richly realized detail'. The multiple ironies of Kipling's story, in which a Janeite society springs up among the trenches of World War I, deal with a manner of 'reading as if for life', but one which is beset around with casual death. The filiations between art and life in Humberstall's tale can be as much the bathetic comedy of recognition as 'a high case of moral attention' ('there was a Miss Bates; just an old maid runnin' about like a hen with 'er 'ead cut off, an' her tongue loose at both ends. I've got an aunt like 'er'[252]). Janeite fondness, too, manifests itself here in oddly sinister ways, Humberstall rechristening the company's guns 'The Reverend Collins', 'General Tilney' and 'Lady Catherine De Bugg';[253] and although reading Austen technically saves his life (his familiarity with Miss Bates secures him entry to the hospital train), this is a fortunate accident in a war full of arbitrary waste, as Kipling sets Humberstall's survival against the knowledge of those whom Jane did not save. 'The Janeites' is tuned to Austen through Kipling's double perspective: respectful of 'dear Jane' and the imaginative meeting place she offers to these socially disparate and culturally dislocated characters, but ever aware of the painful, fatal events which no writing or reading could hope to overcome. As Austen's joke about 'dull Elves' suggests, the novels describe characters becoming more perceptive, and often invite their readers to perform the 'intense scrutiny of particulars'; but they do not imply that the relationship between these levels is 'exemplary'. Indeed, one insight which a reader might gain from a close reading of Austen is a proper sense of the limited nature of the parallel. Brian Southam argues that 'Jane Austen's sense of this close and responsive reader contributed a particular quality to her writing: an intimacy of tone and address which somehow involves us with the author herself',[254] but this only tells half the story: a 'close and responsive reader' may perceive with greater clarity the borders of intimacy. One reason for this is suggested by Marcel Proust, whose insight describes the hopes of writing such as Austen's better than either Leavis or Nussbaum. Proust suggests that 'it is one of the great and wonderful characteristics of good books (which will give us to see the role at once essential and limited that reading may play in our spiritual lives) that for the author they may be called "Conclusions" but for the reader "Incitements" [...] it is at the moment when they have told us everything they could have told us that they give rise to the feeling in us that as yet they have told us nothing'.[255] The act of reading marks a transference, but for Proust, it is not necessarily one of exemplary linguistic plenitude or perceptive delicacy – since it is not an end product but the beginning of a process:

> For as long as reading is for us the instigator whose magic keys have opened the door to those dwelling-places deep within us that we would not have known how to enter, its role in our lives is salutary. It becomes dangerous on the other hand, when, instead of awakening us to the personal life of the mind, reading tends to take its place, when the truth no longer appears to us as an ideal which we can realize only by the intimate progress of our own thought and the efforts of our own heart, but as something material, deposited between the leaves of books like a honey fully prepared by others and which we need only take the trouble to reach down from the shelves of libraries and then sample passively in a perfect repose of mind and body.[256]

Having seen what could and could not be done in the modes of conversational morality, sentimental reading and fictional didacticism, and faced with a multiplicity of possible readerships, Austen, as I shall be exploring in what follows, composed a fictional style which does not depend on either sentimental congruences between text and reader, or on exemplary models; and for all the charades which they depict, her novels are as interested in the setting of puzzles as in the quality of the solutions; the readerly community of romance is turned instead into a starting point for 'the personal life of the mind', composed into that quietness which so many of her readers have noticed.[257] It is one of the most kinetic quietnesses in nineteenth-century literature, one distinct from the dagger-throwing of Edmund Burke, or from Capel Lofft's setting against Burke's 'otherwise resistless edge, the impenetrable shield of Truth and Freedom'.[258] Neither is Austen's eloquence that of a 'vortex'; in September 1814, she wrote in response to the fictional efforts of her niece Anna:

> Devereux Forester's being ruined by his Vanity is extremely good; but I wish you would not let him plunge into a "vortex of Dissipation". I do not object to the Thing, but I cannot bear the expression;—it is such thorough novel slang—and so old, that I dare say Adam met with it in the first novel he opened.[259]

Where *that* novel may have come from is just one of the questions which Austen's writing continues to ask.

INTERLUDE

DIFFERENTIAL NARRATIVE: AUSTEN'S EARLY FICTION

Often carried away by the anti-hero, but rescued either by her Father or the Hero—often reduced to support herself & her Father by her Talents & work for her Bread;—continually cheated & defrauded of her hire, worn down to a Skeleton, & now & then starved to death—. At last, hunted out of civilized Society, denied the poor Shelter of the humblest Cottage, they are compelled to retreat into Kamschatka where the poor Father, quite worn down, finding his end approaching, throws himself on the Ground, & after 4 or 5 hours of tender advice & parental Admonition to his miserable Child, expires in a fine burst of Literary Enthusiasm, intermingled with Invectives again<st> Holder's of Tythes.

Jane Austen, 'Plan of a Novel, according to hints from various quarters' (c. 1816)[1]

In his *Lectures on Rhetoric and Belles Lettres* (published in their collected form in 1783), Hugh Blair analysed the structure of harmonious sentences, arguing for the existence of particularly meaningful and resonant arrangements:

> The structure of periods, then, being susceptible of a melody very sensible to the ear, our next enquiry should be, How this melodious structure is formed, what are the principles of it, and by what laws is it regulated? And, upon this subject, were I to follow the ancient rhetoricians, it would be easy to give a great variety of rules. For here they have entered into a very minute and particular detail; more particular, indeed, than on any other head that regards Language. They hold, that to prose as well as to verse, there belong certain numbers, less strict, indeed, yet such as can be ascertained by rule [...] Wherever they treat of the Structure of Sentences, it is always the music of them that makes the principal object.[2]

Seven years after Blair's work appeared, the fifteen-year-old Jane Austen offered another view of the significant 'structure of periods'; in the fourth letter of *Love and Freindship*, Laura tells her friend's daughter Marianne about the old days:

> Isabel was then one and twenty—Tho' pleasing both in her Person and Manners (between ourselves) she never possessed the hundredth part of my Beauty or Accomplishments. Isabel had seen the World. She had passed 2 Years at one of the first Boarding schools in London; had spent a fortnight in Bath & had supped one night in Southampton.
>
> "Beware my Laura (she would often say) Beware of the insipid Vanities and idle Dissipations of the Metropolis of England; Beware of the unmeaning Luxuries of Bath & of the Stinking fish of Southampton."[3]

This passage turns to gleefully disproportionate and indecorous ends the notion which Blair entertains more seriously, that 'to prose as well as verse there belong certain numbers'. Indeed, Austen is playing not only off 'numbers' in the eighteenth-century sense of prosodic divisions, but off the decorum of mathematical proportion (a technique to which she returns in later works such as *Pride and Prejudice* and *Sanditon*); the expectations set up by the rhythmic 'numbers' of her prose are teasingly out of phase, and out of proportion, with the numbers and quantities narrated therein. 'Person and Manners' stand in rhythmic antithesis to 'Beauty and Accomplishments', but that acoustic balance is set against the gossipy parenthesis '(between ourselves)'; 'the World' is unpacked into its threadbare components in the *diminuendo* of '2 Years [...] a fortnight [...] one night'; and Isabel's clinching 'moral' is so absurd precisely because it gives equal syntactic weight to two qualities which otherwise have little or nothing in common ('the unmeaning Luxuries of Bath [...] the Stinking fish of Southampton'). In a sense, though, Austen spends much of her career forcing 'unmeaning Luxuries' and 'Stinking fish' into unexpected proximity – through her quiet implication of the physical environments in which her novels' emotional events are located, and the habit which embarrassing objects and situations have of appearing at the least convenient times. What the teenage Austen of *Love and Freindship* visits on late eighteenth-century rhetoric gives stylistic form to the perception which I detailed in the Introduction: that even the most well-intentioned social and literary forms can be converted into 'mannerism'.

The syntax of antithetical balance, which *Love and Freindship* and the other juvenilia subject to numerous refractions and distortions, has a particular value to Austen, since 'Johnson in prose' was, according to all the family accounts, among her favourite writing,[4] and Johnson's major prose works, such as *The Rambler* and his preface to Shakespeare, gain much from the clarifying force of antithesis. Take his enquiry, from 1765, into why Shakespeare may have outlived his age:

> The effects of favour and competition are at an end; the tradition of his friendships and his enmities has perished; his works support no opinion with arguments, nor supply any faction with invectives; they can neither indulge vanity nor gratify malignity; but are read without any other reason than the desire of pleasure, and are therefore praised only as pleasure is obtained; yet, thus unassisted by interest or passion, they have passed through variations of taste and changes of manners, and, as they devolved from one generation to another, have received new honours at every transmission.[5]

What Hill has observed of Swift's vulnerability to 'those distortions of meaning which occur when ideas are extracted from the texture of language' could also be applied to Johnson. The 'Preface' is sometimes identified with its most sententious pronouncement ('Nothing can please many, and please long, but just representations of general nature'[6]), a tactic which disregards the fact that Johnson, in context, is presenting his aphorism not as an axiomatic starting-point but as a provisional conclusion which he has drawn from examining the empirical evidence; in this light, his antitheses and parallelisms work to separate out the various causal factors and false clues in the matter of Shakespeare's longevity, for readier comparison and contrast: for example, qualities which might easily be elided and confused ('arguments' and 'invectives', or 'taste' and 'manners'), are carefully distinguished by the rhythmic counterpoint of the prose. Johnson's detractors were not always convinced of the value of this argumentative texture; Archibald Campbell's *Lexiphanes* (1767), which adapts Lucian into an attack on Johnson, warns its dedicatee 'not to suffer those *Lexiphaneses*, those *Shiners*, those Dealers in *Hard Words*, and *absurd phrases*, those *Fabricators* of *Triads* and *Quaternions* [...] There is as great an antipathy between a pure and natural writer, such as your Lordship, and a Lexiphanes, as there is between an elephant and a rhinoceros'.[7] However, Campbell's argument is weakened by his poor ear for Johnson, which leads him to present his target as made of nothing but 'hard words':

CRITICK
What! a new romance, or a second Rasselas of Abyssinia?

J—N
Without dubiety you misapprehend this dazzling scintillation of conceit, in totality, and had you that constant recurrence to my

oraculous dictionary, which was incumbent upon you from the vehemence of my monitory injunctions, it could not have escaped you that the word novel exhibits to all men dignified by literary honours and scientifical accomplishments, two discrepant significations.[8]

Austen's joke about 'Stinking fish', in contrast, is more accurate about Johnsonian style, and more inward with it; registering at once the power of antithetical syntax, and the way in which it can be made to sound in unsuspecting ears as a means of tricking sense *through* sound, *Love and Freindship*'s moment of epistolary absurdity points to a larger characteristic of the juvenilia and *Northanger Abbey*, one which continues to nourish the mature novels, albeit in more supposedly decorous forms. Compressing, relocating, and sometimes collapsing any number of expectations about how fiction goes, Austen discovers her fictional voice in playing the capability of form to organize experience against experience's often bloody-minded habits of resistance, a comic method which produces some bloody-minded works of its own ('But scarcely was she provided with the above-mentioned necessaries, than she began to find herself rather hungry, & had reason to think, by their biting off two of her fingers, that her Children were much in the same situation'[9]).

Blair's account of the 'numbers' of prose concentrates on those intrinsic harmonies which Cicero and Quintilian had attributed to oratorical prose-rhythms; one reason why Eleanor Tilney in *Northanger Abbey* jokes about being 'overpowered with Johnson and Blair'[10] may be that his lectures are less complimentary to 'another species of Composition in prose, which comprehends a very numerous, though, in general, a very insignificant class of Writings, known by the name of Romances and Novels'.[11] However, that 'species of Composition' has its own, necessarily diffuse, kinds of 'numbers': means by which prose fiction divides and patterns itself. Verse writers have at their disposal a range of formal and prosodic models, which they can turn into, for instance, dialogues with their predecessors, or acts of ethical resistance. Forms like the sonnet, with the different weights of association which they have picked up from traditions and accidents of usage, afford numerous opportunities, in that to write in the sonnet form adumbrates not only poetic history, but the larger histories with which poetry engages: consider Geoffrey Hill's twentieth-century sonnet sequence, 'An Apology for the Revival of Christian Architecture in England', which meditates on the continuities and dispersals of English history in a poetic form which is itself a mode of 'Christian Architecture' in language.[12] Novels, of course, are proverbially more diverse in their sources and baggier in their form; the precise formal demarcations between, say, Petrarchan sonnet form and haiku, mean that many criteria in the assessment of verse art are more readily to hand and directly verifiable, whereas the history of novel-criticism is one not only of evaluative arguments, but of disagreements over the very terms in which its own practice should be conducted. But that looseness does not necessarily entail Ian Watt's suggestion that two of the novel's defining characteristics as a literary form are its 'absence of formal conventions' and its 'rejection of traditional plots';[13] rather, the promiscuous parentage of fiction from the eighteenth century onwards allows writers to score off numerous different histories of formal and generic usage, whilst exploring how their form colludes and collides with the less ordered experiences which they are rendering into narrative. Therefore, while fiction does not consistently possess local prosodic and structural features such as metre and stanzaic form, it might be said to have a looser psychological and spatial prosody, taking in the rhetorical divisions of its prose, and the ways in which matter is distributed and organized throughout the body of the book. To a writer like Austen, these qualities are especially fertile, since they allow her to find an expressive style for her circumstances – accommodating her belief in the necessity for form, and her comic awareness that form does not and cannot explain experience. As Margaret Anne Doody puts it: 'To Jane Austen, culture often *is* anarchy'.[14]

Novels do not habitually feature expressive lineation or stanzaic divisions, although the 'mad papers' in *Clarissa*, in which skewed chunks of type mime the heroine's disordered scraps of writing,[15] and the performative blanks, asterisks, dashes and pointing hands which litter *Tristram Shandy*, show that eighteenth-century writers were alert to the possibilities of their *'mise-en-page'*. However, the economic constraints of publication mean that novels feature other potentially creative physical and psychological divisions: while volume divisions are primarily the responsibility of publishers and compositors, novelists can still allude to them, as Sterne has Tristram do repeatedly; and once one gets down to the smaller units, such as the chapters and paragraphs within them, a writer can employ them in a manner not wholly removed from line units, stanzas and verse-paragraphs, inviting a reader to judge how far these divisions do or do not correspond with units of sense. Philip Stevick argues of creative chapter-divisions in eighteenth- and nineteenth-century fiction:

> The eighteenth-century novelists [...] represent the technique of the chapter come full circle, from an unawareness, almost, of its usefulness, to a full exploitation of its power and its variety, to a parody of it. In one sense there is nothing more to be said about the chapter as an aspect of fictional technique. The beginnings and endings, the technical shifts, the relations between chapters in Jane

Austen alone are so subtle and various as to justify a book in themselves. But her chapters do rather little which was not latent in the
technical virtuosity of the eighteenth century.[16]

That said, the fact that Austen's way with chapters is so 'subtle and various'
may be a distinguishing feature in itself.

The most famous comic treatments of plotting in eighteenth-century novels
tend to be deliberate, self-conscious ones. Fielding's *Tom Jones* consistently
jokes about the asymmetry between its perfectly shaped plot and the events it
narrates: the novel's books and chapters can variously contain '*The Time of a
Year*', 'five Pages of Paper', or, indeed, 'little or nothing'.[17] *Tristram Shandy* is,
among numerous other things, a meditation on literal and metaphorical lines:
lines of descent (the male genealogy of the Shandys, now perhaps fatally interrupted by death and impotence), lines of thought (various modes of mental
association), and the real lines, dashes and diagrams which span the novel's
textual spaces, trying to forge sympathetic bonds while demarcating the limits
of those hopes, and of fiction's mimetic power. Typically, Tristram makes the
metaphor of 'plot-lines' comically literal, when, in Volume VI, he traces
graphically the linear movements of his first five volumes (see Fig. 1); he explicates Volume V thus:

> it appears, that except that at the curve, marked A, where I took a
> trip to Navarre,—and the indented curve B, which is the short air-
> ing when I was there with the Lady Baussiere and her page,—I
> have not taken the least frisk of a digression, till John de la Casse's
> devils led me the round you see marked D.—for as for *c c c c c* they
> are nothing but parentheses, and the common *ins* and *outs* incident
> to the lives of the greatest ministers of state; and when compared
> with what men have done,—or with my own transgressions at the
> letters A B D—they vanish into nothing.
>
> In this last volume I have done better still—for from the end of Le
> Fever's episode, to the beginning of my uncle Toby's campaigns,—
> I have scarce stepped a yard out of my way.
>
> If I mend at this rate, it is not impossible—by the good leave of his
> grace of Benevento's devils—but I may arrive hereafter at the excel-
> lency of going on even thus;
>
> ———————————————————————————
>
> which is a line drawn as straight as I could draw it, by a writing-
> master's ruler, (borrowed for that purpose) turning neither to the
> right hand or the left.[18]

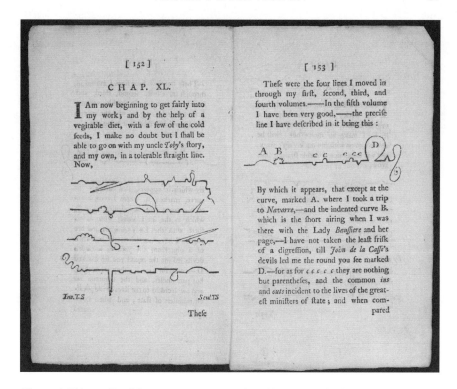

Figure 1. *Tristram Shandy* is, among numerous other things, a meditation on literal and metaphorical lines. Tristram makes the metaphor of 'plot-lines' comically literal when, in Volume VI, he traces graphically the linear movements of his first five volumes.

Austen's juvenilia are less overt about their ironic engagements with convention, but in their own way, they address formal expectations even more rigorously. As a result of the private, occasional nature of their composition (some dedicated, and clearly tailored to individual members of the family), many of the pieces are brief skits – which enables Austen to compress narrative cause and effect into high-speed slapstick. For example, the twelve tiny chapters of 'The Beautifull Cassandra' (so short, on the page, that they resemble poetic epigrams), gain an extra layer of oddity from their author's insistence on providing chapter headings, as one would for a full-length novel, even though the chapters are barely longer than the headings:

CHAPTER THE 4th

She then proceeded to a Pastry-cooks where she devoured six ices, refused to pay for them, knocked down the Pastry cook & walked away.[19]

As it is with titles, so it is with endings: the technique of having chapter endings coincide with significant entrances, exits and transitions means that the Beautifull Cassandra often spends a great proportion of her chapters on the hoof. She 'walked from her Mother's shop to make her Fortune' (Chapter 2); 'She curtseyed & walked on' (Chapter 3); and in Chapter 5, she 'ascended a Hackney Coach & ordered it to Hampstead, where she was no sooner arrived than she ordered the Coachman to turn round & drive her back again'.[20]

The brevity of so many of the juvenile burlesques has other consequences, not least a narrowing of comic focus down to the tiniest elements of Austen's narrative: the causes and effects which link sentences, clauses and cadences to each other are minutely viewed, and often set brilliantly askew. 'The Mystery', a three-page drama which Austen dedicates to her father as 'AN UNFINISHED COMEDY',[21] provides a model in miniature of the kinds of narrative and dramatic reticence on which her mature novels depend. Not only is the 'mystery' itself spoken only once on stage (and that in an inaudible stage direction), but Austen fills the rest of her playlet with references that have no referents:

DAPHNE) My Dear Mrs Humbug howd'ye do? Oh! Fanny t'is all over.
FANNY) Is it indeed!
MRS HUM:) I'm very sorry to hear it.
FANNY) Then t'was to no purpose that I....
DAPHNE) None upon Earth
MRS HUM:) And what is to become of?...
DAPHNE) Oh! thats all settled. (*whispers* MRS HUMBUG)[22]

Likewise, she contrives to stage interruptions before there is even anything to interrupt:

ACT THE FIRST

Scene the 1st

A Garden.

Enter CORYDON.

CORY.) But Hush! I am interrupted.

[*Exit* CORYDON[23]

As in 'The Beautifull Cassandra', the rapid exits with which all three scenes end carry more weight than the events which they curtail. Not that these are the only exit lines with which the juvenilia play fast and loose; where, in Austen's novels of the 1810s, the plots are frequently actuated or precipitated by significant offstage deaths – Mr Dashwood in *Sense and Sensibility*, Mr Norris and Dr Grant in *Mansfield Park*, Mrs Churchill in *Emma* – her teenage burlesques are strewn with comedy corpses. In 'Sir William Mountague', the trivial obstacle of a rival in love is soon disposed of ('Miss Arundel was cruel; she preferred a Mr Stanhope: Sir William shot Mr Stanhope; the lady had then no reason to refuse him'[24]); in 'The History of England', Richard II retires 'for the rest of his Life to Pomfret Castle, where he happened to be murdered', while 'Lord Cobham was burnt alive, but I forget what for';[25] and Sophia's death of 'a galloping Consumption' in *Love and Freindship* resets the deathbed of Le Fever from *Tristram Shandy* as something far less sentimentally edifying:

> "My beloved Laura (said she to me a few Hours before she died) take warning from my unhappy End & avoid the imprudent conduct which has occasioned it..beware of fainting-fits..Though at the time they may be refreshing & Agreable yet beleive me they will in the end, if too often repeated & at improper seasons, prove destructive to your Constitution.....My fate will teach you this..I die a Martyr to my greif for the loss of Augustus....One fatal swoon has cost me my Life....Beware of Swoons Dear Laura...A frenzy fit is not one quarter so pernicious; it is an exercise to the Body & if not too violent, is I dare say conducive to Health in its consequences—Run mad as often as you chuse; but do not faint—".
> These were the last words she ever adressed to me...[26]

While the situation of Sophia's death is rooted in sentimental fiction, the absurd logic of Austen's narrative occupies the territory of Swift's Simon Wagstaff in the preface to *Polite Conversation*: where Wagstaff projects a time when conversational spontaneity ('some sudden surprizing Piece of Wit') can be produced to order, Sophia recommends another form of sentimental response as both reproducible and potentially beneficial ('A frenzy fit [...] is an exercise to the Body'). Moments like this point to a consistent quality of Austen's technique as it works in the burlesques – one which bears on the tone and arrangement of the mature novels.

'To name a sensibility,' argues Susan Sontag, 'to draw its contours and to recount its history, requires a deep sympathy modified by revulsion.'[27] '[D]eep sympathy modified by revulsion' describes well the relationship

Austen's writing has to the literary forms with which it works and, by association, the social circumstances from which those forms emerge. The juvenilia provide an especially focused insight into her more general stylistic practice, in that they deliberately scrutinize the organization of fictional plots, the language of narrative, and even the causality of the lives and deaths which fiction recounts, in order to proclaim her own equivocal victory over those situations which she cannot wholly vanquish. Recognizing that 'genre' can apply to life as well as literature, Austen's juvenilia proceed joyously to set genre adrift from its moorings, defamiliarizing conventional shapes and expectations – an ironic mode ideally suited to Austen, whose 'sympathy' for the world in which she finds herself is checked by the 'revulsion' that world often provokes, and vice versa. Parody plays a prominent part here, but not exclusively; so does bathos, but that word's etymology implies a descent from the heights to the depths, an art of sinking in poetry, while Austen's displacements are often as much lateral as they are vertical. Now more often than not, the coinage of critical terms indicates a question being begged into existence, or another golden calf being forged; the more one needs to invent a term, the more imaginary its referent is likely to be. However, with these caveats, and taking into account Genette's attitude to his own rhetorical figures ('I think, and hope, that all this technology [...] surely barbaric to the lovers of belles lettres, tomorrow will seem positively rustic, and will go to join other packaging, the detritus of Poetics; let us only hope that it will not be abandoned without having had some transitory usefulness'[28]), I shall, from here on, occasionally be employing a term which, I hope, comprehends the multitude of ways in which Austen both reproduces and outflanks the generic conditions with which she is surrounded, refusing to be defined by what confines her: 'differential narrative'.

Doody suggests that in the juvenilia, Austen creates 'a "world of her own", as we say – or that such a world becomes adumbrated'.[29] Her qualification 'as we say' is telling, however, acknowledging that 'world of her own' is a term of art rather than an empirical description. In fact, the alternative reality of the early works is vitally and unavoidably tied to the parody's fictional and non-fictional sources; rather than being a world by itself, it depends on the defined (perhaps over-defined) presence of the world it sends up, and looks forward to another other set of symbiotic multiple worlds, the product of Lewis Carroll's willingly parasitic dependence on Victorian England (in particular Victorian Oxford) as the imaginative underwriting of both Wonderland and Looking-Glass World. In Austen's early burlesques, as later in Carroll, the forms of the everyday waking world are present and correct, but its references and referents are set out of phase, its metaphors are literalized, and logical consequences are pushed to their illogical conclusions; however, because parody needs recognizably to reproduce its targets, this often has the effect of heightening aspects of the originals rather than cancelling them out. For example, 'The Agéd, Agéd Man', Carroll's hilarious take on Wordsworth's 'Resolution and Independence' picks up on the original poem's praise of the leech-gatherer's selfless dedication ('From pond to pond he roamed, from moor to moor;/ Housing, with God's good help, by choice or chance;/ And in this way he gained an honest maintenance'[30]), teasing out from between its lines the economic home truths which it may be glossing over, as the Agéd Man tries repeatedly to touch the speaker for money:

> He said 'I look for butterflies
> That sleep among the wheat:
> I make them into mutton-pies,
> And sell them in the street.
> I sell them unto men,' he said,
> 'Who sail on stormy seas;
> And that's the way I get my bread—
> A trifle, if you please.'[31]

In addition, the closing admonition of Wordsworth's poem ('"God," said I, "be my help and stay secure;/ I'll think of the Leech-gatherer on the lonely moor!"'[32]) gains a wider application by subtly omitting to mention any precise occasions on which the speaker might actually have cause to 'think of the Leech-gatherer' in the future – allowing Carroll, whose poem brims with shiny, useful schemes, to suggest a number of possible cues:

> And now, if e'er by chance I put
> My fingers into glue,
> Or madly squeeze a right-hand foot
> Into a left-hand shoe,
> Or if I drop upon my toe
> A very heavy weight,
> I weep, for it reminds me so
> Of that old man I used to know—[33]

In the early works, Austen, too, brings to the surface the latent greed of her originals. 'They're all on the make, in a quiet way, in Jane',[34] Kipling's Humberstall wryly observes; characters in Jane's juvenilia are often loudly on the make, and when not on the make, under the influence. 'Jack and Alice' grave-facedly recounts the whole Johnson family's being 'carried home, Dead Drunk'[35] after a ball; even social proprieties, in this story, are subject to alcoholic craving, as when Alice 'had too sincere a respect for Lady Williams & too great a relish for her Claret, not to make every concession in her power'.[36] The yoking of 'unmeaning Luxuries' and 'Stinking fish' is only one of many points where the internal logic of particular constructions is found wanting, as decorous or neutral qualities are placed uncomfortably close to harder physical or economic realities. On discovering Lucy caught in a man-trap in 'Jack and Alice', Lady Williams exclaims 'Oh! cruel Charles to wound the hearts & legs of all the fair',[37] and Mr Willmot in 'Edgar and Emma' was 'the representative of a very ancient Family & possessed besides his paternal Estate, a considerable share in a Lead mine & a ticket in the Lottery'.[38] Austen employs all the narrative tropes of the daylight world, but shows them as incapable completely of explaining, containing, or fending off the juvenilia's state of nature, a world occupied by libidinous mercenaries, and in danger of being overrun with an endless supply of dogs ('he regularly sent home a large Newfoundland Dog every Month to his family'[39]). As a result, a reader is invited simultaneously to notice and look beyond these bearings, in an implicit challenge to some of the claims of universal grammarians, ancient and modern. I discussed in Chapter 1 how eighteenth-century grammarians like Harris tried to assimilate every utterance to the working-out of a mental property; in the twentieth century, Formalists such as Vladimir Propp attempted to classify the universal grammar of narrative. Propp's ground-breaking investigation into the 'morphological' family resemblances between Russian folk tales has the salutary effect of concentrating attention on the means by which stories work; however, his larger claims ('Knowing how moves are distributed, we can decompose any tale into its components'[40]) risk reducing narrative solely to its 'locutionary' functions at the expense of the 'illocutionary' and contextual ones – as if a universal grammar might also be a key to all mythologies. Austen's juvenilia provide a pointed test case for various modes of universal grammar, in that one could document any number of recognizable narrative functions without having explained what these bizarre little stories are doing – it is hard to classify generically the functions of a work, when one of its major functions is to fend off genre. Nor is genre the only object of the young Austen's fictional self-defences; in defending Austen against Charlotte Brontë's criticisms, Barbara Everett has pointed to another effect: 'Charlotte Brontë,' she argues, 'was perhaps like Woolf in seeing only what one might call the outside of these romances, given that she defined their writer as cold and passionless. If she had been these things, Jane Austen would probably not have spent a brilliant adolescence so plainly fighting off the task of writing feeling'.[41] It is a distinctive part of Austen's style that the world of the juvenilia is not abandoned in the mature novels, but lurks around and beneath them, threatening continually to emerge, and frequently doing so –

usually at the least decorous moments. The fighting off of feeling meets the writing of feeling, and both are shown to be unpredictable activities – as in *Northanger Abbey*, where the shapes of fiction and conversation share the stage with events which have shapes, and shapelessness, of their own.

As shown by Austen's joke about her readers, and how they might interpret 'the tell-tale compression of the pages' as they near the end of the novel, *Northanger Abbey* is fascinated with all kinds of searching and finding – from the secrets, disclosures, 'sliding pannels and tapestry'[42] which make up the plots of 'horrid' fiction, to the larger means by which people make sense of the world. Henry Tilney latches jokingly on to some of these possibilities when he teases Catherine Morland about what she can expect at the Abbey:

> "How fearfully will you examine the furniture of your apartment!— And what will you discern?—Not tables, toilettes, wardrobes, or drawers, but on one side perhaps the remains of a broken lute, on the other a ponderous chest which no efforts can open, and over the fire-place the portrait of some handsome warrior, whose features will so incomprehensibly strike you, that you will not be able to withdraw your eyes from it. Dorothy meanwhile, no less struck by your appearance, gazes on you in great agitation, and drops a few unintelligible hints. To raise your spirits, moreover, she gives you reason to suppose that the part of the abbey you inhabit is undoubt-edly haunted, and informs you that you will not have a single domestic within call. With this parting cordial she curtseys off—you listen to the sound of her receding footsteps as long as the last echo can reach you—and when, with fainting spirits, you attempt to fasten your door, you discover, with increased alarm, that it has no lock."[43]

Henry offers Catherine a number of tempting cues for her overactive imagin-ation, not only anticipating but practically rehearsing her reaction to the furnishings; he can do this because, as Catherine phrases it, "'Oh, Mr. Tilney, how frightful!—This is just like a book! [...]'".[44] However, in concentrating repeatedly on perceptions and their meanings ('examine', 'discern', 'strike you', 'unintelligible', 'suppose', 'listen', 'discover'), he also furthers *Northanger Abbey*'s examination of the value and limits of 'genres': the numerous ways in which sense is organized, or resists organization, in fictional plots and beyond. Catherine's 'just like a book' might alert a reader to the multiple resonances Austen gives to this exchange: within the plot, it allows Henry gently to pick away at Catherine's habit of translating what she reads directly into how she lives; at the level of narrative, it invites readers to consider the values they are bringing into their reading, the bearings by which they locate themselves in relation to Austen's novel, and novels more generally. Thus *Northanger Abbey* doubly defamiliarizes Gothic 'horrid fiction', setting Catherine loose in a world which does not quite fulfil her ideas of it, but presenting that drama in a form which does not always allow its readers the security of detachment, presenting them with their own range of false leads and red herrings.

Henry's teasing of Catherine about Gothic furniture is an extension of the habit Austen gives him, of standing genially back and noting the ridiculous aspects of what he is obliged to endure, and even, in the case of Mrs Radcliffe, what he enjoys. This is evident from Catherine's first encounter with him in Bath, as he turns the social rituals of the Pump-room into a primer of mannerism recalling Swift's *Polite Conversation*:

> After chatting some time on such matters as naturally arose from the objects around them, he suddenly addressed her with—"I have hitherto been very remiss, madam, in the proper attentions of a partner here; I have not yet asked you how long you have been in Bath; whether you were ever here before; whether you have been at the Upper Rooms, the theatre, and the concert; and how you like the place altogether. I have been very negligent—but are you now at leisure to satisfy me in these particulars? If you are I will begin directly."
>
> "You need not give yourself that trouble, sir."
>
> "No trouble I assure you madam." Then forming his features into a set smile, and affectedly softening his voice, he added, with a simpering air, "Have you been long in Bath, madam?"[45]

These set speeches are set in parallel with the literary 'accomplishments' with which Catherine is fitted out in her 'training for a heroine' ('she read all such works as heroines must read to supply their memories with those quotations which are so serviceable and so soothing in the vicissitudes of their eventful lives'[46]). Tilting at anthologies like Vicesimus Knox's *Elegant Extracts*,[47] even Austen's placement of Catherine's largely misquoted snippets of Pope, Gray and Shakespeare on the page:

> From Pope, she learned to censure those who
> "bear about the mockery of woe."[48]

makes performative fun of the quotations' detachable, portable qualities, 'so serviceable and so soothing' once more recalling Swift's Simon Wagstaff in its suggestion of poetic folk-wisdom as therapeutic, a verbal alternative to smelling-salts for melodramatic heroines. And the particular fictional genre which Austen takes on in the novel is not only chosen because it was enjoying its vogue at the turn of the nineteenth century – the kind of 'horrid' Gothic, much of it translated or imitated from the German, which Catherine consumes, relies for many of its most popular effects on being recognizably 'generic' itself.

Henry's joking prediction about the mysterious chest comes bathetically true at Northanger, as Catherine 'raised the lid a few inches; but at that moment a sudden knocking at the door of the room made her, starting, quit her hold';[49] in reality, of course, the knocking comes not from the General but from Eleanor Tilney's maid, and the chest turns out to be a linen-trunk: 'she sprang forward, and her confidence did not deceive her. Her resolute effort threw back the lid, and gave to her astonished eyes the view of a white cotton counterpane, properly folded, reposing at one end of the chest in undisputed possession!'[50] Austen has more than one target here; being caught breaking into the forbidden chest is the moment which precipitates Caleb Williams's persecution by Falkland in Godwin's novel ('I was in the act of lifting up the lid, when Mr. Falkland entered, wild, breathless, distraction in his looks!'[51]), a guilty primal scene which, shorn of much of its political radicalism, forms the centrepiece of Colman the Younger's much more popular stage version, *The Iron Chest* (1796).[52] The 'white cotton counterpane', however, pastiches a trope common in numerous translated German novels, some of which feature prominently on Isabella Thorpe's recommended reading list. Peter Teuthold's *The Necromancer; or The Tale of the Black Forest* (1794) and Peter Will's *Horrid Mysteries* (1797), teem with conspirators, gangs of robbers, atheistical sects, and symbolically soiled bed-linen:

> I went further in my search, and saw a great number of guns, pistols and swords [...] Perceiving traces of blood on the pillow, I was seized with a sudden terror, my hands trembled violently, the lamp fell to the floor, and I was in the dark.[53]

Matthew Lewis's *The Monk* (1796), which John Thorpe implausibly champions in *Northanger Abbey* as the only decent novel since *Tom Jones* ('I read that t'other day; but as for all the others, they are the stupidest things in creation'[54]), also features bloodstained bedclothes, as Don Raymond recounts his misfortunes ('"Look at the Sheets!" said She as She passed me [...] What was my astonishment, my horror, at finding the sheets crimsoned with blood!'[55]). The symbolism of red staining white, especially in Judaeo-Christian iconography, immediately carries, within the context of Gothic narrative, a complex of associations about the destruction of innocence, which the likes of *The*

Necromancer use, with differing degrees of unsubtlety, as mnemonic devices; *Northanger Abbey*'s 'white cotton counterpane' thus proclaims its resistance to such fictional excesses ('it was not in them perhaps that human nature, at least in the midland counties of England, was to be looked for'[56]), and to overly 'typological' interpretations, whether by characters or readers.

However, the setting of Gothic conventions against mundane reality is only one of many ways in which *Northanger Abbey* declines to do quite what one might expect of it; considered as a whole, Austen's narrative suggests that the debunking of Gothic fiction may be as much of a red herring for the reader as the 'horrid novels' themselves are for Catherine. Volume II, Chapter X opens clearly and forcefully ('The visions of romance were over. Catherine was fully awakened'[57]), but the novel itself neither begins nor ends with this moment of disillusionment. For all the intertextual cross-references which a writer could make at the beginning of the eighteenth century, the fact that novels, in their modern form, had not yet clearly marked themselves as a definable and legitimate literary mode, meant that there was that much less generic precedent on which to draw – a circumstance which arguably allowed some novelists to be more genuinely experimental than would be possible for a writer nowadays. By the time the young Austen was writing her violent burlesques, novelists had long been able knowingly to parody the form in which they were writing, witnessing the growth of a range of widely-held credences about what fiction was supposed to provide. For example, William Beckford (creator of the brilliant, notorious Oriental tale *Vathek*) published in 1796, under the pseudonym of 'Lady Harriet Marlow', his own broadside on the excesses of women's fiction, *Modern Novel Writing, or The Elegant Enthusiast*. The contents-pages of the two volumes themselves read like a 'morphology' of hyperbolic narrative, of the kind Austen later pulls off in 'Plan of a Novel' ('*Rural Picture*', '*Storm at Sea*' '*Terrible Encounter*', '*Important Discovery*', '*Phrenzy, Despair, and Death*'[58]), and some of the contents have a disrespect for decent timing comparable to Austen's juvenilia, as when a delirious death ('O this torrent of lobsters—stop them, they curl the Heavens'[59]) is followed within the space of a page by 'a concert'.[60] In this literary environment, it was not so easy simply to contrast fiction on the one hand to real life on the other, since the increase in fictional production and readership (which so worried Coleridge as part of the 'AWEFUL TIMES' in which he had to work) resulted in fictional texts' making up a proportionately greater part of that reality which writers could represent – a shift which led eventually to novels such as *Madame Bovary*. Charlotte Lennox's fable of misguided reading, *The Female Quixote* (1752), traces the long journey of the heroine Arabella, away from the imaginary world she has learned from a 'great Store of Romances [...] not in the original *French*, but very bad Translations':

> Her Ideas, from the Manner of her Life, and the Objects around her, had taken a romantic Turn; and, supposing Romances were real Pictures of Life, from them she drew all her Notions and Expectations. By them she was taught to believe, that Love was the ruling Principle of the World; that every other Passion was subordinate to this; and that it caused all the Happiness and Miseries of Life. Her Glass, which she often consulted, shewed her a Form so extremely lovely that, not finding herself engaged in such Adventures as were common to the Heroines in the Romances she read, she often complained of the Insensibility of Mankind, upon whom her Charms seemed to have so little Influence. [61]

Although the suddenness with which Arabella resigns herself to the non-fictional world and her subordinate role as wife ('my Heart yields to the Force of Truth'[62]), carries an undertone of bitterness – at the world's inability to match up to her expectations of it, and the dearth of tenable social roles for her – the primary force of Lennox's novel is clear. Such sentiments were still current even as late as Brunton's *Self-Control*, in which, '[h]aving no character of her own, Julia was always, as nearly as she was able, the heroine whom the last-read novel inclined her to personate'.[63] In *Northanger Abbey*, though, the education of the female Quixote is as subject as any other fictional trope to Austen's differential narrative.

Part of this effect is down to the nature of stylistic parody, especially the way in which it depends for its own life and form on the continued existence of the original off which it is feeding, even as it lays equivocal claim to its own identity. Nor is this the only double-take the parodic mode can perform: while a reader must notice some difference of subject matter or scale in order for a parody to work, a writer can create a further comic twist by suggesting ways in which the mismatched style and subject might, in fact, be more deeply akin and appropriate – as, for example, in Austen's juvenilia, where the indecorousness of her forms shows up less honourable motives in her characters. Rather than simply debunking Gothicism, *Northanger Abbey* works the forms of 'horrid fiction' into a more complex comedy of transposition, in which the 'horrid' and the mundane look at times to have swapped subjects: a reader like Catherine Morland, seeking the schemes and conspiracies of Mrs Radcliffe or German romances, is likely to discover laundry-lists or white cotton counterpanes, but a reader looking instead for the reassurances of quotidian non-event may find the 'anxieties of common life' becoming as dangerous in their own way as 'the alarms of romance'[64] – anticipating Freud's thought that 'an uncanny effect is often and easily produced when the distinction between imagination and reality is effaced, as when something that we have hitherto regarded as imaginary appears before us in reality'.[65] Consider those points where Henry Tilney takes up his sister and Catherine for what he sees as lazy usage or overinterpretation:

> "I am sure," cried Catherine, "I did not mean to say any thing wrong; but it *is* a nice book, and why should not I call it so?"
> "Very true," said Henry, "and this is a very nice day, and we are taking a very nice walk, and you are two very nice young ladies. Oh! it is a very nice word indeed!—it does for every thing. Originally perhaps it was applied only to express neatness, propriety, delicacy, or refinement;—people were nice in their dress, in their sentiments, or their choice. But now every commendation on every subject is comprised in that one word."[66]

> "Miss Morland, do not mind what he says;—but have the goodness to satisfy me as to this dreadful riot."
> "Riot!—what riot?"
> "My dear Eleanor, the riot is only in your own brain. The confusion there is scandalous. Miss Morland has been talking of nothing more dreadful than a new publication which is shortly to come out, in three duodecimo volumes, two hundred and seventy-six pages in each, with a frontispiece to the first, or two tombstones and a lantern—do you understand?—And you, Miss Morland—my stupid sister has mistaken all your clearest expressions. You talked of expected horrors in London—and instead of instantly conceiving, as any rational creature would have done, that such words could relate only to a circulating library, she immediately pictured to herself a mob of three thousand men assembling in St. George's Fields […]"[67]

Northanger Abbey's narrative, however, means that Catherine and Eleanor are not the only readers who need to be on their mettle, as Austen sets numerous puzzles of under- and over-interpretation; for instance, by the time a reader comes to Eleanor's confusion about the 'dreadful riot', he or she will already have had to negotiate Austen's incongruous, punning employment of the language of political panic in her description of the Pump-room: 'As for Mr. Allen, he repaired directly to the card-room, and left them to enjoy a *mob* by themselves. With more care for the safety of her new gown than for the comfort of her protégée, Mrs. Allen made her way through the *throng* of men by the door, as swiftly as the necessary caution would allow; Catherine, however, kept close at her side, and linked her arm too firmly within her friend's to be *torn asunder* by any *common effort of a struggling assembly*[68] (italics mine). In this context, the bearings of Gothic fiction are found wanting, not so much because they are opposed to actual reality, but because such generic mechanisms (secret panels, locked trunks, blood-stained sheets, and so on) lead a reader to seek mystery and danger only at certain predetermined points, when, as *Northanger Abbey* comes to illustrate, they may be abroad in less obvious forms within quotidian reality itself.

This carries a particular force with reference to General Tilney: even after Catherine is forced to admit that 'among the English [...] in their hearts and habits, there was a general though unequal mixture of good and bad', she still recognizes 'some actual specks' in the character of the General, 'who, though cleared from the grossly injurious suspicions which she must ever blush to have entertained, she did believe, upon serious consideration, to be not perfectly amiable'.[69] I mentioned how parody can create not only double-takes but 'triple-takes', in which style and subject are found, in fact, to be ironically congruous, and Austen takes advantage of this comic possibility here: the general is not Mrs Radcliffe's Montoni, not the wife-murderer Catherine would have him be, but Catherine is not wholly wrong; her mistake lies not so much in mistaking fantasy for reality, but in feeding experience so insistently through the interpretative template of horrid fiction that she misses his truer faults, the fact that he is, as Kipling's Humberstall calls him, 'a swine of a Major-General, retired, and on the make [...] Turned a girl out of 'is own 'ouse because she 'adn't any money – *after*, mind you, encouragin' 'er to set 'er cap at his son, because 'e thought she had':[70]

> She was guilty only of being less rich than he had supposed her to be. Under a mistaken persuasion of her possessions and claims, he had courted her acquaintance in Bath, solicited her company at Northanger, and designed her for his daughter in law. On discovering his error, to turn her from the house seemed the best, though to his feelings an inadequate proof of his resentment towards herself, and his contempt of her family.[71]

Neither horrid Gothicism nor female Quixotism prepares a reader for this revelation – one which carries that much more weight because Austen has just raised the stakes of her fiction.

As Everett points out, the juvenilia employ various modes of stylistic vandalism in order to fend off 'the task of writing feeling'; Austen could have continued in this vein, but it is hard to see where she could have gone. Whether by choice, or through the dictates of demand, the novels from *Northanger Abbey* onwards take on the fiction of domestic courtship, with the expectations (the writing of feeling included) which that carries with it; however, instead of smoothing over the wrinkles of the juvenilia, romance is found to be potentially just as chaotic. The double-irony of General Tilney's true nature is just one instance where the expected happens unexpectedly, a sign of where Austen's differential narrative begins to distinguish her from her parodic predecessors. For example, while the imaginative longevity of Sterne's masterpiece militates against Johnson's criticism that 'Nothing odd will do long. *Tristram Shandy* did not last',[72] one could argue that its internal energy does run out by the end of the novel. By the time a reader comes to 'The Story of the king of Bohemia and his seven castles' in Volume VIII, the unexpected has been so consistently and predictably elevated into a structural principle that it obvious that Trim's story will never reach its point:

> There was a certain king of Bohemia, but in whose reign, except his own, I am not able to inform your honour—
> I do not desire it of thee, Trim, by any means, cried my uncle Toby.[73]

Austen pulls off the rarer feat of continually shadowing order with chaos, while simultaneously inviting her readers to believe in the resolutions she offers; 'The Janeites' may diagnose acutely the fondnesses of Edwardian taste ('you'd ha' felt your flat feet tingle every time you walked over those sacred pavin'-stones'[74]), but Humberstall remains true ('I read all her six books now for pleasure 'tween times in the shop; an' it brings it all back – down to the smell of the glue-paint on the screens. You take it from me, Brethren, there's no one to touch Jane when you're in a tight place'[75]). Differential narrative, a comic technique which enables Austen to accept the necessity of form without always accepting its causalities, also allows her to become one of the nineteenth century's most penetrating analysts of cliché, mannerism and bad faith, without hardening into (to borrow Gabriel Josipovici's phrase), 'a positivist of the negative'.[76]

The rest of this book will explore what Austen does with this awareness, with particular reference to some of the activities which go on in the novels: flirtation, social ventriloquism and characters' movements in space. Time and again, readers are invited to set their sense and respect for precedent alongside a capacity to be surprised, often by what they most suspect; form – be it social observance or literary genre – is seen to be indispensable but not all-encompassing, so conclusions can be offered without implying that everything is concluded. Henry James mused on novelists' imaginative constraints in his 1907 preface to *Roderick Hudson*. 'Really, universally,' he suggested, 'relations stop nowhere, and the exquisite problem of the artist is eternally but to draw, by a geometry of his own, the circle within which they shall happily *appear* to do so.'[77] In 'The Generous Curate' (1793), Austen comments of young Williams: 'His Character however was perfectly amiable though his genius might be cramped, and he was addicted to no vice, or ever guilty of any fault beyond what his age and situation rendered perfectly excusable. He had indeed sometimes been detected in flinging Stones at a Duck or putting Brickbats into his Benefactor's bed; but these innocent efforts of Wit were considered by that good Man rather as the effects of a lively imagination, than of anything bad in his Nature'.[78] The distinctive effect of Austen's 'lively imagination' is that she can repeatedly draw that circle in which relations 'should happily *appear*' to stop: couples eventually come together, or rediscover the depth of their feelings for each other, years later, in Union Street; somewhere, however, off in the far corner of the frame, is a small figure, 'flinging Stones at a Duck'.

2

FLIRTING

I mean to confine myself in future to Mr Tom Lefroy, for whom I
do not care sixpence.

Jane Austen to Cassandra Austen, 14 January 1796[1]

Have you seen any pleasant men? Have you had any flirting?

Lydia Bennet in Pride and Prejudice[2]

Ars Amatoria

James Edward Austen-Leigh remembered his Aunt Jane speaking, and
wished that others might hear her too; it was a hope only half-forlorn. *A
Memoir of Jane Austen* recalls with pleasure her 'sweet voice, both in singing and
conversation',[3] and prints for the first time some of her familiar letters; with
the proceeds of that work, he was able to supplement the slab in Winchester
Cathedral's north aisle with a brass plaque on a nearby wall. Even the quotation from Proverbs at the bottom of the plaque seems chosen to remind the
public of his aunt's powers of speech: 'She openeth her mouth with wisdom,
and in her tongue is the law of kindness'.[4] For Austen-Leigh to set his aunt
alongside the Biblical 'vertuous woman' whose 'price *is* farre aboue Rubies'[5]
may have been going too far, but Jane Austen did rarely waste her breath.
'What she wrote,' Richard Simpson remarked in 1870, the year of the *Memoir*,
'was worked up by incessant labour into its perfect form'.[6] His words are all
the more judicious for their perceiving the density of Austen's art, and for
their reluctance (rare at the time) to praise Austen herself as intellectually
'small but perfectly formed', a 'creepmouse' among the giants of the
nineteenth-century novel. Brian Southam may be right in claiming the 1870s,
the decade which witnessed the *Memoir* and the centenary of Austen's birth, as
the beginning of serious Austen scholarship[7] – but the excesses of 'gentle-
Janeism' which I discussed in Chapter 1, were still producing what James
memorably dismissed as 'pleasant twaddle'[8] well into this century. One of the
strengths of Simpson's reading lies in his taking Austen's 'form' seriously: 'she
was a critic,' he writes, 'who developed herself into an artist'.[9] Such an artist
would have needed to know her form – both the techniques of her medium

and her own past and potential achievements. Likewise, Simpson's classing the juvenilia as 'exercises, not studies'[10] points to the progression which he traces from *Love and Freindship* through to the mature works.

However, Simpson's comments are cast in the mould of an ancient and rather different progression, as he makes a larger case for Jane Austen as a Platonist: 'Platonist as she was in her feelings, she could rise to contemplate the soul as a family, but not as a republic'.[11] Hence his uses of 'developed' and 'perfect form' may have quite specific applications, senses which pull in subtly divergent directions. Are readers to equate, or even compare, that 'perfect form' which Austen achieved in her works with the final goal of Platonic thought – the transcendence of human contingency in the world of perfect Forms? If anything, the texture of Austen's fiction has more in common with Pope's comedy at neo-Platonism's expense:

> Go, soar with Plato to th'empyreal sphere,
> To the first good, first perfect, and first fair;
> Or tread the mazy round his follow'rs trod,
> And quitting sense call imitating God;[12]

Austen's death-bed request for 'nothing but death',[13] for instance, loses something if one hears it not as a pained and painful joke,[14] the final resignation of a valued life, but as her delivery of a line she had spent her life rehearsing.[15] While Simpson's clear-headed hearing of Austen is so often true to her, it still sounds out of true at points like this; where Charlotte Brontë's letter to Wilson bemoans the fact that Austen spent so much time on messy body parts ('eyes, mouth, hands and feet'), Simpson's emphasis on the 'Platonist' Austen tends in the opposite direction – both writers, after their own fashions, feeling somehow troubled by the superficial, that which is of the surface. Brontë would wish Austen to retreat inward to the 'feeling heart', whereas Simpson would have her reaching beyond the material surfaces of existence to higher things. Austen also has an influential position in the history of the novel as psychological testimony, in which, according to RF Brissenden, 'the emphasis is not on physical action but on reflection, on the inner lives of the characters'.[16] These emphases have their applications, but they are not comprehensive in their coverage. To praise or condemn novelists primarily for their portrayals of individual minds risks ignoring the ways in which those minds – with varying degrees of self-awareness, bewilderment, estrangement and loathing – are imagined to inhabit bodies.[17] An unease about contingency, for example, prompts Simpson to admit of Austen, in a concessive tone which belies his insight: 'Altogether, she is a luminary not beyond the spell of ordinary human magic'.[18]

Simpson's reading, with its implication that the pursuit of ideal forms is the proper business of flawed souls, may speak too lightly of 'ordinary human magic', but he has a point; Austen is not beyond that 'spell', neither is it beyond her (the *OED* credits *Mansfield Park* with the first instance of 'beyond me' as meaning 'to pass [...] comprehension'[19]). Simpson's emphasis on Plato and transcendence says less about Austen's technique than does his description of the 'critic who *developed* herself into an artist' (italics mine).[20] Austen truly 'developed' herself, in that she brought herself to fruition in her art by bringing the whole of herself to bear upon it: in her novels, critical perception and artistic creation became coordinate. The precociously acute twelve-year-old who could describe a character's being 'of so dazzling a Beauty that none but Eagles could look him in the Face',[21] became the writer who could still delight in the piecemeal 'erudition' of Sir Edward Denham in *Sanditon*:

> '[...] But who is perfect? — It were Hyper-criticism, it were Pseudo-philosophy to expect from the soul of high toned Genius, the grovellings of a common mind.'[22]

One thing that had happened in between these two pieces of writing was that Austen, as I have discussed, had reached maturity in an accommodation with the disparate voices around her – moral, political, sociable – an accommodation which was rather a difficult friendship than an acquiescent surrender. Whilst she was hardly prurient, she was canny enough to create in her novels a social acoustic that lived in her world and with the worldly. James Edward Austen-Leigh felt driven, out of loyalty to his aunt's memory, to make several terse protestations of historical fact in a last-minute postscript to the first edition of the *Memoir* ('I have read with astonishment the strange misrepresentation of my aunt's manners [...]', ' In point of fact [...] all intercourse between the families ceased when Jane was little more than seven years old'[23]). The immediate cause for this was Mary Russell Mitford's posthumously published report of what her mother had told her about the young Jane Austen: that she had been 'the prettiest, silliest, most affected, husband-hunting butterfly she ever remembers'.[24] Austen-Leigh was right to object, both to the unlovely, venom-spitting superlatives ('*st* [...]*st* [...] *st* [...] *ct* [...] *sb*') and to Mitford's conflating gossip with historical scruple ('Mamma says'[25]), but he was doing his aunt and her gifts a major injustice if he truly believed that she knew nothing about flirting.

That Austen was versed in the art is evident in her earliest surviving letters to Cassandra, written shortly after her twentieth birthday in January 1796. The accounts of her flirtation with her friends' relative Tom Lefroy bear witness to a sharp knowledge of amatory joking, and to a way with words which her esteemed predecessor Fanny Burney seemed by that time to be losing. The lightness which distinguishes Burney's first novel *Evelina* (1778) springs in part from a knowing – but not disingenuous – feeling for the psychology of convention, and a willingness to include those aspects of young love which everyone knows to be embarrassing, precisely because everyone is guilty of them. In Vol. II, Letter XXI, for instance, Evelina relates her rescue from an indiscreet situation in the pleasure gardens:

> I fancy — that Lord Orville saw what passed; for scarcely was I at liberty, ere he returned. Methought, my dear Sir, the pleasure, the surprise of that moment, recompensed me for all the chagrin I had before felt: for do you not think, that this return, manifests, from a character so quiet, so reserved as Lord Orville's, something like solicitude in my concerns?[26]

'I fancy', 'do you not think', 'something like solicitude': Burney composes Evelina's bashful evasions with consummate skill, as she invites her guardian Mr Villars to confirm what she cannot quite bring herself to venture openly herself – that Lord Orville might, just possibly, care for her. It is convenient that the letter also gives Evelina the chance to dwell on his name, as she does so often throughout the novel. Teenagers in love, of either sex, are wont, however shy they may be out loud, to cherish in private the names of their loved ones, scribbled in margins, murmured into pillows, worked up into codes, charades and florid acrostics; Harriet Smith in *Emma* may be an extreme case, but she is not an exceptional one.[27] For this reason, such habits of licensed hyperbole are as much part of the recognizable precedent of language as more 'quiet' and 'reserved' forms of address. Hence the naturalistic charm and humour in so much of *Evelina*; Burney's heroine appears all the more well-observed for the fact that a reader can recognize even her self-indulgence as something affectingly well-worn. In the act of discharging one obligation, that of keeping her guardian informed, Evelina is seen to discharge another, as she keeps her own affection nourished.

Johnson (not a writer who easily dismissed habit and precedent) singled out Burney's lively sense of occasion and practice, when he paid her the compliment that '*Evelina* seems a work that should result from long experience and deep and intimate knowledge of the world'.[28] The irony of Burney's subsequent career is that her 'long experience' led to *Camilla*, which appeared a few months after Jane Austen's first recorded flirtations, and to which Austen herself was one of the early subscribers. There is no reason to doubt Jane and Cassandra's genuine admiration for the book: it is one of the novels defended by the narrator of *Northanger Abbey*, and the Austen sisters regarded it as a touchstone of others' literary taste (although Jane would, typically enough, joke about the different senses of 'taste' itself at the same time[29]). Nevertheless, as with *Sir Charles Grandison* before it, *Camilla* furnishes few of the roots of Austen's own comedy. Compare, for example, the sly hints of attachment which fall, almost undetected, across Evelina's polite words, with a typical description of love from *Camilla*:

> 'O, my Camilla! my now own Camilla!' cried Edgar, venturing to change the hand of the Mother for that of the daughter; 'what too, too touching words and confessions are these! Suffer me, then, to hope a kind amnesty may take place of retrospection, a clear, liberal, open forgiveness anticipate explanation and enquiry?'[30]

Christopher Ricks has remarked of poetry that 'it is the mark of the true poet that what would be mere convention in others is validated in the art, so that recourse to the word "convention" is just what the poems do not ask'.[31] His comment has wider applications; what seems to have happened to Burney's way with speech at these points in *Camilla* is that it has hardened into 'mere convention'. Where *Evelina* coordinates dramatic exposition with the tones and content of the characters' letters, characters in *Camilla* can descend to talking *in* exposition ('Suffer me, then, to hope', 'a clear, liberal, open forgiveness'). Looking back, in this light, to the ideas of 'perfect form' and 'Platonism', Ricks's words on 'convention' gain further pertinence; he provides a useful working definition of what it means to 'transcend a genre', without disowning one's roots – the attitude which I have called differential narrative. Mrs Mitford may have called the young Austen a 'husband-hunting butterfly', but her metaphor forgets another fact about butterflies: that their adult *imago* stage both transcends and includes those intermediate stages through which they have 'developed' and metamorphosed. That Austen never left her past completely behind her, in developing from critic to artist, can be seen in the odd filiation between her most ostensibly naïve heroine and her most allegedly virtuous one. Catherine Morland's disappointment with the domestic spaces of Northanger ('A moment's glance was enough to satisfy Catherine that her apartment was very unlike the one which Henry had endeavoured to alarm her by the description of'[32]), can never hygienically be separated from Fanny Price's reaction to the Sotherton chapel:

> Fanny's imagination had prepared her for something grander than a mere, spacious, oblong room, fitted up for purposes of devotion – with nothing more striking or more solemn than the profusion of mahogany, and the crimson velvet cushions appearing over the ledge of the family gallery above.[33]

Since *Northanger Abbey* was not published in Austen's lifetime, she cannot be said to have intended her readers to notice the parallel between Catherine and Fanny; nevertheless, the similarity between the two heroines' reactions to rooms shows how her own sense of artistic development was beset around with the possibilities of bathos and embarrassment – as I have said, this was a awkward relationship.

Austen understood well the complex demands which her form and times made upon friendships, as her letters to Cassandra illustrate repeatedly. The two extant letters about young Tom Lefroy can, like *Evelina* before them, make formal politeness convey more personal and flirtatious concerns; but, where Burney takes care to make Evelina's words sound ingenuous and wide-eyed, Austen's correspondence nudges and winks felicitously, even as she wishes her sister a happy birthday: 'In the first place I hope you will live twenty-three years longer. Mr. Tom Lefroy's birthday was yesterday, so you are very nearly of an age'.[34] Not content with this, Austen archly recasts Tom Lefroy as the euphemistic 'my Irish friend', all the more funny considering that, on the evidence of her letter, the real reticence came from Lefroy: 'for he is so excessively laughed at about me at Ashe, that he is ashamed of coming to Steventon, and ran away when we called on Mrs. Lefroy a few days ago'.[35] To have shy boys running away from you is hardly the action of 'Aunt Jane'[36] – at least not in the sense in which Austen-Leigh uses the words. Neither is Austen's comic vamping-up to Cassandra necessarily that of a 'husband-hunting butterfly'. The last we hear of Lefroy's name in the letters is this:

> *Friday.* — At length the Day is come at last when I am to flirt my last with Tom Lefroy, & when you receive this it will be over— My tears flow as I write, at the melancholy idea.[37]

'Flirt my last', 'it will be over': rarely has the old literary truism about love being like death sounded so ingeniously melancholy. These jokes militate against the assumption underpinning Simpson's comments – that however well she combined 'the "tarpaulin phrase" with the demands of art and civility',[38] she still kept the earthly at arms' length in her pursuit of the ideal. That her letter admits how pain can look melodramatic, that she writes it up in a Richardsonian parody ('My tears flow') need not disqualify it as pain. Indeed, something of Austen's loss makes itself felt through the civility two years later:

> of her nephew she said nothing at all, and of her friend very little. She did not once mention the name of the former to *me*, and I was too proud to make any enquiries; but on my father's afterwards

asking where he was, I learnt that he was gone back to London in his way to Ireland, where he is called to the Bar and means to practise.[39]

She never mentions Tom Lefroy again in her surviving correspondence. As I mentioned in Chapter 1, it is always a risky business drawing causal links between life and work – all the more so when the variables involved are a twenty-year-old's flirtation and six of the most famous nineteenth-century English novels. But, by the same token, it would be an impossibly stern and desiccated version of art that could find no room for such modes of affection, as if a work could only be 'literature' if it had its eyes fixed firmly on the heavens. The *amour* with Lefroy in 1796 did not 'cause' *Pride and Prejudice*; all I wish to show is one way in which such unpredictable experiences bear upon a writer's disposition towards the language in which he or she works, and is worked upon. Austen achieved in her fiction a refinement of the comic bravado in these early letters, which can sometimes read as if she is trying to put a brave face on things. The self-critic developed herself into an artist of selves involved with others, chafing and caressing in language.[40]

The anonymous publication of *Sense and Sensibility* in 1811 gave Austen the leisure to remain, as Egerton's title-page records, 'A LADY'; but *Pride and Prejudice* carried with it the responsibility of being identified as 'THE AUTHOR OF "SENSE AND SENSIBILITY"' (see Figure 2), and the potential ignominies of being reviewed as such. Of the novel's two published notices, the *British Critic* adopts the 'tries-hard-could-do-better' tone of a school report:

> It is unnecessary to add, that we have perused these volumes with much satisfaction and amusement, and entertain very little doubt that their successful circulation will induce the author to similar exertions.[41]

and the *Critical Review* falls back upon an easy pun ('The sentiments, which are dispersed over the work, do great credit to the *sense* and *sensibility* of the authoress'[42]). Austen might have had reason to feel that she was, if not exactly being misrepresented, being damned with faint praise; the better of the two reviews, the *Critical Review*, only gestures towards more detailed analysis, noting that 'There is not one person in the drama with whom we could readily dispense;— they have all their proper places'.[43] Irritating as they must have been, such underwhelmed reviews were, however, part of what Austen's calling called her to. Potential misconstruction, condescension and downright tone-deafness were gravitational forces with which her work had to contend,

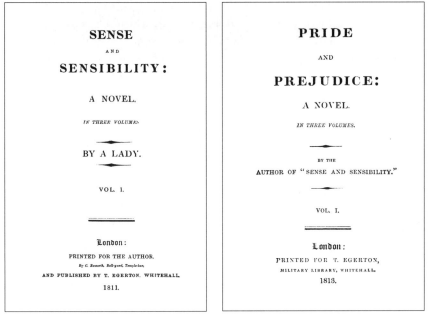

Figure 2. The anonymous publication of *Sense and Sensibility* gave Austen the leisure to remain 'A LADY'; but *Pride and Prejudice* carried with it the responsibility of being identified as 'THE AUTHOR OF "SENSE AND SENSIBILITY"', and the potential ignominies of being reviewed as such.

because they are always pitches in the diverse language of the world from which artists must draw. Geoffrey Hill has remarked:

> That commonplace image, founded upon the unfinished statues of Michelangelo, 'mighty figures straining to free themselves from the imprisoning marble', has never struck me as being an ideal image for sculpture itself; it seems more to embody the nature and condition of those arts which are composed of words.[44]

Austen, in her fiction, is able to work inventively with that 'imprisoning marble', neither ceding to its attendant banality nor believing that one could ever wholly avoid it. She makes a necessity of virtue, by making the necessity of speech the grounds and the expression of virtue; her novels, like so many of the conversations in them, take place within earshot.

In 1817, the year of Austen's death, Coleridge felt the social force of prose less equivocally, as more of a tragic weight in what he variously called 'AWEFUL TIMES', or the 'age of corrupt eloquence':

> In prose I doubt whether it be even possible to preserve our style
> wholly unalloyed by the vicious phraseology which meets us every-
> where, from the sermon to the newspaper, from the harangue of the
> legislator to the speech from the convivial chair, announcing a *toast*
> or sentiment. Our chains rattle, even while we are complaining of
> them. [45]

Coleridge seems surer of focus in describing the symptoms of his irritation
than in pinpointing its cause: his string of metonyms ('the sermon', 'the newspaper', 'the convivial chair') ranges around with an indignant precision which
'vicious phraseology' lacks, perhaps because Coleridge is too afraid of falling
into 'corrupt eloquence' himself. But this is an abstention on Coleridge's part,
potentially as self-defeating as the 'rattle' of which he complains. Neither
rattling chains nor 'imprisoning marble' fits easily when applied to Austen's
comedies; both terms suggest a state of attrition with the language which the
evidence does not uphold. Conversely, as I shall be arguing throughout this
study, neither is Austen guilty of quiescence or quietism, that fabled 'English
Reserve' for which she is often co-opted as an unwitting advocate. As Austen's
letters about Tom Lefroy transcend their genre by owning that young love is
ever poised on the brink of the ridiculous, so the maturity of *Pride and Prejudice*
rises in its own way to such demands by creating a 'sparkling' dramatic
comedy out of the eternal possibility of being misunderstood. Austen chances
her arm with the contexture of prose, where Coleridge would like to wave it
aside dismissively; it is her reward to achieve not the rattling of chains but a
small victory of care. In this novel, romance abides with raillery, 'flyting' with
flirting.

On the surface, it may seem odd to stress the flirtatious aspects of Austen's
writing, since the tendency of many moral commentators at the time – particularly with Evangelicalism in the air – was to recoil from such allegedly
impure motives. Thomas Gisborne, for one, may have provided a cue for
Mansfield Park when he worried about 'the unrestrained familiarity with
persons of the other sex, which invariably results from being joined with them
in the drama'. [46] Writing to Cassandra, Austen 'reviewed' *Pride and Prejudice* in
terms which set such words in context, and set them to rights:

> The work is rather too light, and bright, and sparkling; it wants
> shade; it wants to be stretched out here and there with a long chap-
> ter of sense, if it could be had; if not, of solemn specious nonsense,
> about something unconnected with the story; an essay on writing, a
> critique on Walter Scott, or the history of Buonaparte, or anything
> that would form a contrast, and bring the reader with increased

delight to the playfulness and epigrammatism of the general style. I doubt your quite agreeing with me here. I know your starched notions.[47]

This is a great piece of literary criticism and, like many such pieces, a work of love. Jane's letter flirts with the English language, the truisms of book-reviewing and her sister's tastes in literary reading. Basking in the semantic glow of 'light, and bright, and sparkling', 'wants' initially describes an absence ('it wants shade') only to come alive ('it wants to be') in the long string of alternatives which itself mimes the imagined 'stretching' of the novel; Austen contrives to knock in the process not only abstract etiquette but cosmetic materialism ('the history of Buonaparte') and, with her coinage of 'epigrammatism', the kinds of review she was all to likely to receive. The vigour of her words even spills over into the sisterly rudeness of 'I know your starched notions', which should alert a reader to another notable aspect of this letter. Whatever else she is up to here, Jane Austen is telling a joke – and telling jokes was not something for which the likes of Thomas Gisborne and Mrs West were famous. Marilyn Butler has argued of Austen's letter: 'Although the remedies Jane Austen suggests are intentionally absurd, the critical observation itself reads like a genuine one'.[48] Butler sees, rightly, that Austen's humour can be a serious business; but her 'Although' is itself too schismatic. She makes an attempt (one which Addison and Shaftesbury might have recognized) to co-opt the absurd in the service of the educative – which has the effect of making a good joke sound as if it were too healthily righteous. Jokes and wind-ups, rather than 'instructive sentiments', confer imaginative integrity upon Austen's writing, here and elsewhere.

One ought, however, to note that the word 'flirting' and its cognates do not ostensibly get that good a press in *Pride and Prejudice* – being attached exclusively to Lydia Bennet, a 'husband-hunting butterfly' if ever there were one. Elizabeth warns Mr Bennet that Lydia risks becoming 'A flirt too, in the worst and meanest degree of flirtation',[49] and after Lydia's elopement, she reflects on her sister's priorities – or rather the seeming lack of them: 'Since the —— shire were first quartered in Meryton, nothing but love, flirtation and officers, have been in her head'.[50] Lydia, too, in a dream sequence rare in Austen's fiction (unless one counts Catherine Morland's Gothic fantasies) imagines herself at Brighton:

She saw with the creative eye of fancy, the streets of that gay bathing place covered with officers. She saw herself the object of attention, to tens and to scores of them at present unknown. She saw all the glories of the camp; its tents stretched forth in beauteous uniformity of lines, crowded with the young and the gay, and dazzling with scarlet; and to complete the view, she saw herself beneath a tent, tenderly flirting with at least six officers at once.[51]

At one elegant and ludicrous, Austen's comedy – like the mock-heroic of Pope and Swift, which it recalls here – maintains an inwardness and reciprocity with the object of its disapproval, 'the creative eye of fancy'.[52] Lydia's vision of 'earthly happiness' manages to compact teenage daydream with the rhetoric of Biblical prophecy ('She saw [...] She saw [...] to tens and to scores of them [...] She saw all the glories of the camp [...] she saw'). While Austen may not have been as indulgent towards the grotesque as a later humorist like Flaubert (who certainly saw all the glories of the Camp), her humour shares a world and a language with the likes of Lydia, and makes of that sharing more than just a partition of blame. John Bayley sees her works as 'a peculiar kind of liberation from morality',[53] although, as shown by the Jamesian quotation marks around '"Irresponsibility"' in his essay's title, he seems a little edgy about what that 'peculiar kind' is. The novels provide a peculiar kind of liberation from a particular kind of moralizing, and Bayley touches upon one of their fundamental quirks when he notes that 'Jane Austen's art puts us and herself into a community from which there is no withdrawing; a community in which we are entitled to malice, to misunderstanding, to levity, to thoughtlessness – to anything except the right to detach ourselves and contemplate with the author from outside'.[54] That 'community' which Bayley sketches is primarily a linguistic community, the source of meanings; he tactfully notices that 'malice', 'misunderstanding', 'levity' and 'thoughtlessness' are also elements of the human nature from which language gains its sense, man being a *social animal* with an equal emphasis on both elements. But this is not the whole story; in choosing to focus on characters' involvements in the social medium of speech, Austen fashions an art form which does much with other events 'from which there is no withdrawing' – the growth of understanding, sharing a joke, falling in love.

'...civil disdain...'

Disdaine and Scorne ride sparkling in her eyes,
Mis-prizing what they looke on.
Shakespeare, *Much Ado About Nothing*[55]

To say that Austen's novels are intelligent love stories is to risk bathos; however, that they are intelligent about love as well as being about 'intelligent love' has been less well documented. *Mansfield Park*, for instance, seems more

congenial than the other novels to Simpson's idea that 'the giving and receiv-
ing of knowledge [...] is the truest and strongest foundation of life';[56] yet even
here, there may be more going on than meets the theory. Take Edmund and
Fanny's first impressions of the Crawfords:

> "Well Fanny, and how do you like Miss Crawford *now*?" said
> Edmund the next day, after thinking some time on the subject him-
> self. "How did you like her yesterday?"
> "Very well — very much. I like to hear her talk. She entertained
> me; and she is so extremely pretty, that I have great pleasure of
> looking at her."
> "It is her countenance that is so attractive. She has a wonderful play
> of feature! But was there nothing in her conversation that struck
> you Fanny, as not quite right?"
> "Oh! yes, she ought not to have spoken of her uncle as she did. I
> was quite astonished. An uncle with whom she has been living so
> many years, and who, whatever his faults may be, is so very fond of
> her brother, treating him, they say, quite like a son. I could not have
> believed it!"
> "I thought you would be struck. It was very wrong — very indecor-
> ous."[57]

The two cousins are certainly giving and exchanging information; they are
also, after the peculiar fashion of this novel, chatting each other up (although
they would hardly admit that to themselves). As I have discussed in Chapter 1,
writing can simultaneously put us at a remove from life and bring that life
more sharply and lucidly home; it allows readers to negotiate with other
minds and other experiences, to spend time in reading with characters from
whom they might, with reason, run a mile in real life. Austen shows equanimity in presenting Edmund and Fanny's unwitting courtship as both awkward
and just, without reducing it to a scientific sideshow, The Mating Ritual of the
Cold Fish. There is a comical truth in the way Edmund and Fanny rely on
cues and reassurances ("How did you like her yesterday?"/ "Very well [...] I
have great pleasure of looking at her."/ "It is her countenance [...] But was
there nothing in her conversation that struck you"/ "Oh! yes"/ "I thought
you would be struck"). As a pair of good rural Tories, they like to hear loyalties affirmed, to work towards whatever the righteous equivalent of the
'punchline' is: their chiming conversation affirms the bond between them,
even at a stage of the story where they and the reader might be in need of
reassurance. As Austen's narrative hints darkly under its breath ('after thinking some time on the subject himself'), Edmund's mind and loyalties are from

this point on divided between the urbane sophistication of Mary Crawford and Fanny Price's 'heroism of principle',[58] the good sense of a woman who is, for much of the story, a better representative of his faith than he is himself. This whole passage thrives on the particular dramatic irony that underlies all the central love plots in the mature novels (*Persuasion* perhaps excepted): the hero and heroine form their attachment through conversations not immediately connected with their eventual marriage, in which a reader comes to see and hear more of that end than the characters themselves either suspect or admit. In *Pride and Prejudice*, Darcy and Elizabeth start as sparring-partners; in *Emma*, Knightley moves from being the heroine's better conscience to being her husband; and here in *Mansfield Park*, Edmund and Fanny are saying more about each other than they think they are saying to each other. On one level, Edmund has to cope with the embarrassing recognition that his cousin is always going to tell him just that much more than he would like to know about Mary ('she ought not to have spoken of her uncle as she did'); alongside this, Austen allows the reader to hear those half-acknowledged affinities which will finally draw the two protagonists together. The turn of the nineteenth century was as rich in hopefully fictitious imaginings of love as any other time, so there is a sobering counterweight in Austen's discovering bonds where one would least expect (or hope) to find them.

'If gratitude and esteem are good foundations of affection, Elizabeth's change of sentiment will be neither improbable nor faulty.'[59] *Pride and Prejudice* lends a Johnsonian cadence to a Johnsonian sentiment, to a humane and humorous admission of 'the other less interesting mode of attachment'. Johnson himself was not above staging his own views on marriage as an erudite conversational 'trump', wedding common sense with horse sense:

> BOSWELL: 'Then, Sir, you are not of an opinion with some who imagine that certain men and certain women are made for each other; and that they cannot be happy if they miss their counterparts?'
> JOHNSON: 'To be sure not Sir. I believe marriages would in general be as happy, and even more so, if they were all made by the Lord Chancellor, upon a due consideration of characters and circumstances, without the parties having any choice in the matter.'[60]

That Johnson could do this at all was because he realized the twin forces validating his joke: both the necessary amateur dramatics of courtship and wedlock, and the truth beneath his hyperbole about 'the Lord Chancellor'. A 'due consideration of characters and circumstances' is, after all, a good working definition of prudence in human affairs, not least in the choice of the partner of one's life; a more pertinent question is whether one could trust the Lord Chancellor on this score. In his *Life of Waller,* Johnson is less skittish, bearing witness to the fact that one cannot, and should not, avoid the chaff of human relationships, even as one strives with the recalcitrant matter of human nature. 'Many qualities,' he writes, 'contribute to domestic happiness, upon which poetry has no colours to bestow; and many airs and sallies may delight imagination, which he who flatters them never can approve'.[61] Poetry may not be able to 'bestow' colours on such qualities, but at its best it might decently hope to do them justice by making them part of its spectrum, as Austen's fiction does. I mentioned earlier how the novels' integrity depends on their humour, which is fine up to a point. But this cuts both ways: there is also an important sense in which their humour depends on their integrity, ironic comedy being the recognition of competing perspectives or slants within a larger whole. William Empson's comments on irony are some of the twentieth century's most astute on the topic; of particular relevance to Austen is his assertion that '[t]he value of the state of mind which finds double irony natural is that it combines breadth of sympathy with energy of judgment; it can keep its balance among all the materials for judging'.[62] *Pride and Prejudice* keeps its balance and its head among 'the materials for judging', by admitting that it cannot but be among these 'materials' – not the least of which is the capacity to get a joke.

As she described her flirtation with Tom Lefroy to Cassandra, Austen availed herself of an innuendo more refined than the typographical sauciness of Sterne: 'You scold me so much in the nice long letter which I have this moment received from you, that I am almost afraid to tell you how my Irish friend and I behaved. Imagine to yourself everything most profligate and shocking in the way of dancing and sitting down together'.[63] 'Imagine to yourself' neatly pinpoints the secret of such jokes – and a central quality of Austen's humour – in that it compacts on the page both the huffy indignation of the prude ('Well, just *imagine!*') and the collusion on which innuendo relies ('You're going to have to imagine it for yourself; *I'm* not telling you'), with the result that Cassandra can feel at once bawdy and prim, the initiate and the innocent. Where Austen differs from Sterne's repeated dangling before the reader of Mrs Shandy's '****',[64] is that her joke composes vocally the tug of attitudes which it enacts: she responds to what one might say, as opposed to the sheer unspeakability of Sterne's *mise-en-page*. The intensive 'everything' performs a neat sinking in poetry: it rhymes through 'shocking' and 'dancing' before coming to a bathetic halt in 'sitting'. Here, as in *Northanger Abbey*, Austen gets hysteria to take the weight off its feet. Cassandra Austen was her sister's most sensitive reader, as well as being the tester for her humour – no mean achievement, considering that one of Jane's recurring tricks was to imagine her as ever so slightly prissy ('You scold me', 'I know your starched notions'). No one in English literature stuck their tongue out more elegantly and affectionately than Jane did at Cassandra. Indeed, this very archness was one of the things that Jane's letters asked Cassandra to imagine to and for herself. Of Cassandra's correspondence, we possess only that respectful account of Jane's death which she sent to Fanny Knight: a letter unsurprisingly short on jokes. But it would impugn both Jane Austen's memory and her sister's intelligence if one were to imagine that Jane could have gone on making so many jokes that Cassandra did not get; that would shrink sarcasm into something altogether more spiteful. Austen counted on the fact that her sister would see and hear what she was about. The novels, too, depend on a reader's recognition of what might be going on, all the more so since an ear for context is one of the resources which her characters pick up in the course of their stories. But much as she valued (and ribbed) her sister's opinion, Austen did not compose *Pride and Prejudice* 'for' Cassandra in quite the way she did her letters, although the similarities may be more telling than the differences; she could not rely with the same confidence on the fact that her readers would immediately be on her wavelength. The novel does not baulk at having to manœuvre around the likes of the *British Critic* and the *Critical Review* as it does around Mr Collins or Mrs Bennet. Austen's writing turns the possibility of being mistaken, mis-taken or taken in vain, to good account: 'her characters and her readers see and say more or other than they intended to, so that they and we correct ourselves'.[65] In achieving this, she finds a dramatic form for those abiding concerns which animate her mature work. On the one hand, there is the perennial question of how one balances a serious feeling for community with the rewards of a lively and sarcastic critical intelligence; and on the other, there is her insight into manners at work, the minute portrayal of the ease with which they can slide into mannerism. These interests come into focus in an art which aims lower than Richard Simpson's ideal neo-Platonism, but which is for that reason all the more responsive to the truths of 'intelligent love', to 'everything most profligate and shocking in the way of dancing and sitting down together'.

If sitting down in *Pride and Prejudice* is not always 'shocking', it is often a cause for intrigue and comment. Most famous, perhaps, is that first occasion where Elizabeth and Darcy fail to avoid being in each other's company:

> "Oh! she is the most beautiful creature I ever beheld! But there is one of her sisters sitting down just behind you, who is very pretty, and I dare say, very agreeable. Do let me ask my partner to introduce you."
>
> "Which do you mean?" and turning round, he looked for a moment

at Elizabeth, till catching her eye, he withdrew his own and coldly said, "She is tolerable; but not handsome enough to tempt *me*; and I am in no humour at present to give consequence to young ladies who are slighted by other men. You had better return to your partner and enjoy her smiles, for you are wasting your time with me."[66]

On the basic level of plot, this incident is instrumental in building up a reader's sense of Elizabeth, elaborating on the first sight of the 'second daughter employed in trimming a hat';[67] if nothing else, it is an intelligent piece of plot-exposition to place her next in a dramatic situation where she is not the main actor. But it is so much else. To begin with, there is the stage-direction: 'catching her eye, he withdrew his own and coldly said [...]' As I discuss in greater detail in Chapter 4, Austen was constitutionally alert to what looks can do, and her novels reflect this in the way they begin to give 'catching the eye' – an activity where physics and metaphysics collude – a more assertive and intentional application than in previous usages. Here, although the 'catching' sounds accidental, Austen allows the stranger, more formal 'withdrew his own' to flash back across the familiar and colloquial 'catching her eye'. For a moment, the metaphor seems almost undone and literal, something that should itself arrest a reader's eye. By putting the throw-away temporarily into slow-motion, this point of dictional stress asks a reader to focus more attentively on the setting in which the speech is taking place, and well it should. Considering the subsequent course of the action, it might not be beside the point to consider what Darcy is up to, to think about just what his intentions are by the Bennets' 'second daughter'.

A reader needs to examine the evidence, for evidence is what it is. Austen's staging of this exchange not only gains importance in retrospect, but comes itself as a twice-told tale, the replay of an incident which is originally told in *précis*, with the matter-of-factness of a legal deposition: 'Elizabeth Bennet had been obliged, by the scarcity of gentlemen, to sit down for two dances; and during part of that time, Mr. Darcy had been standing near enough for her to overhear a conversation between him and Mr. Bingley, who came from the dance for a few minutes, to press him to join it'.[68] '[N]ear enough to over-hear': knowing this, what is one to make of Darcy's look over his shoulder, and his dismissive remarks, when one comes to them? Is Darcy merely brushing Elizabeth off, or checking to see whether she's listening? Darcy's words themselves invite close scrutiny, since the only explicit cue for their voicing is 'coldly', which in a passage low on emotive pointings, sounds like a sudden, indignant wince of *style indirect*, as if Darcy has trodden on Elizabeth's toe as well as her pride. A reader must decide how rakishly to let Darcy's 'tolerable' chime against Bingley's 'agreeable', and how to weigh his two contrastive stresses on 'me' against each other. Linguistic practice would dictate that the stronger, italicized '*me*' should stand against the longer chain of pronouns 'You...your...her', and the weaker 'me', having less work to do, should oppose 'She'; but the opposite is true here. R Allen Harris has remarked shrewdly on the role played in *Pride and Prejudice* by personal pronouns, 'the elementary linguistic reflex of self-definition'[69] and by '[r]efined use of italicization'.[70] It is a measure of Austen's transcendence of Richardsonian models that where Richardson's italicizing of pronouns in his revisions aims to forestall moral ambiguity,[71] Austen's italics deliberately set a reader wondering as to what the evidence means. What Darcy's stressed pronoun performs is the drawing-up of the battle lines across which his and Elizabeth's barbs will fly, as they discover one of the old truths about love, that nothing gets one noticed like an insult.

Barbara Hardy has heard this process at work in the novel, and describes it well. She remarks on the 'mutuality of feeling, in which interest, attraction and antagonism have their parts to play' and summarizes it thus: 'The action of strong passion is a relationship, even an intimacy, and of course the *odi* leads to *amo*, as in similar passionate conflicts between Beatrice and Benedict [*sic*]...We see the intimacy of anger and reproach rising into that of affection'.[72] Elizabeth Bennet may not quite be Shakespeare's 'deere Ladie Disdaine',[73] but *Pride and Prejudice* as a work responds acutely to ladies' disdain: both Elizabeth's sharp tongue and Caroline Bingley's jealous *hauteur*. It is not surprising that the novel contains six of Austen's recorded uses of 'disdain', 'The feeling entertained towards that which one thinks unworthy of or beneath one's dignity; scorn, contempt'.[74] Shakespeare's play senses the comic fertility of 'that which one *thinks* unworthy' (italics mine) more finely than the *OED*'s definition. Hero thinks Beatrice 'too disdainful',[75] encapsulating her in those words I have already mentioned: 'Disdaine and Scorne ride sparkling in her eyes,/ Mis-prizing what they looke on'. Part of these lines' power consists in '*ride* sparkling in her *eyes*', which is entirely at home within Hero's speech, yet sits slightly oddly within English idiom. What exactly does it mean for 'Disdaine and Scorne' to ride *in* Beatrice's eyes? Presumably the main sense is that of 'To float or move upon the water; to sail, esp. in a buoyant manner',[76] which would do justice to the buoyancy of the verse, and the flash of 'sparkling'. An impoverished paraphrase of this might run: 'Beatrice thrives so strongly on her pride that disdain and scorn shine in her eyes like sparks on water'. But under that glides the shadow of the more active sense of 'ride', particularly since it is uncertain what 'they' refers to here. If 'they' are not 'Disdaine and Scorne' but Beatrice's eyes, then the two qualities begin to sound like a pair of parasitic sprites, taking her eyes for a joy-ride and reaping the benefits of the eyes' effort ('Mis-prizing what they look on.') 'Ride' and 'eyes' meet in 'Mis-prizing', the act of misjudging value; Beatrice may be not only 'selfe indeared' but self-blinded.

Shakespeare here intertwines aesthetic response with social prudence; Johnson may have accused him of being distracted by the '*ignis fatuus*' of semantic play,[77] but these puns in *Much Ado About Nothing* do more than simply pass the time. As MM Mahood famously emphasized, 'Wordplay was a game the Elizabethans played seriously',[78] and there is much at stake in the doubleness with which Shakespeare invests Hero's speech: a weighing of possibilities, a reckoning of the costs exacted by plumping for one line of hearing over another, and of the kinds of attitude we ourselves might be adopting in so doing. Shakespeare, Eliot contended, 'was occupied with turning human actions into poetry'.[79] If Eliot's words are over-familiar nowadays (they came to seem so to him too),[80] this may be because they describe something central in Shakespeare: a blend of *largesse* and stringency which checks Leavis's attempts to recruit him for 'the Shakespearean use of English'. One transformation which Shakespeare's 'turning' effects is to compose, in his contending intonations, possible attitudes towards those 'human actions' which it depicts; the pun on 'Disdaine' and Beatrice's eyes neither unequivocally celebrates the plenitude of spoken English nor retreats from it into self-reference. Measured against the whole drama of *Much Ado About Nothing*, a comedy of arguments, the grammatical and intonational possibilities in Hero's speech answer to possible (and possibly painful) conflicts of interest about Beatrice: questions about whether her scorn and shrewishness are bad humours extrinsic to her, or whether, as Hero seems to think, the creature known as Beatrice would cease to exist were they to evaporate in love. These are questions in which the play's ending still revels, as one of literature's most belligerent flirtations is both sealed and silenced with a loving kiss: 'Peace I will stop your mouth.'[81] The attitudes which a reader or audience takes towards such ironies need not make one despair of our chances of ever meaning anything to each other; both senses of 'ride' in Hero's speech depend on our recognizing their links to habits and patterns of experience, bearing witness to language as not only sociable but populated. *Much Ado About Nothing* furnishes an imaginative mode of conduct: an imperilled understanding persists amid, and perhaps because of, the counterpoints of 'Mis-prizing'.

If one takes as a criterion Shakespeare's ability to remain uncowed by the weight of words – whilst owning up to the gravitational pratfalls which that weight can cause – then GH Lewes's infamous praise of Austen as 'prose Shakspeare'[82] sounds less enthusiastic; his phrase may not even be an oxymoron. It is reasonable to think, as Lewes did, that Austen's strength as a novelist lies in her command of her form's dramatic dimensions, the way in which her style acts as both correlative and corrective to the varying pulls of

desire and obligation which it describes. A reader feels that pull when first
introduced to Darcy:

> Mr. Bingley was good looking and gentlemanlike; he had a pleasant
> countenance, and easy, unaffected manners. His sisters were fine
> women, with an air of decided fashion. His brother-in-law, Mr.
> Hurst, merely looked the gentleman; but his friend Mr. Darcy soon
> drew the attention of the room by his fine, tall person, handsome
> features, noble mien; and the report which was in general circu-
> lation within five minutes after his entrance, of his having ten
> thousand a year.[83]

Style indirect libre may primarily involve engrafting personalized items of
vocabulary, but the inflections which mark an individual's tone in such narrative are not confined to the semantic: punctuational idiosyncrasy can play its
part as well. Here, for example, the tonal and rhythmic demeanour which
holds 'person', 'features' and 'mien' in balance with commas gives way to a
rush of breathless collective rumour-mongering which the semicolon cannot
hold in check: there is no time for a comma between 'report' and 'which'.
Questions of punctuation and character enrich a similar joke at the beginning
of *Emma*:

> Sixteen years had Miss Taylor been in Mr. Woodhouse's family,
> less as a governess than a friend, very fond of both daughters, but
> particularly of Emma. Between *them* it was more the intimacy of sis-
> ters. Even before Miss Taylor had ceased to hold the nominal office
> of governess, the mildness of her temper had hardly allowed her to
> impose any restraint; and the shadow of authority being now long
> passed away, they had been living together as friend and friend very
> mutually attached, and Emma doing just what she liked; highly
> esteeming Miss Taylor's judgement, but directed chiefly by her
> own.[84]

Austen makes sly comedy of the fact that the 'restraint' which Miss Taylor has
failed to impose is not itself satisfactorily restrained by the semicolon following
it, as a new clause takes off, tending inevitably towards Emma at the end of
the sentence ('but directed chiefly by her own'). Austen's sentences can contain bustles of perspective, and this is particularly appropriate to *Pride and
Prejudice*, since it enables her to depict the growth of knowledge while still facing up to characters who are not sure quite how they feel about each other,
hedged round as they are not only by their own pride and prejudice, but with

what others make of it. The novel invites from a reader not an abstention from opinion but an equity in the face of others' conflicts and attractions: this also encompasses what Brian Southam has described as 'antipathy-at-first-sight [...] The fascination [Elizabeth and Darcy] exert over one another is initially that of character and personality; love comes later. To begin with, each recognises the other to be a challenge. For the first time, each has discovered somebody worth arguing with, worth the exercise of attention and wit'.[85] Southam's criticism perceptively brings together the combative ('challenge') and the affectionate ('attention and wit'), as does *Pride and Prejudice* itself. Where Shaftesbury had imagined 'amicable collision' in which '[w]e polish one another and rub off our corners and rough sides',[86] Austen portrays a riskier friction, one at once more combative and more erotic. Elizabeth and Darcy's aggressive flirtation, combining deep affinity with one-upmanship, strikes sparks off the language which embodies it, shaping the novel's central comic motif, captured by Austen in describing Caroline Bingley's speech-habits: 'an expression of civil disdain'.[87]

Austen habitually keeps her readers on their mettle by describing incidents so as implicitly to ask why things are not otherwise. The opening gossip about Darcy, for example, derives some of its comic force from the mathematical and rhythmical chime between 'five minutes' and 'ten thousand'. In this story, with its exquisite if critically overworked opening ('a single man in possession of a good fortune'[88]), it comes as no surprise that the size of Darcy's income should be a source of interest. More precisely, however, the fact that 'five' and 'ten' stand in mathematical proportion presents further opportunities for humour. Austen's joke is like one of those mathematical problems for children, in which men fill baths using taps: how long would the assembly have taken to react, one might ask, had Darcy's fortune been twenty thousand instead of ten? Elsewhere, Mr Bennet remarks laconically of Darcy's silence ('Mrs. Long told me last night that he sat close to her for half an hour without once opening his lips'[89]), and Elizabeth, nursing Jane at Netherfield, provokes this reaction by announcing that her sister is 'by no means better':

> The sisters, on hearing this, repeated three or four times how much they were grieved, how shocking it was to have a bad cold, and how excessively they disliked being ill themselves; and then thought no more of the matter: and their indifference towards Jane when not immediately before them, restored Elizabeth to the enjoyment of all her original dislike.[90]

In both these latter instances, the sense of Austen's jokes comes from an implicit comparison with what is imagined to be – at least for the purposes of comedy – the right quantity. We get the joke by assuming that half an hour is an impertinently long time for Darcy to keep quiet, and that three or four expressions of concern do not imply any great sincerity. These are particularly specialized examples of what Paul Grice termed 'implicatures', forms of communication which resist exhaustive categorization because they issue from the contingent yet binding circumstances of actual speech:

> I wish to introduce, as terms of art, the verb *implicate* and the related nouns *implicature* (cf. *implying*) and *implication* (cf. *what is implied*). The point of this maneuver is to avoid having, on each occasion, to choose between this or that member of the family of verbs for which *implicate* is to do general duty.[91]

Most simply, an implicature happens when a speaker diverges from linguistic convention so as to adumbrate something not actually stated: what is 'implicated' exists within the earshot of what is said. If, for example, someone were to ask me 'So, what did you think of Andrew Davies's BBC adaptation of *Pride and Prejudice?*' and I answered 'Goodness me, is that the time? How cold it's turned all of a sudden', I would not directly have *stated* my answer to the question, but only someone very ill at ease with English idiom would miss my meaning. Austen's numerical implicatures do not themselves state what their standards are; we take it as said, however, that the numbers we are given are somehow other than expected. Grice's larger case for the essentially interpersonal and cooperative nature of language is salutary; of particular relevance to Austen is his Maxim of Quantity, which he illustrates as follows: 'If you are assisting me to mend a car, I expect your contribution to be neither more nor less than is required. If, for example, at a particular stage I need four screws, I expect you to hand me four, rather than two or six'.[92] It is a maxim without which one would find it difficult to survive, but as flirtation and fiction both demonstrate, one can never be completely sure how much, or how little, one is saying, or being taken to mean.

The skill with which Austen plays off numbers in her own work reflects her grounding of social *nous* in everyday circumstances. The way that Mr Bennet can be so precise in taunting Darcy weighs both his sarcastic expertise (sarcasm being the implicature of opposites) and the pathos of his character and situation; he unerringly has the measure of the circles in which he moves, but unlike his author, he is incapable of investing that knowledge in anything more than a breezy unseriousness, an abstention from familial care which his later trials bring to book. Even so, his remark has some point as well as just bite, as witnessed by Austen's repeating the same joke later in the story, with one telling difference. At Hunsford Parsonage, Darcy's unsuccessful first proposal is prefaced by Elizabeth's wondering why he keeps coming to visit, a suspicion haunted by the words of her own father: 'It could not be society, as he frequently sat there ten minutes together without opening his lips.'[93] From half an hour to ten minutes: Darcy is becoming positively voluble. Similarly, Austen plays out the Bingley girls' insensitive 'three or four times' in the syntactic correspondence of the noun-phrases: the indirect speech of 'how' sounds three times, peaking, appropriately enough, at the word 'themselves', before tailing off into 'and then thought no more of the matter.' The force of Austen's comedy of implication resides in a reader's spotting the possible intentions not only behind but *in* these knowing swerves of communication. If this is an indulgence on which literature depends, a truism about the nature and hopes of poetic speech, Austen reminds us of something which we might notice less readily – it is also a belief which sustains, and is at its best nourished by, the arts of flirtation and courtship.

Regulated Love: an aspect of Jane Austen

"'I am exceedingly gratified," said Bingley, "by your converting what my friend says into a compliment on the sweetness of my temper. But I am afraid you are giving it a turn which that gentleman did by no means intend; for he would certainly think the better of me, if under such a circumstance I were to give a flat denial, and ride off as fast as I could."'[94] Typically for *Pride and Prejudice*, it takes the well-intentioned but not intellectually dazzling Bingley to find Elizabeth's act surprising. Paul Langford has written of the marriage market in eighteenth-century polite culture:

> the very freedom which was necessary for the marriage market to operate satisfactorily created immense risks [...] the game must be allowed to proceed with a careful calculation of the risks involved and an uncomfortable awareness that failure might imperil the stake as well as the prize. All depended on the prudence as well as skill of the players themselves, and in the last analysis parents were onlookers not players.[95]

Austen does much with that 'uncomfortable awareness'. To take one example, Percy Fitzgerald's early twentieth-century reading of Austen has affinities with James's image of 'she-Philistines' (he finds Emma Woodhouse 'rather "middle class"',[96] for instance); and his analysis rings false when discussing courtship. He does not attempt to unsex Austen, praising her 'profoundest knowledge of all the arts that could be employed in this exciting game',[97] but when he comes to see it as 'quite a fine art' he does not move as much as remove the goalposts:

'it has no rule or limits'.[98] On the contrary, I would suggest that what renders 'uncomfortable' the 'awareness' of living in such an environment is one's sense of the 'limits' within which one is constrained to move. There are certain (necessarily vague) repertoires of behaviour which cultures take as indicative of particular intentions, courtship being a prime example – although, as the work of Erving Goffman and Edward T Hall has shown, regional and social differences can occasion grave infelicities of decorum if one is not careful.[99] Modern readers of Austen share the critical apparatus of flirting which Austen describes – nods, winks, pregnant pauses, meaningful looks – but they are apt to take them for granted in ways that Austen's novels do not. In such *coteries* as we see as the social focus of the novels, within the close circles of scrutiny and expectation within which even the youngest turned, the small details and 'implicatures' of behaviour were made to bear greater weights of significance than we might readily accord them nowadays; Langford's mention of 'immense risks' and 'prudence' catches this nicely.

Fanny Burney, a shy person herself, recorded D'Arblay's stammering courtship of her in her journal. The account, whilst remaining one of her funniest pieces of writing, remains respectfully and charmingly attentive to her future husband's efforts, given that D'Arblay's *parvenu* status would, in 1793, still have been a delicate issue, a justifiable cause for hesitancy:[100]

> His look, then, half made me draw back: 'une grace! — une grace!
> — he cried, c'est une grace que j'aye à vous demander — que — —'
> He stopt — — & hid his Face upon my Hand, which he would not
> suffer me to loosen. — I felt half gasping with apprehension of what
> was to follow — & he was long still in his exordium —.
> 'C'est — c'est que — puisque vous ne voulez pas que je vous parle
> — —'
> 'O no! no! no!' I cried.
> 'Eh bien — puisque vous ne me permettez pas — puisque vous me
> defendez de vous parler — — puisque, absolument, vous — —'
> I repeated my negative warmly.[101]

In this kind of polite environment, one route open to people was naturally enough the ability to 'give a turn' to things, to call upon what lay within earshot of their speech, in the hinterland of their assumptions; the art of what we now call implicature afforded the opportunity, however temporary, to keep one step ahead of the game, to transcend the genre. Austen wisely sees no occasion as too small to carry such weight when the need arises – *Pride and Prejudice* is, after all, the book about which she made her famous 'dull Elves' joke ('a "said he" or a "said she" would sometimes make the Dialogue more immediately clear—but [...]'[102]). Pianos are important in more than one of the novels; as a physical centre of polite gatherings, they provide opportunities for testing what one can say, even when Austen's narrative doesn't reveal exactly what the characters *do* say:

> When that business was over, he applied to Miss Bingley and Elizabeth for the indulgence of some music. Miss Bingley moved with alacrity to the piano-forte, and after a polite request that Elizabeth would lead the way, which the other as politely and more earnestly negatived, she seated herself.[103]

The decent remove of reported speech here allows Elizabeth and Caroline's blithe indecencies to stand out in even sharper relief. One can guess what drives Caroline's precipitate movement ('with alacrity'); so the frosty propriety of the qualifying clauses ('a polite request [...] as politely and more earnestly negatived') makes the women's attrition come to sound positively glacial. In addition to the movement of the syntax, the strange technicality of 'negatived' gives the sentence pause. As the *OED* notes, even those senses of 'to negative' which mean simply 'To refuse to countenance' or 'To deny' are derived applications of originally legalistic or philosophical usages.[104] In a brief exercise of mock-heroic parody, which looks back to the legal report of Darcy's entrance, Austen nudges bitchy social conversation back into the orbit of that other tradition of refined insult, the debate; as family friends (and, illegitimately, via Eliza de Feullide, relations) of Warren Hastings, the Austens would have had more chance than most to witness its effects.

To adopt Genette's terms, the *récit* of Elizabeth and Caroline at the piano is rendered more deliberately and heavily than the *histoire* which it describes; and this syntactic and lexical ponderousness is particularly fitting here. It contributes to that paradox which animates Austen's writing: she pulls off the rare achievement of being 'light, and bright, and sparkling' with heavy matter. She is often thought of, with some justification, as a remarkably un-physical writer[105] – not for her Lovelace's fetishistic lingering on Clarissa's clothes, and what they cover:

> Her morning gown was a pale primrose-coloured paduasoy: the cuffs curiously embroidered by the fingers of this ever charming Ariadne in a running pattern of violets and their leaves; the light in the flowers silver; gold in the leaves. A pair of diamond snaps in her ears. A white handkerchief, wrought by the same inimitable fingers, concealed — Oh Belford! what still more inimitable beauties did it not conceal! — And I saw, all the way we rode, the bounding heart; by its throbbing motions I saw it! dancing beneath the charming umbrage.[106]

or Harriet Byron's detailing Charles Grandison's home-economy:

> He seldom travels without a set, and suitable attendants; and, what
> I think seems a little in favour of singularity, his horses are not
> docked: Their tails are only tied up when they are on the road.[107]

or indeed Mrs Radcliffe's attempts to translate Salvator Rosa into words:

> To the south, the view was bounded by the majestic Pyrénées,
> whose summits, veiled in clouds, or exhibiting awful forms, seen,
> and lost again, as the partial vapours rolled along, were sometimes
> barren, and gleamed through the blue tinge of air, and sometimes
> frowned with forests of gloomy pine, that swept downward to their
> base.[108]

However, as I shall be tracing through this book, the imaginative integrity of
Austen's work, the literary accent she found amid the 'Stinking fish' of *Love and
Freindship*, braces itself against a knowledge of the physical world which it
inhabits. As disposition and attitude bear tonally upon her language, the pressures of situated existence weigh upon it, even if they mostly surface in
metaphor or simile. Where late works like *Persuasion* and *Sanditon* attend
directly to bricks, mortar, paint and furniture,

> and further on, in the little green Court of an old Farm House, two
> females in elegant white were actually to be seen with their books &
> camp stools—[109]

they are only amplifying a tone within Austen's writing which sounds variously
throughout her fiction. The turns she gives in pun and metaphor to words and
phrases like 'heart', 'attach', 'catch' and 'beyond me' show her to be alive to
the demands of physical proximity, even when speaking figuratively, which she
does not often do; if she is un-physical, she is also relatively un-metaphorical.

In *Pride and Prejudice*, too, Austen keeps her ear to the ground: an ear for the
little quotidian pointings and stresses which go to make up courtship. It is a
skill conspicuously denied characters like Mary Bennet and Mr Collins, for
whom speech is either strangely weightless, or simply a set of social counters.
It may be tactless for him to say so out loud, but Mr Bennet limns his moralizing daughter precisely ("'While Mary is adjusting her ideas," he continued,
"let us return to Mr Bingley."'[110]) 'Adjusting' is a suitably mechanistic term
for someone who seeks to convert life into aphorism, but manages only 'some
new observations of thread-bare morality'.[111] Austen herself found much that

was 'thread-bare' among the fashionable things of Bath, as when she tartly forewarned Cassandra about Miss Holder: 'She has an idea of your being remarkably lively; therefore get ready the proper selection of adverbs, & due scraps of Italian and French'.[112] Mary's half-witted abstractions may initially be harmless and amusing, but as the stakes get higher, and the novel itself becomes noticeably less 'light, and bright, and sparkling', her voice comes to sound increasingly out of tune with the demands of her situation. When the full extent of what Lydia has done becomes clear, a reader can hear, in parallel with Elizabeth, the grind as a joke stops being funny. Mary cultivates just the wrong type of elegance, like a woman wearing a ballgown to a funeral:

> "This is a most unfortunate affair; and will probably be much talked of. But we must stem the tide of malice, and pour into the wounded bosoms of each other, the balm of sisterly consolation."
>
> Then, perceiving in Elizabeth no inclination of replying, she added, "Unhappy as the event must be for Lydia, we may draw from it this useful lesson; that loss of virtue in a female is irretrievable — that one false step involves her in endless ruin — that her reputation is no less brittle than it is beautiful, — and that she cannot be too much guarded in her behaviour towards the undeserving of the other sex."
>
> Elizabeth lifted up her eyes in amazement, but was too much oppressed to make any reply. Mary, however, continued to console herself with such kind of moral extractions from the evil before them.[113]

Elizabeth's silence at this moment is eloquently damning, and Austen's narrative has its own ways of speaking silently. Mary's 'moral extraction' is all the more painful for the fact that we, unlike Elizabeth, cannot simply lift up *our* eyes in amazement. To hark back to the distinction I made earlier, this is an example of Austen's style working as 'corrective' as well as 'correlative'; casting a chill over the suspension-marks of polite conversation, she creates what is almost a typographical 'alienation effect'. There is an awed helplessness in the way a reader's eye has to be dragged horizontally across each of Mary's false endings, since the long dash is itself a false ending: it provides the stop which we might wish Mary to reach, whilst reminding us ominously that it is not a full stop, that Mary will continue to compound her felony (Sterne, in contrast, revels in the dash as false ending, and fashions his version of pastoral around deferred conclusions and cheating death.).

Like Mary, Mr Collins is all the more ridiculous for his habit of reacting to things before they happen, 'with the determined air of following his own inclination';[114] if ever Austen drew a caricature in DW Harding's sense ('the identifying peculiarity is not only exaggerated but recurrent [...] and its repetition takes the place of any extended exploration'[115]) then it is here. Collins becomes so identified with his wearisome catchphrases that Elizabeth, even as she gazes at Darcy with entranced disgust, can lip-read one half of the exchange: 'Her cousin prefaced his speech with a solemn bow, and though she could not hear a word of it, she felt as if hearing it all, and saw in the motion of his lips the words "apology," "Hunsford" and "Lady Catherine de Bourgh." — It vexed her to see him expose himself to such a man'.[116] Aptly enough, the accents and syllables of 'civil disdain' sound beneath Darcy's reply, delivered 'with an air of *distant civility*'[117] – though Austen may also be remembering *Clarissa* here.[118] Collins' proposal to Elizabeth, however, is hilarity of a different, sterner order; Harding's thought-provoking essay does not provide any clear suggestion as to where and why one might draw the line between 'character' and 'caricature', reckoning more by the number of words people get to say. When Collins treats the risky business of courtship as a foregone conclusion, there is more at stake:

> "[...] But the fact is, that being, as I am, to inherit this estate after the death of your honoured father, (who, however, may live many years longer,) I could not satisfy myself without resolving to chuse a wife from among his daughters, that the loss to them might be as little as possible, when the melancholy event takes place — which, however, as I have already said, may not be for several years. This has been my motive, my fair cousin, and I flatter myself it will not sink me in your esteem. And now nothing remains for me but to assure you in the most animated language of the violence of my affection."[119]

One might rightly be exasperated, as Elizabeth is, by a man who proposes marriage in a style approaching *oratio obliqua* ('to assure you in the most animated language'), but Collins' refusal to understand anything he doesn't wish to allows Austen to show serious perplexity entangled with comic breadth. Elizabeth is in a logical cul-de-sac, a 'catch-22': "I know not how to express my refusal in such a way as may convince you of its being one."[120] Collins' circular argument resembles the manœuvre in psychoanalysis, where to deny that one is neurotic is proof of neurosis, because one would not deny it otherwise.[121] Nothing, it seems, can change Collins' mind: 'As I must therefore conclude that you are not serious in your rejection of me, I shall chuse to attribute it to your wish of increasing my love by suspense, according to the usual practice of elegant females'.[122] That last phrase is an extraordinary moment in Austen's work. Her feeling for wit is often traced back through

Johnson to Pope, but here, amid the 'playfulness and epigrammatism', the writing once more possesses some of the darker energy of Swift. A reader perceives simultaneously a polite society for which manners held serious importance, and the lunacy which is the *reductio ad absurdum* of those manners, as Collins confounds 'usual practice' with universal rules.

Flyting and flirting converge to serve Austen's turn; one reason that Elizabeth and Darcy thrive is that their 'disdain' itself lives within the ambience of 'usual practice', even as they come to learn how much more there is to life than that. As Elizabeth begins to become conscious of her change of feelings ('she lay awake two whole hours endeavouring to make them out'[123]) the narrative begins to unpack the 'civil disdain' which has been the novel's keynote:

> It was not often that she could turn her eyes on Mr. Darcy himself; but, whenever she did catch a glimpse, she saw an expression of general complaisance, and in all that he said, she heard an accent so far removed from hauteur or disdain of his companions, as convinced her that the improvement of manners which she had yesterday witnessed, however temporary its existence might prove, had at least outlived one day. When she saw him thus seeking the acquaintance, and courting the good opinion of people, with whom any intercourse a few months ago would have been a disgrace; when she saw him thus civil, not only to herself, but to the very relations whom he had openly disdained, and recollected their last lively scene in Hunsford Parsonage, the difference, the change was so great, and struck so forcibly on her mind, that she could hardly restrain her astonishment from being visible.[124]

She has learned to hear this 'accent' through the long process of her conversational sparring with Darcy, a courtship sustained by 'usual practice' as well as by the knowing turns with which each has sought to trump or outsmart the other, making it far from clear exactly what the twist is:

> "Are you consulting your feelings in the present case, or do you imagine that you are gratifying mine?"
> "Both," replied Elizabeth archly; "for I have always seen a great similarity in our turn of minds. — We are each of an unsocial, taciturn disposition, unwilling to speak, unless we expect to say something that will amaze the whole room, and be handed down to posterity with all the eclat of a proverb."
> "This is no very striking resemblance of your own character, I am

sure," said he. "How near it may be to *mine*, I cannot pretend to say.
— *You* think it a faithful portrait undoubtedly."
"I must not decide on my own performance."[125]

'This simultaneity of tonal layers,' noted Reuben A Brower in his prescient
1951 essay, 'can be matched only in the satire of Pope, where [...] the reader
feels the impossibility of adjusting his voice to the rapid changes in tone and
the difficulty of representing by a single sound the several sounds he hears as
equally appropriate and necessary [...] No speaking voice could possibly
represent the variety of tones conveyed to the reader by such interplay of
dialogue and comment'.[126] One undertow to Brower's argument, which he
does not explore at length, is what we might make of such composition: what,
indeed, it might make of us. No *speaking* voice could fully represent such
speeches, it is true; but voices can be tensed creatively against what they cannot say so as to arbitrate in just those situations which we witness in Elizabeth
and Darcy's flirting. As readers, we need both our sense of speech, and our
sense of how confused feelings can exert more pulls than speech can handle,
in order to do their words justice. They are, for a start, a long way from the
duetting effects which Austen achieves at times in *Mansfield Park*. 'Do you
imagine', 'I am sure', 'I cannot pretend to say', 'I must not decide': little units
of social speech here carry the variety of ironic stresses and distresses that go
with fascination, attraction, suspicion and one-upmanship. Much humour
and truth sounds in the contrast between Darcy's pronouns ('you [...] your
[...] you [...] you [...] mine') and Elizabeth's ('I [...] our [...] we [...] we') Even
as Elizabeth delights in 'archly' thwarting him, she strikes a deeper nerve –
deeper even than she suspects – in her 'great similarity in our turn of minds.'
It is telling that Darcy finds it necessary to return, with nettled (and italicized)
insistence, to his initial contrast ('*mine* [...] *you*'). Elizabeth begins to hear an
accent; Darcy begins, even as he disclaims the ability, to catch a tone:

> "I certainly have not the talent which some people possess," said
> Darcy, "Of conversing easily with those I have never seen before. I
> cannot catch their tone of conversation, or appear interested in
> their concerns, as I often see done."[127]

Reading what Austen makes of these speeches, readers are also invited to
reflect on intentions, and to hear accents; we can recognize possible intentions, get the joke, even when local stresses may fall athwart our own pitch. As
an admirer of Johnson, and as a comedian, Austen was never one to look
down on 'usual practice': most relationships may not begin in fascinated disgust, but they do, by and large, partake of that 'less interesting mode of

attachment' which animates *Pride and Prejudice*, a comedy of love at second opinion. As we can never say *exactly* when we learned to speak,[128] neither can we say exactly when our feelings evolved into that frightening abstract noun, which English presses into service to signify so much, and to signify nothing:

> Elizabeth's spirits soon rising to playfulness again, she wanted Mr. Darcy to account for his having ever fallen in love with her.
> "How could you begin?" said she. "I can comprehend your going on charmingly, when you had once made a beginning; but what could set you off in the first place?"
> "I cannot fix on the hour, or the spot, or the look, or the words, which laid the foundation. It is too long ago. I was in the middle before I knew that I *had* begun."[129]

This looks forward to the historic moment of narrative reticence which attends the proposal in *Emma* ('What did she say? - Just what she ought, of course. A lady always does'[130]). Because of the material nature of text, we can move both ways along the time-line in reading – something which, of course, we cannot do in immediate experience, which is fatally governed by 'time's arrow'.[131] A reader is able, unlike Darcy, to go back over 'the words, which laid the foundation'; but the narrative *coup* of Austen's novel is that a reader is no better off than he is when it comes to pinpointing 'the hour, or the spot, or the look'. Austen is not high-handed or dismissive towards 'timeless moments', particularly in *Persuasion*; still, she makes her readers aware of how difficult it might be to presume that they could 'spot' where love starts: is it in *this* arch look, *this* contrastive stress, *this* pregnant pause? Such presumption would bear comparison with the absurdly precise moment which Larkin's speaker affects to pinpoint (but cannot pin down) in 'Annus Mirabilis':

> Sexual intercourse began
> In nineteen sixty-three
> (Which was rather late for me) –
> Between the end of the *Chatterley* ban
> And the Beatles' first LP.[132]

A reader can see and hear love in *Pride and Prejudice*; but it registers in the tonal amplitude of flirting, in feelings that are 'in the middle' before they know that they have begun.

To be in the middle before one knows that one has begun: much the same happens when a person opens his or her mouth, even if it is for the first time. Thus arose that style of which Austen makes such refined and influential use.

Style indirect allows narrative prose to aspire to the condition of poetic drama, since it must remain attentive both to those personal traits and turns of consciousness which it preserves, and to their existence 'in the middle' of something larger than themselves. Martha Nussbaum has suggested that 'social democracy and the art of the novel are allies', which, as I have discussed in Chapter 1, presupposes an essential righteousness of poetic purpose which may not stand up to the evidence; nevertheless, she is right to suggest that *style indirect* affords a means for language to work as a social medium.[133] Sentences carry personal weight, but at their end they cannot but be called to account, since the grammatical logic of the style requires the inscape of individual perspective to meet the larger view of third-person narrative. In a novel so aware of what one can and cannot say within earshot ('she could perceive that the chief of it was overheard by Mr. Darcy'), the technique is of particular value:

> When they sat down to supper, therefore, she considered it a most unlucky perverseness which placed them within one of each other; and deeply was she vexed to find that her mother was talking to that one person (Lady Lucas) freely, openly, and of nothing else but of her expectation that Jane would soon be married to Mr. Bingley. — It was an animating subject, and Mrs. Bennet seemed incapable of fatigue while enumerating the advantages of the match.[134]

Such storytelling does, however, have its detractors. The return to third-person narration in novels such as Austen's has been construed as betraying the epistolary novel to the authorities; in some critical accounts, the external narration of nineteenth-century novels comes to be seen as a linguistic analogue to the authoritarian mechanisms of surveillance which some nineteenth century societies imagined.[135] Take, for example, Nicola J Watson's comments on Scott's *Guy Mannering*, a work which, like *Pride and Prejudice* and *Emma*, encloses letters within third-person narrative: 'That authority socializes, relativizes, and contextualizes the reader, who, no longer the privileged, secret voyeur of intimate passions constructed by the epistolary, becomes instead the acquiescent spectator of critical readings performed by an omniscient narrator on a series of transfixed embedded texts'.[136] Watson's own reading is predicated on the assumptions that anything external to the self is *de facto* inimical to that self, and that sincerity is the exclusive preserve of those individual and 'intimate passions' which epistolary fictions record. But this is by no means certain; against such emphases, one could set Käte Hamburger's insistence that '[e]pic fiction is the sole instance where third-person figures can be spoken of not, or not only as objects, but also as subjects, where the subjectivity of a third-person figure *qua* that of a third-person can be portrayed',[137] and Dorrit Cohn's analysis of Austen's stylistic legacy:

> The pattern set by Jane Austen unfolds throughout the nineteenth century: precisely those authors who, in their major works, most decisively abandoned first-person narration (Flaubert, Zola, James), instituting instead the norms of the dramatic novel, objective narration, and unobtrusive narrators, were the ones who re-introduced the subjectivity of private experience into the novel: this time not in terms of direct self-narration, but by imperceptibly integrating mental reactions into the neutral-objective report of actions, scenes, and spoken words.[138]

Both Hamburger and Cohn recognize that third-person narration need not be repressively 'panoptic', and that in its nineteenth-century forms, it need not embody so categorical a shift from one mode of consciousness to another. For a start, fictional narrative is not the only artistic medium in the eighteenth and nineteenth centuries in which the dialogue of personal perspectives with more social or interpersonal viewpoints carries aesthetic weight. One of the central fields of enquiry in Wordsworth's preface to *Lyrical Ballads*, for example, is the mediation which metrical form embodies, between social and personal voices. 'The Poet thinks and feels in the spirit of the passions of men,' Wordsworth argues. 'How, then, can his language differ in any material degree from that of all other men who feel vividly and see clearly?'[139] When he comes specifically to discuss the effects of metre, he sets the older and more ostensibly 'impersonal' ballad forms against the immediacy of Richardson's narrative style:

> The end of Poetry is to produce excitement in co-existence with an over-balance of pleasure. Now, by the supposition, excitement is an unusual and irregular state of the mind; ideas and feelings do not in that state succeed each other in accustomed order. But, if the words by which this excitement is produced are in themselves powerful, or the images and feelings have an undue proportion of pain connected with them, there is some danger that the excitement may be carried beyond its proper bounds. Now, the co-presence of something regular, something to which the mind has been accustomed in various moods and in a less excited state, cannot but have great efficacy in tempering and restraining the passion by an intertexture of ordinary feeling, and of feeling not strictly and necessarily connected with the passion [...] there can be little doubt but that more

pathetic situations and sentiments, that is, those which have a greater proportion of pain connected with them, may be endured in metrical composition, especially in rhyme, than in prose [...] This opinion may be further illustrated by appealing to the Reader's own experience of the reluctance with which he comes to the re-perusal of the distressful parts of Clarissa Harlowe, or the Gamester.[140]

Instead of the direct mapping of sentimental reader-response which Words-worth perceives in Richardson ('more pathetic situations and sentiments'), metrical verse, with its less inward and subjective associations, can provide an external, acoustic measure for emotion; moreover, the traditions of usage attached to particular verse forms ('old ballads'[141]), allow a poem's voice to be heard and viewed as part of a longer narrative of comparable and contrasting instances. But this is not to imply that the individual voices and stories within poems are entirely constrained by external precedent: accentual-syllabic metres can only structure a reading, never completely dictate it. Thus, a reader's arbitration, between the demands of metrical form and the specific pulls of imagined voicings, can witness the larger resonances of a poem, whilst also registering the ease or difficulty with which its voices yield to or resist the marshalling of form.

Nor is such mediation even the exclusive preserve of verbal art forms; visual art also often makes much of those interminglings of texture and circumstance which I mentioned earlier under the heading of 'contexture' – an aspect brought into particular focus in portraiture. 'The excellence of Portrait-Painting,' wrote Reynolds, 'and we may add even the likeness, the character, and countenance [...] depend more upon the general effect produced by the painter, than on the exact expression of the peculiarities, or minute discrimination of the parts'.[142] This is true in some cases, but what one sees in much late eighteenth- and early nineteenth-century portraiture is, rather, an active combination of 'general effect' and 'minute discrimination'. The visual synecdoche of clothing and specific objects, the simultaneous appeal to different points of view and sight-lines within the frame, can com-bine to create and implicate interpersonal narratives within an individual portrait. For example, Michael Rosenthal comments on Gainsborough's *An Officer of the Fourth Regiment of Foot* (Plate 2): 'There may be a narrative here, to do with duty involving service overseas, as that vessel, sailing dangerously close to the shore, may hint, and how this conflicts with the instincts of a pri-vate man, as the sitter's gazing down and out to our right, in an apparently melancholy fashion, suggests'.[143]

As portraiture developed in the nineteenth century, such complex visual techniques themselves gained in power. Ingres' portraits are always attuned to the social and narrative resonances of fashionable clothing, but in his 1816 portrait of Madame de Senonnes (Plate 3), and his 1845 portrait of the Comtesse D'Haussonville (Plate 4), the sitters' relationship to their physical surroundings sets up a dialogue between seeing and being seen, one focused by the presence of mirrors.[144] Centred among some of the domestic trappings of her status, with her chin resting comfortably on her hand, the Comtesse D'Haussonville directly addresses a viewer's eye with her own look: within her own plane, she is at ease, and Ingres does this justice. However, one of her material possessions is the mirror before which she stands; hence a viewer's eye cannot but be drawn to that perspective which she cannot directly control – the smaller, more distant virtual image of the back of her head and neck, in which her left forefinger does not appear nearly as comfortable or poised (she could be squeezing a pimple, for all we know). The reflected image does not cancel out or invalidate the Comtesse's direct self-projection, but it does contextualize it, reminding a viewer that, among other things, someone else might be staring at the ungainly back of their head as they study the portrait. *Style indirect* can perform comparable feats of dual perspective in language, holding personal and external sight-lines within the same frame; it can bring us close to the thoughts and opinions of its characters even while looking at the backs of their necks, at the awkward figures they don't wholly know they are striking from that angle. 'La visibilité est un piège' ['visibility is a trap'], says Foucault of the Panopticon; but then he is describing what is (in both senses) a visionary scheme of punitive surveillance. Wordsworth's feeling for metre and its associations, the implied narrativity of Gainsborough and Ingres, Austen's way with *style indirect*, all portray, in their own ways, the dialectic of seeing and being seen, of hearing and being heard (or misheard) as one of the sometimes awkward, but unavoidable, conditions of being in a world with other people – *polyopticon* might describe it better.[145] To privilege private and 'intimate passions', as Nicola Watson does in her reading of Scott, has an honourable pedigree in early modern and Enlightenment thinking,[146] but it is not an incontestable position. An attentive reader of third-person narratives will not be an 'acquiescent spectator', as Wolfgang Iser has analysed at length;[147] and the 'omniscient narrator', an inaccurate term of art, is overdue for burial. Such readings undervalue one of the most enduring aspects of narrative: if we exist for ourselves in the first person (and occasionally the second), it is both chastening and heartening to know that we exist to others in the second and third. It is, at least, an explanation for why people enjoy reading and hearing stories about other people. Narrative can attend to all these aspects, neither glossing over salient particulars nor forgetting larger patterns; another way of reading the relationship between narrative and social structures can be found in Alasdair MacIntyre: 'that the self has to find its moral identity in and through its membership in communities,' he maintains, '[…] does not entail that the self has to accept the moral *limitations* of the particularity of those forms of community.'[148] As speakers, readers, writers and agents, people are all in the middle before they know that they have begun; but that need not be where they stop.

Jane Austen lived in the middle of it all, spending much of her life with one of the two people directly responsible for putting her there in the first place. She complained of her mother's reading of *Pride and Prejudice* that 'she cannot speak as they ought'.[149] This was unfair on Mrs Austen, since no one person could speak out loud the whole drama in which Elizabeth and Darcy are involved, even in a novel which invites imaginative performance as much as does *Pride and Prejudice*. But her remark had a ring of truth; Mrs Austen could not speak as the characters ought, perhaps because she did not speak quite as her daughter did. DW Harding published 'Regulated Hatred' – probably the single most influential piece of twentieth-century Austen criticism, and rightly so – in 1940. It was a welcome emphasis, seeking to question those who sought to enshrine 'gentle Jane' as the lady-laureate of 'English Reserve', as if practical, analytical intelligence in a woman were somehow unfeminine. Mrs Austen features prominently in Harding's account. 'Most children,' he writes, 'are likely to have some conflict of attitude towards their mother, finding her in some respects an ideal object of love and in others an obstacle to their wishes and a bitter disappointment. For a child such as Jane Austen who actually was in many ways more sensitive and able than her mother, one can understand that this conflict may persist in some form for a very long time'.[150] This is fair enough; but the combative associations of the phrase 'regulated hatred' might blind a reader to the simpler (and perhaps more disturbing) truth which Harding perceives. All the contradictory pulls in human relationships which Harding describes so eloquently could, with equal plausibility, be seen as elements of love; to call them 'regulated hatred' would be to imply that they are not pulls which any reasonable person might feel. After the original having of children, the next biggest wrench people face is having to acknowledge that their children aren't themselves; it is normal to feel the tension between wanting children in one's own image, and the atoning yet liberating realization that one has created a person, a social animal – which is one reason why parents can spend so much time and effort trying to make sure that their children have a better life than they did. The bad parents in Austen's fiction are united in being unable to make that second recognition: Mr Woodhouse imagines Emma as his female emanation, Sir Walter Elliot prefers Elizabeth to Anne because she is 'very like himself',[151] and Mrs Bennet looks suspiciously like a grown-up version of Lydia ('Had Lydia and her mother known the substance of her conference with her father, their indignation would hardly have found expression in their united volubility').[152] The flirtatious form of *Pride and Prejudice* is able to make a reader think about how children are both like and unlike their parents – and, more generally, about how people are both like and unlike each other. A comedy in which tones chime, jar and tease, the story is the model of a particular, tricky decency – a love far from Plato but no less intelligent for that.

It is Elizabeth and Darcy's achievement to begin a marriage that preserves at least something of their distinctive charm. *Pride and Prejudice* finds room for such fragile victories, since they constitute the 'spell' which it is not 'beyond'. One need not share Austen's conservatism to appreciate what her turn of mind led her to – a style which weighs personal trumps against 'usual practice' within her mother tongue. Whether love will survive the entropic tests of time, whether people will go on getting each other's jokes: these are mortal questions of which *Pride and Prejudice* makes longer-lasting comedy. By never presuming to be beyond the ambience of imperfection and misunderstanding, the novel finds the 'perfect form' for events that are ordinary, human and occasionally magical. 'Mamma says': Austen-Leigh defended his aunt against that accusation as best he could. But there is an irony, both humorous and poignant, in the fact that he chose to commemorate her with the *éclat* of a Proverb, with 'The wordes of King Lemuel, the prophecie that his mother taught him'.[153]

3

THROWING THE VOICE

On the stage he was natural, simple, affecting,
'Twas only that, when he was off, he was acting:
Oliver Goldsmith, 'Retaliation'[1]

Absent Friends

In a letter to Cassandra of January 1801, Austen made a remark about one aspect of her writing – one which it might be tempting to read as stating a position, rather than striking a pose. She wrote: 'I have now attained the true art of letter-writing, which we are always told, is to express on paper exactly what one would say to the same person by word of mouth; I have been talking to you almost as fast as I could the whole of this letter.'[2] Austen is aware here of belonging and adding to an ongoing tradition of epistolary rhetoric ('which we are always told'), but her very knowingness might complicate attempts to read her remark as definitive or unironic. Norman Page uses her words as the basis of a larger inference about the power of letters in the period: 'In the absence of the telephone,' he argues, 'letters were also capable of suggesting something of the tone of the speaking voice.'[3] However, he may be speaking more truly than he purposes in calling attention to that 'something of the tone of the speaking voice'; the distance between Page's writing (1972) and Austen's (1801) may render his implied contrast rather too trusting. As a twentieth-century critic, used to the assumed intimacies of telecommunication, his phrase offers the 'something' as an extenuating factor for writing, in contrast to the alleged self-sufficiency of 'the telephone'.

There is indeed much to be made of the contrast between the two means of expression. The 'communications revolution' truly deserves the name – not least because one of its effects, as with other revolutions before it, has been to alter the parameters and resources of the language available to describe it. From the perspective of an age predicated on telecommunication, it is natural to cast 'something of the tone of the speaking voice' as a consolation, maybe even as an afterthought; but this may misrepresent how Jane and Cassandra Austen saw things. Letter writers at the turn of the nineteenth century were not cowed by their insufficiency, their inability to provide a service which they did not yet know to be possible. Austen's letters are suffused with an awareness that she could only ever provide 'something' of speech; but as writing creates through its constraints, so she placed that very incompleteness at the centre of her art.

Janet Gurkin Altman has offered a useful formulation for the relationships between intimacy and distance in letters: 'Given the letter's function as a connector between two distant points, as a bridge between sender and receiver, the epistolary author can choose to emphasize either the distance or the bridge.'[4] Distance is the logical prerequisite to all letter writing (even if the distance involved is, as at the end of *Persuasion*, no greater than the length of a room), and it naturally features strongly in both ancient and modern accounts of writing. Angel Day, in *The English Secretary* (1586), brought distance and intimacy together in his terms:

> An Epistle, therefore, is that which vsually we in our vulgar, doe tearme a Letter, and for the respectes thereof is called the messenger, or familiar speach of the absent, for that therein is discouered whatsoeuer the minde wisheth in such cases to have deliuered [...] the declaration of euerie letter, is no more then what the minde willeth in all occasions to haue performed [...][5]

More recently, Freud's *Civilisation and Its Discontents* (1930) claimed:

> With every tool man is perfecting his own organs, whether motor or sensory, or is removing the limits to their functioning [...] Writing was in its origin the voice of an absent person; and the dwelling-house was a substitute for the mother's womb, the first lodging, for which in all likelihood man still longs, and in which he was safe and felt at ease.[6]

The 'familiar speach of the absent'; 'the voice of an absent person': both Day and Freud recognize the animating paradox of writing in general, and letter writing in particular. As Freud's terms imply, the cave or house cannot wholly replace the womb, and what writing so often records, in its quests after and approximations of the absent voice, is how much of the person is absent even *in* their voice. We can remember the desired cadences of an ex-lover or the familiar accent of a dead relative, go over the written records of their time in our lives, even trace with our fingers the indentations still left in the sheets by their acts of writing – yet be left with a heightened sense of their own physical absence, at the moment when we are most haunted, tormented, or comforted by their words. Austen's 'true art of letter-writing', whatever else it may be, needs to maintain both the distance and the affinity between the flesh-and-blood person and the 'something' of them which is expressible in writing; thus, it inevitably exists in a dramatic context. I discussed in Chapter 1 how acts of readerly attention and involvement can create a context, or even an imaginative stage, for silently-speaking literary texts, and furthermore, how such readings can bear, however obliquely, on more immediate encounters and relations. Austen's letters, working within a form commonly associated with intimacy, pose their own questions about how immediate such encounters truly are.

Looking back to the letter of 3 January 1801, it is not only Austen's self-aware 'we are always told' which conflates spontaneity with 'usual practice' (in Mr Collins's phrase from *Pride and Prejudice*); as well as combining voice and writing ('to express on paper [...] I have been talking'), Austen qualifies 'I have been talking' not with time but with text, with the comical, Sternean 'the whole of this letter'. It is realizing this difference between lived and textual time which so animates and exasperates the narrator in Volume IV of *Tristram Shandy*:

> I am this month one whole year older than I was this time twelve-month; and having got, as you perceive, almost into the middle of my fourth volume – and no farther than to my first day's life – 'tis demonstrative that I have three hundred and sixty-four days more life to write just now, than when I first set out [...] at this rate I should just live 364 times faster than I should write [...][7]

Exasperating to the fictional Tristram, this discrepancy allows the private Austen to appear, paradoxically, more quirkily personified to Cassandra by emphasizing her own absence. Part of this effect derives from one of the inherent problems of time in writing. To someone reading Volume IV of Sterne's novel on its first publication in late 1760, 'this month' might just have conveyed an illusion of synchronicity, but as the book grows older, the captured present in the text remains, distant but not wholly irredeemable, to be brought alive and elicited in the act of reading.[8] The epistolary voice lacks the spatial and temporal accountability of immediate speech: in a typical face-to-face conversation, the interlocutors are aware at least of the time-lapses between their words and the replies they receive, and of the speech's basic physical location. Neither of these points of orientation is explicit or guaranteed in letters, a fact which, as I will discuss later, licenses some of the abuses of epistolary distance in the fiction of Richardson and Laclos. But the potential slippages between speaking and writing, and between sender and receiver, are worked into a new stage for intimacy in the texture of Austen's letters.

The measurement of time-spans in textual terms plays a part in many of Austen's most familiar exchanges with Cassandra – so much so that it becomes a shared and habitual joke in itself. Her letter of 1 November 1800 carries its trust across distance:

> You have written I am sure, tho' I have received no letter from you since your leaving London; — the Post, & not yourself must have been unpunctual.[9]

While the archness of 'I am sure' and 'must have' recurs more pointedly in the novels in the selfish mouths of Mrs Norris and Mrs Elton, here the phrases have more the weight of sisterly sarcasm. Even the relief of Jane's anticipation is narrated in 'letter-time':

> Your letter is come; it came indeed twelve lines ago, but I could not stop to acknowledge it before, & I am glad it did not arrive till I had completed my first sentence, because the sentence had been made ever since yesterday, & I think forms a very good beginning.[10]

Jane's words strengthen the bond of voice between the sisters, but they also recast the letter's opening as a cliché or a stock formula, as often happens in her early parodies of epistolary fiction. Take, for example, 'A Letter from a Young Lady, whose feelings being too Strong for her Judgement led her into the commission of Errors which her Heart disapproved', a piece whose content belies the pious associations of its opening, and whose imagined present tense offers an absurd version of Richardson's 'writing to the moment':

> Many have been the cares & vicissitudes of my past life, my beloved Ellinor, & the only consolation I feel for their bitterness is that on a close examination of my conduct, I am convinced that I have strictly deserved them. I murdered my father at a very early period of my Life, I have since murdered my Mother, and I am now going to murder my Sister.[11]

Although this little skit was collected for Austen's cousin Eliza De Feuillide, it is likely that Cassandra read it too – in which case, one wonders what she made of the repeated 'I am now going to murder my Sister'. That said, the basic comic effect is not so far removed from the 'very good beginning' which Austen retains, even after her sister's letter has rendered it unnecessary. As shown by 'twelve lines ago', Austen is stressing the letter's existence as a textual object: part of a shared repertoire of references, a game which she is playing with her sister, like charades or *bouts-rimés*. 'Letter-time' partially removes the writing from immediate experience, yet in its own way it shows Austen's commitment to her words. Fictional schemers such as Richardson's Lovelace and Laclos' Valmont often use the written present merely to torment their victims with what they cannot share; Austen, in contrast, figures her sister in a compensatory illusion, by allowing her written or imagined speech into the frame of the letter. Rather than employing distance to fend off or to conceal information from the interlocutor, this is writing whose object comes to collaborate by implication in the original moment of composition.

Nothing can lessen the physical distance between the sisters, but letters have their compensations. Austen's repeated references in the letters to the real-time circumstances of their writing ('I have just asked Caroline if I should send her love to her godmama, to which she answered "Yes"'[12]), coupled with her framing of so many comments as replies to Cassandra's unheard voice:

> I need not therefore be above acknowledging the receipt of yours this morn^g; or of replying to every part of it which is capable of an answer; & you may accordingly prepare for my ringing the Changes of the Glads & Sorrys for the rest of the page.[13]

create an intimacy for the two written voices which is more than just a hopeful whim. Where formality, either in conversation or correspondence, demands a greater reliance on pre-existing and external observances (the complex protocols of early nineteenth-century social introduction, for instance, or the precise modes of address in a formal letter), familiar correspondence can either dispense with such formalities altogether, or (as I have discussed in Chapter 2) play knowingly with their habitual expectations so as to fashion in-jokes and idiolects from the public currency of social talk. Keats, writing two years after Austen died, famously described and performed letter-writing's resourceful way with convention:

> Writing has this disadvantage of speaking – one cannot write a wink, or a nod, or a grin, or a purse of the Lips, or a *smile – O law!* One can<not> put ones finger to one's nose, or yerk ye in the ribs, or lay hold of your button in writing – but in all the most lively and titterly parts of my Letter you must not fail to imagine me as the epic poets say – now here, now there, now with my pen on my ear, now with my elbow in my mouth. O my friends you loose the action – and attitude is every thing as Fusili said when he took up his leg

like a Musket to shoot a Swallow just darting behind his shoulder.
And yet does not the word mum! go for ones finger beside the nose.
I hope it does.[14]

A useful reminder that writing may involve not only the voice but the body of
an absent person ('does not the word mum! go for one's finger beside the
nose'), Keats's letter also simultaneously registers, and sets comically askew,
those referents, out in the world of lived experience, from which his writing
has become loosened, but not set adrift: such proverbial touchstones as *Hamlet*
('O my friends you loose the action' is itself only a 'loose' wink and nod at
'loose the name of Action'), and the anatomical possibilities of the human
body (you try putting your elbow in your mouth).[15] The gadding-about of
Keats's page-directions is therefore not the only swerving which his brother
and sister-in-law are invited to imagine: Keats's familiar letter invites readerly
reception into his act of writing, by offering received wisdoms with added,
personal freight. This is a capacity in which Austen's letters to Cassandra
revel; and, like Keats's letters after them, they achieve their intimacies by
being open to and open about their dramatic nature. Erving Goffman noted
the modern phenomenon of the 'telephone voice' as early as 1959;[16] in
Austen's letters, the sisters' exchanges are conducted in a particular epistolary
voice.

Austen's remarks on the 'true art of letter-writing' tap into and play off a
complex of thoughts on the art, which runs from Cicero through Sterne, but
which came to carry a particular force, and to raise any number of unexpected problems, in the course of the eighteenth century, owing to writers'
increasing consciousness of those vexed relations between 'artfulness' and
'naturalness' which I detailed in Chapter 1. Even the oldest thoughts on epistolary rhetoric are, for example, alert to what one would now call the
context-dependency of letters. Cicero himself worried about such matters:

> Quaerenti mihi iamdiu, quid ad te potissimum scriberem, non
> modo certa res nulla, sed ne genus quidem litterarum usitatum
> veniebat in mentem. Unam enim partem et consuetudinem earum
> epistolarum, quibus, secundus rebus, uti solebamus, tempus
> eripuerat [...][17]

> [I have been wondering for some time what would be the best thing
> to write to you; not only did no definite theme occur to me, but the
> customary style of letter-writing did not suit. For one convention of
> correspondence, to which we were accustomed in better times, has
> been taken by force from us by current events [...]]

Angel Day listed the three prerequisites for a letter as being 'Aptnesse of wordes and sentences', 'Breuity of speach', and 'Comelinesse in deliuerance touching the person or cause':

> as it is most decent that in the matter we make choice of, we giue vnto euerie cause his proper and orderly effect: so it is euery way as conuenient to afford a like *Decorum* to those to whome our letters are directed.[18]

By the beginning of the eighteenth century, the issue had become more overtly qualified. David Marshall has detected a slippery area between character and performance, which is remarked upon as early as Shaftesbury's works:

> Is the character of a person something essential and individual or a role to be enacted, a figure that represents a self? Could it be all of these, and if so, could a self exist apart from its representation, before its enactment? What would be the difference between a representation of the self and a counterfeit or false representation, between the self's essence and its status as a fictive role?[19]

That said, in some eighteenth-century writing – and in some more recent accounts of it – one can often find a more insistent emphasis on one of the two poles which Marshall mentions: 'the self's essence' rather than the 'fictive role'. This is reasonable enough, given the existence of an interpretative tradition, founded on a reading of Cicero's letters, of seeing familiar correspondence as an act of unmasking or revelation; whether the evidence supports so cleanly a separation between 'essence' and 'role' is less clear. Hugh Blair, placing correspondence in 'a kind of middle space between the serious and amusing species of Composition', tapped into the 'Ciceronian' view of letter-writing: for Blair, it is 'a conversation carried on upon paper',[20] an art whose greatest Roman exponent 'lays open himself and his heart, with entire freedom'.[21] However, this view does not go unqualified in the lecture; as Blair points out, 'It is childish indeed to expect, that in Letters we are to find the whole heart of the Author unveiled. Concealment and disguise take place, more or less, in all human intercourse.'[22] The adjectives with which Blair checks himself on this point are telling: Cicero may lay open his heart 'with entire freedom', but nowhere is it suggested that he is exposing his 'whole heart'.

One complication in writing is the fact that to be unguarded in a letter to a friend does not necessarily commit a writer to categorical sincerity. Take, for instance, the case of two friends sharing a joke about a third party behind his or her back; these jokes often involve deliberate impersonations, which would rightly be unacceptable if performed in front of their object, but which most people know to occur (whether or not they admit to perpetrating them themselves). In such a case, it would be difficult to draw the line where 'essence' stops and 'role' begins – indeed, one might say that the writer's skill in the latter validates the former rather than vitiating it. Cicero himself was not above such jokes, as when lampooning the speech-impediment of the statesman Hirrus: 'de Hillo (balbus enim sum) [...] Sed (balbi non sumus) ad rem redeamus.'[23] ['in Hillus's case (if you'll excuse the lisp)...But (to drop the lisp), back to the matter in hand.'] Instances like this militate against modern versions of the 'Ciceronian' theory, such as GF Singer's argument, from 1933, that familiar letters draw aside all the veils of protective subterfuge, cracking the shell of fiction to lay bare the true author. Pope's letters, he claims 'are definitely familiar in composition. This familiarity enables us to see the personality of the author with an absolute clearness of portraiture.'[24] Similarly, Cicero's letters are, on this account, 'the true Cicero'.[25] But if one takes the shell from a snail, one does not speak of having discovered the 'true' snail; what one is left with is a creature which required the shell in order to deserve its name.

Samuel Johnson was suspicious of those who claimed the ability to discern personality 'with an absolute clearness of portraiture', because he recognized that humans, in their earthly lives, are genetically and theologically predisposed to some degree of moral myopia, whether viewing others or themselves. If one's own self is always partly occluded, Johnson's writings repeatedly suggest, then the authority with which one can pronounce on others will be crucially – though perhaps salutarily – compromised. This recognition prompts a running metaphor about sight and blindness in Johnson's writing. In *The Rambler*, for example, he refers wryly to those 'that imagine themselves to have looked with more than common penetration into human nature',[26] and in his review of Soame Jenyn's *Free Inquiry into the Nature and Origin of Evil*, he questions the author's claim to another kind of superhuman sight:

> This is a treatise, consisting of six letters, upon a very difficult and important question, which, I am afraid, this author's endeavours will not free from the perplexity which has entangled the speculatists of all ages, and which must continue while *we see* but *in part*.[27]

Given this chastened, but never complacently negative, facing up to the limits of human vision, it is not surprising that Johnson should not have been easily convinced by claims for the spontaneity and 'absolute clearness' of Pope's letters, as seen in the 'Life of Pope':

Of his social qualities, if an estimate be made from his Letters, an opinion too favourable cannot easily be formed; they exhibit a perpetual and unclouded effulgence of general benevolence and particular fondness. There is nothing but liberality, gratitude, constancy, and tenderness. It has been so long said as to be commonly believed, that the true characters of men may be found in their letters, and that he who writes to his friend lays his heart open before him. But the truth is, that such were the simple friendships of the 'Golden Age,' and are now the friendships only of children. Very few can boast of hearts which they dare to lay open to themselves, and of which, by whatever accident exposed, they do not shun a distinct and continued view; and, certainly, what we hide from ourselves we do not show to our friends. There is, indeed, no transaction which offers stronger temptations to fallacy and sophistication than epistolary intercourse. In the eagerness of conversation the first emotions of the mind often burst out before they are considered; in the tumult of business, interest and passion have their genuine effect; but a friendly letter is a calm and deliberate performance, in the cool of leisure, in the stillness of solitude, and surely no man sits down to depreciate by design his own character.

Friendship has no tendency to secure veracity; for by whom can a man so much wish to be thought better than he is, as by him whose kindness he desires to gain and keep? Even in writing to the world there is less constraint; the author is not confronted with his reader, and takes his chance of approbation among the different dispositions of mankind; but a letter is addressed to a single mind, of which the prejudices and partialities are known, and must therefore please, if not by favouring them, by forbearing to oppose them.[28]

'It has been so long said as to be commonly believed': given that he knew of the *Lectures on Rhetoric and Belles Lettres*, via Boswell, before their publication, Johnson may be tilting obliquely at Blair in this passage,[29] but he also takes issue with a broader view, according to which familiarity involves a greater clarity than other forms of communication. In particular, he shows how the running metaphors of visual art and portraiture may be inadequate to sum up letter writing ('lay open', 'exposed', 'a distinct and continued view', 'hide from ourselves', 'show to our friends'). Bruce Redford has suggested that Johnson represents the most pertinent counterweight in the eighteenth century to the view of letters as intimate portraits: 'It is the Johnson of the letters to Hester Thrale,' he argues, 'who exemplifies the far end of the spectrum, the widest possible divorce between *ex cathedra* and *sub rosa* selves.'[30] The play of distance between those selves may be puzzling or deceitful; it may come to embody what Coleridge described as 'the mind's self-experience in the act of thinking';[31] but in Johnson's letters, as in Austen's after them, the writing is at least partly animated by drama – a successful and 'deliberate performance'.

Alasdair MacIntyre has claimed Austen as 'the last great imaginative voice' of an Aristotelian tradition in which '[p]olitics and philosophy were shaped by dramatic form'.[32] Austen's letters are both performative and sincere, since they work with the letter-writer's confinement to writing (which can itself be assumed as a role), yet work up their raw materials so that their intended reader can recognize and engage with the character which that writing creates. Take, for example, the letter which Austen, staying in Southampton, wrote to Cassandra at Godmersham Park on 10–11 January 1809: a particularly illuminating instance, since Austen's opening gambit is ostensibly to claim that she has nothing to write about. 'I am not surprised my dear Cassandra, that you did not find my last Letter very full of Matter, & I wish this may not have the same deficiency;—but we are doing nothing ourselves to write about, & I am therefore quite dependant upon the Communications of our friends, or my own Wit.'[33] One common reaction to a reading of Austen's correspondence is to complain that the letters are (especially considering their writer's fame) about 'nothing'. For all Austen's occasional references to the research, publication and family readings of the major novels, there is nothing in the surviving correspondence to compare with Richardson's letters to Lady Bradshaigh and Lady Echlin, no extended critical reflection on the novelist's fictional techniques and aesthetics. But, as so often in Austen's writing, what the letters lack in overt 'Matter' they make up for in the movement of her 'Wit' through the available materials.

Refusing to be put off by the supposed lack of 'Matter', Austen ranges promiscuously through distant war stories from La Coruña ('The St Albans perhaps may soon be off to help bring home what may remain of our poor Army'), domestic needlework ('pray let Marianne know, in private, that I think she is quite right to work a rug for Uncle John's Coffee urn'), card-games ('The preference of Brag over Speculation does not greatly surprise me'),[34] Mrs Sykes's novel *Margiana, or Widdrington Tower* ('We are just going to set off for Northumberland to be shut up in Widdrington Tower, where there must be two or three sets of Victims already immured under a very fine Villain'), and more frightening tales from the newspapers ('a sad story of a Mrs Middleton, wife of a Farmer in Yorkshire, her sister & servant being almost frozen to death in the late weather'[35]). Fanny in *Mansfield Park* has to seize upon the objects around her to construct her 'nest of comforts',[36] and Austen achieves similar effects with what she has to hand in this letter: the various subjects are recast dramatically as they are written about. Austen's surface tone is deliberately gossipy, refusing to make any clear stylistic separation between events of international importance and domestic trivia, but the letter is emphatically not *spoken* gossip – not least because of its typically self-aware humour about its written status. As Austen qualifies talking in terms of text in January 1801, so, eight years later, she pays equal attention to both halves of the metaphor of 'talking upon paper'. By writing of the impending Battle of Corunna and 'Uncle John's Coffee urn' in the same way, she approximates something of the unpredictable way in which history enters actual lives – even at times of heightened tension – and something of the way in which such events are gossiped about. But beyond that, her letter works its seeming trivia into a distinctive epistolary voice, one which exists between speech and writing. RW Chapman, introducing his pioneering edition of the letters, made what is still one of the finest analyses of their appeal, and its potential limits:

> But the enchantment which enthusiasts have sometimes found in these letters will not be universally admitted. It will be admitted by those only in whose own experience little things—like nicknames, or family jokes, or the arrangement of the furniture—are insepar-able from the deeper joys, and even from the deeper sorrows of life; and by those only who find wisdom and humanity in this corres-pondence, as well as—or in spite of—its devotion to minutiae.[37]

Despite his concessive 'as well as—or in spite of', Chapman senses well the intimate connection between 'little things' and weightier matters; 'minutiae' in Austen's writing become charged particles in her microscopic parables of discernment. However, it is in the very act of writing that the 'enchantment' Chapman discusses is created; and in the letters to Cassandra, Jane's voice is brought to life in the tone in which her writing arranges details. Mary A Favret has productively questioned a tendency in criticism to read eighteenth-century letters too readily as private and interior spaces. 'Throughout the eighteenth century,' she argues, 'the letter's ability to define and confine per-sonal experience had already been subject to a centripetal force which carried the private into the public realm, offering the individual's most intimate self for mass consumption.'[38] Her point, however, is primarily rooted in economic matters, and underplays the extent to which such a transaction between the 'intimate self' and public currency is also played out stylistically, at the small-est levels.

One of the most striking moments in the letter of 10–11 January 1809 is Austen's characteristic little literary-critical joke about her current reading: 'We are just going to set off for Northumberland to be shut up in Widdrington

Tower, where there must be two or three sets of Victims already immured under a very fine Villain.' As befits the author of *Northanger Abbey*, Austen's joke manages to present Mrs Sykes's fictional plot as if it were part of the real events around her ('We are just going to set off for Northumberland') whilst at the same time punning slyly on the novel's subtitle to point up its material existence as a book (is she 'shut up' in 'Widdrington Tower' or '*Widdrington Tower*'?). Redford has noted of Johnson's letters to Mrs Thrale that their humour 'depends for its effect on an ear attuned to the rhythms and inflections of speech, and on a mind quick to respond to half-buried allusions',[39] and his analysis could apply to Austen's letters as well. Austen's epistolary voice lives off a shared pattern of habits and private references. For example, the comedy of the repeated tickings-off she gives her sister requires Cassandra to offer herself as a stooge:

> You used me scandalously by not mentioning Ed. Cooper's Sermons;—I tell you everything, & it is unknown the Mysteries you conceal from me.[40]

By disproportionately yoking the melodramatic 'novel slang' phrase 'used me scandalously' to the respectable 'Sermons', Austen pouts sulkily at Cassandra across the space of their writing, while protecting the intimacy of their friendship through intentional and personal ironies of scale.

Carol Houlihan Flynn remarks of the letters that Austen often 'seems to be exploring the limits of a stream of consciousness located somewhere between Sterne and Samuel Beckett, one that represents her own awareness of the endless nature of her domestic tasks'.[41] Flynn's points of comparison are illuminating, since much of the humour and pathos of both Sterne and Beckett derive from their focus on how life and writing overlap, contend, and sometimes cancel each other out. More particularly, Austen's letters are comparable to *Tristram Shandy* and *Murphy* in their parodic awareness of certain conventions and expectations of writerly decorum: psychological and rhetorical patterns which they both include and outflank. I have discussed ways in which Austen's juvenilia often throw the expected rhetorical periods of eighteenth-century writing creatively out of kilter; her letters achieve comparable effects with expectations of what does and does not belong in a familiar letter, depending on a reader's being attuned not only to 'the rhythms and inflections of speech' but to those of writing. On 24 January 1809, she has a dig in passing at Hannah More's new novel *Coelebs in Search of a Wife*: 'You have by no means raised my curiosity after Caleb;—My disinclination for it before was affected, but now it is real; I do not like the Evangelicals.—Of course I shall be delighted when I read it, like other people, but till I do, I dislike it.'[42] Six days later, she explains her misreading of her sister's handwriting, but her apology is, typically, not a straightforward one:

> I am not at all ashamed about the name of the Novel, having been guilty of no insult towards your handwriting; the Dipthong I always saw, but knowing how fond you were of adding a vowel wherever you could, I attributed it to that alone—& the knowledge of the truth does the book no service;—the only merit it could have, was in the name of Caleb, which has an honest, unpretending sound; but in Coelebs, there is pedantry & affectation.—Is it written only to Classical Scholars?[43]

Austen skilfully manipulates the form of polite apology ('having been guilty of no insult towards your handwriting') so she can then get away with insulting her sister's handwriting ('knowing how fond you were of adding a vowel wherever you could'), but her joke does not stop there. She also scores off the 'pedantry & affectation' of More's title, matching the 'honest, unpretending sound' of 'Caleb' with her own English variant, 'Dipthong': where Cassandra adds vowels, Jane drops consonants. Once again, 'knowing how fond you were' places Austen's game within a private catalogue of wind-ups: an aspect of familial affection which she also affords to that rare pair of happy fictional siblings, Henry and Eleanor Tilney in *Northanger Abbey*. A frequent move in the letters to Cassandra involves Jane's testing the boundaries of propriety, seeing how near the edge of acceptability she can go without falling over it – and then sometimes deliberately jumping anyway. As early as May 1801, one can see her turning the markers of epistolary decorum to more creative and unsettling ends. Her letter begins by presupposing, and repeating, what Cassandra ought by now to have heard ('You know from Elizabeth I dare say', 'James I dare say has been over to Ibthrop by this time'[44]). So far, this is only informative; but when Austen subtly changes the way she qualifies her words, matters become more complicated:

> I then got Mr Evelyn to talk to, & Miss Twisleton to look at; and I am proud to say that I have a very good eye at an Adultress, for tho' repeatedly assured that another in the same party was the *She*, I fixed upon the right one from the first.[45]

This is indeed 'daring to say', its playfulness providing what Austen's fictional speeches rarely provide: direct pointing for the voice.

There are even moments in the letters when Austen's 'deliberate performance' is so self-conscious as to cast doubt on those, from many ideological positions, who have identified the open-ended nature of familiar letters with a generic, essentialist 'female' speech and writing: this is one of those instances where the opposing forces occupy some of the same ground. In 1922, Otto Jespersen's breakthrough work of historical linguistics claimed: 'Women much more often than men break off without finishing their sentences, because they start talking without having thought out what they are going to say',[46] and GF Singer alleged that '[t]here are few of us who have not, at one time or another, suffered from the lengthy outpourings that only a female correspondent may send us'.[47] On the other side of the fence come claims such as Virginia Woolf's, about Austen's turning critically on the 'male' sentence ('Jane Austen looked at it and laughed at it and devised a perfectly natural, shapely sentence proper to her own use and never departed from it'[48]). For all that she did laugh at certain kinds of rhetorical flourish perpetrated by eighteenth-century men, Austen was wise enough to know that her sentences could neither be entirely 'proper' to her (in the sense of being her own particular property, like Woolf's 'Room of One's Own'), nor always 'perfectly natural'. Her 'written voice' is more akin to that which Gabriel Josipovici has divined in literary texts: one 'which avoids […] both the biographical and the textual temptations'.[49] In other words, it cannot be entirely assimilated either to the flesh-and-blood Jane Austen or to the impersonal forces of '*langue*' or '*écriture*'. Even more importantly, Austen's comic targets are not confined to what might be called 'male sentences', as witnessed by her most Sternean moment, the extraordinary letter which she wrote to Cassandra from London on 15 September 1813 – or as she put it herself:

Henrietta St Wednesday – ½ past 8 —

Here I am my dearest Cassandra, seated in the Breakfast, Dining, sitting room, beginning with all my might. Fanny will join me as soon as she is dressed & begin her Letter.[50]

At the beginning of her letter, Austen keys into her running joke with her sister, by being slightly too precise about her timing ('½ past 8'), and follows Fielding's *Shamela* in rendering 'writing to the moment' absurd[51] ('in the Breakfast, Dining, sitting room'). But there is more to come:

Sace arrived safely about ½ past 6. At 7 we set off in a Coach for the Lyceum – were at home again in about 4 hours and ½ – had Soup & wine & water, & then went to our Holes. Edward finds his quarters very snug & quiet. – I must get a softer pen. – This is harder. I am in agonies. – I have not yet seen Mr Crabbe. – Martha's Letter is gone to the Post. –

I am going to write nothing but short Sentences. There shall be two full stops in every Line. Layton and Shear's *is* Bedford House. We mean to get there before breakfast if it's possible. For we feel more & more how much we have to do. And how little time. This house looks very nice. It seems like Sloane Sᵗ moved here. I believe Henry is just rid of Sloane Sᵗ – Fanny does not come, but I have Edward seated by me beginning a letter, which looks natural.

· ·

Let me be rational & return to my two full stops.

I talked to Henry at the Play last night. We were in a private Box – Mʳ Spencer's – Which made it much more pleasant. The Box is directly on the Stage. One is infinitely less fatigued than in the common way. – But Henry's plans are not what one could wish. He does not mean to be at Chawton till yᵉ 29.[52]

One reason Emma Woodhouse is so troubled by Miss Bates is that she can divine in the spinster's domestic glossolalia something of herself, or of what she herself might one day become; and critics such as Carol Houlihan Flynn have noted the stylistic similarity between some of Austen's own letters and the 'parasyntactic, always obliging Miss Bates, who sees and reports *every thing* with a flat, undistinguished, decidedly unbecoming zeal'.[53] The crucial difference is, of course, that Miss Bates's creator knows what she's doing. This letter turns the Richardsonian trope of the sentimental correspondent with her tremblingly sincere pen into bathetic slapstick ('I must get a softer pen. – This is harder. I am in agonies'), and its deliberate burlesque of 'short sentences' at once admits the fact that *some* women talk like Miss Bates, and mocks any idea of prattling as a universal trait of women's language.

Austen-Leigh's *Memoir* of his aunt has been read as a founding document in the legend of 'Gentle Jane', and it has its undeniable moments of fondness; but its very title, like that of Hallam Tennyson's account of his father, does not pretend to the objectivity of a 'Biography', and what it lacks in critical detachment it gains in intimacy with the social and familial pragmatics of its subject. Therefore, Austen-Leigh's account of his aunt Jane's in-jokes is telling:

> She was as far as possible from being censorious or satirical [...] The laugh which she occasionally raised was by imagining for her neighbours, as she was equally ready to imagine for her friends or herself, impossible contingencies, or by relating in prose or verse some trifling anecdote coloured to her own fancy, or in writing a fictitious history of what they were supposed to have said or done, which could deceive nobody.[54]

Austen-Leigh is overly anxious about the possibility of his aunt's being 'censorious and satirical', and the clerical shades in his phrasing ('imagining for her neighbours [...] for her friends or herself' carries an unmistakable undertone of 'loue thy neighbor as thy selfe'[55]) further the effect. Nevertheless, he makes a pertinent point about the nature of Austen's jokes, in particular their status as 'occasional' or 'party pieces'. The fact of Cassandra Austen's censoring the letters by fire, and the absence of much direct and explicit self-revelation in the surviving letters, have led some, naturally enough, to conjecture that the Austen of the lost correspondence must have been radically different. 'No one who reads the *Memoir*,' remarks DW Harding, 'can doubt that she followed this programme naturally and well and that it reflected part of her personality. It is equally evident that the novels would not have been what they are unless she had at the same time been a very different person.'[56] That people have 'insides' to their characters is indisputable; indeed, as I shall explore later in this chapter, such a perception is central to *Emma*. It is less certain that the 'lost Austen' is any more privately revelatory or confessional than the one we know; as the juvenilia witness her 'fighting off the task of writing feeling', so the letters may show her fighting off the confessional demands of sentimental correspondence. One of the letters' many fascinations – and one reason why they so illuminate the novels – is that Austen's personality often makes itself felt not so much in 'hidden depths' but in the distinctive ways in which it stirs the surface.

If one reads the letters as a whole, one can readily detect a markedly different tone of epistolary voice in letters not addressed to Cassandra: a tone more overtly decorous than the sisters' comic idiolect. For example, when the Rev. James Stanier Clarke asked her to include someone not unlike himself in her next novel ('the Habits of Life and Character and enthusiasm of a Clergyman—who should pass his time between the metropolis & the Country'[57]), Austen fobbed him off with disingenous brilliance: 'I think I may boast myself to be, with all possible Vanity, the most unlearned, & uninformed Female who ever dared to be an Authoress'.[58] Conversely, when advising her niece Fanny Knight on matters of love, she measured her written tone to the demands of that situation, practising the circumspection which her letter recommends to Fanny:

> but when I think how very, very far it is from a *Now*, & take everything that *may be*, into consideration, I dare not say " determine to accept him." The risk is too great for *you*, unless your own Sentiments prompt it.[59]

Different contexts demand particular responses and tones; and it is in this light, I would suggest, that the more famously barbed moments in Austen's letters ought to be viewed. If she could sometimes hope 'to express on paper exactly what one would say to the same person by word of mouth', she also knew what letters could offer her as a safety valve, a means of saying to her sister what the demands of spoken politeness would *not* allow her to say. As William Milns suggested in 1794, '[i]t is not enough to consider well the nature of the subject on which we are going to write: we should be no less attentive to the rank, fortune and temper of the persons with whom we correspond [...] The least indecorum in this respect will often render a letter ridiculous, or offensive'.[60]

Reminding Cassandra of her enduring interest in trivia in September 1813, she spoke of herself in resonant phrasing:

> Well, there is some comfort in the Mrs Hulberts not coming to you—& I am happy to hear of the Honey.—I was thinking of it the other day.—Let me know when you begin the new Tea—& the new white wine.—My present Elegancies have not yet made me indifferent to such Matters. I am still a Cat if I see a Mouse.[61]

In its way, this has a greater claim to being the byword of Austen's letter-writing than any remarks about 'talking on paper'. For her to imagine her relationship to domestic trivia as that of 'Cat' to 'Mouse' would be significant enough in itself, but the phrase also has its memories of Hamlet's 'antic disposition', in which essence and role become inseparable ('I am but mad North, North-West: when the Winde is Southerly, I know a Hawke from a Handsaw'[62]). Austen's familiarity with her sister allows her to get away with venting her sharper frustrations, knowing that her remarks are for Cassandra's mind's ear alone; furthermore, her annoyance is often transfigured into art. Her letter of 12–13 May 1801, for example, complains earnestly about 'Another stupid party last night':

> I respect Mrs Chamberlayne for doing her hair well, but cannot feel a more tender sentiment. – Miss Langley is like any other short girl with a broad nose & wide mouth, fashionable dress, & exposed bosom.[63]

The anger and ennui are palpable and unfeigned; but that anger is a novelist's anger: Austen's precise *cadenza* of focal points in describing Miss Langley ('hair', 'nose', 'mouth', 'dress', 'bosom') wins a more organized comic victory from the constraints of social dullness, the writer rising above her circumstances even as she looks down her nose. Perhaps the most notorious remark in the surviving letters comes on 27 October 1798: 'Mrs Hall of Sherbourn was brought to bed yesterday of a dead child, some weeks before she expected, owing to a fright. – I suppose she happened unawares to look at her husband.'[64] The joke is a vicious one – although its very insensitivity may feel the limits of sympathy with others' grief more decently than any easy pretence at inwardness at such a time. Such instances form part of the larger texture of Austen's life and work, a life and work much devoted to the minute analysis of true and false feelings, and to the perennial difficulties of telling the two apart.

'Seldom, very seldom,' muses the narrator of *Emma*, 'does complete truth belong to any human disclosure; seldom can it happen that something is not a little disguised, or a little mistaken'.[65] Like Johnson before her, Austen had to balance her desire to communicate in writing against her knowledge that such communication will never be wholly transparent; having seen what could happen to the hopes of Ciceronian and sentimental correspondence, she needed to find other ways of writing her voice across space. To that end, her letters and juvenilia swerve in and out of step with received expectations, sounding out what one can and cannot say – what is and is not possible, or permissible, in writing. As Josipovici puts it: 'Trust without suspicion is the recipe for a false and meretricious art; but suspicion without trust is the recipe for a shallow and empty art'.[66] The rest of this chapter will explore the extent to which a comparable sense in Austen underwrites 'the perfect happiness of the union' at the very end of *Emma*: the novel's points of romantic and narrative convergence gain their force by admitting the number of ways in which they may otherwise have gone awry. While Austen could trust that her epistolary voice would reach Cassandra – sometimes in spite of, and sometimes because of the medium of writing – she could not be so sure when writing to others, whether less intimate correspondents or the unknown audience for her novels. *Emma's* masterly analysis of deception and self-deception is alive to what can happen to our voices and words once they enter the unpredictable spaces that divide people from each other. Whether accidentally or deliberately, words' detached nature can turn them into instruments of ventriloquial trickery and possession; conversely, they can prove awkwardly tenacious, returning on us like psychological heartburn – a quality which fictional narrative, with its potentially more structured patterns of memory and echo, is especially effective at highlighting. Steven Connor has meticulously described this 'essential paradox of the voice':

> My voice defines me because it draws me into coincidence with myself, accomplishes me in a way which goes beyond mere belonging, association, or instrumental use. And yet my voice is also essentially itself and my own in the ways in which it parts or passes from

me. Nothing else about me defines me so intimately as my voice, precisely because there is no other feature of myself whose nature it is thus to move from me to the world, and to move me into the world. If my voice is mine because it comes from me, it can only be known as mine because it also goes from me. My voice is, literally, my way of taking leave of my senses. What I say goes.[67]

In *Emma*, Austen composed a comic romance around the many 'comings' and 'goings' of people's words, but it was only her most complete exploration to date of a concern which can be seen working even in the juvenilia, and which takes on greater force in her most extended surviving epistolary fiction, one nourished by two of the eighteenth century's most famous portraits of epistolary deceit. Therefore, it is to *Lady Susan* that I now turn.

Parading Propriety: Lady Susan

Those letters are only good, which contain the natural effusions of the heart, expressed in unaffected language. Tinsel and glitter, and laboured phrases, dismiss the friend and introduce the authoress.

Thomas Gisborne, *An Enquiry into the Duties of the Female Sex*[68]

The opinions of James Wildman of Chilham Castle on the merits of *Emma* have not (unlike those of Austen's closer circle) been recorded, but Austen's letter to Fanny Knight from March 1817 gives a good idea of what they must have been:

I am very much obliged to you my dearest Fanny for sending me M[r] Wildman's conversation, I had great amusement in reading it, & I *hope* I am not affronted & do not think the worse of him for having a Brain so very different from mine, but my strongest sensation of all is *astonishment* at your being able to press him on the subject so perseveringly—and I agree with your Papa, that it was not fair. [...] He & I should not in the least agree of course, in our ideas of Novels & Heroines;—pictures of perfection as you know make me sick & wicked—but there is some very good sense in what he says, & I particularly respect him for wishing to think well of all young Ladies; it shews an amiable & a delicate Mind.—And he deserves better treatment than to be obliged to read any more of my Works.[69]

Austen's objection to 'pictures of perfection' has rightly passed into Janeite legend alongside her 'little bit (two Inches wide) of Ivory',[70] although readers' emphasis often falls more on her avoidance of 'perfection' than on her suspicion of 'pictures'. The Johnsonian scepticism about psychological transparency and its metaphors, which I mentioned above, is equally in evidence here as it is in *Lady Susan* – a work particularly fascinated by the lures of appearance. In Letter 6 of *Lady Susan*, Catherine Vernon sounds out the novella's keynote when she remarks on the sister-in-law's 'happy command of Language, which is too often used I beleive to make Black appear White'.[71] Black and white are the shades of morality in which many of *Lady Susan*'s characters would like to be able to deal, but they are not the tones in which Austen writes her story; her concern is with the numerous shades of grey created by 'command of Language', and what that 'command' can make 'appear' or hide from view – especially in familiar letters.

It is perhaps appropriate that accidents of literary history have conspired to make *Lady Susan* appear dislocated within Austen's *oeuvre*, since some of its readers have themselves found it difficult to assimilate to the published novels. Mary Augusta Austen-Leigh, for example, attributed the work's peculiarity to a foundation in family legend: she wrote of the 'horrified indignation' which 'may have seized upon Jane Austen's soul when the story of an unnatural and brutal mother was made known to her, overpowering her fancy to so great a degree that she was at last impelled to seek relief in gibbeting this repulsive creature by setting down her character in writing'.[72] More recently (and more soberly), Margaret Drabble pondered: 'What a pity it is that she never, in her mature work, returned to the subject of a handsome thirty-five-year-old widow.'[73] Whether it is a matter of imaginative sources or of subject-matter, both Austen-Leigh and Drabble notice something about *Lady Susan* which does not quite square with their respective impressions of Austen's other writing; this tonal dislocation has been sharpened by *Lady Susan*'s own history. Although it was not published until JE Austen-Leigh included it in the *Memoir* in the 1870s, *Lady Susan*'s fair copy dates from 1805, and Brian Southam has convincingly dated its composition to around 1793–4;[74] therefore, whatever its seeming idiosyncrasies, the novella occupies a pivotal place in the development of Austen's writing, between the juvenilia and the original versions of *Sense and Sensibility*, *Pride and Prejudice* and *Northanger Abbey*. In this context, it is all the more illuminating; since *Elinor and Marianne*, the embryonic, epistolary version of *Sense and Sensibility*, is now lost, *Lady Susan* is Austen's only surviving epistolary work in a non-burlesque mode. The novella may be, as Roger Gard calls it, a 'single effect';[75] something of an experiment, a set-piece or a side-track, but that circumstance does not cut it off completely from the body of work to which it belongs: all side-tracks, however circuitously, lead to Steventon.

Indeed, *Lady Susan*'s most disquieting characteristic may not be its distance from but its uncomfortable proximity to the more familiar works, from the 1790s and elsewhere. For example, the absurd, exaggerated emotional reactions of *Love and Freindship* find more comically sombre echoes in the novella. Austen ends Letters 8 and 9 of *Love and Freindship* with the characters becoming overpowered by sentiment:

> Never did I see such an affecting Scene as was the meeting of Edward & Augustus.
> "My Life! my Soul!" (exclaimed the former) "My Adorable Angel!" (replied the latter) as they flew into each other's arms. It was too pathetic for the feelings of Sophia and myself – We fainted Alternately on a Sofa.
>
> Adeiu
Laura[76]

> The beautifull Augustus was arrested and we were all undone. Such perfidious Treachery in the merciless perpetrators of the Deed will shock your gentle nature Dearest Marianne as much as it then affected the Delicate Sensibility of Edward, Sophia, your Laura, & of Augustus himself. To compleat such unparalelled Barbarity we were informed that an Execution in the House would shortly take place. Ah! what could we do but what we did! We sighed & fainted on the Sofa.
>
> Adeiu
Laura[77]

Part of the joke here is a temporal *reductio ad absurdum*, akin to the effect of watching film footage speeded up: what seems natural in 'real time' can appear comical even when replayed ever so slightly too fast (compare modern viewers' reactions to the frame-speeds of early newsreels, however grave their subject-matter – 'comedy is tragedy speeded up', as Norman Holland notes[78]). Thus Austen achieves a great deal simply by piling a great deal of plot-matter into too short a narrative space, as she does elsewhere by reducing the one-thousand-plus pages of *Sir Charles Grandison* to fifty-two small pages of dramatic manuscript; Brian Southam aptly terms this the 'comedy of abridgement'.[79] But Austen's comic compression of events also highlights certain expectations – of how sentimental responses should follow specific events naturally and promptly, almost as physiological reflexes. To chuckle at a joke in a letter, expecting one's correspondent to do the same, as Austen did in her letters to Cassandra, requires only a modicum of reciprocal imagination, but the sentimental correspondence sent up in *Love and Freindship* demands much more: Laura hopes that the rendition of her woes will literally set off a sympathetic vibration of woe in Marianne ('Such perfidious treachery [...] will shock your gentle nature [...] as much as it then affected the Delicate Sensibility of Edward'), even though such a reaction might, logically, lead to Marianne's fainting over her letter. Send-ups like this pose a challenge to that aspect of Richardsonian sentiment which John Mullan has identified:

> The body's visible fluctuations are symptomatic of the sensibility which cannot be disguised, but which is supposed not to be spoken. It is a corpus of irrepressible signs [...] Women are bound together – in Richardson's extraordinary version of femininity – in tears, postures and movements instantly understood. This is his version of essential sociability. It is a condition that he can only ever imagine.[80]

Mullan's final qualification is telling: Richardson could present the sympathetic pulses of 'female bonding' as an ideal, but it was in practice an ideal which, especially in *Clarissa*, became more clearly defined the more it was shown to be inadequate to the circumstances of his plots. It is this double-irony at the heart of *Clarissa*, in combination with Laclos' chilly parodies of emotion in *Les Liaisons dangereuses* (where Valmont toys with and rejects the idea of 'faire une nouvelle Clarisse' ['or even to set her asleep, as in Clarissa'][81]), which nourish *Lady Susan* – a novella unsettlingly and hilariously alert to the unsociable ends to which 'essential sociability' can be turned.

Lady Susan arrives at the home of her brother-in-law and his wife, quick to observe her surroundings, but also quick to sense what she can gain by being seen in the right light:

> The house is a good one, the Furniture fashionable, & everything announces plenty & elegance. Charles is very rich I am sure; when a Man has once got his name in a Banking House he rolls in money. But they do not know what to do with their fortune, keep very little company, and never go to Town but on business. We shall be as stupid as possible. I mean to win my Sister in law's heart through her Children; I know all their names already, & am going to attach myself with the greatest sensibility to one in particular, a young Frederic, whom I take on my lap & sigh over for his dear Uncle's sake.[82]

Her plan sounds more like an empirical experiment than an emotional reconciliation, taking that emphasis on '*extérieur brillant*' and 'observation', which underpins Chesterfieldian manners, to vicious extremes. In 1749, Chesterfield had advised his son in matters of style. 'Gain the heart,' reads his letter, 'or you gain nothing; the eyes and the ears are the only roads to the heart. Merit and knowledge will not gain hearts, though they will secure them when gained. Pray have that truth ever in your mind. Engage the eyes by your address, air, and motions: soothe the ears by the elegance and harmony of your diction; the heart will certainly follow; and the whole man, or woman, will as certainly follow the heart.'[83] Lady Susan can so readily assume the tone and diction of conduct literature, because decorum for her exists precisely as text-book material: a rhetorical repertoire which can be trotted out at will, with no cost to herself; compare, for example, her aphoristic formulae ('Consideration & Esteem as surely follow command of Language, as Admiration waits on Beauty') with Chesterfield's ('Engage the eyes […] the heart will certainly follow'). The cause-and-effect of her emotive plotting is clear in the timing with which she relates it to her confidante Alicia Johnson: not only does she 'aim to win my Sister in law's heart through her children', but the progress of natural affection is noted deliberately in advance, its stages ticked off as if they were items on a checklist ('I know all their names already, & am going to attach myself with the greatest sensibility to one in particular'). Even more shockingly matter-of-fact is how she reveals the symptoms of innate sentimental authenticity – those 'visible fluctuations' analysed by Mullan – to be, potentially, less a matter of reflex than of planning. Like Chesterfield before her, Lady Susan knows that 'observation' covers both sententiousness and narcissism; and in the phrase 'whom I take on my lap & sigh over for his dear Uncle's sake', she manages to step back and observe herself from a distance – even when her sentiments are meant to be most actively involved and engaged. In the 'Inquiry Concerning Virtue or Merit', Shaftesbury had claimed: 'lest any should imagine that with themselves that an inferior degree of natural affection, or an imperfect partial regard […] can supply the place of an entire, sincere, and truly moral one […] and give us that enjoyment of participation and community which is so essential to our happiness; we may consider first, that partial affection, or social love in part, without regard to a complete society or whole, is itself an inconsistency, and implies an absolute contradiction'.[84] However, this philosophically optimistic view of hypocrisy as both easily detectable and logically self-defeating finds no room for instances which lack 'sincere, and truly moral' affection, but adopt its outward forms – the very events in which Austen's fiction is most interested, which are everywhere in *Lady Susan*, and to which one might apply Susan Vernon's own words about her daughter's schoolmistress: 'a parade of propriety'.[85]

One of the distinctive stylistic features of epistolary narrative is hinted at within the plot of *Persuasion*, as Mrs Smith uses one of Mr Elliot's letters to reveal the truth about his economic and emotional scheming to Anne, who, even as she suffers 'the shock and mortification of finding such words applied to her father', still reminds herself 'that no private correspondence could bear the eye of others'.[86] Epistolary fiction, on the other hand, thrives on breaking these contracts, and depends for its being on 'the eye of others'; a reader of *Clarissa* or *Lady Susan* needs to peer over characters' shoulders, at multiple acts of writing, and, crucially, at multiple acts of reading, inference and interpretation (one reason why Richardson's novel has become a *locus classicus* for reader-response theory and post-structuralism).[87] Part of the vicarious thrill of the novel-in-letters is the mobility it offers, the ability to see plotting as it is conceived, received at the other end, and variously delayed, intercepted and forwarded in between – a freedom circumscribed when one realizes that, in the absence of external narration, one's own interpretations may be limited or suspect. For all the protagonist's dominance over her story, and over those around her, *Lady Susan* is full of attempted 'readings' of her and the possible significance of her behaviour. Both Reginald De Courcy and his sister Catherine Vernon are particularly keen to work out exactly what Lady Susan is up to on her visit to Churchill, but for different reasons: where Catherine is suspicious in Letter 3 ('I cannot make up my mind, till I better understand her real meaning in coming to us'[88]), Reginald, in the next letter, treats her like a prodigious curiosity:

> I congratulate you & Mr Vernon on being about to receive into your family, the most accomplished Coquette in England. As a very distinguished Flirt, I have been always taught to consider her; but it has lately fallen in my way to hear some particulars of her conduct at Langford, which prove that she does not confine herself to that sort of honest flirtation which satisfies most people, but aspires to the more delicious gratification of making a whole family miserable [...] What a Woman she must be! I long to see her, & shall certainly accept your kind invitation, that I may form some idea of those bewitching powers which can do so much [...] by all that I can gather, Lady Susan possesses a degree of captivating Deceit which must be pleasing to witness and detect.[89]

However, once a reader returns, two letters later, to Lady Susan, it is not only his or her perspective that shifts, but the entire balance of power, as it transpires that Reginald's role as dispassionate observer is in fact one created for him by that 'most accomplished Coquette':

He is lively & seems clever, & when I have inspired him with greater respect for me than his sister's kind offices have implanted, he may be an agreable Flirt. There is exquisite pleasure in subduing an insolent spirit, in making a person pre-determined to dislike, acknowledge one's superiority. I have disconcerted him already by my calm reserve; & it shall be my endeavour to humble the Pride of these self-important De Courcies still lower, to convince Mrs Vernon that her sisterly cautions have been bestowed in vain, & to persuade Reginald that she has scandalously belied me. This project will serve at least to amuse me, & prevent my feeling so acutely this dreadful separation from You & all whom I love.[90]

'This project': here Austen places her protagonist most firmly (if ironically) in a line of descent which runs from eighteenth-century epistolary fiction onwards, one in which the signs of sentiment and 'essential sociability' can be paraded as counters, parts of a 'project' to stave off social ennui, and which involves readers both inside and outside the plot in complex emotional detective work – the libertine tradition which she knew through *Clarissa*, and quite plausibly through *Les Liaisons dangereuses*.

Clarissa, or the History of a Young Lady has gained a history of its own since 1748, in particular that history of revision in successive editions, with the aim of rendering its instructive sentiments more direct, and of forestalling ambiguity, however forlorn the latter hope may have been.[91] As Mullan reminds us, 'the space between precept and interpretation may be one in which literary criticism can now discover plural meanings and a conventionally valued freedom for the reader, but we should recognize that Richardson's endeavour was to make this space disappear'.[92] That said, the fact that Richardson needed to 'endeavour' at all in this direction shows that the novel as it originally stood was not, in his opinion, quite fulfilling the remit of the first edition's editorial preface ('to caution parents against the undue exertion of their natural authority over their children [...] and children against preferring a man of pleasure to a man of probity'[93]); indeed, it may be the mark of *Clarissa*'s superiority to *Pamela* and *Grandison* that the novel grows beyond Richardson's original design for it, taking on a life of its own. When Johnson famously told Boswell that 'if you were to read Richardson for the story you would hang yourself', he indicated that *Clarissa*'s focus is less on the movements of plot than on the analysis and reflection to which that plot gives rise. The novel's extreme length is largely down to its profusion of descriptive details, but these details are not all scenic. For all its renderings of physical features, whether the precise posting-place for Clarissa's clandestine exchanges with Anna Howe ('The lane is lower than the floor of the wood-house, and in the side of the wood-house the boards are rotted away down to the floor for half an ell together'[94]) or the unpleasant looks of her approved suitor ('Mr Solmes removed to his first seat, and fell to gnawing the head of his hazel, a carved head, almost as ugly as his own'[95]), Richardson's narrative is even more given to the minute, extended scrutiny of emotional responses, symptoms which fictional correspondents and real readers are challenged to trace back to their causes.

In effect, *Clarissa* tries to maintain a double focus, training its eye at once on the external '*throbs*' and '*glows*'[96] of the sensitive body, and inward towards a mental terrain which turns out to be as rugged and treacherous as any Gothic landscape; this double perspective is particularly well served by the epistolary form, since, despite Richardson's valuing of writing 'to the moment', what would conventionally be thought of as the plot of an epistolary novel exists, strictly speaking, at one remove from its text. John Preston has noted of *Clarissa* in particular, and the fiction of letters in general, that 'the actual process of writing, the text itself, is the action. It is not a description or a narration of the action, though it contains many such descriptions [...] it is the telling that constitutes the novel, not what is told. The words in this novel are the acts.'[97] Thus, in keeping with the novel's double perspective, the true *histoire* of *Clarissa* is made up of the many acts of writing in which its events are set down: a succession of phenomenological meetings in which emotional response converges with the bodily movements that write it down and narrate it. In *Clarissa*, though, these meetings are always uneasy ones, less sentimental harmonies than mind/body problems; the very difficulty of linking the cause and effect of emotion is what eventually, and destructively, brings Clarissa Harlowe and Robert Lovelace together.

It has frequently been noted of Clarissa and Lovelace that their perverse relationship depends on the progressive collapse of the opposition that the novel initially appears to be offering between them.[98] In fact, over the course of the narrative, if they do not quite change places, each begins unconsciously to take on some of the other's characteristics, and nowhere is this clearer than in the way their experience of emotional symptoms converges: Clarissa learns to dissemble, and Lovelace finds himself being sincere against his will. Terry Castle has described the Clarissa Harlowe of the novel's opening well, calling her 'a naïve exegete' who 'reads the world as if it were an "open book" – a transparent source of meaning';[99] for example, as Clarissa relates an awkward irruption of feeling into an interview with her estranged mother, she trusts implicitly in the external shorthand of emotion, both in herself and Mrs Harlowe:

> If children would always be children—parents—And there she stopped.

She then went to her toilette and looked in the glass, and gave half a sigh—the other half, as if she would not have sighed could she have helped it, she hemmed away.

I don't love to see the girl look so sullen.

Indeed, madam, I am not sullen—And I arose and, turning from her, drew out my handkerchief, for the tears ran down my cheeks. I thought, by the glass before me, I saw the *mother* in her softened eye cast before me—But her words confirmed not the hoped-for tenderness.

One of the provokingest things in the world is to have people cry for what they can help!

I wish to heaven I could, madam!—and I sobbed again.

Tears of penitence and sobs of perverseness are mighty well suited!—You may go up to your chamber. I shall talk with you by and by.

I curtsied with reverence—

Mock me not with outward gesture of respect. The heart, Clary, is what I want.

Indeed, madam, you have it. It is not so much mine, as my mamma's!

Fine talking!—As somebody says, if words were duty, Clarissa Harlowe would be the dutifullest child breathing.

God bless that somebody!—Be it whom it will, God bless that somebody!—And I curtsied and, pursuant to her last command, was going.[100]

Despite her mother's suspicion of 'outward gesture of respect', Clarissa still holds to her belief in the authenticity of tears and curtseys, and it is such a belief that eventually allows Lovelace to achieve her abduction; she may quote with approval Elizabeth Carter's 'Ode to Wisdom'('She sees through ev'ry fair disguise,/ That all, but VIRTUE'S solid joys,/ Is vanity and woe'[101]), but when the crisis arrives, Clarissa's skill in sentimental close reading deserts her. Lovelace's chivalrous repertoire seems convincing ('Who can bear, said he, with an ardour that could not be feigned, his own sweet eyes glistening, as I thought, who can bear to behold such sweet emotion?'[102]), as does the fear of discovery which precipitates her flight:

I was offering the key to the lock, when starting from his knees, with a voice of affrightment loudly whispering, and as if out of breath, *They are at the door, my beloved creature!* And taking the key from me, he flew to it, and fluttered with it as if he would double-lock it.

And instantly a voice from within cried out, bursting against the door, as if to break it open, and repeating its violent pushes: *Are you there?—Come up this moment!—this moment!—Here they are—Here they are both together!—Your pistol this moment!—your gun!* [...] He at the same moment drew his sword, and clapping it naked under his arm, took both my trembling hands in his; and, drawing me swiftly after him: Fly, my charmer; this moment is all you have for it! said he—[103]

Richardson, however, immediately stages a brilliant moment of narrative withholding, as he makes the reader privy to an alternative version of the same events: Lovelace's instructions to Joseph Leman, told out of chronological sequence, which unpicks the confidence of Clarissa's account. 'If you hear our voices parleying,' he prescribes, 'keep at the door, till I cry Hem, hem, twice: but be watchful for this signal, for I must not hem very loud, lest she should take it for a signal [...] Then you are to make a violent burst against the door, as if you'd break it open, drawing backward and forward the bolt in a hurry; then with another push, but with more noise than strength, let the lock give way, cry out (as if you saw some of the family): Come up, come up, instantly!—Here they are! Here they are!'[104]). '[W]ith a voice of affrightment loudly whispering'; 'till I cry Hem, hem, twice': this moment of dark, nasty comedy is one of the great shocks of eighteenth-century fiction. At the heart of the supreme novel of sentiment, Richardson finds the faultline which was to become the undoing of sentimentalism, as his narrative breaks the fundamental contract of emotional response: the two versions of Lovelace's whisper show conclusively that the sentimental 'metonymy of the body'[105] need have no absolute basis, that what sounds like a spontaneous outburst of sentiment can be a theatrical cue.

The recognition which dawns on a reader at this point eventually dawns on Clarissa, too, not least when she finally makes good her escape from Mrs Sinclair by contriving to disguise herself as the servant Mabel; so successful is this transformation, in fact, that it poses questions as to whether character itself in *Clarissa* is essential or reproducible at will ('Without turning her face, or answering, she held out her hand, pointing to the stairs; which they construed as a caution for them to look out in her absence; and supposing she would not be long gone, as she had not formally repeated her caution to them, up went Will tarrying at the stairs-head in expectation of the supposed Mabel's return'[106]). Tony Tanner relates that the future comedian David Baddiel noted how the senses of 'propriety' and 'property' began to shift and converge in the latter half of the eighteenth century, 'propriety' being almost exclusively applicable to matters of ownership;[107] it is appropriate that in *Clarissa*, whose plot is set in motion by a monetary bequest, and in which

Clarissa herself becomes an economic chattel in the Harlowes' dealings with Solmes, the very currency of emotion risks becoming just that: not so much a series of practices as the circulation of worn coinage.

The shock of Clarissa's abduction clearly inspired the central point of mental torture in the novel which did for the moral traditions of the French *ancien régime* what Richardson had done with the culture of English sentiment: Laclos's *Les Liaisons dangereuses* (1782), which had appeared in English as *Dangerous Connections* as early as 1784, and which Austen may well have known in the original via her flirtatious Continental cousin Eliza De Feuillide.[108] Recasting the concerns of *Clarissa* in the terms of what Gard has called 'a kind of heroic code, perhaps that of a debased chivalry',[109] Laclos takes even further the fear that personality may have shrunk to nothing but successive acts of self-presentation, and 'articulates the impossibility of a return to nature or to a transparent subjectivity'[110] – a fear which underpins Valmont's extraordinary address to the Présidente de Tourvel, the (professed) object of his affections, in Letter 48. He has set out, like Lovelace before him, to fulfil a project, a strategy distanced from feeling ('Voilà ce que j'attaque; voilà l'ennemi digne de moi, voilà le but où je prétends atteindre [...] J'ai bien besoin d'avoir cette femme pour me sauver du ridicule d'en être amoureux' ['that is the object I attack; that is the enemy worthy of me; that is the point I intend to carry [...] I must possess this woman, lest I should be so ridiculous as to be in love']111]), only his is more overt in its sexual cruelty, as witnessed by the stark contrast between the 'sentimental' and 'libertine' versions of the same event. In Letter 48, Valmont tells Tourvel:

> Jamais je n'eus tant de plaisir en vous écrivant; jamais je ne ressentis, dans cette occupation, une émotion si douce et cependant si vive. Tout semble augmenter mes transports: l'air que je respire est brûlant de volupté; la table même sur laquelle je vous écris, consacrée pour la première fois à cet usage, devient pour moi l'autel sacré de l'amour; combien elle va s'embellir à mes yeux! j'aurai tracé sur elle le serment de vous aimer toujours! Pardonnez, je vous en supplie, au désordre de mes sens. Je devrais peut-être m'abandonner moins à des transports que vous ne partagez pas: il faut vous quitter un moment pour dissiper une ivresse qui s'augmente à chaque instant, et qui devient plus forte que moi.

> [Never did I before experience so much pleasure in writing to you. Never did I feel in this pleasing employment so sweet, so lively an emotion! Everything conspires to raise my transports! The very air I breathe wafts me luxurious pleasure; even the table I write on, now, for the first time, consecrated by me to that use, becomes to me a

sacred altar of love; how much more lustre will it not hence derive in my eyes! I will have engraven upon it my oath ever to love you! Forgive, I beseech you, my disordered sense. I ought, perhaps, to moderate transports you do not share in. I must leave you a moment to dissipate a phrenzy which I find growing upon me: I find it too strong for me.][112]

However, a reader will come to this account having just read Valmont's less metaphorical rendition for the Marquise de Merteuil, in which the true nature of that desk is revealed:

Cette complaisance de ma part est le prix de celle qu'elle vient d'avoir, de me servir de pupitre pour écrire à ma belle Dévote, à qui j'ai trouvé plaisant d'envoyer une Lettre écrite du lit et presque d'entre les bras d'une fille, interrompue même pour une infidélité complète, et dans laquelle je lui rends un compte exact de ma situation et ma conduite. Émilie, qui a lu l'Épitre, en a ri comme une folle, et j'espère que vous en rirez aussi.

[This condescension is a return for that she has just had for me, in submitting to serve me as a desk to write to my lovely devotee, to whom it struck me as a pleasant thought, to write in bed with, and almost in the arms of, a girl, where I was interrupted by a complete infidelity. In this letter I give her an exact account of my conduct and situation. Emily, who read the epistle, laughed immoderately, and I expect it will make you laugh also.][113]

For all the emotive hyperbole of Valmont's address to Tourvel ('mes transports'), it is telling that the Présidente is imagined only to remind her of what she cannot share, rendering her as impersonal as Valmont's formulaic raptures, drawn from chivalric iconography; whereas his co-conspirator is invited to laugh along with him; compare Letter 9 of *Lady Susan*, in which Alicia Johnson writes of Sir James Martin: 'I scolded him for making Love to Maria Manwaring; he protested that he had been only in joke, & we both laughed heartily at her disappointment, & in short were very agreable'.[114] Valmont's vocabulary bristles with emotive but imprecise resonances, which the Présidente, being a 'naïve exegete' herself, takes largely at face value, despite the fact that among the thicket of abstract nouns with which he presents her ('plaisir', 'amour', 'ivresse'), the actual 'moment' Valmont is narrating, the one thing she should be most eager to share, is deliberately and repeatedly withheld.

In the end, however, it is with Valmont as with Lovelace before him; both accidentally discover the double irony of libertinism, one which Austen puts to comically creative use in *Lady Susan*. Christine Roulston argues that 'Valmont's surrender to the role of lover erases the distinction between seeming and being; the desiring self and the libertine self are conflated, as Valmont becomes the product of his own narrative'.[115] To put it another way, if the schemes of Lovelace and Valmont show the relationships between the heart and its signs not to be essentially transparent, their eventual destinies reveal the double-edged logic of that fact: if the marks of sentiment can at times be feigned, unfeigned emotion can, by the same token, creep up unannounced on the most detached libertine. For all Lovelace's professions to Belford ('Well sayest thou, that mine is *the plottingest heart in the world*'[116]), he comes to find that the heart which those plots are designed to avoid will not always do what it is told, sometimes appearing to plot against him, turning him into a sentimentalist despite himself:

> All hands at work in preparation for London. What makes my heart beat so strong? Why rises it to my throat in such half-choking flutters, when I think of what this removal may do for me?—I am hitherto resolved to be honest: and that increases my wonder at these involuntary commotions. 'Tis a plotting villain of a heart: it ever was; and ever will be, I doubt. Such a joy when any roguery is going forward!—I so little its master!—A head likewise so well turned to answer the triangular varlet's impulses. No matter. I will have one struggle with thee, old friend; and if I cannot overcome thee, I never will attempt to conquer thee.[117]

It is the very unpredictability of human hearts which so fascinates Austen in *Lady Susan*; even as her comedy questions letters' ability to present the heart transparently, the linguistic contexture of its narrative invites readers to consider what Hardy was later to call 'the persistence of the unforeseen'.[118]

As early as the first letter of *Lady Susan*, as Catherine Vernon suspects, there may be more to the protagonist's visit than there first appears. 'I can no longer refuse myself the pleasure of profitting by your kind invitation when we last parted',[119] writes Lady Susan, who subsequently claims 'I long to be made known to your dear little Children, in whose hearts I shall be very eager to secure an interest'.[120] The 'debased chivalry' which lies behind Lovelace and Valmont finds a determinedly parochial Austenian counterpart here, as 'profitting' and 'secure an interest' drag the language of feeling into the realm of material greed: an intermingling which comes to define the atmosphere of *Lady Susan*. For example, Lady Susan's announcement that she is 'going to attach myself with the greatest sensibility to one in particular, a young Frederic', is immediately followed by the dramatic irony of Catherine Vernon's scrutiny of her: 'Her address to me was so gentle, frank & even affectionate, that if I had not known how much she has always disliked me for marrying Mr Vernon, & that we had never met before, I should have imagined her a very attached friend'.[121] 'Attach' and its derivatives hold a particular interest for Austen (indeed, the *OED* credits *Sense and Sensibility* as the source of one of the verb's usages, 'to win or attract the attention'[122]), playing as they do between emotional and stubbornly physical applications; as Lovelace and Valmont are by nature parasitic upon the conventions of decorum, and on the body of literary *exempla*, so, aptly enough, Lady Susan's use of 'attach myself' comes to sound like the action of a leech or a limpet. Even 'Manwaring', the name of the man whom she has snatched from the heart of his family, is suggestive in this context; it is shadowed vocally in English pronunciation, by 'manner' (the protective screen on which Lady Susan depends), and on the page, by the possibilities that this brilliant widow is someone of whom a 'man' must 'beware', and (in this work full of performative surface) that she might 'wear' men as others display trophies.

If, as I have been arguing, Richardson discovers, in the act of creating *Clarissa* as a work of sentimental didacticism, the mirror image of such intentions, and Laclos applies this perception to the worn-down modes of military honour which were to be at once swept aside and perversely reabsorbed by the events of the French Revolution, Austen is one of the first major imaginative voices to inhabit the space left by sentimentalism – a chronicler of how one might get by in the knowledge that no language is intrinsically any more sincere than another. *Lady Susan* and the novels of the 1810s respond to this situation, not with despair, but by exploring the further implications of what epistolary fiction discovered. In his excellent study of *Clarissa* and its engagement with eighteenth-century readership, Tom Keymer describes the field of response which the novel affords in practice, rather than in its own morally edifying theory; although Austen's methods go beyond Richardson's in many ways, much of what Keymer argues about *Clarissa* could still apply to *Lady Susan*: 'The reader, unaided, must become a judge of all the difficulties thrown up by the text, and make his own construction, in the end, of all the evidence and pleas with which he is assailed. And in responding to this challenge he will develop capacities of understanding by which, thereafter, to light his way through the actual twilit, probationary state of which the novel is only a vast image'.[123] While *Lady Susan* is only a 'single effect' next to the 'vast image' of *Clarissa*, it does prompt a shift of focus in terms of how a reader is asked to make sense of the conflicting 'evidence and pleas' with which he or she is presented by the characters' letters. *Lady Susan* inherits from Richardson and

Laclos its portrayal of epistolary writers and readers, engaged in presenting, parading and decoding words, appearances and their links back to their causes; but another mark of Austen's differential narrative is that it offers an alternative trajectory of reading, one not so dependent on the Cartesian division between inside and outside that underpins sentimental correspondence. Tellingly, one way Austen offers that path is in her treatment of that object (if indeed it is an object) whose 'natural effusions' letter-writers, in both Ciceronian and sentimental traditions, were at pains to reveal or express 'in unaffected language': the heart.

There is no one simple way in which hearts work in Austen's fiction: they can sometimes become, like the blushes to which they are physiologically related, embarrassing physical tokens of sensibility, as with Catherine Morland, whose 'heart beat quick' to complement 'a cheek flushed by hope, and an eye straining with curiosity';[124] but elsewhere they take on more metaphysical applications. *Lady Susan* sees Austen beginning to recognize within her form the possibilities offered by punning and wordplay, comic techniques which go on to have a more extensive life in *Northanger Abbey* and the mature novels; particularly noticeable here is what she does with words like 'catch', 'attach' and 'heart', which bridge the sentimental and material worlds. Unlike its great epistolary models, *Lady Susan* ends not with fatal duelling but with a bathetic series of anti-climactic accidents, as Reginald just happens to arrive at the Johnson's house at the same time as the outraged Mrs Manwaring ('She came to this house to entreat my Husband's interference, & before I could be aware of it, everything that you could wish to be concealed, was known to him [...] All is by this time known to De Courcy, who is now alone with Mr Johnson'[125]); finally, as Austen offers her short third-person coda, it is clear that matters are much as they were. This particular plot may have been foiled (more by accident than design); Frederica Vernon is safe from her mother's interference; Lady Susan, though, lives to fight another day, leaving the work ironically suspended, as befits Austen's little display of 'regulated hatred', between a heroine of whom the story cannot approve, and a supporting cast of, at best, righteous dullness: a plague on both their houses.

Lady Susan may feature much of the obsessive watching and emotional detection familiar from Richardson ('She may be Reginald's Wife. Heaven forbid it!—but why should I be quicker sighted than anyone else?'[126]); however, it is not these that bring the story to its conclusion. That is not to say that the characters have learned nothing by the end, but the hint offered by the conclusion points towards a different mode of understanding: 'Very little assistance to the State could be derived from the Epistolary Intercourse of Mrs Vernon & her neice, for the former soon perceived by the stile of Frederica's Letters, that they were written under her Mother's inspection, & therefore deferring all particular enquiry till she could make it personally in Town, ceased writing minutely or often'.[127] I have discussed above how the texture of Austen's own letters to Cassandra depends less on the revelation of hidden depths than on their distinctive inflections of the surface, and as suggested by what Catherine Vernon has learned to do, *Lady Susan* prompts a reader to look beyond the language of sentimental exposure and concealment – not least in matters of the 'heart'. If hearts can still at times be the competitive prizes familiar from earlier novels, other instances in *Lady Susan* offer different possibilities. In Letter 6, for example, Catherine warns Reginald about Lady Susan, remarking that '[i]f her manners have so great an influence on my resentful heart, you may guess how much more they operate on Mr Vernon's generous temper'.[128] Even Lady Susan, who would ideally not have to bother with such trifles ('you know my reasons—Propriety & so forth'[129]), finds herself disparaging 'that Heart which seems always debating on the reasonableness of it's Emotions';[130] and in defeat, she is forced to admit 'I have little heart to jest'.[131] In tracing the range of 'heart' across the dramatic space offered by Austen's text, a reader may come to sense that the heart can be more than simply an object or commodity, to be won or lost in love, and which is revealed or hidden in writing, but a capacity which one can exercise. Alongside the emotional vocabulary of sentimentalism, eighteenth-century thought also employed 'heart' in theological and philosophical contexts, and in more capacious senses – as, for example, in the writings of Joseph Butler, whose sermons repeatedly suggest 'heart' as a mode of emotional intelligence. '[T]o get our heart and temper formed to a love and liking of what is good,' he argues, 'is absolutely necessary in order to our behaving rightly in the familiar and daily intercourses amongst mankind';[132] he also provides a definition of the heart as something more than a trophy: 'the whole system, as I may speak, of affections, (including rationality,) which constitute the heart'.[133] It is this kind of moral vocabulary that Austen begins to graft on to the stock of sentiment in *Lady Susan*, as she takes into new territory those 'capacities of understanding' which Keymer sees Richardson as asking of his readers.

'Men should be what they seeme', and women too, but they often fail to be so or contrive to be otherwise – whether in person or in writing. Austen's comedy realizes this as the inevitable condition within which it lives, and on which it feeds; implicit throughout her own correspondence is the knowledge of what will always remain 'a little disguised', and *Lady Susan* is one testament to what she managed to do in the absence of absolute emotional transparency. Even as she follows Richardson and Laclos, she points towards the achievement of her own work – her discovery of a comic language that inhabits those spaces between people and words, and invites its readers to work with and through opacity. *Lady Susan* may be a 'single effect', but its after-effects are many, as the novel's techniques and comic fascinations are revisited and recast in *Northanger Abbey* and the novels of the 1810s; the accent of *Emma*'s author is already alive and well in *Lady Susan*, if one has the heart to catch it.

Emma the Ventriloquist

> I use the words you taught me. If they don't mean anything any more, teach me others, or let me be silent.
>
> Clov in Samuel Beckett, *Endgame*[134]

Steven Connor notes that the turn of the nineteenth century (and therefore the period of Austen's life) was an important cusp in the history of ventriloquism. 'For the eighteenth century,' he writes, 'ventriloquism had seemed fascinating, and dangerously spiced with the demonic and supernatural; from the nineteenth century onwards, ventriloquism would continue to have these associations but would be fringed with a sense of the tawdry and the ridiculous as well. The very fact that ventriloquism became and remained a fundamentally comic entertainment suggests the presence of this ambivalence.'[135] It is an ambivalence which offers much to *Emma*, Austen's most technically ambitious novel, in which the social slapstick of Highbury exists alongside darker intimations of mortality and irreparable loss, and the comic business of throwing the voice across space can stumble unexpectedly into the gaps of understanding that separate people from each other. Characters in *Emma* regularly commend (and judge) each other according to their skill with musical instruments;[136] but a reader does not have to look too far beneath comments, such as Emma's remark to Mrs Elton that 'Highbury has long known that you are a superior performer';[137] in order to find other performances taking place. More than any of the other novels, *Emma* is interested in all forms of 'dictating', in those acts by which people make others subject to their wills along with their words. Unlike Austen's first two published novels, *Emma* has no long-lost epistolary prototype, no equivalent of *Elinor and Marianne* and *First Impressions*; nevertheless, it is aware in its own way of the power of letters, and, more generally, of the power and limitations of speaking as from a distance. At its centre, of course, stands the figure of Emma Woodhouse, whose adventures in social and amatory ventriloquism, together with their attendant slip-ups, are the novel's motive force. Throwing the voice becomes, in the course of Austen's narrative, more than a stylistic device: indeed, it is the very medium within which she comes to apprehend how repentance might operate in the world of polite conversation – a repentance which demands more of the voice and the imagination than Marianne's regret in *Sense and Sensibility*, with 'two words just articulate through her tears, "Tell mama,"'.[138]

1. Jane Austen's Epitaph in Winchester Cathedral. The epitaph remembers 'the extraordinary endowments of her mind', but makes no mention of that mind's literary productions.

2. Thomas Gainsborough, 'An Officer of the Fourth Regiment of Foot'
c.1776–80. Gainsborough's use of the coast and the ship within his portrait
may imply the insistent pressures of the public world upon the military
individual.

3. Jean-Auguste-Dominique Ingres, 'Madame de Senonnes', c.1814–16. The presence of mirrors in Ingres' portraits sets up a creative dialogue between seeing and being seen, and between real and virtual images.

4. Jean-Auguste-Dominique Ingres, 'The Comtesse d'Haussonville', 1845. The
   reflection does not cancel out the Comtesse's self-projection, but it does
   contextualize it, reminding the viewer that someone else might be staring at
   the back of *their* head as they study the portrait.

Emma's first great conversational showdown with her rival Augusta Elton provides one of the novel's central moments:

> "When you have seen more of this country, I am afraid you will think you have over-rated Hartfield. Surry is full of beauties."
>
> "Oh! yes, I am quite aware of that. It is the garden of England, you know. Surry is the garden of England."
>
> "Yes; but we must not rest our claims on that distinction. Many counties, I believe, are called the garden of England, as well as Surry."
>
> "No, I fancy not," replied Mrs. Elton, with a most satisfied smile. "I never heard any county but Surry called so."
>
> Emma was silenced.[139]

There is more to this little exchange than the comedy of seeing Emma meet her match. The clash of egos, each woman claiming the intellectual high ground and insisting on top billing in the conversation, spills over into the glacially polite 'I believe' and 'I fancy not', tokens of civility sharpened into weapons as they pass through clenched teeth. This is not the only point in *Emma* at which characters talk *at* others rather than *to* them (Miss Bates, for one, might be said to do this much of the time), but it brings home with particular force the fact that '[e]ach of us being a main character in his own drama plays subordinate parts in the dramas of others, and each drama constrains the others'.[140] Aptly enough for a comedy of voices' going astray, part of this effect is down to a small but resonant curiosity of voice: in this case, the grammatical 'voice' of Austen's narrative. Austen often invites her readers to have a more attentive ear for situations than her characters are displaying, and 'Emma was silenced' merits a closer examination than its length might suggest. The sentence, short in itself, is, however, one of the rare occasions in the novel on which Emma is made either the subject of a passive verb or the object of an active one: as such, the minute grammatical shift from 'silent' to 'silenced' enacts a little pragmatic recoil, as the heroine reaches the limits of her own influence. Emma's own thoughts, translated with varying degrees of obviousness into *style indirect libre*, form the prism through which the narrative is refracted at the reader, and it is a measure of her overbearing fluency in the early sections of the novel that those thoughts only sound out of kilter when they run aground on stubborn realities. The little *éclaircissements* along Emma's path are often registered, acoustically and grammatically, by passive verbs and monosyllables, as Emma becomes momentarily less certain of her own fluency and control.

Elton's designs on Emma, for example, should come as no great shock to an attentive reader, although they are an unconscionable time dawning on the heroine herself, even though we detect them partly through the screen of her own biased perceptions. Austen achieves this daring comic effect by arranging events so that even when we are constrained to see things through her eyes, we do not necessarily hear them with her ears. Suspicions might well be alerted as early as the sixth chapter, when Elton speaks of her influence on Harriet 'with a sort of sighing animation, which had a vast deal of the lover'[141] – though Emma does not stop to think *whose* lover he could be. Likewise, she manages to miss Elton's pre-Freudian slip about his skill at charades:

> "Oh, no! he had never written, hardly ever, any thing of the kind in his life. The stupidest fellow! He was afraid not even Miss Woodhouse"—he stopt a moment—"or Miss Smith could inspire him."[142]

However, when even Emma can no longer ignore the facts, Austen's prose delivers them with a hard clarity ('It really was so'[143]), an awkward chime which cuts through what Emma has conspired to ignore or to repress. Compare the sentence's brevity and heavy stresses with 'Emma was silenced': these are the moments when sententious volubility finds itself wanting. Likewise, once Emma's guilt about her rudeness on Box Hill is fully before her, it sounds in a form whose very terseness rounds on the elegance of her original remark, its 'mock ceremony':[144] 'The truth of his representation there was no denying. She felt it at her heart.'[145] Emma may have 'lived nearly twenty-one years in the world with very little to distress or vex her',[146] but at this reverse, she 'was vexed', 'was most forcibly struck', and 'Time did not compose her'.[147]

Perhaps the most important quality of the sentence 'Emma was silenced' is the fact that it is an echo. Adam Piette argues that some form of mnemonic echoing is one of the basic features of fictional narrative:

> A novelist must, almost by definition, be acutely concerned with memory, as the act of creation is essentially a continual act of memory-creation, -accretion, and -synthesis, the imagination at constant service to the characters' memories [...] Memory work is an essential part of the work of the writer, and it is in his or her contact with language, from both a semantic and an acoustic point of view, that the work is done. Though writing has been primarily described as an act of the imagination, prose fiction is above all an act of imaginative remembering, and there is no writer who does not reflect on this strange human power, be it faculty, treasure house, or computer store.[148]

It is not only the wills of other characters within a plot which can 'constrain' the subjectivities of individuals: narrative discourse itself is a lexical and poetic creation which works with, above and beyond the particular characters and actions it represents. A novelist may make practical use of connections through time as basic memorial devices (nineteenth-century serial fiction is a case in point, as I mentioned in the Interlude); he or she may make the whole text of the work a structure of repetitions and distortions, inviting the reader to experience, intellectually and acoustically, the processes by which characters and events are connected, however perilously, across time. At more local levels, those phonemic and rhythmic repetitions which Piette calls 'prose rhymes'[149] allow novelists to dramatize the pressures exerted by the past on characters' minds, as they seek to recover or escape their connections to other times.

Austen gives *Emma* a richer patterning of narrative echoes than her other novels, not least because Emma Woodhouse spends so much of the book trying to make others echo her words and, by implication, her thoughts. Throughout the novel, sounds, phrases and rhythms resonate unpredictably between dialogue, *style indirect* and external narration. If *Lady Susan* deals much in the language of egotistical self-viewing, *Emma* is the Echo to the earlier novella's Narcissus: Austen can make the most seemingly casual conversational indelicacies reappear embarrassingly. As Emma's presumptions come back to haunt her, Austen's echoing prose performs the return of the repressed: as surely as any slips of the tongue, repetitions within Emma's consciousness become what Freud called 'a mode of self-betrayal',[150] the unexpected reappearance of '*incompletely suppressed psychical material, which although pushed away by consciousness, has nevertheless not been robbed of all capacity to express itself*'.[151] Elton declares his desires to their true object, and what is so unsettlingly comic about Emma's dawning realization is that the truth crystallizes out of her own words and thoughts. When she first plots to 'improve' Harriet, we are told:

> *She* would notice her; she would improve her; she would detach her from her bad acquaintance, and introduce her into good society; she would form her opinions and manners. It would be an interesting, and certainly a very kind undertaking; highly becoming her own situation in life, her leisure, and powers.[152]

With a ghastly irony, the full backfiring of that particular plan is rendered as a parodic echo:

> Instead of forgetting him, his behaviour was such that she could not avoid the internal suggestion of "Can it really be as my brother

imagined? can it be possible for this man to be beginning to transfer his affections from Harriet to me?—Absurd and insufferable!"— Yet he would be so anxious for her being perfectly warm, would be so interested about her father, and so delighted with Mrs. Weston; and at last would begin admiring her drawings with so much zeal and so little knowledge as seemed terribly like a would-be lover, and made it some effort with her to preserve her good manners.[153]

As well as marking the limits of Emma's control, 'Emma was silenced' is itself a guilty repetition, since in her flustered silence, a reader can hear Harriet Smith, bewildered in her turn by Emma's presumptuous attitude to Robert Martin:

> "You think I ought to refuse him then," said Harriet, looking down.
> "Ought to refuse him! My dear Harriet, what do you mean? Are you in any doubt as to that? I thought—but I beg your pardon, perhaps I have been under a mistake. I certainly have been mis-understanding you, if you feel in doubt as to the *purport* of your answer. I had imagined you were consulting me only as to the wording of your answer."
> Harriet was silent. With a little reserve of manner, Emma con-tinued:
> "You mean to return a favourable answer, I collect."[154]

It is the ventriloquist's comeuppance to have her words and deeds thrown back in her face. The allusive and acoustic depth of Austen's text offers a stylistic counterpoint at times when characters act as if they could curl up and watch their words' effects from a distance, disclaiming all responsibility for them. But even actions and opinions of which one is ashamed live on, in that future actions and words are shaped by their memory – a circumstance par-ticularly well served by the structural conditions of fiction. Whether a novel's timespan is one of 24 hours or several generations, its text takes its own time; and within that time of reading, repetitions and evolutions become models in miniature of how the memory retains and loses events over larger lifespans. For all its poetic justice, 'Emma was silenced' is not the whole story of the novel, and any reading of *Emma* which attempts to treat that reversal as if it were a *précis* of the whole plot is bound to be insufficient. For one thing, the sentence does not only echo back but forwards, connecting Emma's errors to her eventual happiness, in ways that are not so simply punitive.

In my discussion of *Lady Susan*, I noted Tanner and Baddiel's observations on the convergence of 'property' and 'propriety' in late eighteenth-century English usage. *Lady Susan* and *Emma*, for their part, also illustrate an fruitful overlap between the materialistic and spiritual senses of 'possession', between 'the holding or having of something (material or immaterial) as one's own, or in one's control' and '[t]he fact of a demon possessing a person; the fact of being possessed by a demon or spirit'.[155] Following the leads of Richardson and Laclos, *Lady Susan*, as we have seen, portrays a world in which the signs of emotional sincerity and spontaneity can be collected and displayed like so many objects; *Emma* takes even further the novel's exploration of commodities and capacities, and the fraught process of telling them apart. To this end, Austen gets much comic mileage out of ventriloquism, and the various related forms of social *legerdemain* by which characters attempt to 'possess' and control others. Connor offers a pertinent insight into how this may have come about:

> In between the solidification of these two functions – ventriloquism as superhuman utterance from the late classical period to the end of the eighteenth century, and ventriloquism as sub- or inhuman utterance characteristic of the period since the end of the nine-teenth century – was the brief period of ventriloquism's appearance as the manipulation of human voices, as a dramaturgy. It is in this period that the questions *what?* and *where?* asked of the unlocated voice mutate into the question *who?* Ventriloquism becomes an affair of dramatization and colloquy, and a medium for exploring the relations between selves and their voices.[156]

This distinction is comparable to the shift between Austen's experiments with epistolary form and the polyphonic narrative she creates in the mature novels. After treating the 'unlocated voice' of the letter in *Lady Susan*, Austen deals in 'dramatization and colloquy'. Characters in *Emma* often need to maintain a certain distance between themselves and their words (Jane Fairfax and Frank Churchill, for example), only to find that the novel has other ideas, strewing their paths with banana skins and rendering 'the relations between selves and their voices' considerably less predictable.

The value of various kinds of 'possession' is one which Austen addresses in her opening sentence:

> Emma Woodhouse, handsome, clever, and rich, with a comfortable home and happy disposition, seemed to unite some of the best bless-ings of existence; and had lived nearly twenty-one years in the world with very little to distress or vex her.[157]

As I discussed in the previous chapter, the opening of *Pride and Prejudice* raises questions as to how 'universally acknowledged' its 'truth' really is; *Emma*'s opening becomes more suggestive and filled with implicature the longer one considers it. 'Emma Woodhouse' governs the sentence's grammar as the name's bearer dominates the scene of Highbury, but what exactly she does govern is more open to question; 'handsome, clever, and rich, with a comfortable home and happy disposition' reels off her possessions like the list of an empress's dominions. However, the modal qualifiers 'seemed' and 'some', especially coming in such quick succession, immediately call the opening words into question – one pertinent question being whether to be 'handsome, clever, and rich' necessarily corresponds to 'the best blessings of existence', or even to 'some' of them. This is brought home at the beginning of Vol. II, Chapter IV, where Mrs Elton, even before she has arrived in Highbury, is 'discovered to have every recommendation of person and mind; to be handsome, elegant, highly accomplished, and perfectly amiable'.[158] That Emma only 'seemed to unite' her blessings suggests someone embarrassed by her riches, unable to fit together the parts of a happy life into anything that truly feels like one. For all Emma's hyperactive matchmaking in the early parts of the novel, a reader may also sense what her activity is only just managing to fend off: the atmosphere (in Barbara Everett's brilliant phrase) of 'inescapable mundanity, as of the experience of endlessly swimming through gruel'.[159] In attempting to give her possessions meaning, Emma's first recourse is to that other mode of 'possession', of which her ventriloquial adventures are the most famous examples.

Ventriloquial possession – where characters either consciously inhabit others with their words, or find themselves unwittingly mouthing words from elsewhere – has a long literary pedigree, taking in the Weïrd Sisters' antitheses (which come to infect the whole of *Macbeth*) and the prelude-and-recapitulation form of Joyce's 'Sirens', and its potential for both comic and uncanny effects does not pass Austen by. In a letter to Cassandra in October 1808, she noted with wry disapproval 'a wedding in the Salisbury paper, which has amused me very much, Dr Phillot to Lady Frances St Lawrence. *She* wanted to have a husband I suppose, once in her life, and *he* a Lady Frances.'[160] The possessiveness which Austen skewers on her indefinite article recurs in *Emma*, where the heroine's first thoughts about Harriet are phrased in just such words: 'She had ventured once alone to Randalls, but it was not pleasant; and a Harriet Smith, therefore, one whom she could summon at any time to a walk, would be a valuable addition to her privileges'.[161] These coolly rational terms could almost come from Lady Susan; they make no distinction between people and things to be collected. Harriet comes to sound like something with which Emma can 'accessorize', a tame lapdog to take out for walks, rather than a human being, let alone a friend. Even Mrs Weston, when trying to defend Emma's behaviour towards Harriet, cannot help describing Harriet as 'a new object of interest'.[162] The vocabulary of material possessiveness which pervades *Lady Susan* returns here: for example, after Emma has rejected Elton's advances, she rightly surmises that 'he only wanted to aggrandize and enrich himself; and if Miss Woodhouse of Hartfield, the heiress of thirty thousand pounds, were not quite so easily obtained as he had fancied, he would soon try for Miss Somebody else with twenty, or with ten',[163] and, sure enough, we are later told that 'he had gained a woman of 10,000*l*. or thereabouts'.[164] '[O]bject', 'obtained', 'gained a woman': Austen was never one to downplay hard material necessities, but the confluence of 'propriety' with 'property' is shown up in a less flattering light at such moments.

'With insufferable vanity had she believed herself in the secret of everybody's feelings':[165] if Austen's treatments of epistolary form score off the 'Ciceronian' metaphors of visual transparency, *Emma* shows her to be equally aware of their acoustic equivalent, of what one might call 'trans-audibility'. Emma's attempts to turn Harriet into her reassuring personal echo depend upon Harriet's unawareness of being imposed upon – as if her naïvety, coupled with her indeterminate status as 'the natural daughter of somebody',[166] made her a blank for Emma's own vocal signature. Austen's narrator tells the reader that Mr Woodhouse 'was fond of society in his own way',[167] intimating not only that he likes society 'after his own fashion' but that he only responds to others when they adopt his personal tastes and eccentricities ("Mrs. Bates, let me propose your venturing on one of these eggs. An egg boiled very soft is not unwholesome."[168]). He resembles Tristram Shandy's 'hobby-horsical' Uncle Toby, only stripped of the rosy tints of Sterne's narrative; and his daughter appears to have inherited some of his most distinctive qualities, since even her solicitude is cast in her own image:

> "These are the sights, Harriet, to do one good. How trifling they make every thing else appear!—I feel now as if I could think of nothing else but these poor creatures all the rest of the day; and yet, who can say how soon it may all vanish from my mind?"
> "Very true," said Harriet. "Poor creatures! one can think of nothing else."[169]

Emma's mistake is to cross over from hearing her own words echoed in others to hearing her thoughts. This works, up to a point, with Harriet, since she lacks Emma's ironic mobility around words: therefore, like Othello before her, she is vulnerable, being unable to hear the difference between decorum and imposition, even when Emma comes on like *The English Secretary*:

> "Yes. But what shall I say? Dear Miss Woodhouse, do advise me."
>
> "Oh, no, no! the letter had much better be all your own. You will express yourself very properly, I am sure. There is no danger of your not being intelligible, which is the first thing. Your meaning must be unequivocal; no doubts or demurs: and such expressions of gratitude and concern for the pain you are inflicting as propriety requires, will present themselves unbidden to *your* mind, I am persuaded. *You* need not be prompted to write with the appearance of sorrow for his disappointment."
>
> "You think I ought to refuse him then," said Harriet, looking down.
>
> "Ought to refuse him? My dear Harriet, what do you mean? Are you in any doubt as to that? [...]"

That typographical 'alienation-effect' which I discussed at work in *Pride and Prejudice* is in evidence here, as Austen italicizes '*your*' and '*You*' in a speech where Harriet has no real power whatsoever. 'But do not imagine that I want to influence you',[170] claims Emma. And Brutus is an honourable man.

Yet for all her powers of conversational suggestion, Emma does not always listen that closely herself. *Pride and Prejudice* follows the likes of *Lady Susan*, in that Elizabeth Bennet's disillusionment is described primarily in terms of visual revelation: 'Of neither Darcy nor Wickham could she think, without feeling that she had been blind, partial, prejudiced, absurd.'[171] Although *Emma* is not without such descriptions ('She saw it all with a clarity which had never blessed her before [...] What blindness, what madness, had led her on!'[172]), Austen focuses more frequently on Emma's insufficiently attentive ear for the little nuances of the world around her: as Nancy Struever puts it, 'Emma, in short, is morally tone-deaf'.[173] Nowhere is this more evident than in her dealings with Harriet and Elton, which Austen arranges in ironic parallel. Emma assumes that, because Elton, like Harriet, repeats her words, he has the same intentions in doing so. However, Harriet echoes Emma because (at least initially), she knows no better, or feels socially bound not to disagree; despite the similar overall shape of his replies, there is more happening in Elton's words:

> "I have perhaps given her a little more decision of character, have taught her to think on points which had not fallen in her way before."

"Exactly so; that is what principally strikes me. So much super-added decision of character! Skilful has been the hand."[174]

Elton's final words exalt Emma's influence more than its object, as he repeatedly praises Emma's drawing above Harriet the sitter; there is more than dumb parroting going on here, but Emma cannot be bothered to hear it. Illocutionary force is not simply determined by speakers: even to 'take something differently' can work as a dramatic check, turning ventriloquial speech into an implicit dialogue. Above all, identity of words cannot guarantee identity of intention – an instructive warning in Austen's age of prescriptive etiquette, as it is in the present-day culture of intellectual chiming-in.[175] Elton may share his desire for social and material advancement with Collins in *Pride and Prejudice*, but unlike the earlier clergyman – and despite first appearances – he is no fool. The bluff surface of Elton's behaviour hides, from a superficial listener like Emma, the truth that 'echoing' is not his natural mode of speaking, but one adopted deliberately in pursuit of an ulterior motive: 'Miss Woodhouse of Hartfield, heiress of thirty thousand pounds'. In retrospect, what seems to be another ventriloquial performance by Emma comes to sound more evenly matched. Elton's first echo comes after he is interrupted by Emma, prevented from exercizing even the nominal power of finishing a sentence, and Austen plants a red herring in the text by cutting his speech off with the typographical gag of the long dash ("'If it were possible to contradict a lady," said the gallant Mr. Elton—'[176]). But he is in fact all too eloquent, given the opportunity; unlike Harriet, he echoes Emma because he recognizes that, being in love with the sound of her own voice, she might well love someone who speaks in her own words. Indeed, he assumes that she has been playing along with him, 'according to the usual practice of elegant females':

"I am very much astonished, Mr. Elton. This to *me!* you forget yourself—you take me for my friend—any message to Miss Smith I shall be happy to deliver; but no more of this to *me*, if you please."
"Miss Smith!—Message to Miss Smith!—What could she possibly mean!"—And he repeated her words with such assurance of accent, such boastful pretence of amazement, that she could not help replying with quickness,
"Mr. Elton, this is the most extraordinary conduct! and I can account for it only in one way; you are not yourself, or you could not speak either to me, or of Harriet, in such a manner. Command yourself enough to say no more, and I will endeavour to forget it."[177]

There is a poetic justice in this moment: a ventriloquist meets an impressionist, and neither can quite hear the other.

Matters are different, if never foolproof, for a reader, not least because those imaginative tonalities which a reader brings to a novel themselves depend on a larger condition of 'tone-deafness' – namely, the fact that novels (as I have noted before) speak to us without telling us exactly how they sound. Austen does not ask of her readers the kind of lachrymose emotional transference which Lady Bradshaigh brought to her reading of Richardson;[178] rather, a reader's necessary distance from empathetic identification with the characters (an inwardness which may be bought too cheaply) challenges and allows them to sense what those characters might be missing, even when their thoughts are uppermost in the narrative. The Box Hill incident is just such a moment:

> "Oh! very well," exclaimed Miss Bates, "then I need not be uneasy. 'Three things very dull indeed.' That will just do for me, you know. I shall be sure to say three dull things as soon as ever I open my mouth, shan't I?—(looking round with the most good-humoured dependence on every body's assent)—Do not you all think I shall?"[179]

'You know', 'shan't I', 'Do not you all think'; as if these prompts were not enough, Austen inserts the extraordinary bracketed stage direction in the middle of Miss Bates's speech – one which, given Austen's relative lack of adverbial qualifications, is all the more prominent. Miss Bates may be no Falstaff ('I am not onely witty in my self, but the cause that wit is in other men'[180]), but the stage direction, compounded by the page directions of the parentheses, suggests she is at least partly aware of the ridiculous figure she makes, and that she has, therefore, partly pre-empted Emma's joke at her expense – which makes it all the more embarrassing that Emma can then so completely misunderstand her cue. Struever suggests that Austen's interest in 'strong common-sense oppositions' is 'subservient to the "minute distinctions" which Hume had stipulated as the moralist's concern';[181] 'minute distinctions' certainly play a central role in *Emma*, since so much of the novel's pleasure and perplexity is found in its peripheral vision, in the far corners of the narrative frame. These 'distinctions' foster a sense of readerly tact: of when to be touched by words and when to leave decently alone, when to care, not to care, and sit still. Such quotidian practices as tact form part of the ethical cement of communities, because there may not be a universally applicable maxim for every conceivable occasion; besides, too great a reliance on 'general civility' has, as one of its logical conclusions, Lady Susan. So it is that the movement of *Emma* leads

Austen's characters down twisted and thorny paths, beset both by the larger resonances of actions and the embarrassing recognition of what remains irreducibly particular. Unlike *Sense and Sensibility* and *Pride and Prejudice*, the novel has no abstract moral qualities in its title to tempt the unwary, and refuses to be teased through interpretative hoops; indeed, even those moral qualities with which it deals do not operate simply as things to be submitted to or to be possessed like so many ethical 'brownie-points' – another reason why the novel does not begin and end with 'Emma was silenced'. Tanner has perceptively suggested: 'The real "evil" or terror in *Emma* is the prospect of having no one properly to talk to, no *real* community, in fact.'[182] Hence, of course, all the talking *at*, and ventriloquial speculation, in which Emma indulges. However, talking and listening take on even greater force as the novel progresses. Emma's accomplishments are listed in the opening sentence like isolated members of a community, coexisting but only seemingly united. The power that will bring them into harmony has been there all the time: it is Emma's own voice, but it takes her – and the reader – the whole novel to find it.

'There is one line of thought,' wrote Mary Augusta Austen-Leigh,

> one grace, or quality, or necessity, whichever title we like to know it by, apparent in all her works. Its name is – Repentance [...] this incident recurs in all her novels, neither being dragged in as a moral nor dwelt upon as a duty, but quietly taking its place as a natural and indispensable part of the plot.[183]

Austen-Leigh's customarily physical diction serves her better here than in her shocked reaction to *Lady Susan*, as she contrasts 'dragged in' with 'quietly taking its place'. But the century's distance between *Emma* and *Personal Aspects of Jane Austen* occasions a different unease in her words, as she conflates a 'line of thought' with 'this incident'. Austen's feeling for the charge of particular moments does not imply that repentance is confined to specific incidents, climactic reversals after which order reigns; her differential narrative provides conventional points of *peripeteia* without offering them as explanations or solutions: they just happen that way, and the plot moves on. This is another of Austen's parodic jokes at rhetoric's expense: the points at which the plots of her novels intersect are not necessarily the most important ones. Take Emma's response, when Knightley has rebuked her for persuading Harriet to reject Martin's advances: 'She was sorry, but could not repent.'[184] In 1920, Mary Augusta Austen-Leigh was writing in the age of the *OED*, and the weight which the dictionary's first edition affords 'sorry' and 'repent' extenuates some of her unease, since its own definitions seem not to encompass quite the sense or spirit in which Austen uses them:

Sorry [...] 1. Pained at heart; distressed, sad; full of grief or sorrow. In later use frequ. in weakened sense, and often employed in the phrase 'I'm sorry' to express mere sympathy or apology.

Repent [...] 1. *refl.* To affect (oneself) with contrition or regret for something done [...]
3. *intr.* To feel contrition, compunction, sorrow or regret for something one has done or left undone; to change one's mind with regard to past action or conduct through dissatisfaction with it or its results.[185]

Whilst *Emma* may sharply dramatize what it means to be 'pained at heart', the emphasis on inward sentiment in both the *OED* definitions telescopes the strength which the antithesis would have possessed for Austen's readers. 'Johnson in prose' was, after all, among her favourite reading, and Johnson's definitions from 1755 capture more of the depth of contrast on which Austen draws in *Emma*:

SORRY, adj.

1. Grieved for something past. It is generally used of slight or casual miscarriages or vexations, but sometimes of greater things. It does not imply any long continuance of grief.

To REPENT, v.n.

[...] 3. To have such sorrow for sin, as produces amendment of life.[186]

Even an Anglican of such fluency and commitment as Johnson could find room within the scope of 'repent' for the older and more external *poenitentiam agere*. To produce 'amendment of life' is by definition not the work of a moment, although the change may be sparked off, as it is in *Emma*, by a moment of beatific self-knowledge, of 'clearness which had never blessed her before'. When Mrs Weston explains the truth about Frank Churchill and Jane Fairfax, Austen phrases Emma's response as a pun which echoes throughout the latter stages of the novel: 'Emma began to listen better'.[187] As befits this novel, the verb form marks it out as both a single watershed and the beginning of a longer habit.

This habit, a process encompassing past, present and future, is a tricky and wide-ranging one, and cannot simply be defined as or confined to 'the moment when a key character abandons her error and humbly submits to objective reality'.[188] But if Emma is culpable in the early part of the novel for treating others as echo chambers, then it fits too snugly to make her punishment consist in her becoming a passive receptacle for 'objective reality'. Seeing things as they are may in fact be as much a struggle as a submission, a matter not only of conceding but of knowing what one has a right to expect. If Emma has no one to talk to at the beginning of the novel, Austen charts through the plot her learning to converse with the world, a process enacted for readers in her return to the unpredictable density of that language in which we also belong, often despite ourselves. As Emma finally experiences the force of her feelings, Austen's narrative relates: 'Her own conduct, as well as her own heart, was before her in the same few minutes.'[189] This kind of insight takes imagination, not the detached fancy of the 'imaginist':[190] that selfishness so stubborn as to demand a little corner of the dictionary all to itself. There is a deep irony at work here: the more Emma learns of her own heart, the more she knows that she cannot so readily know other peoples'. The unpredictable echoing of words between the novel's different levels of narrative offers Austen great comic possibilities: Emma the ventriloquist, who once 'believed herself in the secret of everybody's feelings', now comes to worry about Harriet in Knightley in familiar-sounding words – words which, however, echo ones she cannot possibly have read:

> Mr. Knightley to be no longer coming there for his evening comfort!—No longer walking in at all hours, as if ever willing to change his own home for their's!—How was it to be endured? And if he were to be lost to them for Harriet's sake; if he were to be thought of hereafter, as finding in Harriet's society all that he wanted; if Harriet were to be the chosen, the first, the dearest, the friend, the wife to whom he looked for all the best blessings of existence [...][191]

Whereas Emma, of course, can only muster '*some of* the best blessings of existence' (italics mine). Long before Iris Murdoch, Austen's fiction concedes that its characters, and even its 'caricatures' (in DW Harding's sense), are partially and necessarily opaque,[192] and the end of *Emma* takes to its conclusion that sceptical play with the eighteenth-century language of emotional transparency and revealed hearts, which Austen picks up from sentimental fiction and subjects to such withering comic scrutiny in *Lady Susan*. Three times between the Box Hill picnic and Emma's wedding, the novel, like *Tristram Shandy* before it,[193] reminds the reader that humans do not possess Momus's ideal window into the soul. Reflecting on her conduct towards Jane, Emma muses:

> it mortified her that she was given so little credit for proper feeling, or esteemed so little worthy as a friend: but she had the consolation

of knowing that her intentions were good, and of being able to say to herself, that could Mr. Knightley have been privy to all her attempts of assisting Jane Fairfax, could he even have seen into her heart, he would not, on this occasion, have found anything to reprove.[194]

Then, on the news of Frank and Jane's engagement, Harriet innocently reproves Emma's social myopia, by praising her insight:

> "Had you any idea," cried Harriet, "of his being in love with her?—You, perhaps, might.—You (blushing as she spoke) who can see into everybody's heart; but nobody else—"
> "Upon my word," said Emma, "I begin to doubt my having any such talent [...]"[195]

Even Mr Woodhouse, 'fond of society in his own way', is given a version of the image after his own mind, as Austen drags the sense of 'heart' within the orbit of his hypochondria:

> Poor Mr Woodhouse little suspected what was plotting against him in the breast of that man whom he was so cordially welcoming, and so anxiously hoping might not have taken cold from his ride. – Could he have seen the heart, he would have cared very little for the lungs [...][196]

The inability to see into hearts, however, neither can nor does prevent people from understanding others, although it does fill the space between them with those misfires, gaffes and social indelicacies on which Austen's comedy thrives.[197] Hearts that are not directly visible or accessible can be approached by riskier and more circuitous routes: through acquaintance and familiarity; through talking and listening, whether polite debate or the exploratory banter of sexual desire. Emma's beginning to 'listen better' also licenses her to speak out, as when she accepts Knightley, with a feeling of self-worth that is neither humble nor submissive ('She felt for Harriet, with pain and contrition, but no flight of generosity run mad, opposing all that could be probable or reasonable, entered her brain.'[198]). Chastened she may be, but Emma's will is no less strong than at the beginning of the novel; it is just that she now knows what, and whom, she wants. Many factors have combined to further, and hinder, that knowledge: patience, *amour propre*, sacrifices, suspicions, and sometimes a resolve bordering on the bloody-minded. Hence it is appropriate that Austen should end the reader's engagement with *Emma* by narrating a form of private and public conversation which comprehends all these and more: the celebration of a marriage.

Weddings lend themselves readily to fictional endings – witness the prevalence of the 'Wedding' function at the end of Propp's plot-diagrams of folk- and fairy-tales[199] – and one reason for this, in addition to the economic and biological imperatives, is that a writer can close his or her story by implying the beginning of another. But this carries its own hazards, as GK Chesterton observed when he argued that the protagonist's marriage to Agnes Wickfield at the end of *David Copperfield* rang false. 'The fairy tales said,' he claimed, 'that the prince and princess lived happily ever afterwards: and so they did. They lived happily, although it is very likely that from time to time they threw the furniture at each other. Most marriages, I think, are happy marriages; but there is no such thing as a contented marriage. The whole pleasure of marriage is that it is a perpetual crisis.'[200] Now 'perpetual crisis' is an exaggeration, and perhaps only a confirmed bachelor like Chesterton could speak so sunnily of woe that is in marriage, since he could afford to do so; nevertheless, his joke touches on a home truth. There may well not be, at least in marriage as we know it, an end to 'talking it over'. It can hardly be coincidental that both Anglican and Catholic marriages are sanctified by stylized and dramatic patterns of call and response, prompt and echo – for instance, the exchange in the Common Prayer service ('I N. take thee *N.* to my wedded wife/ 'I *N.* take thee N. to my wedded husband'). As Chesterton's joke suggests, one of the risks a person takes in marrying another is that the quotidian talk in which they discover and cherish that which they love in their partner may decline, almost imperceptibly, into a routine of bickering; but the pain of having one's most sensitive nerve hammered upon is so painful precisely because it is, like a fallen angel, the wreck of a beautiful shape. Knowing what hurts one's lover is as much the fruit of intimacy as knowing what makes them happy. Only a certain kind of couple could truly be said to thrive in a marriage that was 'a perpetual crisis': Austen ends *Emma,* a work which unsparingly faces up to solipsism and loss, with a marriage that is a perpetual conversation.

The ritualistic formality of the Common Prayer marriage service may appear to iron out the wrinkles of 'real' relationships; but part of its purpose is, after all, to enshrine a vision of mutuality, to give its participants something at which to aim; and in this, it is both like and unlike any marriage we might encounter either inside or outside fiction. Knightley's proposal moves nervously through the actual and momentary in search of a longer-lasting achievement – showing that Emma is not the only character whose fluency is checked in the latter stages of the novel. In order to win Emma, he must brave the trial of her will and words, becoming in the process both prompter and echo.

Austen weighs his risk in the unwontedly heavy stage- and page-directions which interrupt the assurance of his speech:

> "Emma!" cried he, looking eagerly at her, "are you, indeed?" —
> but checking himself —"No, no, I understand you—forgive me—I
> am pleased that you can say even so much.—He is no object of
> regret, indeed! and it will not be very long, I hope, before that
> becomes the acknowledgement of more than your reason.—
> Fortunate that your affections were not farther entangled!—I could
> never, I confess, from your manners, assure myself as to the degree
> of what you felt—I could only be certain that there was a prefer-
> ence—and a preference which I never believed him to deserve.—
> He is a disgrace to the name of man.—And is he to be rewarded
> with that sweet young woman?—Jane, Jane, you will be a miserable
> creature."[201]

'Emma was silenced' also finds its counterpoint in the proposal scene, in the familiar stresses of 'He was silent'.[202] For all his supposed status as a 'com-pletely reliable' figure of intellectual authority,[203] it turns out that the whole of Knightley's happiness is chanced on something beyond his control, which could well be irrevocably lost. A proposal must prompt the right answer in order to succeed, and in moving from silence to speech, the novel restores the power of Emma's voice:

> "My dearest Emma," said he, "for dearest you will always be,
> whatever the event of this hour's conversation, my dearest, most
> beloved Emma—tell me at once. Say 'No' if it is to be said."—She
> could really say nothing.—"You are silent," he cried, with great
> animation; "absolutely silent! at present I ask no more."
>   . . . .
> "[...] God knows, I have been but a very indifferent lover.—But
> you understand me.—Yes, you see, you understand my feelings—
> and will return them if you can. At present, I ask only to hear, once
> to hear your voice."[204]

In one of the most famous moments in Austen's writing, Knightley hears that voice, we do not; but Austen reveals just enough of Emma's reply to make it clear that it too is a prompt: 'She said enough to show that there need not be despair—and to invite him to say more himself.'[205] The betrothal and marriage breed a vocal familiarity which compensates for the inability to see into hearts, in which the willing exchange and echoing of words becomes a kind of caress:

"Oh! I always deserve the best treatment, because I never put up with any other; and, therefore, you must give me a plain, direct answer. Are you quite sure that you understand the terms on which Mr. Martin and Harriet now are?"

"I am quite sure," he replied, speaking very distinctly [...][206]

But before the wedding, Emma and Knightley's familiarity has still more uncanny effects; in this novel of ventriloquism and impressionism, it is only fair that Austen should also provide a little moment of romantic ESP. Reading Frank Churchill's apologetic letter, Emma reflects that 'he had suffered, and was very sorry—and he was so grateful to Mrs. Weston, and so much in love with Miss Fairfax, and she was so happy herself, that there was no being severe';[207] Knightley manages an apparently psychic echo, as he tunes in on Emma's *style indirect* and voices one of her thoughts directly:

He proceeded a little farther, reading to himself; and then, with a smile, observed, "Humph!—a fine complimentary opening:—But it is his way. One man's style must not be the rule of another's. We will not be severe."[208]

Lovers, both consciously and unconsciously, continually pick up on one another's words, caressing and teasing them by turns. As the narrator of *Sense and Sensibility* observes, 'though a very few hours spent in the hard labour of incessant talking will dispatch more subjects than can really be in common between any two rational creatures, yet with lovers it is different. Between *them* no subject is finished, no communication is even made, till it has been made at least twenty times over.'[209] One could argue that these small amatory contentions serve merely to palliate or disguise the danger of larger crises. That said, the minute circumstances which cause them, what a person hears in their loved one, also makes up part of what they 'see' in them, explaining why others 'cannot understand what he sees in her', or vice-versa. In John Updike's words: 'A tribe segregated in a valley develops an accent, then a dialect, and then a language all its own; so does a couple.'[210] The enclosed and semi-private nature of lovers' talk is one reason why the pragmatics of endearment can sound obscure, masonic, tacky, or just plain boring, to anyone outside the particular relationship. On the inside, though, affection's idiolects may afford comforts less susceptible to, if never insulated from, the accidents of bodily decline. Beyond the sequence of her plotting, Austen offers the very end of *Emma* as a complex model in narrative of what this might imply. The novel's opening sentence describes an illusory union ('seemed to unite some of the best blessings of existence'), whereas its closing sentence at least points towards a more productive one. The word 'perfection' floats teasingly round the latter part of *Emma*, notably on Box Hill, as the clue to Mr Weston's fawning, phonetically suspect (and, given what Emma has just done to Miss Bates, spectacularly ill-timed) conundrum:

> "I doubt it's being very clever myself," said Mr. Weston. "It is too much a matter of fact, but here it is.—What two letters of the alphabet are there, that express perfection?"[211]

Knightley, his words laden with directed implicature, points out that '*Perfection* should not have come quite so soon';[212] and, true to form, it doesn't. Austen hints at things to come after Emma has accepted the proposal ('Within half an hour, he had passed from a thoroughly distressed state of mind, to something so like perfect happiness, that it could bear no other name'[213]); but it takes the novel's final phrase to wed the two, as the syllables of 'perfect happiness' settle into the phonemic embrace of 'perfection', in the words '*perfect* happiness of the un*ion*'[214] (italics mine).

'[P]ictures of perfection as you know make me sick & wicked': the novelist who could compare her own verses jokingly to 'Homer & Virgil, Ovid & Propria que Maribus'[215] would have known the full charge her phrase carried. 'Pictures of perfection' for Austen denote not only fictional portrayals of unimpeachable – and therefore unattainable – virtue, but images of 'perfection' at its etymological roots: 'completing, consummating, finishing, accomplishing', and 'The fact or condition of being perfected or completed'.[216] Endings in fiction, like so many other climaxes with the power to satisfy, are radically equivocal. For one thing, they are, like sleep, rehearsals for (if not inoculations against) our own endings – only more troubling than sleep, since we are conscious to experience these intimations of mortality, of the first event that we will no longer be there to experience; as Wittgenstein remarked, 'Death is not an event in life: we do not live to experience death'.[217] Moreover, they present the dilemma of 'perfection' in all its senses, 'the tension or dissonance between paradigmatic form and contingent reality'.[218] To put matters more simply, too little closure frightens readers with the spectre of absolute, random contingency, where nothing is connected to anything else; and too complete or too neat a closure risks transforming characters into ciphers, the automata of an external controlling force. *Emma*'s conclusion is not, however, a static picture of perfection, but what Barbara Everett has suggestively dubbed 'Hard Romance': a state both hard-headed and perilous, 'hard to destroy and hard to achieve'.[219] Lionel Trilling's generous insight into the ending is particularly appropriate here:

> This England, especially as it is represented in *Emma*, is an idyll.
> The error of identifying it with the actual England ought always to
> be remarked. Yet the same sense of actuality that corrects the error
> should not fail to recognize the remarkable force of the ideal that
> leads many to make the error.[220]

An idyll cannot be exactly like everyday life, or it wouldn't offer anything to which to aspire; by the same token, it cannot be entirely removed from that life, or there would be no imaginative bridge possible between the two worlds. One of Austen's most challenging achievements in *Emma* is to preserve the rewards of romantic fulfilment while deliberately exposing them to threats which could destroy them utterly. In this, *Emma* might seem initially to resemble a novel like *Tom Jones*, in which Fielding stages an elaborate display of narrative escapology for his readers, repeatedly getting Tom into apparently intractable (and often potentially fatal) scrapes, only to rescue him at the last moment, by revealing some fact, hitherto withheld, which extricates and excuses him. This bravado is of a piece with the essentially sanguine, post-Shaftesburian outlook of *Tom Jones*, in which Fielding's plot becomes a Providential force, and in some ways the most 'rounded' character in the story;[221] therefore, by the novel's latter stages, a reader may well get so accustomed to this manoeuvre that she or he treats its every appearance as 'crying wolf'. *Emma* allows its readers no such leisure. While the precedent of Austen's novels, as established by the authorial branding on the title-pages ('BY THE | AUTHOR OF "PRIDE AND PREJUDICE," | *&c. &c.*'), might have led her first audiences to surmise that the new novel would end the same way as the previous works had done, *Emma* arranges matters so as to make the anticipated and wished-for ending by no means a foregone conclusion. This is most obviously achieved in the way Austen so deliberately besets Emma round with possible alternative versions of herself: there, but for the grace of God, goes Emma.

Even setting aside their family connection, it is not surprising, after 'nearly twenty-one years' together, that Mr Woodhouse and his daughter should share so many traits; but this is not the only parallel implicated by the novel. Mrs Elton, despite her vulgarisms, threatens to usurp Emma's social supremacy in Highbury; Austen hints ominously at further parallels between the women in the transformation of names from 'The charming Augusta Hawkins'[222] to 'Mrs. Elton' – the latter, of course, being the title which Emma herself might have assumed in different circumstances. Likewise, Emma voices an anxiety about Miss Bates which also reflects obliquely back on herself, when Harriet unconsciously hits on a raw spot:

"But then, to be an old maid at last, like Miss Bates!"

"That is as formidable an image as you could present, Harriet; and if I thought I should ever be like Miss Bates! so silly—so satisfied—so smiling—so prosing—so undistinguished and unfastidious—and so apt to tell every thing relative to every body about me, I would marry to-morrow. But between *us*, I am convinced there never can be any likeness, except in being unmarried."[223]

Emma may be convinced, but she doesn't sound convincing – in this novel so full of uncanny and unconscious echoes, the very accuracy with which she reproduces Miss Bates's verbal mannerisms ('so silly—so satisfied') furthers this; Austen has Emma parody Miss Bates long before the latter has a direct speech in the novel, so the effect of imitation is almost reversed. Neither is the single common factor of 'being unmarried' a small consideration; Emma may believe that 'it is poverty only which makes celibacy contemptible',[224] but the novel is not so sure. In her Steventon years, Austen herself had witnessed the awkward position of Mrs Stent, whose reduced circumstances and sheer social unavoidability must have contributed to her imagination of Miss Bates. 'Poor M[rs] Stent!' she wrote to Cassandra in 1805. 'it has been her lot to be always in the way; but we must be merciful, for perhaps in time we may come to be M[rs] Stents ourselves, unequal to anything & unwelcome to everybody.'[225] Ten years later, Miss Bates worries Emma because she sees all too clearly in the spinster the ghost of a possible Emma-yet-to-be: someone reduced to being an unreflective channel for 'every thing relative to every body' but herself, worn by gossip and time almost into a non-character, a mere conduit for the third person:

"Oh! yes—Mr. Elton, I understood—certainly as to dancing—Mrs. Cole was telling me that dancing at the rooms at Bath was—Mrs. Cole was so kind as to sit some time with us, talking of Jane; for as soon as she came in, she began inquiring after her, Jane is so very great a favourite there [...]"[226]

The world of *Emma* is unusual in that it is an idyll still subject, as elsewhere in Austen's fiction, to the demands of economic necessity, but the lot of the spinster Miss Bates also points up an unpalatable but inescapable fact about Highbury, and about the world of its childless, forty-year-old creator – that it times itself by a 'biological clock'. *Emma* depicts pastoral as continually invaded and menaced by time, particularly unsettlingly in the portrayal of Jane Fairfax, who provides the most complex counterfactual version of the heroine. When Wayne Booth wonders 'what Emma's story would be if seen

through Jane Fairfax' or Mrs. Elton's or Robert Martin's eyes',[227] he hints at
Jane's status as the heroine of *Emma*'s repressed plot: the back-story that takes
place in the interstices of that novel which Austen does choose to narrate, the
one focused on Emma Woodhouse. On a day-to-day level, Jane is a persistent
irritant to the heroine, since she provides a ready (and almost identically-
aged) yardstick by which others can measure and judge Emma; but she trou-
bles Emma on subtler levels. If Miss Bates reflects back what an unmarried life
might make of Emma, Jane embodies the awful possibility of what Emma's
prospects might be if the last of her possessions ('handsome, clever, and rich')
were to be taken away. Whether or not Austen imagined Jane Fairfax as not
long for the world after the novel's end (as the family reports would have it),[228]
her status is felt, repeatedly and insistently, as ephemeral, fragile, under
threat. It is hard not to read the rumour back into the text once one knows of
it, given that Jane's time in *Emma* is marked by so many references to tran-
sience. On her first appearance, the account of her comfortable life with the
Campbells is undercut by 'the sobering suggestions of her own good understanding to remind her that all this might soon be over';[229] within two further
paragraphs, a reader is presented with a bizarre extended metaphor, which
sets being a governess on a par with being a nun, not without reason:

> With the fortitude of a devoted noviciate, she had resolved at
> one-and-twenty to complete the sacrifice, and retire from all the
> pleasures of life, of rational intercourse, equal society, peace and
> hope, to penance and mortification for ever.

After this description, to be told that Jane 'had never been quite well since the
time of [the Campbells'] daughter's marriage',[230] in conjunction with Mrs
Elton's quoting from Gray's *Elegy*,[231] offer many temptations, in the light
of the family legend; but the possibility of Jane's death is not necessary to
Austen's effect here. However long she may or may not live, Jane Fairfax,
unless she can secure a man like Frank Churchill, is not long for *this* world:
economic necessity will force her out of the world of Highbury, one which,
for all its evident inanity and restriction, is nevertheless a charmed place.
Highbury is where the grubbily worldly shares the same space with the
other-worldly – a feeling heightened by its being a place at once topographically precise and literally 'utopian', physically incapable of occupying the
triangulation-points provided for it. RW Chapman noted: 'in fact, no possible
place is at once 16 miles from London, 9 from Richmond, and 7 from Box
Hill; the precision of these figures was perhaps designed to preclude the possibility of a false identification.'[232] Barbara Everett rightly divines more
profound possibilities:

> But Highbury is not a pastoral place. It is a romance place. Given
> an exact topography, as if locatable on a map – 16 miles from
> London, nine from Richmond – its locations turn out to be self-
> contradictory; so that, like the island in *The Tempest*, Highbury is
> real, but nowhere. Its reality is that the people in it live naturally
> […][233]

In its placing of everyday details and mythical archetypes within the same
frame, *Emma* has some famous eighteenth-century precedents, notably
Clarissa's layering of obsessively detailed, domestic 'virtual reality' over older
motifs from fairy tales; but Everett locates an older source: Shakespeare's late
plays, the romances, in which the most mundane signs become the means to
come upon wonders. Like Prospero's island, and like the phantom coastline of
Bohemia in *The Winter's Tale*, Highbury is indeed a romance place; and like
Shakespeare's romance places, it is a field of dreams which can still turn into
mud:

> "Dirty, sir! Look at my shoes. Not a speck on them."
> "Well! that is quite surprizing, for we have had a vast deal of rain
> here. It rained dreadfully hard for half an hour, while we were at
> breakfast. I wanted them to put off the wedding."[234]

When Victorians such as Whately, Macaulay and Lewes attempted to
canonize Austen as 'prose Shakspeare', their habitual points of comparison
were the comedies: *Much Ado About Nothing*, *Twelfth Night*, *The Merry Wives of
Windsor*. During Austen's working life, however, Romantic Shakespeare criticism was raising to prominence plays such as *Hamlet* and *The Tempest*; as
Jonathan Bate notes: 'The presence of Hamlet in Romantic discourse usually
indicates that the artist is examining his own self […] The self was a central
problem for the Romantics; Shakespeare was thus brought to the centre of
their thinking […]'.[235] Unsurprisingly, *The Tempest* figures large as an emblem,
even an allegory of imagination – but not only because of the challenges to
belief presented by the play's supernatural machinery. Coleridge's account of
the play strikes what is now a familiar note in describing Prospero as 'the very
Shakespeare himself, as it were of the tempest';[236] however, *The Tempest* also
prompts one of his most meticulous accounts of dramatic illusion:

> […] I find two extremes of critical decision; — the French, which
> evidently presupposes that a perfect delusion is to be aimed at, —an
> opinion which needs no fresh confutation; and the exact opposite to
> it, brought forward by Dr. Johnson, who supposes the auditors

throughout in the full reflective knowledge of the contrary. In evinc-
ing the impossibility of delusion, he makes no sufficient allowance
for an intermediate state, which I have before distinguished by the
term, illusion, and I have attempted to illustrate its quality and
character by reference to our mental state, when dreaming. In both
cases we simply do not judge the imagery to be unreal; there is a
negative reality, and no more.[237]

In his *Characters of Shakespear's Plays*, Hazlitt remarks that Shakespeare possesses 'the same insight into the world of imagination that he has into the
world of reality [...] His ideal beings are as true and natural as his real characters'.[238] For both critics, *The Tempest* focuses their attention on the shifting
relations between 'reality', 'illusion' and 'delusion', and between 'ideal beings'
and 'real characters', relations which continued to collide and cross-fertilize in
literature as the century went on.[239] Such relations are especially pertinent to
The Winter's Tale and *The Tempest*, since it is essential to their romance endings
that both plays tender the possibility of regenerative marriages, whilst keeping
their counsel as to whether those marriages will or will not prevail – and it is
here that *Emma* is most in Shakespeare's debt. The romantic crux in *The
Tempest* comes with the discovery of Miranda and Ferdinand in V.i., in particular that exchange between Miranda and Prospero, one which has been
rendered so familiar by anthologies and Aldous Huxley, that everyone who
knows it also thinks he or she 'knows how it goes':

Alo.   If this proue
           A vision of the Island, one deere Sonne
           Shall I twice loose.
Seb.   A most high miracle.
Fer.   Though the Seas threaten they are mercifull,
           I haue curs'd them without cause.
Alo.   Now all the blessings
           Of a glad father, compasse thee about:
           Arise, and say how thou cams't heere.
Mir.   O wonder!
           How many goodly creatures are there heere?
           How beauteous mankinde is? O braue new world
           That has such people in't.
Pro.   'Tis new to thee.[240]

What Josipovici says about the ending of *The Winter's Tale* could equally well
be applied here. 'These things,' he argues, 'do not simply exist or not exist; it is

required of us that we awake our faith in them. That does not require an effort of the will but an openness to the new, to whatever time will bring.'[241] In *The Tempest*, the 'openness to the new' is embodied in Prospero's four monosyllables, words also open to mistrust and world-weariness: "Tis new to thee.' The contextual pressure of Sebastian's wise-cracking 'A most high miracle' cannot but tell on Prospero's line, but it does not dictate its sense. Neither can the accentual-syllabic patterns of blank verse do so, for reasons I have discussed in the previous chapter. It is entirely plausible, and even probable, that Prospero does say "Tis *new* to *thee*', his words falling into the worn tick-tock of iambic regularity much as Miranda's wonder will soon succumb to the pressures of the 'real world'. This is, however, a man addressing his only child, and now his only hope, and it is hard to give his words a terminal stress without also lending them a mocking accent – but however strongly he remonstrates with Miranda, nowhere in the play does Prospero scoff at her. For all the pulls of worldly knowledge upon Prospero's line, it still cocoons within itself the fragile possibility of "*Tis* new to thee', of Prospero's sudden recall, as if from a past life, of that 'openness to the new' which he once possessed, but which can now only reside in his daughter. *The Tempest* does not settle the question; what little we are told of the future away from the island is itself phrased optatively:

> and so to *Naples*,
> Where I hope to see the nuptiall
> Of these our deere-belou'd, solemnized,
> And thence retire me to my *Millaine*, where
> Euery third thought shall be my graue.[242]

Furthermore, the conceit of the epilogue makes it clear that Prospero will not even get that far without the audience's indulgence. Poised on the cusp of belief and disillusionment whilst endorsing neither, Shakespeare's romance ending has an extraordinary impunity and inscrutability; the rest, as they say, is silence.

Emma's romance ending similarly avails itself of non-committal silence, with the added advantage of not being designed to be staged aloud (although Austen, living in the age of Kemble's *Tempest*, would almost certainly have only known "Tis new to thee' as a printed line herself);[243] like *The Tempest*, the ending has also exercized generations of readers, many of them eager to make the novel's mind up for it. Chesterton claimed: 'The fairy tales said that the prince and princess lived happily ever afterwards,' but Austen's mature novels do not do so. None of them features much of what Genette calls 'external prolepsis',[244] that is, foreshadowings of any future plot beyond the end of the narrative, an 'ever after'; but *Emma* takes this reticence to its furthest extent.

The sparseness of foretelling in Austen comes into relief when set in comparison with her predecessors. Mrs Radcliffe, for example, reassures the readers of *Udolpho* that Emily and Valancourt are restored to 'the securest felicity of this life, that of aspiring to moral and labouring for intellectual improvement—to the pleasures of enlightened society, and to the exercise of the benevolence, which had always animated their hearts'.[245] Burney narrates Camilla's wedding ('Dr. Marchmont united them; and Edgar, glowing with happiness, now purified from any alloy, received from the same revered hand, and owed to the same honoured voice, the final and lasting possession of the tearful, but happy Camilla'[246]), then provides several further pages of proleptic summary before the novel closes. Likewise, the 'ever after' was to gain even greater prominence in Victorian fiction, whether Little Dorrit's 'modest life of usefulness and happiness'[247] or the 'incalculably diffusive'[248] future life of Eliot's Dorothea Brooke. Albeit with her tongue in her cheek, the young Austen could conclude *Evelyn* with a vision of 'perfect happiness' in the future ('M^r & Mrs Gower resided many years at Evelyn enjoying perfect happiness the just reward of their virtues'[249]); her mature endings do not possess such long sight or such unequivocal confidence. *Sense and Sensibility* offers the most certain proleptic guarantees, not only for Elinor and Marianne ('there was that constant communication which strong family affection would naturally dictate'[250]), but even for Willoughby ('He lived to exert, and frequently to enjoy himself'[251]). But in her next two novels, what Austen does reveal about life after the climactic marriages is not exclusively sanguine. Whatever happens to Elizabeth and Darcy after *Pride and Prejudice*, Lydia and Wickham wear down into mutual tolerance ('His affection for her soon sunk into indifference; her's lasted a little longer'[252]), while in *Mansfield Park*, Austen's narrator achieves a masterstroke of implicature about Henry Crawford's future, by seeming, like Tristram Shandy, to fend off the inference:

> That punishment, the public punishment of disgrace, should in a just measure attend *his* share of the offence, is, we know, not one of the barriers, which society gives to virtue. In this world, the penalty is less equal than could be wished; but without presuming to look forward to a just appointment hereafter, we may fairly consider a man of sense like Henry Crawford, to be providing for himself no small portion of vexation and regret [...][253]

Elizabeth, Darcy, Fanny and Edmund are at least partially protected from the attrition of time by the fact of how little their narratives actually reveal about them; but the other stories which cluster around them are not such as to inspire great trust in a 'happy ever after'.

Even in comparison with its immediate predecessors, *Emma* is unusually tight-lipped about the afterlife of its plot, but Austen's *coup* in this novel is to recognize that if endings in fiction are little apocalypses, reading furnishes the eschatology of writing – as I have discussed, this is a paradox which Proust grasped later, when he wrote that

> for the author they may be called 'Conclusions' but for the reader 'Incitements'. We feel very strongly that our own wisdom begins where that of the author leaves off, and we would like him to provide us with answers when all he is able to do is to provide us with desires.[254]

Kipling's critical and creative rereading of Austen in 'The Janeites', likewise, arranges matters so that the afterlife of Austen's novels, within Humberstall's story of an ill-sorted community of readerly affection, is paralleled with the framing fantasy of Austen's personal afterlife, and her marriage in heaven:

Instantly the under-
    standing Seraphim
Laid their fingers on their lips
    And went to look for him.
Stole across the Zodiac,
    Harnessed Charles's Wain,
And whispered round the Nebulae
    "Who loved Jane?"
In a private limbo
    Where none had thought to look,
Sat a Hampshire gentleman
    Reading of a book.
It was called *Persuasion*,
    And it told the plain
Story of the love between
    Him and Jane.
He heard the question
    Circle Heaven through —
Closed the book and answered:
    "I did – and do!"
Quietly and speedily
    (As Captain Wentworth moved)
Entered into Paradise
    The man Jane loved![255]

The beauty of this is that it manages to be Austenian even as it sends up Janeites ('a Hampshire gentleman/ Reading of a book'), responding to the emotional pull of 'Aunt Jane' whilst admitting, in the same breath, how ludicrous the whole business is; Kipling cross-hatches his vision of Paradise with more awkward actualities. Seraphim, for one thing, cannot flit in their customary manner if they are so visibly and semantically earthed by the enjambment of 'under/ standing'; to whisper 'around' anything as ill-defined as 'the Nebulae' would be a feat, even for angels; and the connection of 'plain' and 'Jane' set up in Kipling's rhymes tells its own story. Kipling's verse, though, also weaves in Austen's writing ('(As Captain Wentworth moved)'), alongside a declaration of love ("I did – and do!"): the poem itself may be what James called a 'ponderous *amoroso*', but its affection is no less sincere for that fact.

Some more recent critical reactions to *Emma* have not always possessed Kipling's circumspection. Following DW Harding's timely focus on 'Regulated Hatred', a certain critical consensus has built up, according to which the ending of *Emma* cannot possibly be sincere, since no novelist as clever as Austen could truly have believed in such a confection. Famous instances of this interpretative slant are those of GB Stern, Marvin Mudrick and Edmund Wilson;[256] even Wayne Booth, 27 years after defending the end of the novel against such accusations, found himself having to backtrack a little: 'Though I still see the claim as, at best, only half of what should be said, I now think my rejection of it was too simple. In *Emma*, we play doubled roles much more intricate than are demanded by fantastic elements like gold-laying geese. On the one hand, we must see the ending as indeed a happy one, not in the least ironic, given the world of the conventional plot, a world that we are to enter with absolute wholeheartedness. And yet, simultaneously, we are asked to embrace standards according to which the ending can only be viewed as a fairy tale or fantasy.'[257] The number of 'continuations' of Austen's works which sprang up after her commercial resurgence in the 1990s similarly testifies to a desire which her endings awaken and nourish, the desire to know 'how it turns out' – and what better way to know than to write it yourself? Emma Tennant's *Emma in Love* (1996), for example, picks up the narrative four years after the wedding and gives us secret cross-dressing, lesbian crushes, and Miss Bates's gossip declining into Tourette's Syndrome[258] – all of which Austen's original allows for, but only because, in its reticence, it allows for practically anything.

This is as it should be, since romance endings are all about wish-fulfilment, and a reader's wishes can be as fulfilled by couples' living *un*happily ever after as by the opposite. However, such responses are only half of the effect; since what romance gives with one hand, it takes away with the other. *Emma*'s ending lives on in readerly speculation, but its crowning double irony is its silence, reminding the reader that any conjecture he or she might frame is just that: speculation. At the end of *Lady Susan*, the narrator poses the question:

> Whether Lady Susan was, or was not happy in her second Choice—I do not see how it can ever be ascertained—for who would take her assurance of it, on either side of the question? The World must judge from Probability.[259]

Northanger Abbey closes by leaving it 'to be settled by whomsoever it may concern, whether the tendency of this work be altogether to recommend parental tyranny, or reward filial disobedience.'[260] By the time of *Emma*, Austen can compact such questions into the novel's final silence; plot and narrative, closure and contingency, narrow to an apex in 'the perfect happiness of the union' – then vanish into a blank which is as finally unknowable as the urge to fill it is irresistible. That lifelong scrutiny of the distance and closeness between selves and words, which Austen conducts in her letters, in her epistolary fictions, and on into the mature novels, gives rise in *Emma* to one of the greatest ventriloquial tricks in nineteenth-century fiction: after all the novel's echoes and awkward repetitions, the final phrase of the narrative invites a reader to project his or her own 'ever after', providing a space into which readers can throw their voices, only to echo them straight back, in a final act of novelistic passive resistance. DA Miller's fascinating analysis of closure in Austen discusses in depth the tendency of her narrative form 'to disown at an ideological level what it embraces at a constructional one',[261] but Miller's casting of the paradox in polarized or dialectical terms does not entirely fit *Emma*: this is a novel that has it both ways at once.

Austen has, throughout the story, threatened the romance by surrounding it with characters unfulfilled within or without marriages, and with possible alternative versions of Emma herself. She then has the audacity to present a romance ending which depends on a marriage, whilst all the time amassing an ever larger weight of equivocal or worrying precedent. Not only are Emma and Knightley surrounded by people whose marriages are far from 'perfect', but the couple's vows (like Emma's acceptance, a significantly unnarrated speech) are those same words which those people, and generations before them, have spoken for the same purpose. This is, though, one reason why marriage offers Austen such a suggestive motif for intimacy and distance: in repeating the old words, two people place themselves within a longer and less personal narrative, but it is not a completely impersonal one. Firstly, the service bears the individual inflections of the partners' own names (say, 'I Emma take thee George'); more fundamentally, no two people in such a situation, whatever the evidence to the contrary, could fully believe that things would not, by some miracle, be different for them. 'The World must judge from Probability', supposedly, and *Emma* gives a reader more than enough to be going with; but its silence makes it clear that any conclusions drawn will be probabilistic ones, not facts. Despite all appearances to the contrary, it is as impossible to say definitively how *Emma* 'turns out' as it is to be wholly at one with the intimacy of others, or to achieve that 'absolute clarity' at which senti-mental correspondents aimed – we share the words, but not the timbres which fully give them meaning. The brilliant doubleness of *Emma*'s ending is that it weighs the banality, and the attrition, against which the lovers' hopes are tensed, within the same words. Instead of offering any simple oppositions between the 'real' and the 'ideal', the plaited strands of Austen's narrative implicitly recognize the idealizing impulse as part of that reality which novels represent. That a honeymoon will one day be over is an analytical proposi-tion: the very etymology of the word implies that one's honey will start to sour as soon as the moon starts waning,[262] and it is this that lends the 'hardness' of risk and of durability to *Emma*. '[T]he perfect happiness of the union': that last phrase is an idyll, but an idyll won and made out of the phonemes of 'perfec-tion' and 'perfect happiness', words indelibly stained by the hurt and thought-lessness they have witnessed over the course of the novel. Closure and contin-gency meet, the sentence ends, and the rest is silence. Like the marriage which it describes, the last sentence is an act of hope in the ambience and in the teeth of experience; unlike any relationship, however, it deliberately stops just before the 'ever after', and remains poised endlessly on the brink. But fiction and life would be much less fun if matters were otherwise.

4

HABIT AND HABITATION

> giving way
> To a comparison of scene with scene,
> Bent overmuch on superficial things,
> Pampering myself with meagre novelties
> Of colour and proportion, to the moods
> Of Nature, and the spirit of the place,
> Less sensible.
>
> Wordsworth, *The Prelude* (1805 text), Book Eleventh[1]

> *Decor* is the keeping of a due *Respect* between the *Inhabitant*, and the *Habitation*.
>
> Henry Wotton, *The Elements of Architecture*, 1624[2]

Jane Austen in Space

Henry Austen and Alfred Tennyson were both fond of Jane Austen. The first was her elder brother, by turns a banker, a bankrupt and a cleric; the latter became Poet Laureate. These different circumstances go some way towards explaining the two men's different reactions to her. Austen's authorship of her novels may have been an open secret in certain quarters of the literary world during her later life, but the first official public confirmation came in the 'Biographical Notice of the Author' which Henry Austen appended to *Northanger Abbey* and *Persuasion* when they first appeared in 1818:

> The following pages are the production of a pen which has also contributed in no small degree to the entertainment of the public. And when the public, which has not been insensible to the merits of "Sense and Sensibility," "Pride and Prejudice," "Mansfield Park," and "Emma," shall now be informed that the hand which guided that pen is now mouldering in the grave, perhaps a brief account of Jane Austen will be read with a kindlier sentiment than simple curiosity.

> Short and easy will be the task of the mere biographer. A life of
> usefulness, literature, and religion, was not by any means a life of
> event.[3]

The sense of priorities that could bracket 'literature' in Jane Austen's life between 'usefulness' and 'religion' makes the 'Biographical Notice' comparable, at least on the surface, to the black slab which her eldest brother James placed in the North Aisle of Winchester Cathedral; Austen's epitaph (Plate 1) features an evasive reference to 'The benevolence of her heart, the sweetness of her temper, and the extraordinary endowments of her mind' – so evasive, in fact, that it never mentions directly her occupation as a novelist. Austen, could she have read these words, might have appreciated their reticence, given that she would reputedly hide her writing under a blotter if she heard someone approaching. However, the epitaph's description of Austen is also, whether by accident or design, oddly close to her own account of what Edmund Bertram comes to cherish in Fanny Price ('the sweetness of her temper, the purity of her mind, and the excellence of her principles'[4]), and what may be fine for a fictional character may rather undersell her creator.

The question of what constitutes a fitting memorial is a perennial one, which repeatedly exercized writers in the eighteenth and nineteenth centuries. In his early *Essay on Epitaphs* (1740), Johnson suggested: 'The best subject for epitaphs is private virtue; virtue exerted in the same circumstances in which the bulk of mankind are placed, and which, therefore, may admit of many imitators.'[5] There is dignity in Johnson's vision of the public afterlife of individuals' endurance, but it is less certain whether his 'in the same circumstances' thereby excludes from consideration anything about the deceased that may be too personal to admit of 'many imitators'. Johnson had to face these contradictions more directly four years after the *Essay*, when he set out, in the *Life of Savage*, to do justice to the divergent and sometimes conflicting roles of personal friend, and public biographer; and in this case, he found himself obliged to pay more attention to his subject's quirks: 'Mr. *Savage* related another Fact equally uncommon, which, though it has no Relation to his life, ought to be preserved.'[6] Writing in 1809, in the first of his 'Essays upon Epitaphs', Wordsworth addressed more directly the curious double status of the epitaph, standing on the border between the ephemeral body and the eternal soul:

> The composition and quality of the mind of a virtuous man, con-
> templated by the side of the grave in which his body is mouldering,
> ought to appear, and be felt as something midway between what he
> was on earth walking about with his living frailties, and what he
> may be presumed to be as a Spirit in heaven.[7]

For all the insistent piety of his tone, Henry Austen in the 'Biographical Notice' displays a circumspection akin to Wordsworth's, in recognizing that he mourns a figure who was, even before she died, already 'midway between' her personal self and what the public presumed her to be. In writing of 'the production of a pen which has already contributed [...] to the entertainment of the public', he zooms in on the tool of his sister's trade, and also appeals to the convention by which 'pen' stands metonymically for 'writer' (compare 'Let other pens dwell on guilt and misery' in *Mansfield Park*[8]). Henry Austen had been the mediator between his sister and her publishers during her life, and in setting up his imaginative conjunction of the mortal author and her potential public 'afterlife', he half redeems the cliché of 'mouldering in the grave', a phrase which in this context bridges literary posterity and the nasty facts of bodily decay. Whatever other effects the 'Biographical Notice' may have had in fixing a certain image of Austen for public reception, passages like this partake of at least some of their subject's spirit, in that they embellish fact with disposition – a distant relation, but still a relation, of those novels in which disposition becomes event.

Henry Austen's words saw his late sister across the bar between her life's work and the life of her 'Works'; fifty years after Jane Austen's death, Tennyson still found enough in her published works to inspire a personal attachment. Hallam Tennyson's *Memoir* of his father (1897) relates the events of the summer of 1867, with a fine eye for detail:

> On August 23rd my father left for Bridport. He was led on to Lyme by the description of the place in Miss Austen's *Persuasion*, walking thither the nine miles over the hills from Bridport. On his arrival he called on Palgrave, and, refusing all refreshment, he said at once: "Now take me to the Cobb, and show me the steps from which Louisa Musgrove fell."[9]

There is a dry comedy in the poise with which Hallam Tennyson narrates the 58-year-old poet's walking 'the nine miles over the hills from Bridport'; however, his words are also attuned to what his father may have read and valued in *Persuasion* to lead him on to Lyme. The precisely detailed circumstances ('nine miles', 'refusing all refreshment', 'at once') point to an action as poetic as it was precipitate. Tennyson's was the reaction of a sensitive and affectionate reader, responding to Austen's posthumous hold on the Victorian imagination; but that response is not completely removed from the more familiar memories that Tennyson would have read in the 'Biographical Notice', even before he came to the story of Louisa Musgrove at the Cobb. Both Tennyson and the writer of the 'Biographical Notice' had places in their

hearts for Jane Austen; even without any personal knowledge of the flesh-and-
blood author, Tennyson forged an imaginative relationship with her works by
cherishing that precise location, 'the steps from which Louisa Musgrove fell' –
recalling as he did so the habits of Anne Elliot in the novel he so admired:

> no sooner had such an end been reached, than Anne, who had been
> a most attentive listener to the whole, left the room, to seek the
> comfort of cool air for her flushed cheeks; and as she walked along a
> favourite grove, said, with a gentle sigh, "a few months more, and
> *he*, perhaps may be walking here."[10]

At the most basic level, it is neither strange nor insignificant that places in
the heart should be given to places on the map. Human events take place in
space and time; they possess that quality which phenomenologists, following
Hegel, have termed *Dasein* or 'being in the world'. Therefore, since experience is embodied, one might reasonably expect those embodiments to have
some bearing on how people see things to matter in their lives. The spatial
and temporal placing of events can comfort or torture us with the knowledge
of what happened where and when, ranging from the intensely private (the
first kiss) to the catastrophically public ('Where were you when Princess Diana
died?'), and many habitual observances, whether rules of thumb or Orders of
Service, depend on there being a time and place for everything. In my discussion of Austen's juvenilia, I pointed out that fictional narrative itself is a
matter of space as well as time – a circumstance from which Austen, like
Sterne before her, draws much comic strength. As well as playing literally off
the book as a visual and material object, novelists can compose space in other,
more metaphorical ways. Narrative, in its differential relationship to story,
engages its readers in a form of parallax movement, and *style indirect libre*, inso-
far as it tries to depict its subjects from inside and outside at once, implies a
three-dimensional perspective. Genette offers a perceptive summary of the
pervasive spatial metaphors in criticism's descriptive languages:

> il existe entre les catégories du langage et celles de l'étendue une
> sorte d'affinité, qui fait que de tous temps les hommes ont emprunté
> au vocabulaire spatial des termes destinés aux applications les plus
> diverses [...][11]

> There is a kind of affinity between the categories of language and
> those of space, with the result that people have borrowed terms
> from the vocabulary of space which they have then applied in the
> most diverse contexts [...]

Aujourd'hui la littérature – la pensée – ne se dit plus qu'en termes de distance, d'horizon, d'univers, de paysage, de lieu, de site, de chemins et de demeure: figures naïves, mais caractéristiques, figures par excellence, où le langage *s'espace* afin que l'espace, en lui, devenu langage, se parle et s'écrive.[12]

Nowadays, literature – thought itself – can only speak of itself in terms of distance, universe, landscape, place, location, site, paths and habitation: naïve but typical rhetorical figures, in which language *spatializes itself,* in order that space might itself become language, might speak and write itself.

Despite the brilliance of Genette's insight here, he still suggests this 'spatializ-ation' as primarily a modern characteristic ('Aujourd'hui'), which may not entirely fit the evidence. The increasing 'technologizing of the word' in the nineteenth and twentieth centuries clearly rendered literature more spatially self-conscious;[13] but Richardson, Sterne and Austen knew, too, how far value – whether economic or psychological – depended on location.

Things would, however, be tediously convenient if the associations of meaning with place were always readily and exactly comparable. One relief for fallible humans is that habit allows them to take certain gestures and situa-tions for granted; but this does not imply that every time and place carries an accessible, detachable baggage of significance for anyone who comes along. As Austen's writing demonstrates so extensively, the same ambiguities which render conventional certainties desirable may also prevent them from work-ing in practice. A world in which the significance of every situation were to be completely measurable in advance would take to ludicrous extremes a men-tality which was gaining a particular ascendancy in Austen's lifetime, and has continued to expand apace ever since – the cult of existential travel. The modern aesthetics of sightseeing travel have their roots firmly in the growth of 'picturesque' tourism that began towards the end of the eighteenth century; in both old and new forms, the fundamental premise is that one can imbibe and collect the essential aura of the places one visits, often as a cumulative index of one's own worth or sensitivity. Travel may broaden the mind, but an activity which sets so much store by the aggregate weight of experience always risks declining into a kind of commodity-fetishism, something more akin to the modern hobbies of trainspotting or stamp collecting. In this chapter, I shall explore how Austen's treatments of space and time in works like *The Watsons, Mansfield Park, Persuasion* and *Sanditon* show a complex understanding of the value of location, whilst sending up many cherished popular beliefs about the topic, at all levels – from broad matters of genre and literary allusion to the smallest architectonics of her narrative. One of the catchphrases of late twentieth-century existential tourism saw travelling as a means of 'finding oneself'; Jane Austen had to 'find herself' in the world in which she found herself.

For all its good intentions, there had been a distinctive shift in the cult of the picturesque by Austen's time. A genre which had aimed to provide its readers with a frame for their imaginations had increasingly to deal with a perverse, but not unpredictable consequence: that some of those readers were now paying more attention to the qualities of the frame than to anything portrayed therein. William Gilpin, whose works did more than any other writers' to popularize picturesque tourism in late eighteenth-century Britain, foresaw (and tried to forestall) potential accusations of artifice in the preface to his *Observations* on Cumberland and Westmorland from 1786:

> The ground indeed, which the author hath taken, that of examining landscape by the *rules of picturesque beauty*, seems rather a deviation from *nature* to *art*. Yet, in fact, it is not so: for the *rules of picturesque beauty*, we know, are drawn from *nature*: so that to examine the face of nature by these rules, is no more than to examine nature by her own most beautiful exertions. Thus Shakespear:
> ⸻There is an art,
> Which does mend Nature – change it rather: but
> That art itself is Nature ⸻[14]

Gilpin's attempt to naturalize art taps into a tradition that runs back through various familiar Augustan versions of the 'argument from design' and beyond – the basic premise being that the rules of art are, at root, also products of the same nature that produced the landscape. The cast of Gilpin's language plays off the deist metaphors of the landscape as bodily lineament ('the face of nature'), subtly assimilates matters of fact to terms of art ('drawn from *nature*' suggests that the rules of art are both derived from nature, and a faithful artistic depiction of them, as one might say 'drawn from life'), and even manages a little 'improvement' of its own. There is a certain irony in Gilpin's quoting Polixenes' defence of the 'art/ Which does mend Nature – change it rather' to justify his own practice, since his own way with Shakespeare's lines does much the same thing. By silently changing 'The art itself is Nature' into 'That art itself is Nature', Gilpin himself 'mends' Shakespeare's original, the more emphatic 'That' of his misquotation once again highlighting the 'art' at Nature's expense.

Gilpin's hopes were understandable ones, and it is hard to overestimate the influence in the period of his guides to the Wye Valley and the Lakes. His insistence on the possibility – even the necessity – of imaginative licence with regard to landscape, influences a variety of literary works, although it is a licence which, in its original context, he grants primarily to pictorial art:

> he who works *from imagination* — that is, he who culls from nature the most beautiful parts of her productions — a *distance* here; and there a *fore-ground* — combines them artificially; and removing every thing offensive, admits only such parts, as are *congruous*, and *beautiful*; will in all probability, make a much better landscape, than he who takes all as it comes; and without selecting beauties, copies only what he sees presented in each particular scene.[15]

However, by becoming structural templates, defining not just the order in which their readers visited the 'sights', but how they viewed them once there, Gilpin's Tours had other potentially less healthy effects. As early as 1802, Charles Lamb remarked in passing on some of them, as he related his own travels among the Lakes and the Lake Poets:

> So we have seen Keswick, Grasmere, Ambleside, Ulswater (where the Clarksons live) and a place at the other end of Ulswater, I forget the name, to which we travelled on a very sultry day over the middle of Helvellyn. – We h[a]ve clambered up to the top of Skiddaw, & I have waded up the bed of Lodore. In fine I have satisfied myself, that there is such a thing as that, which tourists call *romantic*, which I very much suspected before: they make such a spluttering about it, and toss their splendid epithets around them, till they give as dim a light, as four oClock next morning the Lamps do after an illumination. Mary was excessively tired, when she got about half way up Skiddaw, but we came to a cold rill (than which nothing can be imagined more cold, running over cold stones) & with the reinforcemt. of a draught of cold water, she surmounted it most manfully. – O its fine black head & the bleak air a top of it, with a prospect of mountains all about & about, making you giddy, & then Scotland afar off & all the border countries so famous in song & ballad –. It was a day that will stand out, like a mountain, I am sure, in my life.[16]

The humour and zest of Lamb's account derive in part from his switching, almost without warning, between his genuine delight in the landscape and his sharply sarcastic feeling for what he sees picturesque tourism to be imposing upon it. Not only does he tilt at the tourists' 'spluttering' and 'splendid

epithets', but he also deliberately unpicks the tidying and 'improving' effects
of picturesque description, as conventional terms of art are brought into
uncomfortable, ironic contact with some of the circumstances they seek elsewhere to smooth over, or exclude. The 'cold rill' which refreshes Mary Lamb
may sound picturesque in isolation, but Lamb's insistent repetition ('nothing
can be imagined more cold', 'cold stones', 'cold water') renders the water's
temperature unmissably literal, as if his whole letter has caught a chill from it;
likewise, the precision with which he kills his own metaphor ('It was a day that
will stand out, like a mountain'), insists on the sheer workaday bulk of the
scene he views, and the 'prospect of mountains all about & about' the top of
Skiddaw is also allowed to reach its logical, indecorous conclusion ('making
you giddy'). For all his avowed metropolitan urbanity, Lamb is suitably
impressed by Skiddaw ('Still Skiddaw is a fine Creature',[17] he concedes later
in the same letter), whilst refusing wholly to abandon himself to what he could
already distinguish as the formulaic rhapsodies of picturesque tourism. By the
1810s, such rhapsodies had crystallized from formula into cliché. Malcolm
Andrews has argued of picturesque travellers, '[t]here is something of the big-
game hunter in these tourists, boasting of their encounters with savage land-
scapes, "capturing" wild scenes, and "fixing" them as pictorial trophies in
order to sell them or hang them up in frames on their drawing-room walls';[18]
this acquisitiveness, implicit in Gilpin's silent appropriation of *The Winter's
Tale*, became more self-conscious in the early nineteenth century, an impulse
caught precisely in a work with which Austen was familiar[19] – William
Combe's immensely popular verse skit, *The Tour of Doctor Syntax, in Search of the
Picturesque*:

> "Your sport, my Lord, I cannot take,
> "For I must go and hunt a lake;
> "And while you chase the flying deer,
> "I must fly off to *Windermere*.
> "'Stead of hallooing to a fox,
> "I must catch echoes from the rocks.
> "With curious eye and active scent,
> "I on the *picturesque* am bent.
> "This is my game; I must pursue it,
> "And make it where I cannot view it.[20]

Doctor Syntax, Combe's quixotic parson, is brazenly untroubled by any
illusions about the aesthetic worth of his picturesque tour of Gilpin country:

> "I'll ride and *write*, and *sketch* and *print*,
> "And thus create a real mint;

> "I'll *prose* it here, I'll *verse* it there,
> " And *picturesque* it ev'ry where.[21]

> "For tho' your wisdom may decry it,
> "The simple folk will surely buy it.
> "I will allow it is but trash,
> "But then it furnishes the cash."[22]

The picturesque desires to 'touch up' and silently to change the landscape ('And make it where I cannot view it') are viciously exaggerated in Combe's doggerel, whose rhymes depict those desires as debased forms of commercial alchemy: Doctor Syntax's 'trash' is transfigured miraculously into 'cash'. Like so many other significant rhymes in literary history, the collision which Combe arranges between 'trash' and 'cash' takes a cultural temperature, bringing two qualities connected more diffusely in the world at large into a direct spatial and acoustic parallel, as it witnesses the processing of landscape into a readily consumable commodity. In *Sanditon*, Austen's last, unfinished fiction, places and names similarly become so vulnerable to commercial exploitation that 'spirit of the place' could almost be the name of a proprietary medicine. Mr Parker, the presiding commercial genius of Sanditon, has, for instance, few qualms about turning the important place names of recent history into 'heritage brands':

> when we reach Trafalgar House—which by the bye, I almost wish I had not named Trafalgar—for Waterloo is more the thing now. However, Waterloo is in reserve—& if we have encouragement enough this year for a little Crescent to be ventured on—(as I trust we shall) then, we shall be able to call it Waterloo Crescent—& the name joined to the form of the Building, which always takes, will give us the command of Lodgers.[23]

The picturesque was only one of many areas of early nineteenth-century experience to be affected, often problematically, by an interest in placing and position. As I have discussed in Chapter 2, much of *Pride and Prejudice* reads like a primer for reading the significance of social and amatory gestures – only, in this case, it is a primer where many of the entries and their definitions have been transposed, rendering the whole interpretative process that much more unpredictable. Likewise, as the focus in linguistic study shifted in the eighteenth century from semantic correspondence to grammatical and performative functions, so writers came to pay more attention to the fact that rhetoric in practice is often a matter for the eye as well as the ear. In *Polite*

Conversation, Swift's enthusiast Wagstaff suggests that 'there is hardly a polite Sentence in the following Dialogues, which doth not absolutely require some peculiar graceful Motion in the Eyes, or Nose, or Mouth, or Forehead, or Chin; or suitable Toss of the Head, with certain Offices assigned to each Hand'.[24] Tristram Shandy, that great fictional encyclopaedist of eighteenth-century rhetorical figures, pays his own back-handed tribute to this interest, tracing it nostalgically back to the Ancients:

> It is a singular stroke of eloquence (at least it was so, when elo-
> quence flourished at Athens and Rome, and would be so now, did
> orators wear mantles) not to mention the name of a thing, when you
> had the thing about you, *in petto*, ready to produce, pop, in the place
> you want it. A scar, an axe, a sword, a pinked doublet, a rusty hel-
> met, a pound and a half of pot-ashes in an urn, or a three-halfpenny
> pickle pot,—but above all, a tender infant royally accoutred.[25]

In addition, he provides his own absurd modern version, as he describes Trim's 'meaningful' bodily attitude while he reads the sermon on Conscience:

> He stood before them with his body swayed, and bent forwards just
> so far, as to make an angle of 85 degrees and a half upon the plain
> of the horizon;—which sound orators, to whom I address this,
> know very well, to be the true persuasive angle of incidence;—in
> any other angle you may talk and preach;—'tis certain;—and it is
> done every day;—but with what effect,—I leave the world to
> judge![26]

Such accounts are not solely the province of eighteenth-century literature; for example, Gilbert Austin's rhetorical treatise *Chironomia* (1806), tries to sum-marize the history of '[t]he management of the voice, the expression of the countenance, and the gesture of the head, the body, and the limbs', which 'constitute the external part of oratory'.[27] Austin offers some suggestive analy-ses, stressing how gestures often form part of the context determining what his twentieth-century namesake John was to call illocutionary force. 'A slight movement of the head,' he notes, 'a look of the eye, a turn of hand, a judicious pause or interruption of gesture, or a change of position in the feet often illu-minates the meaning of a passage, and sends it full of light and warmth into the understanding'.[28] *Chironomia*, however, makes larger claims, which are more difficult to sustain with confidence: in laying out his '*New Method*' for the notation of meaningful gestures, Austin is too sanguine about the precision of those meanings. He even goes so far as to provide a comprehensive set of diagrams, illustrating the arrangements of arms, eyes, and body which correspond to particular emotional states:

> Fig. 83. In the appeal to conscience, the right is laid on the breast, the left drops unmoved, the eyes are fixed upon the person addressed; sometimes both hands press the breast.[29]

One need only compare and contrast Lady Susan's posturing ('whom I take on my lap & sigh over for his dear Uncle's sake') or Henry Tilney's 'forming his features into a set smile' to sense what Austin is missing: that the verbal and gestural languages of sincerity are as open to scheming or parody as any others; and that the overall effect of speech may owe as much to reticence, awkwardness and misprision as it does to '[t]he stroke of the gesture [...] on the accented syllable of the emphatical word'.[30]

What Jane Austen, Combe and Wordsworth variously noticed about the cult of the picturesque was that its ostensibly primary object of interest – the landscape – could often be relegated to a secondary role, as a mere pretext for the rituals of aesthetic reception. Travellers would follow in the predetermined footsteps of Gilpin or Thomas Gray, position themselves at the prescribed 'stations', and take in the views – often looking away from the landscape itself towards its reflection, seeing in the Claude Glass, darkly. One way in which Wordsworth's poetry came to resist the demands of static 'prospect' was in its insistence on mobile sight lines within the landscape. According to Hazlitt's account in 'My First Acquaintance with Poets', even the composition of the Lake Poets' work was inseparable from motion: 'Coleridge has told me,' Hazlitt writes, 'that he himself liked to compose in walking over uneven ground, or breaking through the straggling branches of a copse-wood; whereas Wordsworth always wrote (if he could) walking up and down a straight gravel-walk, or in some spot where the continuity of his verse met with no collateral interruption'.[31] Whether literally or metaphorically, walking and pacing pervade Wordsworth's poetry and criticism, from Lucy's dwelling 'amongst the untrodden ways' to the poet's own thoughts on the timing and significance of metrical 'footfalls' in verse; and some of his most accomplished poetry implicitly challenges the prescriptions of picturesque viewing by moving the eye of the beholder more actively around, thereby changing the view itself.

Hugh Sykes Davies has suggested of Wordsworth that '[t]here is a real sense in which most of his greatest poetry is a continued, and ever varied attempt to express the positive side of his criticism of the 'picturesque' – to show more fully what it omitted, how it distorted, by putting in its place a much deeper feeling for Nature and its relation with human perception'.[32] In works such as *The Prelude*, this is achieved through shifts of perspective, and parallax movement, most notably in the 'stolen boat' sequence of Book First. Wordsworth recalls his younger self, rowing away from the shore he is viewing:

> A rocky steep uprose
> Above the cavern of the willow-tree,
> And now, as suited one who proudly rowed
> With his best skill, I fixed a steady view
> Upon the top of that same craggy ridge,
> The bound of the horizon – for behind
> Was nothing but the stars and the grey sky.
> She was an elfin pinnace; lustily
> I dipped my oars into the silent lake,
> And as I rose upon the stroke my boat
> Went heaving through the water like a swan –
> When from behind that craggy steep, till then
> The bound of the horizon, a huge cliff,
> As if with voluntary power instinct,
> Upreared its head. I struck, and struck again,
> And, growing still in stature, the huge cliff
> Rose up between me and the stars, and still
> With measured motion, like a living thing
> Strode after me.[33]

Visual parallax and foreshortening take on moral dimensions in the movement of Wordsworth's lines: the young man initially imagines himself in control, as monarch of all he surveys, a feeling reinforced by his recourse to more conventional picturesque viewing ('a steady view', 'The bound of the horizon'). But the further he rows, the more his prospect is shown to have been a subjective, vulnerable one ('till then/ The bound of the horizon'), as the animistic cliff seems to chase him across the water. In this episode, as in many other parts of *The Prelude*, the deeper psychological resonances of the landscape are discovered in its resisting or moving beyond the *a priori* templates of picturesque aesthetics, from 'rules of mimic art'[34] towards the 'prospect in my mind'.[35] It is not coincidental that Wordsworth conveys his disillusionment with the picturesque in much the same manner as he regrets some of the Godwinian excesses of his youth ('the philosophy/ That promised to abstract the hopes of man/ Out of his feelings'[36]): in both instances, he feels that practice has been damagingly superseded by general precept.

Although she was politically unsympathetic to Godwinism, Austen's only surviving reference to Godwin in her own letters is more concerned with matters of fashion, as she describes Mr Pickford, a visitor to Bath in 1801; '*He is as raffish in his appearance,*' she writes, 'as I would wish every Disciple of Godwin to be'.[37] Her double-edged treatment of picturesque aesthetics, however, has affinities with Wordsworth, as it does with Combe: whether observing the decline of polite manners into mannerisms, the clichés of sentimental and Gothic 'novel slang', or the taste for picturesque touring and 'improvement', Austen pinpoints and resists the commodification of experience. Both in her representations of physical spaces, and in the spatial and temporal structures of her narratives, her writing invests much thought and feeling in 'location'; but as the rest of this chapter will show, she remains ever alert to the thought that 'the spirit of the place' may not be where we expect to find it.

Austen had personal reasons to be particularly attuned to what Oliver Sacks has described as a '*linguistic* use of space',[38] as witnessed by a remark in her letter to Cassandra from 28 December 1808:

> We spent friday Even^g with our friends at the Boarding House, & our curiosity was gratified by the sight of their fellow-inmates, Mrs Drew & Miss Hook, Mr Wynne & Mr Fitzhugh, the latter is brother to Mrs Lance, & very much the Gentleman. He has lived in that House more than twenty years, & poor Man, is so totally deaf, that they say he c^d not hear a Cannon, were it fired close to him; having no cannon on hand to make the experiment, I took it for granted, & talked to him a little with my fingers, which was funny enough. — I recommended him to read Corinna.[39]

Sign language of any description was not among the standard set of female accomplishments at the time, so it would be reasonable to assume that 'finger-spelling' – which is what Austen seems to have been doing here – was a skill she picked up in order to communicate with her brother George. A gestural alphabet is a particularly (and necessarily) stylized form of that larger repertoire of social theatre, of which Austen makes so much in her fiction; but it depends on a direct symbolic correspondence between denotation and connotation, in ways about which Austen's fictional treatments of space are more wary. Places and objects in the novels are often significant, even as Austen remains deliberately tight-lipped about what those precise significances are. In the *Memoir*, James Edward Austen-Leigh is characteristically circumspect in recording Mr Austen's decision to move from Steventon Rectory in 1800, an event which clearly had an effect on the rector's younger daughter: 'The loss of the first home,' writes Austen-Leigh, 'is generally a great grief to young persons of strong feeling and lively imagination; and Jane was exceedingly unhappy when she was told that her father, now seventy years of age, had determined to resign his duties to his eldest son, who was to be his successor in the Rectory of Steventon, and to remove with his wife and daughters to Bath'.[40] By 1913, Austen-Leigh's son and grandson had worked this up into the more dramatic account: 'Tradition says that [...] the shock of the intelligence was so great to Jane that she fainted away'.[41] The latter version may make for a more immediately racy piece of literary biography, but it is at best conjecture and rumour ('Tradition says'); moreover, Austen's complex and wide-ranging investment of feeling in places is shrunk into symbolic reflex by the image of her fainting at the loss of her home – whether or not the story is true. David Nokes has questioned the ease with which this version of the story has gained currency: 'Austen's biographers have been happy to repeat a story which accords so well with their own views of how she *ought* to have reacted. Imagine her anguish! [...] There is a tendency for them to wax indignant on her behalf at such a forced removal'.[42] However, he does not point out that while the apocryphal fainting fit may accord with some biographers' vision of 'dear Aunt Jane' – since it conflates literary and pathological 'sensitivity' – it does not accord with much of Austen's own fictional practice. For instance, modern readers would not be able imaginatively to follow Tennyson to 'the steps from which Louisa Musgrove fell' if the resonances of literary moments yielded themselves up with the ease of a swoon. Austen's novels understand and demonstrate writing's capacity to *respond* to events as well as reacting to them; as words have their being within a language in which they can pick up the most unpredictable associations, so fiction's events, its choices, accidents and 'Acts of God', carry with them the unpredictable weight of the larger world of embodiment around them. Fictional happenings can also imply non-events, what Eliot called 'the passage we did not take/ Towards the door we never opened';[43] and the most seemingly ephemeral, throwaway moments can, within the larger structures of Austen's narratives, turn out to be the most important.

A major contributory factor to this technique is Austen's relative abstemiousness in descriptive narration; as I discussed in Chapter 2, her major novels are nowhere near as physically and topographically precise as the works of Richardson or Radcliffe. Nikolaus Pevsner, one of the twentieth century's leading authorities on British architecture, has argued that 'she is without exception vague, when it comes to describing buildings',[44] and one would search the mature novels in vain for many extended architectural passages. But 'describing buildings' is not the only way in which narrative can be architectural, for what Austen's fiction may lack in cornices, bay-windows, and flying buttresses, it makes up for in its intellectual physique – in the pitches and contours of its syntax, and in the architectonics of its plots. Neither, in fact, is she 'without exception vague' in such matters; one could, for example, speculate about the counterfactual maturity Austen might have come to, had she followed the example of her own abandoned fragment, composed between 1804 and 1805, the work which James Edward Austen-Leigh called *The Watsons*. As with *Lady Susan*, the fragment's position in time between the juvenilia and the published novels makes it an object of particular historical interest; like *Lady Susan*, however, it is also fascinating for the light it sheds on the development of Austen's narrative style – not least because it challenges the idea of that development as a smooth, evolutionary progress. As I shall go on to explore in this chapter, *Mansfield Park* may have more in common with *Northanger Abbey* than with this later fragment. *The Watsons* is at once a source of and a possible alternative path for Austen's mature fiction – a strange, inchoate cluster of recognizably Austenian motifs and cadences that never exist in quite the same relations before or afterwards. A reader coming to *The Watsons* from the major novels will recognize many protoypes: the heroine, Emma Watson, has a father who 'was sickly & had lost his wife',[45] looking forward to another Emma W. a decade later; Mrs Edwardes' 'reserved air, & a great deal of formal Civility'[46] anticipate *Pride and Prejudice*; and the name 'Musgrave' eventually begets the Musgroves of *Persuasion*. The narrative manner of *The Watsons*, in contrast, is oddly distinctive; Nokes has gone as far as to suggest that Austen's abandoning the work was less to do with her father's death in 1805 than with 'the hard, cynical tone of the piece' which 'deterred her from ever returning to it'.[47] It is not only the tone of the piece that is hard: it is also full of descriptive hardness. Even by Austen's standards, *The Watsons* is particularly unsparing in its observations of the harsher economic motives and realities of the country gentry, who inhabit a world in which all the physical and psychological surfaces of domestic life are likewise exposed and displayed, from Emma Watson's skin ('very brown, but clear, smooth and glowing'[48]) to the dimensions of the ballroom in 'the Town of D. in Surry':

> The cold & empty appearance of the Room & the demure air of the small cluster of Females at one end of it began soon to give way; the inspiriting sound of other Carriages was heard, & continual accessions of portly Chaperons, & strings of smartly-dressed girls were received, with now & then a fresh gentleman straggler, who if not enough in Love to station himself near any fair Creature seemed glad to escape into the Card-room.[49]

Austen's narrative is unusually attentive to details here, but the parallel rhythms in which it links those details together ('inspiriting sound of other Carriages', 'accessions of portly Chaperons', 'strings of smartly-dressed girls'), look back to the absurd antitheses of *Love and Freindship*, and betray the kind of weary, dazed quality that often appears in Austen's personal descriptions of comparable social events to her sister. This is the flip side of that provincial mundanity which Austen later depicts in Highbury, another Surrey location; if Emma Woodhouse's experience of her environment is one of 'endlessly swimming through gruel' (in Everett's phrase), Emma Watson's is one of continually bumping into and rubbing up against hard, unforgiving surfaces.

Austen turns the vocabulary of picturesque space to more tawdry and claustrophobic effect here: in addition to the above reference to the 'gentleman straggler [...] not enough in Love to station himself near any fair Creature', Emma Watson finds her own movements checked by social and spatial expectations:

> Miss E. gave her a caution to be at hand, in a manner which convinced her of M^{rs} E's holding it very important to have them both close to her when she moved into the Tearoom; & Emma was accordingly on the alert to gain her proper station. It was always the pleasure of the company to have a little bustle & croud when they thus adjourned for refreshment;— the Tearoom was a small room within the Cardroom, & in passing thro' the latter, where the passage was straightened by Tables, Mrs E. & her party were for a few moments hemmed in.[50]

Joseph A Kestner has argued that '[i]f one explores the inner structure of certain novels, it becomes evident that geometric spatiality is a major form of their construction', and cited the example of Madame de la Fayette's *Princesse de Clèves*, in which 'the use of dances, points forming geometric patterns, symbolizes the complex relationship among the Princess, her husband, and the Duc de Nemours'.[51] *The Watsons* makes its own use of significant, even ritualized movements through space, but these references to 'stations', for example, recast those bearings by which picturesque tourists oriented themselves as both confined and confining. Not only are the nested rooms uncomfortably cramped ('the Tearoom was a small room within the Cardroom [...] M^{rs}. E. & her party were for a few moments hemmed in') but Austen offers the extraordinary observation that this is in fact a deliberate contrivance on the Edwardes' part ('It was always the pleasure of the company to have a little bustle & croud'). Like James after her, Austen was a poet of domestic pathology, and moments like this in *The Watsons* betray an uncanny insight into characters' mental inhabiting of three-dimensional physical space, and into the various uses of that quality which Adam Phillips has recently explored under the heading of 'clutter':

Clutter, as chaotic accumulation, could be both a thwarting and a source of revelation. One might think of the difference as being two different kinds of unconscious work, the good mess and the bad mess – the mess that can be used, and the mess that stultifies. It may be a more productive distinction than the one between clutter and pattern.[52]

That said, it is not so easy in Austen's fragment to draw the line between 'the good mess and the bad mess', partly because *The Watsons* narrates almost everything at the same pitch of descriptive intensity: that 'hardness' which Nokes attributes to the work emerges in its absence of contour, and if everything in a narrative is equally meaningful, one could argue that nothing is. Although it may hint at much of what is to follow in Austen's fiction, *The Watsons* cannot be described as the palette from which she drew. To begin with, the metaphor of the artist's palette to describe a writer's early work is limited in its application; a palette holds single tints, which the artist then combines in more complex mixtures, an analogy which only holds if one imagines writers' developments as evolutionary progressions. This would be applicable to Richardson, whose writing does become progressively more dense in its descriptions from *Pamela* to *Grandison*; for Austen, however, as for the likes of Flaubert and Beckett after her, it is often more a matter of learning which layers she can productively scrape off her 'little bit (two inches wide) of ivory'. In *The Watsons*, the intensity of detail with which Austen renders physical space produces, like *Lady Susan*, a 'single effect' – in this case, one of social, sexual and economic claustrophobia; in the major novels of the 1810s, she learns selectively to reapply some of these techniques, in order further to explore the double nature of what fiction can offer – the reassurance of pattern and design, sharing the same space with contingencies that cannot be reduced to schemes of meaning, that are just *there*. To borrow Phillips's remarks on clutter, Austen's mature fiction also 'counsels us to be wary of the pre-emptive imposition of pattern, of the compulsive sanity of reassuring recognitions'.[53] In a period when the resonances of place and time were often becoming aesthetically regimented in advance, these novels reserve the right creatively to displace such expectations. Hegel, in his *Philosophy of Right*, was of the opinion that the social life of the family was the first step in the synthesis of 'ethical life':

> Thus, the disposition [...] is to have self-consciousness of one's individuality *within this unity* as essentiality which has being in and for itself, so that one is present in it not as an independent person but as a *member*.[54]

Mansfield Park, *Persuasion* and *Sanditon* tell another truth, no less important in its way: that we can also learn the facts of our social nature by tripping over the furniture, or over our relatives.

The Gate, the Ha-ha and the Sofa: Mansfield Park

> Common to the original sense of the word is the idea of bounded-ness, demarcation, the drawing of lines to mark off and order. This easily extends to the chart or diagram of the demarcated area, which in turn modulates to the outline of the literary work. From the organized space, plot becomes the organizing line, demarcating and diagramming that which was previously undifferentiated. We might think here of the geometrical expression, plotting points, or curves, on a graph by means of coordinates, as a way of locating something, perhaps oneself.
>
> Peter Brooks[55]

> I live chiefly on the sofa, but am allowed to walk from one room to another.
>
> Jane Austen to (?) Frances Tilson, (?) 28/29 May 1817[56]

From its earliest nineteenth-century readers to its most famous twentieth-century critics, *Mansfield Park* has prompted telling overlaps of critical reaction and vocabulary – many of which claim to discern a different focus in this novel compared to the other major works. It is, for example, the only one of the longer novels which Austen herself named after a place;[57] *Northanger Abbey* was titled after her death by James and Cassandra Austen, and as such, the title *Mansfield Park* could be seen as pointing towards something distinct from the interlinked humours and character traits in the titles of its immediate predecessors, *Sense and Sensibility* and *Pride and Prejudice*. Collecting the opinions of her family and friends about her latest work, Austen must have been both amused and frustrated by the tone of disappointed expectation which sounded repeatedly amid the admiring notices: Edward Austen Knight thought it 'Not so clever as P. & P.'; Anna Lefroy 'liked it better than P. & P.' but 'could not bear Fanny'; Mrs Austen '[t]hought Fanny insipid'; Austen's distant relative Fanny Cage 'did not much like it – not to be compared to P. & P. – nothing interesting in the Characters – language poor. – Characters natural & well supported – Improved as it went on. –'[58]. In the 1950s, Lionel Trilling wrote the single most famous twentieth-century essay on *Mansfield Park*, one which bears comparison with the reactions of those earliest readers:

Perhaps no other work of genius has ever spoken, or seemed to speak, so insistently for cautiousness and constraint, even for dullness. No other great novel has so anxiously asserted the need to find security, to establish, in fixity and enclosure, a refuge from the dangers of openness and chance.

There is scarcely one of our modern pieties that it does not offend [...] It scandalizes the modern assumptions about social relations, about virtue, about religion, sex, and art. Most troubling of all is its preference for rest over motion [...] Yet *Mansfield Park* is a great novel, its greatness being commensurate with its power to offend.[59]

Trilling's words are not only greatly influential but representative of a broad consensus of opinion that is not confined to the middle of the last century – the fundamental point of agreement being that *Mansfield Park* is, in some way that is hard to define precisely, 'not quite like the others' (indeed, as Austen herself pointed out to John Murray, even Walter Scott managed to review *Emma* without mentioning its immediate predecessor).[60] It is open to question whether *our* 'modern pieties' are exactly the same as Trilling's, or whether – in 1950s America, after all – everyone felt quite as liberated as he did about 'religion, sex, and art'; nevertheless, that 'troubling' persists. I recall, in the late 1990s, a group of English teachers from various schools remarking to me how hard it was to 'sell' *Mansfield Park* to their students when it came back round as a set text. *Pride and Prejudice* presented no difficulties, they told me, and this was not just because of the contemporary televisual appeal of Colin Firth and Jennifer Ehle as Darcy and Elizabeth in Andrew Davies' BBC adaptation. The students' reactions to *Mansfield Park*, on the other hand, were not unlike Humberstall's initial response to the novels in 'The Janeites': "'Twasn't as if there was anythin' *to* 'em, either [...] They weren't adventurous, nor smutty, nor what you'd call even interestin".[61] What the students regretted was that *Mansfield Park* lacked not only the 'epigrammatism' of *Pride and Prejudice*, but also that novel's feeling of eventfulness: certain expectations had been frustrated.

In what follows, I shall suggest that such responses are exactly what *Mansfield Park* aims for, but that far from being a weakness in the novel, the quality which prompts these readings is its peculiar strength. For example, looking back at Trilling's remarks, one can see how he not only describes the book's power to trouble, but is troubled by it as he does so. For all his assertiveness of tone, he qualifies himself twice in the space of one sentence ('*Perhaps* no other work of genius has ever spoken, *or seemed to speak*', italics mine), and, less than a page later, makes a similar swerve when locating *Mansfield Park* in Austen's *oeuvre*: '*Mansfield Park* was published in 1814, only

one year after the publication of *Pride and Prejudice*, and no small part of its
interest derives from the fact that it *seems to* controvert everything that its predecessor tells us about life' (italics mine).[62] The subliminal exasperation which
surfaces in Trilling's repeated recourse to the language of 'seeming' ironically
pinpoints exactly what this novel achieves so well: a quality of elusiveness, a
comedy of frustrated expectations. Whatever a reader thinks *Mansfield Park* is
up to at any moment, it is all too likely to do something different – or, still
more challengingly, to do nothing at all. From the loco-descriptive associations of its title (which link it with a tradition taking in the likes of Dyer's
'Grongar Hill' and Pope's 'Windsor-Forest'), through the events of its plot, to
the spatial and temporal arrangements of those events within its narrative discourse, *Mansfield Park* is all about place and placement, or more specifically
about *displacement*, as it plays games of hermeneutic hide-and-seek with a
variety of fictional, aesthetic and social conventions. It is a great novel, its
greatness being commensurate with its power to frustrate.

This ability to defamiliarize space and time owes much to the subtly but
insistently spatial cast of language with which Austen imbues her novel. In
one of the most influential late twentieth-century readings of the novel,
Edward W Said identifies this aspect of its technique. 'After Lukacs and
Proust,' he comments, 'we have become so accustomed to thinking of the
novel's plot and structure as constituted mainly by temporality that we have
overlooked the function of space, geography and location [...] Like many
other novels, *Mansfield Park* is very precisely about a series of both small and
large dislocations and relocations in space'.[63] Fanny edges her way onto the
scene of Mansfield, finding the rooms in the house 'too large for her to move
in with ease',[64] and part of the book's own movement is encompassed by the
change between that initial reaction and her eventual excursion back to
Portsmouth – her parental, but no longer her spiritual home ('The smallness
of the house, and the thinness of the walls, brought everything so close to her,
that, added to the fatigue of her journey, and all her recent agitation, she
hardly knew how to bear it').[65] Likewise, the rhythms and diction of the
novel's final sentences not only describe, but psychologically locate, a place:

> Equally formed for domestic life, and attached to country pleasures,
> their home was the home of affection and comfort; and to complete
> the picture of good, the acquisition of Mansfield living by the death
> of Dr Grant, occurred just after they had been married long enough
> to begin to want an increase of income, and feel their distance from
> the paternal abode.
>
> On that event they removed to Mansfield, and the parsonage
> there, which under each of its two former owners, Fanny had never

been able to approach but with some painful sensation of restraint or alarm, soon grew as dear to her heart, and as thoroughly perfect in her eyes, as every thing else, within the view and patronage of Mansfield Park, had long been.[66]

In the last sentence, the long *style indirect* flinch ('which [...] alarm'), delaying the main verb 'grew' for so long that a reader runs short of imagined breath, mimes Fanny's instinctive 'sensation of restraint' – fittingly enough for a character who has so often felt herself, and been made to feel, 'in the way'. Here, however, the intercession of her feelings is finally rewarded, Austen's language bringing together the different senses and registers which have been played off against each other over the course of the novel. '[A]s dear to her heart, and as thoroughly perfect in her eyes'; 'within the view and patronage of Mansfield Park': the prose intertwines emotional affect, sensory pleasure and economic hard-headedness, so that Mansfield parsonage seems at once a just desert and a nice place to entertain friends – especially since it provides all the joys of the grounds without the expense.

   This conclusion, however, is only the last in a long series of often painful and awkward mappings of the psychological on to the spatial throughout the novel. Perhaps the most directly painful of these for Fanny is Mrs Norris's insistence that the young arrival in the household should, in all senses of the phrase, 'know her place'; it is typical of *Mansfield Park*'s comedy that Fanny's place should turn out to be at the moral centre of Mansfield, whilst Aunt Norris and Maria are cast into outer darkness, 'where, shut up together with little society, on one side no affection, on the other, no judgment, it may be reasonably supposed that their tempers became their mutual punishment'.[67] In earlier parts of the novel, though, Fanny is more at the mercy of her aunt's attempts to keep her where she wants her. The role Mrs Norris adopts, or imposes, in the organization of the theatricals is typical ('I *am* of some use I hope in preventing waste and making the most of things. There should always be one steady hand to superintend so many young ones'[68]), since she spends so much of the rest of the novel trying to be a stage manager; she even takes upon herself the task of trying psychologically to 'condition' Fanny for the subordinate, second-class existence she wishes her to have at Mansfield. It is Mrs Norris who initially travels to Northampton and 'thus regaled in the credit of being foremost to welcome her'[69] – which provides the opportunity for some characteristically pre-emptive efforts:

   Mrs Norris had been talking to her the whole way from Northampton of her wonderful good fortune, and the extra-ordinary degree of gratitude and good behaviour which it ought to

produce, and her consciousness of misery was therefore increased
by the idea of its being a wicked thing for her not to be happy.[70]

Similarly, Fanny's 'nest of comforts' in the East Room is circumscribed in
advance by her aunt's demands ('Mrs. Norris having stipulated for there
never being a fire in it on Fanny's account, was tolerably resigned to her having the use of what nobody else wanted'[71]); but much earlier in Volume I, the
Bertrams' plans to lodge Fanny with her are thwarted in an extraordinary
passage which blends dialogue, *style indirect* and narratorial sarcasm:

> "And I am quite convinced that your being with Mrs. Norris, will
> be as good for your mind, as riding has been for your health – and
> as much for your ultimate happiness, too."
> So ended their discourse, which for any very appropriate service it
> could render Fanny, might as well have been spared, for Mrs.
> Norris had not the smallest intention of taking her. It had never
> occurred to her, on the present occasion, but as a thing to be care-
> fully avoided. To prevent its being expected, she had fixed on the
> smallest habitation which could rank as genteel among the build-
> ings of Mansfield parish; the White house being only just large
> enough to receive herself and her servants, and allow a spare room
> for a friend, of which she made a very particular point;—the spare-
> rooms at the parsonage had never been wanted, but the absolute
> necessity of a spare-room for a friend was now never forgotten.[72]

As I have discussed, *Mansfield Park* is full of anticipation and expectation, but
Mrs Norris's attempts to mould the physical and psychological world in
advance, according to her own straitened specifications, take this to a pathological extreme, with more malevolent intent and effect than comparable
instances in *Pride and Prejudice* and *Emma*. 'To prevent its being expected': so
obsessive is her desire to control space that she deliberately chooses the 'small-
est habitation' possible, still keeping that needless spare room 'for a friend',
like a phantom limb.[73]

In the creation of Mrs Norris's miserly neurosis, Austen's art (as so often in
Mansfield Park) bears comparison with that of Wordsworth. Christopher Ricks
has commented sensitively on Max Beerbohm's caricature *Wordsworth in the
Lake District – at cross-purposes*. 'The pressure there,' he argues, 'of *in* is enough
to make *at* sound as if it ought to signify a location (at the crossroads, say); the
implication is that "at cross-purposes" is a haunt of Wordsworth – as indeed it
is.'[74] In this light, the moment at which Mrs Norris comes closest to explaining
herself becomes particularly suggestive:

"Lady Bertram, I do not complain. I know I cannot live as I have done, but I must retrench where I can, and learn to be a better manager. I *have been* a liberal housekeeper enough, but I shall not be ashamed to practice economy now. My situation is as much altered as my income. A great many things were due from poor Mr. Norris as clergyman of the parish, that cannot be expected from me. It is unknown how much was consumed in our kitchen by odd comers and goers. At the White house, matters must be better looked after. I *must* live within my income, or I shall be miserable; and I own it would give great satisfaction to be able to do rather more – to lay by a little at the end of the year."[75]

'I *must* live within my income': Austen's comic and stylistic *coup* here is to recognize, like Wordsworth, that a prepositional phrase can work locatively as well as simply adverbially. Mrs Norris's behaviour and language become so defined by her ruling passion that, in the context of *Mansfield Park*, 'within my income' has more of the character of a physical location, the dwelling place of Mrs Norris's psyche, than an economic condition; and her pre-emptive stage-management of Mansfield's rooms finds a corollary in the way her speech forces others prejudicially into corners, or onto the retreat. 'Me! a poor helpless, forlorn widow, unfit for any thing, my spirits quite broke down'; 'Nobody that wishes me well, I am sure, would propose it'; 'I am sure in his heart he could not wish me to do it'; 'Here am I a poor desolate widow':[76] this is prejudice in its most radical form, literally judging everything in advance. Not content with dictating others' movements, Mrs Norris's very sentences are structured in advance, with their combination of emotional blackmail and modal insistence ('I am sure'), so as to make wherever she feels herself comfortable appear as if it were the moral high ground. Indeed, when, long before her widowhood, she insists that 'I should be the last person in the world to withhold my mite upon such an occasion',[77] 'mite' suggests that she is, whether consciously or not, already casting herself as the Biblical 'poore widow' who 'threw in two mites, which make a farthing'.[78] Refashioning the absurd *idée fixe* of Mr Collins from *Pride and Prejudice* into a nasty study of the psychopathology of everyday life, Austen's creation of Mrs Norris also renders DW Harding's otherwise illuminating attempt to distinguish between 'character' and 'caricature' especially problematic. I mentioned in Chapter 1 that Collins fulfils Harding's criteria for 'caricature' ('attention is then concentrated on a few features or a small segment of the personality'[79]); Harding, however, makes a significant qualification when he comes to Mrs Norris, rightly pointing out that she may not be nearly as amusing to the other characters as she is to a reader:

When we think of Mrs Norris and Fanny Price it is inescapable
that the figure which *we* are invited to ridicule can certainly be no
laughing matter to the heroine. The technique of caricature constitutes communication on a different level between the author and
her readers. It assures us that although the heroine may be distressed and in a material sense endangered by the caricatured figure
the danger and trouble will always remain external, the threat will
not be to the values which make her the heroine.[80]

Here, as elsewhere in his critical writing, Harding is sharply attentive to the
fact that the ethical worlds of fiction, and of its readerships, are contiguous but
not identical. However, it is less certain whether the 'danger and trouble' of
Mrs Norris remains safely 'external' in either dimension; rather, she trespasses
over the borders of caricature to become a material threat to the other characters, and the miserly skeleton at the narrative's feast.

In *Pride and Prejudice*, Collins's peculiar relationship to the world around
Longbourn consists in his being the *reductio ad absurdum* of manners which are
otherwise treated in earnest by the characters, a figure whom devotion to
social observance and 'usual practice' has transposed almost entirely into
third-person caricature; Mrs Norris is oddly troubling, in different ways, to
the characters and readers of *Mansfield Park*, since her jealous guarding of
physical and psychological space is only a pathological exaggeration of a more
diffuse and pervasive concern, throughout the novel, with matters of social
and spatial division, with placings and arrangements – and events' often wilful
failure to comply with those arrangements. In her 'dull Elves' letter to
Cassandra of 29 January 1813, Austen both reviewed her 'own darling child'
Pride and Prejudice and did some research for the new novel which she was
already writing, the work in progress that was to become *Mansfield Park*. 'I am
glad to find your enquiries have ended so well,' she writes to her sister. '—If
you c[d] discover whether Northamptonshire is a Country of Hedgerows, I sh[d]
be glad again.'[81] One one level, this simply testifies to Austen's care about the
topographical accuracy of her mature fiction, the contract on which the
impossible romance location of Highbury in *Emma* is predicated; but it cannot
be coincidental that she should have been so interested in the fictional potential of 'Hedgerows': structures at once natural and artificial, which can work
as physical, economic and emotional divisions.

Mansfield Park is full of both real and illusory borders and demarcations,
between minds, bodies, social classes and physical locations, and it is not only
characters such as Mrs Norris who are subject to the attendant pres-sures.
Much in the novel, for instance, hinges on the social propriety of a particular
spatial metaphor: that of being 'out' or not. Edmund Bertram may attend

more to the spirit than the letter of such observances ('She has the age and sense of a woman, but the outs and not outs are beyond me'[82]), but he is in a minority. Mary Crawford voices the more common view of the distinction:

> "And yet in general, nothing can be more easily ascertained. The distinction is so broad. Manners as well as appearance are, generally speaking, so totally different. Till now, I could not have supposed it possible to be mistaken as to a girl's being out or not. A girl not out, has always the same sort of dress; a close bonnet for instance, looks very demure, and never says a word. You may smile – but it is so I assure you – and except that it is sometimes carried a little too far, it is all very proper [...]"[83]

but it soon transpires from Tom Bertram's experience that it may not be as broad as they would imagine or prefer it to be:

> "[...] I made my bow in form, and as Mrs. Sneyd was surrounded by men, attached myself to one of her daughters, walked by her side all the way home, and made myself as agreeable as I could; the young lady perfectly easy in her manners, and as ready to talk as to listen. I had not a suspicion that I could be doing any thing wrong. They looked just the same; both well dressed, with veils and parasols like other girls; but I afterwards found that I had been giving all my attention to the youngest, who was not *out*, and had most excessively offended the eldest. Miss Augusta ought not to have been noticed for the next six months, and Miss Sneyd, I believe, has never forgiven me."[84]

While there is a charming absurdity in Tom's incredulous 'both well dressed, with veils and parasols like other girls' (as if girls not 'out' are normally distinguishable by an extra head or similar), one has only to compare 'Miss Augusta ought not to have been noticed for the next six months' with '[t]o prevent its being expected' to see that Mrs Norris exists at only one remove from the rest of her family.

Nor is the distinction between 'out' and 'not out' the only metaphor of space which takes on a social or material force in the novel; even as he disclaims any aptitude in such matters, Edmund animates yet another one ('the outs and not outs are beyond me'). Whether or not one believes the *OED*'s citation of *Mansfield Park* as the first recorded instance of this particular usage ('(colloq.): to pass his comprehension'), it is fitting that Austen should have been among the first to employ a colloquialism which maps the discourse of mind onto that of location. Perhaps the most important instance of a word which inhabits such different dimensions is 'disposition', which runs like a *leitmotiv* through the narrative (more than a quarter of all its appearances in Austen are in this novel). Austen's applications of the word habitually span the range of Johnson's definitions ('Order; method; distribution'; 'Tendency to any act or state'; 'Temper of mind'; 'Predominant inclination'),[85] but the link implied, in *Pride and Prejudice*, between Elizabeth's softening towards Darcy and her first view of his grounds, suggests another sense:

> It was a large, well-proportioned room, handsomely fitted up. Elizabeth, after slightly surveying it, went to a window to enjoy its prospect. The hill, crowned with wood, from which they had descended, receiving increased abruptness from the distance, was a beautiful object. Every disposition of the ground was good; and she looked on the whole scene, the river, the trees scattered on its banks, and the winding of the valley, as far as she could trace it, with delight.[86]

Given the process of picturesque viewing which Elizabeth follows here, and the concentration of picturesque terms ('surveying', 'prospect', 'abruptness', 'object', 'trace it'), Austen is clearly also aware of such architectural and pictorial resonances of 'disposition' as, for example, '[t]he due arrangement of the several parts of a building, *esp.* in reference to the general design'. *Mansfield Park* is fascinated by the articulate and shifting relationships between its 'several parts' and its 'general design', but as a novel, it cannot invest in picturesque rhetoric even the quizzical attachment shown by Elizabeth Bennet. 'Romantic' poetry has a small part to play in *Persuasion*, as a means by which Benwick cultivates his grief ('how ranked the *Giaour* and *The Bride of Abydos*; and moreover, how the *Giaour* was to be pronounced'[87]), and in *Sanditon*, contemporary verse is inevitably tainted by its being part of Sir Edward Denham's shallow repertoire – although the accuracy with which Austen sends him up suggests more than a casual acquaintance with the poetry itself:

> He began, in a tone of great Taste & Feeling, to talk of the Sea & the Sea shore—& ran with Energy through all the usual Phrases employed in praise of their Sublimity, & descriptive of the *undescribable* Emotions they excite in the Mind of Sensibility.
>
> . . . .
>
> "[...] But while we are on the subject of Poetry, what think you Miss H. of Burns Lines to his Mary? – Oh! there is Pathos to madden one!—If ever there was a Man who *felt*, it was Burns.— Montgomery has all the Fire of Poetry, Wordsworth has the true soul of it –"[88]

Nevertheless, as I have been discussing, much of what Austen does with the organization (and the unpredictability) of places, parallels that great Wordsworthian work-in-progress which she was never to know – *The Prelude*. One could conjecture broadly about what Hazlitt was to immortalize in 1825 as *The Spirit of the Age*, but such a broad sweep is unnecessary. *Mansfield Park* and *The Prelude* have a major literary source in common, one in which a heart-felt affection for rural peace and the 'spirit of the place' is continually shadowed and menaced by the dangers which lurk therein – the poetry of William Cowper, where, in Donald Davie's phrase, 'Horror starts, like Charity, at home'.[89]

Following Henry Austen's account of his sisters' chosen reading in the 'Biographical Notice' ('[h]er favourite moral writers were Johnson in prose, and Cowper in verse'),[90] James Edward Austen-Leigh offered his own summary: 'Amongst her favourite writers, Johnson in prose, Crabbe in verse, and Cowper in both, stood high'.[91] The two relatives are similarly united in treating the verse writers who formed Austen's taste as if their influence were either negligible, or so obvious as not to require explanation. Henry Austen takes pains to point out his sister's debts to Richardson's *Grandison*, while maintaining that 'her taste secured her from the errors of his prolix style and tedious narrative',[92] while Austen-Leigh is relieved that 'the native sense of herself and those with whom she lived, saved her from the snare into which a sister novelist [Fanny Burney] had fallen, of imitating the grandiloquent style of Johnson'.[93] As for Austen's critical and creative engagement with poets, however, the most these accounts can offer is Austen-Leigh's passing mention of his aunt's whimsical thought that 'if she ever married at all, she could fancy being Mrs Crabbe',[94] which is of a piece with that tendency (which I mentioned in Chapter 1) of nineteenth-century writers like Charlotte Brontë and Richard Simpson, to deny or downplay 'poetry' in Austen's writing. For instance, when Austen-Leigh reproduces his aunt's longest surviving poem, 'To the Memory of Mrs Lefroy', he does so with a concessive, apologetic swerve: the lines are 'given, not for their merits as poetry, but to show how deep and lasting was the impression made by the elder friend on the mind of the younger'.[95] Admittedly, Austen's verse can hardly be argued to be a significant contribution to Romantic poetry; but this does not negate the influence of verse poets such as Cowper on the prose poetry of the novels.

Austen's letters are evidence of the currency of Cowper as a poetic touch-stone in late eighteenth-century reading practice. For instance, her letter to Cassandra of 18 December 1798 relates Mr Austen's reading Cowper aloud as a kind of poetic *digestif* for Christmas: 'We drink tea at half after six.—my father reads Cowper to us in the evening, to which I listen when I can'.[96] Likewise, the canonical force of Cowper at Steventon shows in the ease with which Austen can appropriate Cowper's 'Verses, supposed to be written by Alexander Selkirk', in a letter of September 1813: 'I am now alone in the Library, Mistress of all I survey – at least I may say so & repeat the whole poem if I like it, without offence to anybody.—'[97] Rural ease, edifying reading, 'the cups/ That cheer but not inebriate': it is as if some of the situations imagined in Cowper's masterpiece, *The Task*, have come to life, and come to shape the very manner and location in which the poem is read. One could simply interpret this as an ideological and commercial success: proof that the imaginative domesticity so often figured in Cowper's poems – and immortalized in the public image of the gentle recluse with what Austen termed his 'Tame Hares & Blank verse'[98] – had found its natural target market in the shires. One could read Cowper and thank God that one didn't live in London, 'opulent, enlarged and still/ Increasing London'.[99] However, to focus only on this aspect of Cowper's 'domesticity' would be to put too much emphasis on the famous apostrophe from *The Task* ('Domestic happiness, thou only bliss/ Of Paradise that has survived the fall!'[100]).

Perhaps as a reaction to so many idealizations of hearth and home in Victorian writing and beyond, readers can nowadays lapse with equal complacency into understanding 'domestic' and 'domesticity' as terms of derogation, denoting states or actions at best irrelevant, at worst harmfully repressive; so much so, that one might easily miss not only the force of the imperilled Horatian ideal which *The Task* upholds, but the clear-headed rigour with which Cowper's poetry documents the range of pleasures (mostly fleeting) and pains (all too lasting), which fall under the heading of the 'domestic'.[101] In Cowper, domesticity exists less as a Platonic ideal or an all-encompassing metaphor than as a field of empirical enquiry in which the finer resonances of embodied living inevitably run up against the irreducible clutter of objects in the world. Book I of *The Task*, 'The Sofa', opens with the mock-Virgilian (and mock-Miltonic) invocation:

> I sing the SOFA. I, who lately sang
> Truth, Hope, and Charity, and touch'd with awe
> The solemn chords, and with a trembling hand,
> Escap'd with pain from that advent'rous flight,
> Now seek repose upon an humbler theme;[102]

Considering the evidently ironic tone of the opening lines, a reader – particularly one familiar with 'Truth', 'Hope' and 'Charity', Cowper's more earnest Evangelical satires from 1782 – would notice some piqued pride in that stressed 'I', as if the poet/speaker can barely believe that he has taken on such a flimsy commission. However, by the end of the poem, as Cowper takes a retrospect of his original commission from his patron Lady Austen ('the Fair commands the song'[103]), it feels more as though one of the many tasks which *The Task* has set itself has been to find a poetic form in which 'the SOFA' – a conventionally silent and unsung piece of furniture – can coexist with those large Evangelical abstractions, 'Truth, Hope, and Charity'.

Martin Priestman has offered a sharp insight into how Cowper might achieve this mapping: 'a key,' he suggests, 'to much that is characteristic in Cowper can be found in a certain kind of mental geography; or perhaps, given Cowper's armchair interest in travel, topography'.[104] Cowper's verse and prose are drawn to the often painful interfaces between the mental and solidly physical worlds – and to those occasions on which events in one world have noticeable effects in the other. 'On the Death of Mrs Throckmorton's Bullfinch', for example, derives both its sick comedy and its existential chill from the failure of physical contrivances:

> Above, below, in all the house,
> (Dire foe alike of bird and mouse)
>   No cat had leave to dwell,
> And Bully's cage supported stood
> On props of smoother-shaven wood,
>   Large-built and latticed well.
>
> Well-latticed, but the grate, alas!
> Not rough with wire of steel or brass
>   For Bully's plumage sake,
> But smooth with wands from Ouse's side,
> With which, when neatly peel'd and dried
>   The swains their baskets make.[105]

The crowning irony in this poem is that the material preparations for Bully the bullfinch's comfort ('supported', 'props of smoother-shaven wood', 'Not rough with wire', 'neatly peel'd and dried') serve only to assist the 'badger-colour'd' rat, that force of destructive external nature:

> For, aided both by ear and scent
> Right to his mark the Monster went—
>   Ah, Muse! forbear to speak,
> Minute, the horrors that ensued,
> His teeth were strong, the cage was wood—
>   He left poor Bully's beak.[106]

Indeed, Cowper would never have lived to write *The Task* or this poem had he not himself been subject to the failure of material planning. *Adelphi*, the harrowing spiritual autobiography in which he recounts his mental collapse of 1763 and his subsequent Evangelical rebirth, gains some of its peculiarly disquieting force from its inability or unwillingness wholly to separate spiritual suffering from its physical circumstances. Cowper notably recounts one of his suicide attempts, with a matter-of-factness that is anything but prurient:

> My garter was made of a broad scarlet binding with a sliding buckle being sewn together at the ends; by the help of the buckle I formed a noose and fixing it about my neck, strained it so tight that I hardly left a passage for breath or the blood to circulate. The tongue of the buckle held it fast. At each corner of the bed was placed a wreath of carved work fastened by an iron pin which passed up through the midst of it. The other part of the garter therefore which made a loop I slipped over one of these and hung by it some seconds, drawing up my feet under me that they might not touch the floor. But the iron bent, the carved work slipped off, and the garter with it.[107]

The specific features of the suicide apparatus are rendered all the more unpleasant by the fact that they seem initially to be offering Cowper a gruesome parody of ordered, manufactured convenience, making dying, rather than living, easier ('by the help of the buckle', '[a]t each corner of the bed', 'fastened by an iron pin'), only for a deeper providential plan to assert itself, as it does with Bully's cage, in the collective failure of these mechanisms. As Cowper remarks later in *Adelphi*, '[t]here is that in the nature of salvation by grace when it is truly and experimentally known which prompts every person to think himself the most extraordinary instance of its power'.[108] Even poems written when his illness was in remission, such as his contributions to the *Olney Hymns* (1779), derive their force from often surprising conflations of theological and spatial perspectives. After all, the one stanza of Cowper which has passed into folk wisdom is the opening of 'Light Shining out of Darkness':

> God moves in a mysterious way,
> His wonders to perform,
> He plants his footsteps in the Sea,
> And rides upon the Storm.[109]

In *Peri Bathous*, Pope berates 'The MIXTURE OF FIGURES, which raises so many images, as to give you no image at all',[110] and judged by those standards, Cowper's hymn would not bear much examination (not that Cowper, who thought Pope's version of Homer 'bloated and tumid',[111] would have been too worried about that), but the sheer insistence of his mixed metaphors ('plants his footsteps', 'rides upon the Storm') witnesses the ubiquity of divine grace which the hymn is trying to convey; grace, it seems, knows no boundaries, including those of Augustan poetic convention.

Cowper's complex achievement in *The Task*, encompassed in Coleridge's description of 'divine Chit chat',[112] is to ground the earnest religious impulses which drive 'Truth', 'Hope' and 'Charity', within the more occasional and associationist poetic forms with which he had been experimenting in the years between 1782 and 1785. Few English poems move so wilfully and unpredictably as *The Task*, between contingent trivia and Christian eschatology, between the cracking of the 'satyric thong' and the dressing of cucumbers with steaming manure. Cowper defended his form, and its seeming disregard of symmetry and proportion, in a letter of 1788:

> Have you seen the account of five hundred celebrated Authors now living? I am one of them; but stand charged with the high crime and misdemeanor of totally neglecting method. An accusation which, if the gentleman would take the pains to read me, he would find sufficiently refuted. I am conscious at least myself of having laboured much in the arrangement of my matter, and of having given to the several parts of every book of the Task, as well as to each poem in the first volume, that sort of slight connection which poetry demands; for in poetry (except professedly of the didactic kind) a logical progression would be stiff, pedantic, and ridiculous.[113]

As *The Task* proceeds, the physical and the metaphysical collude, and contend, in surprising fashions, but for all the poem's famously quotable lines ('God made the country, and Man made the town',[114] amongst others), it is eventually impossible to abstract a single strand of resolution from the work – a fact which would support readings of *The Task* as a poem about 'process' rather than product.[115] Nowhere is this felt more keenly than in that aspect of the poem which bears most influentially on *Mansfield Park*: its equivocal treatment of rural leisure, focused through the 'SOFA' of its opening line. The shifting emotional and ethical resonances of sofas in *The Task* find echoes in Austen's own sense of the unpredictable importance of the objects in her domestic worlds. For all Cowper's talk of 'rural ease',[116] 'ease' itself is the one activity (if activity it be) about which *The Task* is most ambivalent, leading to that audible, self-exculpatory squirm in Book I:

> Oh may I live exempted (while I live
> Guiltless of pamper'd appetite obscene)
> From pangs arthritic that infest the toe
> Of libertine excess. The SOFA suits
> The gouty limb 'tis true; but gouty limb,
> Though on a SOFA, may I never feel:
> For I have loved the rural walk[117]

However, by the beginning of Book IV, the sofa has regained its positive value as an essential property of the domestic theatre, a comfortably composed nest from which news of the bustling world outside can be contemplated at leisure ('Now stir the fire, and close the shutters fast,/ Let fall the curtains, wheel the sofa round').[118] Priestman writes of this double bind in the poem: 'the ideal of ease, once attained, immediately turns into the anti-ideal of neglecting work';[119] it is one of Cowper's finest achievements to chart the means by which rural tranquillity and retirement can be their own undoing. The paradox of leisure is one which *The Task* never conclusively resolves, a creative worry which it bequeaths to *Mansfield Park*, that novel which holds it in amused respect. Like Cowper before her, Austen registers the duplicity of leisured life through the refusal of objects and places to maintain comfortably stable meanings; but, as I shall go on to discuss, she takes this treatment even further than her poetic ancestor, thereby posing larger puzzles for her readers about the fundamental nature of fictional plotting and literary symbolism. Adam Phillips notes clutter's ability to be 'both a thwarting and a source of revelation'; Austen challenges her readers to recognize both the psychological suggestiveness of inhabited space, and those instances where a door may simply be a door.

The ill-fated amateur theatricals become the abiding preoccupation of the latter part of *Mansfield Park*'s first volume, and in the words of Tony Tanner's now classic analysis, they 'explore the profound implications of "acting" and "role-playing" for the individual and society';[120] but to afford too exclusive an emphasis to these events would be to ignore the innumerable, less overt domestic *coups de théâtre* with which *Mansfield Park* is littered. For example, as the casting of *Lovers' Vows* takes place, and Fanny is prevailed upon to take part, not all the emotive stage business is happening on stage:

> "Do not urge her, madam," said Edmund. "It is not fair to urge her in this manner.— You see she does not like to act.— Let her choose for herself as well as the rest of us.— Her judgment may be quite as safely trusted.— Do not urge her any more."
> "I am not going to urge her," —replied Mrs. Norris sharply, "but I

shall think her a very obstinate, ungrateful girl, if she does not do what her aunt and cousins wish her—very ungrateful indeed, considering who and what she is."

Edmund was too angry to speak; but Miss Crawford looking for a moment with astonished eyes at Mrs. Norris, and then at Fanny, whose tears were beginning to show themselves, immediately said with some keenness, "I do not like my situation; this *place* is too hot for me"—and moved away her chair to the opposite side of the table close to Fanny, saying to her in a kind of low whisper as she placed herself, "Never mind, my dear Miss Price—this is a cross evening,—everybody is cross and teasing—but do not let us mind them;"[121]

Mary's spontaneous act of comfort and solidarity, moving her chair near to the distressed Fanny Price, is just one of the many 'dislocations and relocations in space' which Said sees at work in the novel. The rehearsals for *Lovers' Vows* are only the most stylized example of meaningful 'blocking' in the novel. Those little, unsignposted disclosures in Austen's narrative, regarding characters' movements around the furniture and the gardens, and the very movements of their eyes and bodies around their environment, can implicate further back-stories or suggest psychological unease, but they do not always do so; and even when they do, as in the incident of Mary's chair, it is not always precisely indicated quite what such implicatures are. It is clear that Mary's movement is emotionally suggestive, but less clear exactly what difference it makes to the social charge of the occasion, especially given the circumstances under which she has moved to the table in the first place, in reaction to Edmund's obduracy:

> "*That* circumstance would by no means tempt me," he replied, "for I should be sorry to make the character ridiculous by bad acting. It must be very difficult to keep Anhalt from appearing a formal, solemn lecturer; and the man who chooses the profession itself, is, perhaps, one of the last who would wish to represent it on the stage."
>
> Miss Crawford was silenced; and with some feelings of resentment and mortification, moved her chair considerably nearer the tea-table, and gave all her attention to Mrs. Norris, who was presiding there.[122]

As I discussed with reference to Darcy's glance over his shoulder in *Pride and Prejudice*, and Gilbert Austin's taxonomy of emotive postures in *Chironomia*, the rhetoric of gesture is more a matter of broad repertoires than geometric precision, and Austen is not above employing what Burke called 'judicious obscurity'[123] in such matters. Like Wordsworth ('a sense sublime/ Of something far more deeply interfused'[124]), she feels the connotative power of '*something*; that favouring *something* which every body who shuts their eyes while they look, or their understandings while they reason, feels the comfort of'.[125]

A particularly tantalizing example of significant, but not precise, movements comes in Volume I, Chapter 11. On this November evening, the Bertram household is divided spatially between the window and the piano ('Miss Crawford was standing at an open window with Edmund and Fanny looking out on a twilight scene, while the Miss Bertrams, Mr. Rushworth, and Henry Crawford, were all busy with candles at the pianoforte'[126]). The ostensible conversational topics of ordination and religious economics, as so often in Austen, offer a platform, or a screen, for other suggestions:

> "Poor William! He has met with great kindness from the chaplain
> of the Antwerp," was a tender apostrophe of Fanny's, very much to
> the purpose of her own feelings, if not of the conversation.[127]

As the conversation proceeds, the division between the window and the piano gains new and various shades of performative complexity:

> "We cannot prove the contrary, to be sure—but I wish you a bet-
> ter fate Miss Price, than to be the wife of a man whose amiableness
> depends upon his own sermons; for though he may preach himself
> into a good humour every Sunday, it will be bad enough to have
> him quarrelling about green geese from Monday morning till
> Saturday night."
> "I think the man who could often quarrel with Fanny," said
> Edmund, affectionately, "must be beyond the reach of any ser-
> mons."
> Fanny turned further into the window; and Miss Crawford had
> only time to say in a pleasant manner, "I fancy Miss Price has been
> more used to deserve praise than to hear it;" when being earnestly
> invited by the Miss Bertrams to join in a glee, she tripped off to the
> instrument, leaving Edmund looking after her in an ecstacy of
> admiration of all her many virtues, from her obliging manners
> down to her light and graceful tread.[128]

Fanny's bashful response to her cousin's compliment moves in one direction, only for Edmund's attention to be drawn the opposite way ('looking after her in an ecstacy of admiration'); but, for a while at least, Fanny has 'the pleasure of seeing him continue at the window with her, in spite of the expected glee; and of having his eyes soon turned like her's towards the scene without'.[129] While, over at the piano, the young women prepare for the three-part harmony of the glee, Fanny and Edmund take part in a little two-part harmony of their own by the window – an astronomical version of talking about the weather, in which much is taking place beneath the neutral surfaces of speech:

> "*You* taught me to think and feel on the subject, cousin."
> "I had a very apt scholar. There's Arcturus looking very bright."
> "Yes, and the bear. I wish I could see Cassiopeia."
> "We must go out on the lawn for that. Should you be afraid?"
> "Not in the least. It is a great while since we have had any star-gazing."
> "Yes, I do not know how it has happened." The glee began. "We will stay till this is finished, Fanny," said he, turning his back on the window; and as it advanced, she had the mortification of seeing him advance too, moving forward by gentle degrees towards the instrument, and when it ceased, he was close by the singers, among the most urgent in requesting to hear the glee again.[130]

Until Mary begins singing, this exchange seems to be another of those righteous chat-ups of which I wrote in Chapter 2; but as soon as he hears Mary's voice, Edmund is pulled back from the garden and the stars ('turning his back on the window'), drawn towards the piano by a genteel version of siren-song, moving in space as the glee moves through time ('as it advanced', 'seeing him advance too'). As David Selwyn has perceptively noted, even Mary's musical instrument of choice, the harp, offers possibilities for spatial flirtation: '[t]he "elegant" harp, reflecting in its graceful curves the shape and posture of the female form, becomes an extension of the body itself; and it is a body at which it is now legitimate to look closely, as the eye is drawn by the seductive sounds emanating from it'.[131]

Given this interplay between viewing, hearing and movement in *Mansfield Park*'s treatments of rooms, it is appropriate that the novel should begin to expand the usage of another spatial metaphor. At the end of the book, Austen's narrative asks of Edmund's transfer of attachment from Mary to Fanny, 'what was there to add, but that he should learn to prefer soft light eyes to sparkling dark ones'.[132] Similarly, Fanny's resistance to Sir Thomas over Crawford's suit requires her to protect her vision: she is described 'with eyes cast down',[133] 'with her eyes fixed upon one of the windows',[134] and picturing her uncle's frown 'though she dared not lift up her eyes'.[135] However, when she is called back from Portsmouth, her eyes have more authority: on the journey to Mansfield with Edmund, 'Fanny watched him with never-failing solicitude, and sometimes catching his eye, received an affectionate smile, which comforted her; but the first day's journey passed without her hearing a word from him on the subjects that were weighing him down.'[136] As with the psychological sense of 'beyond me', pinpointing watersheds in English usage can rarely be foolproof; nevertheless, the *OED* credits Austen with extending the semantic range of 'catching the eye' beyond simply denoting the way in which the eye is struck by objects or people (as one might say 'That antique mirror just caught my eye'). In *Lady Susan, Pride and Prejudice* and *Mansfield Park*, the phrase also describes those moments when characters' eyes actively meet, whether by accident or design. Yet another instance in Austen's language of the bodily and the psychological occupying the same space, 'catching the eye' offers further evidence of her distance from those context-independent packagings of location to which the 'stations' of picturesque tourism were sometimes reduced. Space in *Mansfield Park*, be it physical (as in Volume I, Chapter 11), or textual, is always psychologized space, and therefore subject to the parallax effects produced by changes of perspective; after all, it is of the first importance whose eyes are being caught, and by whom. Of the mental landscape of houses, Gaston Bachelard has remarked:

> thanks to the house, a great many of our memories are housed, and if the house is a bit elaborate, if it has a cellar and a garret, nooks and corridors, our memories have refuges that are all the more clearly delineated [...] In its countless alveoli space contains compressed time. That is what space is for.[137]

This only tells half the story, however: by being so insistently metaphorical ('countless alveoli'), Bachelard downplays a point which Austen, like Cowper before her, knew from experience, that space is also for living in, often uncomfortably. Rooms in *Mansfield Park* are inevitably rooms attached to memories and experiences, occupied by people with attitude – 'attitude' being, like 'disposition', both a turn of mind and a bodily posture – and this cannot but tell on the flexible, unpredictable ways in which they gain (or lose) significance. For instance, all the subtle social pragmatics in the novel's eleventh chapter suddenly evaporate on Edmund's retreat, leaving Fanny stuck in what is suddenly a less romantic and suggestive location: 'Fanny sighed alone at the window till scolded away by Mrs. Norris's threats of catching cold'.[138]

As much of Cowper's poetry places the spiritual sublimely or bathetically in contact with the physical, so Fanny's outbursts of righteousness are sometimes 'earthed', either by events or by Edmund. The most famous instance of such an effect is, not coincidentally, the scene which features the novel's most blatant reference to *The Task*; Fanny's reaction to the news about Sotherton's trees is understandable enough, but Austen – not above quoting from Cowper herself – is, like Edmund, amused by how ready she is with Cowperian 'soundbites':

> Fanny, who was sitting on the other side of Edmund, exactly opposite Miss Crawford, and who had been attentively listening, now looked at him, and said in a low voice,
> "Cut down an avenue! What a pity! Does not it make you think of Cowper? 'Ye fallen avenues, once more I mourn your fate unmerited.'"
> He smiled as he answered, "I am afraid the avenue stands a bad chance, Fanny."[139]

For all the novel's many notable set pieces (*Lovers' Vows*, the locked gate at Sotherton), *Mansfield Park*'s narrative texture renders it problematic to concentrate exclusively on such set pieces; even more challengingly, it raises questions as to whether its own most prominent sequences are necessarily its most important ones – which may explain some of that quality of exasperation which permeates its critical history. There is no doubt that Fanny's 'nest of comforts' in the East Room is Fanny's cocoon against her general neglect, and the more pointed antagonism of Mrs Norris. Furnished with Crabbe's *Tales* and Johnson's *Idler*, it is a space in which furniture and its emotional resonances are as one:

> The comfort of it in her hours of leisure was extreme. She could go there after any thing unpleasant below, and find immediate consolation in some pursuit, or some train of thought at hand.—Her plants, her books—of which she had been a collector, from the first hour of her commanding a shilling—her writing desk, and her works of charity and ingenuity, were all within her reach;—or if indisposed for employment, if nothing but musing would do, she could scarcely see an object in that room which had not an interesting remembrance connected with it.— Every thing was a friend, or bore her thoughts to a friend [...][140]

The strangeness of furniture's being 'a friend' (comparable to the activity of singing the sofa) reveals how the importance of objects for Fanny is an effect of her emotional investment in them – and as such, not easily or exhaustively measurable. In this light, it becomes debatable as to how far one can speak of 'symbolism' in *Mansfield Park*, and indeed in Austen's whole *oeuvre* – especially when one considers those characters who avail themselves most ostentatiously of physical symbols. DW Harding was wary of overly abstracted schemata of meaning in literature, arguing: 'In the greater part of fiction and drama the interest of the events and people in their own right comes first; we grow uneasy if we feel that they have been sought out for the purpose of conveying or illustrating a theme';[141] this follows on from Keats's suspicion of 'poetry that has a palpable design upon us—and if we do not agree, seems to put its hand in its breeches pocket'.[140] Harding pinpoints one excess of 'iconic' signi-fication in literature, but he also describes the attitude of some of Austen's characters towards objects. Henry Crawford, for one, picks up and plays with objects as if they were stage props, seeking them out 'for the purpose of con-veying or illustrating a theme':

> Mr. Crawford smiled his acquiescence, and stepping forward to Maria, said, in a voice which she only could hear, "I do not like to see Miss Bertram so near the altar."[143]

> "And for the world you would not get out without the key and with-out Mr. Rushworth's authority and protection, or I think you might with little difficulty pass around the edge of the gate, here, with my assistance; I think it might be done, if you really wished to be more at large, and could allow yourself to think it not prohibited."[144]

Alongside the amateur theatricals and the game of 'Speculation', the Sotherton altar and the locked gate are probably the most discussed 'symbols' in the novel; what is discussed less often is that these scenes are composed so as to be flip and conspicuous, to stick out as self-regarding exceptions in a novel whose larger narrative is more reticent as to what objects represent (if indeed they 'represent' anything at all), which invites a reader to imagine rela-tionships more complex and frustrating than 'If $x = 1$ then $y = 2$'. For one thing, although the locked gate may be the most visible means of division and spatial organization in Rushworth's grounds, it is not the only one; there is also the ha-ha, a feature whose very name derives from its ability to surprise: 'A boundary to a garden, pleasure-ground, or park, of such a kind as not to interrupt the view from within, and not to be seen till closely approached'.[145] Simon Varey has observed of architecture's divisions of space that 'there are other, far from illusory, boundaries that have no tangible existence';[146] within the architecture of Austen's narrative, for every suggestively locked gate there exist any number of fictional ha-has, into which characters and readers may stumble without warning.

Whether ostentatiously centre stage or hovering menacingly at the margins, placement does not automatically guarantee anything in *Mansfield Park*. Said sheds light on some important areas of the narrative, as he traces ways in which the sources of the Bertram wealth in Antigua disturb the novel's peripheries, however much they are anxiously marginalized; but his attempt to 'calibrate the signifying power of the references to Antigua'[147] is more problematic. The phrase 'calibrate the signifying power' is predicated on there being a stable exchange rate between denoted signifier and connoted resonance, when the truth of *Mansfield Park* is murkier and more contingent: it seems to turn on where you are, or who. To suggest that there is a constant currency of symbolism in the novel would be, in effect, to deny that one feature which owes most to the precedent of Cowper, namely Austen's running joke about sofas. *The Task* recognizes that the sofa is a location for both dignified *otium* and indolent sloth:

> but neither sleep
> Of lazy Nurse, who snores the sick man dead,
> Nor his who quits the box at midnight hour
> To slumber in the carriage more secure,
> Nor sleep enjoy'd by Curate in his desk,
> Nor yet the dozings of the Clerk, are sweet,
> Compar'd with the repose the SOFA yields.[148]

Cowper's poem faces this paradox (without ever resolving it), oxymoronically, by resorting to ideas such as 'instructive ease',[149] and suggesting that 'There is a pleasure in poetic pains/ Which only poets know'.[150] The duplicity of the sofa affords Austen the most wicked and disturbing joke in *Mansfield Park*: Fanny may retreat to the corners of rooms, and to the sofa, in order to feel safe from an uncaring world, but she is not alone in such actions – which renders her attachment to Mansfield's furniture rather tricky. Austen does not provide a reader with any means overtly to distinguish Fanny's righteous occupancy of the sofa from her aunt Bertram's indolent half-life: as Mrs Norris remarks, 'it is a shocking trick for a young person to be always lolling on a sofa'.[151] Fanny's longing for her 'nest of comforts', and her desire to be comfortable, cannot but chime disquietingly with Lady Bertram's outburst when her niece returns from Portsmouth, about the only occasion in the novel when Lady Bertram's indolence deserts her:

> Fanny had scarcely passed the solemn-looking servants, when Lady
> Bertram came from the drawing room to meet her; came with no

indolent step; and, falling upon her neck, said, "Dear Fanny! Now I shall be comfortable."[152]

Not that Lady Bertram is the only character with whom the novel sets up an uncomfortable parallel; as any attempts to set Elinor and Marianne Dashwood in diametric ethical opposition are thwarted by the very existence of Margaret, the third sister,[153] there is in *Mansfield Park* the subliminal suggestion that Fanny forms only one apex of a triangle of peripheral observers and silent auditors, alongside her aunt – and Pug, scarcely narrated but everywhere implied, another vaguely gendered onlooker of events at Mansfield.[154] Symmetries and connections here obtrude unexpectedly upon a reader's responses, to startling effect, while what Phillips calls 'the pre-emptive imposition of pattern' is often found wanting, as Austen's differential narrative plays its most daring games with what plots can and cannot do to organize experience.

Readers of verse are accustomed (and freshly sensitized, in each act of reading), to those means by which poems locate themselves in space and time: the placement of lines and stanzas in relation to the white space of the page; the acoustic prospects and retrospects set up by rhymes; the prosodic marshallings of pulse and breath. However, as I touched upon earlier, it is possible to speak of a psychological prosody of fictional narrative: an admittedly more nebulous complex of expectations about the temporal and spatial arrangements of *histoire* by *récit*. 'We might think of plot', argues Peter Brooks, 'as the logic or perhaps the syntax of a certain kind of discourse, one that develops its propositions only through temporal sequence and progression.'[155] Brooks's comparison of plotting to a 'syntax' is apposite, but as he acknowledges elsewhere, it can also operate as a kind of hermeneutic map, a textual placing which operates over and above any significant locations within the story itself. *Mansfield Park* makes much of the possibilities which this offers, but much of the frustration which some of its readers have felt may be to do with the way in which, over the course of the novel, that map is defamiliarized. As this book has been exploring, Austen was all too aware of the numerous *a priori* templates for experience with which she was surrounded – etiquette, picturesque aesthetics, literary genre, amongst others – but the politically conservative *Mansfield Park* is, in its own peculiar way, her most truly radical narrative response to them. *Northanger Abbey* has as its basic comic premise the way in which over-reliance on the referents of a particular fictional genre cause one to lose focus on objects truly worthy of attention; *Mansfield Park* takes this one step further, finding absurd humour in the thought that this might be true not only for 'horrid novels' but for *all* novels. As elsewhere, Austen's writing recognizes the necessity of form and order, while maintaining that form and order do not in and of themselves explain anything; the methods of *Mansfield Park* are nothing like as visibly self-referential as those of *Tristram Shandy*, but Austen contrives as least as many ironic discrepancies between the rhetoric of fiction and the events it renders.

As befits a novel so adept at frustrating its readers' expectations, *Mansfield Park* opens with an account of frustrated expectations – in this case, the financial and matrimonial expectations of the young Lady Bertram's sisters:

> All Huntingdon exclaimed on the greatness of the match, and her uncle, the lawyer, himself, allowed her to be at least three thousand pounds short of any equitable claim to it. She had two sisters to be benefited by her elevation; and such of their acquaintance as thought Miss Ward and Miss Frances quite as handsome as Miss Maria, did not scruple to predict their marrying with almost equal advantage. But there certainly are not so many men of large fortune in the world, as there are pretty women to deserve them. Miss Ward, at the end of half a dozen years, found herself obliged to be attached to the Rev. Mr. Norris, a friend of her brother-in-law, with scarcely any private fortune, and Miss Frances fared yet worse.[156]

Three sisters and their respective fortunes: as in *Clarissa*, and in Austen's own teenage sketch 'The Three Sisters', older folk-tale motifs are visible through the naturalistic fabric; but Austen sets the folk tale askew by explicitly pointing out that those fortunes initially have little to do with matters of just desert. Maria Ward becomes Lady Bertram through 'good luck' and what many 'predict' does not come to pass; something is set out of joint (though nothing as specific as Mr Parker's ankle at the beginning of *Sanditon*), thus setting the tone for much of what is to follow. Tony Tanner has described the novel as 'a stoic book in that it speaks for stillness rather than movement, firmness rather than fluidity, arrest rather than change, endurance rather than adventure';[157] while that account encompasses *Mansfield Park*'s ethical and political priorities well, the novel is narratologically less demure, more mobile. As the opening of Chapter 1 puts matters out of joint, so the topography of Austen's subsequent narration is often comically out of phase with the events it relates: imagine, for instance, a Proppian diagram for *Mansfield Park*'s story, and consider how in-adequately such a 'morphology' would describe the way the novel actually moves. It is as if Austen has traced her narrative over the top of her story, and then, deliberately and repeatedly, moves her tracing to one side or another, with the result that what might be peaks of action in another novel often coin-cide with narrative troughs, and vice versa; much of readers' puzzlement may derive from this fact – that *Mansfield Park* reproduces so many of the conventional prosodic markers of early nineteenth-century plotting, while declining to locate its own important transitions at those points.

One comic effect of this technique is the repeated failure of 'prediction' as the novel progresses. There can be few other nineteenth-century novels, with the exception of Flaubert's *L'Éducation sentimentale*, that trail so many forthcoming attractions which then either fail to arrive, or are barely narrated when they do so. In the former category come such non-events as the performance of *Lovers' Vows*, Pug's phantom puppies, and Henry Crawford's speculative 'improvements' to Thornton Lacey – not to mention the various abortive marriage plans of the Crawford siblings. In the latter category, the much-anticipated wedding of Maria to Rushworth becomes so emotionally evacuated by the time it finally takes place, that it is narrated first in the pluperfect ('before the middle of the same month the ceremony had taken place'[158]). Set this comedy of non-event alongside the earnest, Evangelically-leaning moralism with which some critics have identified the novel, and it looks to have more in common with *Waiting for Godot* (whose author thought Austen had 'much to teach' him[159]) than it has with Hannah More or Maria Edgeworth. 'A life of usefulness, literature, and religion, was not by any means a life of event,' wrote Henry Austen; part of *Mansfield Park*'s genius is its ability to comprehend 'usefulness, literature, and religion' in much the same order, resulting in the peculiar status it affords to 'event'. One of the (by now) axiomatic observations about *Mansfield Park* involves the marginalization of larger political and ideological events and issues such as slavery and the Napoleonic wars, but even those events to which the novel lays more direct claim are narrated at some temporal or spatial remove. At times, *Mansfield Park* reads as if it is taking place in its own wings, as many of its significant sequences of transition happen somewhere else; one reason why the book has lent itself so uneasily to filming may be that it consists of a long series of what would be, if translated into the grammar of cinematic narration, 'reaction shots'.

Melodramatic events, such as Henry's elopement with Maria, are distanced, delayed, and inevitably partly attenuated, by being rendered in reports and letters; in the case of Maria's shame, the information does not even reach Fanny at Portsmouth in the right order. Mary's letter arrives in advance of the news to which it refers:

> Fanny stood aghast. As no scandalous, ill-natured rumour had reached her, it was impossible for her to understand much of this strange letter. She could only perceive that it must relate to Wimpole Street and Mr. Crawford, and only conjecture that

something very imprudent had just occurred in that quarter of the world, and to excite her jealousy, in Miss Crawford's apprehension, if she heard it.[160]

Similarly, when Fanny finally does find out the truth the next day, she receives it in a queasy parody of Cowperian 'retreat'. At the beginning of Book IV of *The Task*, 'The Winter Evening', the newspaper is delivered from a physical distance ('He comes, the herald of a noisy world,/ With spatter'd boots, strapp'd waist, and frozen locks,/ News from all nations lumb'ring at his back'[161]), and consumed in comfort:

> Now stir the fire, and close the shutters fast,
> Let fall the curtains, wheel the sofa round,
> And while the bubbling and loud-hissing urn
> Throws up a steamy column, and the cups
> That cheer but not inebriate, wait on each,
> So let us welcome peaceful evening in.
>
> . . . .
>
> This folio of four pages, happy work!
> Which not ev'n critics criticise, that holds
> Inquisitive attention while I read
> Fast bound in chains of silence, which the fair,
> Thought eloquent themselves, yet fear to break,
> What is it but a map of busy life
> Its fluctuations and its vast concerns?[162]

Austen's version remembers the claustrophobic surfaces of *The Watsons* ('the cups and saucers wiped in streaks, the milk a mixture of motes floating in thin blue, and the bread and butter growing every minute more greasy than even Rebecca's hands had first produced it'[163]), and, in narrating the revelation indirectly through the coarse Mr Price, removes the safety of journalistic distance that underpins Cowper's scene:

> [...] Fanny was first roused by his calling out to her, after humphing and considering over a particular paragraph—"What's the name of your great cousins in town, Fan?"
>   A moment's recollection enabled her to say, "Rushworth, Sir."
>   "And don't they live in Wimpole Street?"
>   "Yes, Sir."
>   "Then, there's the devil to pay among them, that's all. There,

(holding out the paper to her)—much good may such fine relations do you. I don't know what Sir Thomas may think of such matters; he may be too much of the courtier and fine gentleman to like his daughter the less. But by G— if she belonged to me, I'd give her the rope's end as long as I could stand over her. A little flogging for man and woman too, would be the best way of preventing such things."[164]

Austen's sidelining of the narrative watersheds of *Mansfield Park*'s plot inevitably refocuses a reader's attention on those apparent troughs or plateaus with which he or she is left instead – the murkier and less conspicuous parts of the narrative which might form the default background of another story, but which are offered as the main matter here. Once again, her way with prose can be compared to what Wordsworth's verse does to reanimate the 'spirit of the place' in resistance to the 'rules of mimic art'. Ricks's emphasis on Wordsworth's prepositional poetics, and Hugh Sykes Davies's scrutiny of 'the essentially incantatory qualities' of his 'cumulative tautologies',[165] both attest to the shifts of attention in Wordsworthian verse towards those unglamorous portions of language which do so much of the essential work, and to the means by which much of his poetry gains its force from the cumulative, iterative arrangement of words, phrases and particles ('thing', 'something', 'sense of', 'not un-'[166]) which might well look banal or fatuous if considered in isolation. In the field of Austen studies, JF Burrows's invaluable statistical analyses of the language of the novels have revealed the degree to which Austen's subtlety also depends upon the work done by particles and auxiliaries, and challenged 'the assumption [...] that, within the verbal universe of any novel, the very common words constitute a largely inert medium while all the real activity emanates from more visible and more energetic bodies'.[167] What Burrows observes at work in Austen's vocabulary also pertains to the larger structure of her plots: as shown by the proximity of the ha-ha to the gate at Sotherton, it is not always the most visible divisions that are the most pertinent. Wordsworth was perhaps the greatest English poet of the non-event, who created a genre of loco-*non*-descriptive poetry in 'Yarrow Unvisited', first published in 1807, which records the speaker's *not* going somewhere, in order to protect the sanctity of his mind's eye ('We have a vision of our own;/ Ah! why should we undo it?'[168]). His biggest non-event is recorded in the sixth book of *The Prelude*, in which, after just failing (through no fault of his own) to coincide with Coleridge at Cambridge, he and his friend Robert Jones fail to notice that they have, imperceptibly, already achieved the object of their Swiss journey, a moment which Paul De Man called 'a missed high point'.[169]

> Hard of belief, we questioned him again,
> And all the answers which the man returned
> To our inquiries, in their sense and substance
> Translated by the feelings which we had,
> Ended in this—that we had crossed the Alps.[170]

For a novelist working under the material conditions of eighteenth- and nineteenth-century publication, one economic necessity which could nevertheless be turned to creative ends was the division of novels into volumes; such very visible partitions, as many have remarked, offer possibilities for Austen's larger narrative rhythms. Joseph A Kestner has gone as far as to suggest that '[t]he three volumes of Jane Austen's *Pride and Prejudice* or *Emma* were required by the demands of the circulating libraries, but frequently one may see the form of the syllogism in such tripartite arrangements. The novels present a major premise, minor premise, and conclusion'.[171] It is questionable whether the intellectual correspondence of the volume divisions in *Pride and Prejudice* and *Emma* is quite as neat as Kestner makes it sound; moreover, it is noticeable that he does not include *Mansfield Park* in this list. It is a wise omission, since the novel does something rather different with its divisions. Rather than ending Volumes I and II with climactic shifts, Austen ends them with 'missed high points'; Volume I ends in anticlimax, with the evaporation of the theatricals:

> They *did* begin—and being too much engaged in their own noise, to be struck by an unusual noise in the other part of the house, had proceeded some way, when the door of the room was thrown open, and Julia appearing at it, with a face all aghast, exclaimed, "My father is come! He is in the hall at this moment!"[172]

while the gap between Volumes II and III is only that of a night's sleep ('Fanny had by no means forgotten Mr. Crawford, when she awoke the next morning'[173]) – not that a night's sleep is meaningless, as the woman who had been engaged overnight to Harris Bigg-Wither would have known. One result of the novel's reluctance overtly to signpost significance is that a reader is invited to shift his or her attention to what might be happening in the less notable peripheries of *Mansfield Park*, a shift which can suddenly touch on depths of repressed emotion. Either of the possible ways in which the Crawfords and Mansfield might become united pains Fanny over long stretches of the novel, but her reticence makes that pain hard to measure. As the Crawfords prepare to leave, Mary tries a little emotional blackmail by appealing to Fanny's emotional attachment to special places:

Fanny was affected. She had not foreseen anything of this, and her feelings could seldom withstand the melancholy influence of the word "last." She cried as if she had loved Miss Crawford more than she possibly could; and Miss Crawford, yet farther softened by the sight of such emotion, hung about her with fondness, and said, "I hate to leave you. I shall see no one half so amiable where I am going. Who says we shall not be sisters? I know we shall. I feel that we are born to be connected; and those tears convince me that you feel it too, dear Fanny."

Fanny roused herself, and replying only in part, said, "But you are only going from one set of friends to another. You are going to a very particular friend."[174]

There are a number of conflicting emotions at work here, but they are not spelt out. 'Who says we shall not be sisters?' asks Mary; two chapters later, one tiny, unheralded reference casts retrospective light on this and other moments in Fanny's history of unease. At Portsmouth, her sisters Susan and Betsey are seen squabbling over something; it turns out to be a silver knife, which Susan claims: "'It was very hard that she was not to have her *own* knife; it was her own knife; little sister Mary had left it to her on her death-bed, and she ought to have had it to keep herself long ago [...]".'[175] Suddenly the experience of listening to someone named Mary asking 'Who says we shall not be sisters?' feels that much more painful – a hint not proffered by suggestive symbolism or the 'high points' of narrative. This is one of so many barely implicated shades and sub-plots in *Mansfield Park*, another division 'of such a kind as not to interrupt the view from within, and not to be seen till closely approached'.

Flaubert is often credited with having brought the 'modern' narrative consciousness into being: for Kestner, his distinguishing achievement lies in *L'Éducation sentimentale*'s repudiation of 'ascending climactic art';[176] for Brooks, in the novel's 'deconstructions of the contents of education and the sentiments, its critical examination of systems of meaning applied to life – or claimed to be immanent to life'.[177] Perhaps, though, one of the reasons *Mansfield Park* has so puzzled its readers is that it is a novel ahead of its time, in that many of those innovations in narrative understanding and misunderstanding attributed to Flaubert's novel, which closes by remembering a hitherto unnarrated event ('C'est là que nous avons eu de meilleur! dit Deslauriers'[178]), can be seen at work in Austen's text. Like Cowper and Wordsworth before her, Austen re-orders conventional associations of meaning with place, and with textual space, recognizing the extent to which novels can and cannot tell us 'how things go', as noted subtly by Roger Gard, one of the few critics to sense fully the affinities of *Mansfield Park* to Flaubert:

The idea of totally pervasive, immanent meaning or sets of meanings in a work of art [...] is very attractive, but it can wish away also the irreducible, to itself, unportentous, non-transitive nature of some of the (as it were uncontrolled) particulars in works of art – especially novels; it can tidy out and forget uniqueness and distinction and even inconsequence in favour of an insistence on the seemingly grander, and at any rate more communicable, possibilities offered by the detection and elaboration of inter-connected significances – which can then be applied to the world. So when reading critics, one often wants in reaction to stop and say "wait – this is just *this* and not other, this is Mary, this is the East room..." and so on.[179]

Like the Flaubert of *L'Éducation sentimentale* after her, Austen offers any number of potentially meaningful connections and symmetries, then proceeds to demonstrate her matter's irreducibility to those patterns, to insist on clutter (a feature which militates against George Levine's citation of *Mansfield Park* as the representative example of pre-Darwinian, teleological narrative, which is allegedly 'consonant with the world described in natural theology').[180] These mismatches and slippages are, however, turned to more directly ethical ends in *Mansfield Park* than in Flaubert; this may be where the novel's 'morality of conversation' does its work. For example, early in Volume I, the fifteen-year-old Fanny is coming to terms with the possibility of moving in with Mrs Norris, a thought which does not fill her with hope:

> "I can say nothing for her manner to you as a child; but it was the same with us all, or nearly so. She never knew how it was to be pleasant to children. But you are now of an age to be treated better; I think she *is* behaving better already; and when you are her only companion, you *must* be important to her."
> "I can never be important to any one."
> "What is to prevent you?"
> "Every thing—my situation—my foolishness and awkwardness."[181]

The best part of three volumes later, the roles have been reversed; the Bertram girls are departed in disgrace, and with them all hope of Edmund's marrying Mary Crawford; and as Fanny comes into new prominence, the rhythm of Austen's prose ironically recalls Fanny's early opinion of herself, 'her own first feelings'. As I discussed in the previous chapter, *Emma*, the novel which succeeds *Mansfield Park*, depends on the figure of echo for many of its comic effects, and is particularly interested in the force of intentional or unintentional repetitions; it is typical of *Mansfield Park* that a tempting narrative symmetry leads only to a bathetic pratfall. A lesser novelist might have turned the rhythmic echo into a point of melodramatic reversal, with Edmund finally declaring the feelings which readers may have been wishing him to reveal; Austen makes of it something far more cruelly and comically profound:

> By eight in the morning, Edmund was in the house. The girls heard his entrance from above, and Fanny went down. The idea of immediately seeing him, with the knowledge of what he must be suffering, brought back all her own first feelings. He so near her, and in misery. She was ready to sink, as she entered the parlour. He was alone, and met her instantly; and she found herself pressed to his heart with only these words, just articulate, "My Fanny—my only sister—my only comfort now."[182]

Fanny may be 'pressed to his heart', but she still hasn't got her man; she has to wait, and so do Austen's readers – leading to the extraordinary implications of the novel's final chapter, in which levity and hellishness meet in surprising fashions.

'Let other pens dwell on guilt and misery. I quit such odious subjects as soon as I can, impatient to restore every body, not greatly in fault themselves, to tolerable comfort, and to have done with all the rest'.[183] It is difficult easily to discern moral proportion in this chapter; at times, the tone of the narrative has some of the archness of the end of *Northanger Abbey*; yet nowhere else in her writing does Austen sound as much like Dante or Sartre as in the exile of Maria and Mrs Norris ('it may be reasonably supposed that their tempers became their mutual punishment'), and in Henry Crawford's being doomed to spend the rest of his life in the knowledge of the woman he has lost, 'the woman whom he had rationally, as well as passionately loved'[184]. How true it is – 'Nessun maggior dolore/ che ricordarsi del tempo felice/ nella miseria'.[185] Nor is this all a reader is told; at the end of a novel full of failed predictions, Austen's narrator looks back at those significant non-events, at what might have been. Of Henry Crawford, we are told: 'Could he have been satisfied with the conquest of one amiable woman's affections, could he have found sufficient exultation in overcoming the reluctance, in working himself into the esteem and tenderness of Fanny Price, there would have been every probability of success and felicity for him [...] Would he have persevered, and uprightly, Fanny must have been his reward – and a reward very voluntarily bestowed – within a reasonable period from Edmund's marrying Mary'.[186] This counterfactual insight is so matter-of-fact in its tone, that it would be easy to miss its full implications, until one comes to the shift in Edmund's affections from Mary to Fanny:

> I purposely abstain from dates on this occasion, that every one may be at liberty to fix their own, aware that the cure of unconquerable passions, and the transfer of unchanging attachments, must vary much as to time in different people.—I only intreat every body to believe exactly at the time when it was quite natural that it should be so, and not a week earlier, Edmund did cease to care about Miss Crawford, and became as anxious to marry Fanny, as Fanny herself could desire.[187]

Nowhere in this last chapter is there anything to suggest that the narratorial voice is any less trustworthy here than elsewhere – allowing Austen to achieve her novel's more daring feat at this point, as she pulls the rug out from underneath herself, and from *Mansfield Park*'s notions of moral desert. The novel presents Fanny as deserving, and (eventually) as coming into her own; in effect, Austen gives a reader the 'Before' and 'After' stages of a didactic work, only to turn round and reveal that the connection between those stages may be as much an effect of happy accidents as of moral causality; had things been ever so slightly different, Henry would be married to Fanny, and Edmund to Mary. In the novel's final and most comprehensive displacement, the wished-for conclusion has been reached, but, it transpires, by a surprising and unsignposted alternative route; and the matter of the novel itself is seen to have been clearing the ground for something to come, 'something evermore about to be'.

'God moves in a mysterious way,/ His wonders to perform,' wrote Cowper, and the ways in which the narrative of *Mansfield Park* emphasizes humans' limited power to locate and dictate meaning and event may display the most complex religious sensibility in Austen's fiction – akin, perhaps, to WH Auden's idea that any truly religious art must bear the formal marks of Original Sin.[188] Then again, the novel may just be one of the most elusive portrayals in English fiction of the ineradicable contingencies of art and experience; either way, what becomes clearer in the last few pages is that *Mansfield Park* (like that great poem which existed in 1813, but which Austen was never to know) is a prelude. 'With such a regard for her, indeed, as his had long been'; 'as every thing else, within the view and patronage of Mansfield Park, had long been': as the pluperfects indicate, the novel up to this point has been waiting for something to happen, and it finally comes back into phase as it catches up with Fanny; after three volumes packed with unfulfilled expectations, it closes by looking forward to its most important event, one which it cannot and does not narrate – whatever it is that takes place after its own ending. Whether that be one far-off divine event, to which its whole creation moves, or merely a modest life of 'usefulness, literature, and religion', *Mansfield Park* does not tell. What we are told ('On that event they removed to Mansfield') is that it is a homecoming, of sorts; then again, 'Horror starts, like Charity, at home'.

Moving Furniture: Persuasion and Sanditon

> Are you so little loved, so little esteemed, that there is not a single person in your family, or among your connections [...] on whom your sentiments and conduct would operate either in the way of recommendation or the contrary? If this supposition be possible, how must you have lived?
>
> Thomas Gisborne, *An Enquiry into the Duties of the Female Sex*, 1797[189]

> Who can endure a Cabbage Bed in October?
>
> *Sanditon*, 1817[190]

Even before Austen died, the tourists were growing in number, as witnessed by the holidaying population of Sanditon; and with her posthumous literary canonization in the nineteenth century, she increasingly became part of the landscape herself. 'Now take me to the Cobb, and show me the steps from which Louisa Musgrove fell,' begged Tennyson in 1867; in 1935, Samuel Beckett made his own Austen pilgrimage to Winchester and Bath (finding the experience more beneficial than that of Stratford-upon-Avon, which was 'unspeakable, everything His Nibs up to the vespasienne universelle'[191]). Literary locations can become, like the 'stations' of picturesque travel guides, just so many stops on the cultural tourist trail, but they can also provide public, shared spaces in which successive readings and responses meet; and in this, they bear a vital relationship to literary texts themselves. Tennyson and Beckett, both writers fascinated by decay, permanence and the permanence of decay ('The woods decay, the woods decay and fall'), took delight in revisiting the special places of Austen's fiction – places which, like the novels themselves, had outlasted their creator, now 'mouldering in the grave'. Part of Tennyson's attachment may have derived from the intellectual and emotional timbre of his age, one marked by large contentions about the understanding of space and time, as TS Eliot remarked; 'Tennyson,' Eliot wrote, 'lived in a time which was already acutely time-conscious: a great many things seemed to be happening, railways were being built, discoveries were being made, the face of the world was changing. That was a time busy in keeping up to date. It had, for the most part, no hold on permanent things, on permanent truths about man and God and life and death'.[192] Both critically distanced from Tennyson and sympathetically attuned to him, Eliot's words themselves comprehend the creative dilemma which Tennyson worked up into *In Memoriam* (even if he didn't 'work it out' there). For to have a 'hold on permanent things' is at once an achievement and a *memento mori*: holding is something which hands do, hands being parts of bodies, bodies being anything but 'permanent things'. The form of Tennyson's writing may have few affinities with Austen's, but his imaginative investment in Louisa Musgrove's fictional fall is evidence that *Persuasion*, like *In Memoriam* after it, is of its time by living in time, its longevity braced against its existence in a world in which things and people do pass away; Henry Austen's 'Biographical Notice' is all the more poignant for being appended to the first printing of *Persuasion*, a novel which attempts to gain its own 'hold on permanent things'. Completed as Austen began to slip slowly and painfully out of life, it tells a story which moves in the other direction – of a woman coming back to life in space and time, recovering her voice and her rightful place. Like Louisa's fall, the whole novel can seem 'all done in rapid moments', but Austen composes and weighs those moments so as to connect them to larger spans of time; *Persuasion*'s clutter reveals how moments contain other moments and are in turn contained by them. If it is a book about rebirth, however, it is, like *Mansfield Park*, a novel about furniture.

Austen was the first to point out that none of her writing was composed for 'dull Elves', but *Persuasion* invites an intensity of readerly application greater than in any of her previous fictions; a reader needs imaginatively to inhabit its physical and textual spaces in ways that would simply not be possible amid the more sparely rendered worlds of *Sense and Sensibility* and *Pride and Prejudice*. This is most apparent in Austen's simply providing *more* information to work with: locations, distances, sizes, time-lapses and colours. Take, for example, Sir Walter's dismissive treatment of Kellynch's new tenant, Admiral Croft:

> "And who is Admiral Croft?" was Sir Walter's cold suspicious inquiry.
>
> Mr. Shepherd answered for his being of a gentleman's family, and mentioned a place; and Anne, after the little pause which followed, added—
>
> "He is rear admiral of the white. He was in the Trafalgar action, and has been in the East Indies since; he has been stationed there, I believe, several years."
>
> "Then I take it for granted," observed Sir Walter, "that his face is about as orange as the cuffs and capes of my livery."[193]

Austen arranges the scene so as to make Sir Walter's bad joke intersect with her own good one at his expense; within the sentence, the word 'orange' catches the ear as garishly as that colour on a servant's clothes might catch the eye, and if one looks more closely, it transpires that this is the only instance of the word in all Austen's fiction.[194] As I mentioned in Chapter 2, one has only to compare Austen's narrative with the descriptive opulence of *Udolpho* to see that detail in her works tends not to be simply mnemonic. Barbara Hardy has noted that 'Jane Austen's brilliant and solid chronicle of social objects goes beyond a psychological record, which fills the world with things in order to dramatize individual attitudes and appetites [...] She also knows that life in her society is lived with and through things'.[195] The colour of a servant's cuffs, the distance from Kellynch to Uppercross, Mrs Clay's having 'freckles, and a projecting tooth, and a clumsy wrist'[196] – Austen's last fictions notice all these in greater detail than any other work apart from *The Watsons*, and turn them to more creative purposes than the 1805 fragment. Nor is this a matter only for the eye. Living where she did, and reading as she did, Austen knew all about dung, both from experience and from *The Task*'s 'stercorarious heap',[197] and her last two works begin to develop their narrative sense of smell; in *Persuasion*, Mrs Croft's care prevents her carriage from falling 'foul of a dung-cart';[198] in *Sanditon*, Mr Parker's distaste for his former house comes partly from 'the yearly nuisance of its decaying vegetation' ('Who can endure a Cabbage Bed in October?'[199]). Austen's noticing in *Persuasion* and *Sanditon* recognizes 'things' not just as adjuncts and symbolic projections of the mind, but as objects which bear upon, muddy, and sometimes thwart existence – as shown by her treatment of colour. Her amused interest in the 'off-stage' lives of her characters was such that she could, in her letters to Cassandra, sometimes sound like a mother interested in the progress of her children, as she pondered novels which were themselves variously a 'sucking child' and a 'darling Child' to her. In May 1813, she joked to her sister that she had even seen a real portrait of one of her own characters, on a visit to London:

> Henry & I went to the Exhibition in Spring Gardens. It is not thought a good collection,, but I was very well pleased—particularly (pray tell Fanny) with a small portrait of Mrs Bingley, excessively like her. I went in hopes of seeing one of her Sister, but there was no Mrs Darcy;—perhaps however, I may find her in the Great Exhibition which we shall go to, if we have time;—I have no chance of her in the collection of Sir Joshua Reynolds's Paintings which is now shewing in Pall Mall, & which we are also to visit.—Mrs Bingley's is exactly herself, size, shaped face, features & sweetness; there never was a greater likeness. She is dressed in a white gown,

with green ornaments, which convinces me of what I had always supposed, that green was a favourite colour with her. I dare say Mrs D. will be in Yellow.[200]

Noticing colours, however, was to gain an altogether more grim significance in her life, as she surveyed the visible evidence of her own impending death. The disease which eventually killed her had begun to appear before she finished *Persuasion*, and in March 1817, four months before she died, she mentioned her finished manuscript in a letter to Fanny Knight: 'Do not be surprised at finding Uncle Henry acquainted with my having another ready for publication'.[201] After a customary quip about the new work ('You may *perhaps* like the Heroine, as she is almost too good for me'), her letter moves on, almost without warning, to the particulars of her own malady:

> Many thanks for your kind care for my health; I certainly have not been well for many weeks, & about a week ago I was very poorly, I have had a good deal of fever at times & indifferent nights, but am considerably better now, & recovering my Looks a little, which have been bad enough, black & white & every wrong colour. I must not depend upon being ever very blooming again. Sickness is a dangerous Indulgence at my time of Life.[202]

There is a brave gallows humour in Austen's telling herself off for being ill when she knows it is bad for her health, at once acknowledging the facts of mortality and scoring comic points off them. It is a gallows humour which takes on even more surreal forms in the creative work of her last months, which she had finally left off writing five days before this letter; for example, one of Sanditon's selling points as a resort (at least according to Mr Parker), is that, as befits a place whose very name is repeated like a magic shibboleth, it has the power to cure all ills. 'The Sea air & Sea Bathing together,' we are told, 'were nearly infallible, one or the other of them being a match for every Disorder, of the Stomach, the Lungs or the Blood; They were anti-spasmodic, anti-pulmonary, anti-sceptic, anti-bilious & anti-rheumatic'.[203] (Whatever Sanditon's powers, one thing it cannot prevent is scepticism, and it is tempting to see a suggestive, almost Keatsian misspelling in Austen's 'anti-sceptic'.[204]) Perhaps the most extreme comedy of bodily decay pertains to the hypochondriac Parker siblings, who 'must either be very busy for the Good of others, or else extremely ill themselves';[205] even at a time when she could barely move from a sofa herself, Austen was pushing her fictional characters to ever more indecorous, 'hobby-horsical' extremes: 'I sh^d have been with you at all hazards the day after the rec^pt of your Letter, though it found me suffering under a more severe attack than usual of my old greivance, Spasmodic Bile & hardly able to crawl from my Bed to the Sofa'.[206] In relating Diana Parker's account of various afflictions, Austen manages to combine the claustrophobia of *The Watsons* with the gleeful sadism of the juvenilia and the numerical improprieties of *Pride and Prejudice*:

> If indeed a simple Sprain, as you denominate it, nothing w^d have been so judicious as Friction, Friction by the hand alone, supposing it could be applied *instantly*.—Two years ago I happened to be calling on Mrs Sheldon when her Coachman sprained his foot as he was cleaning the Carriage & c^d hardly limp into the House—but by the immediate use of Friction alone steadily persevered in, (& I rubbed his Ancle with my own hand for six Hours without Intermission)—he was well in three days [...] I doubt whether Susan's nerves w^d be equal to the effort. She has been suffering much from the Headache and Six Leaches a day for 10 days together releived her so little that we thought it right to change our measures—and being convinced on examination that much of the Evil lay in her Gum, I persuaded her to attack the disorder there. She has accordingly had 3 Teeth drawn, & is decidedly better, but her Nerves are a good deal deranged. She can only speak in a whisper—and fainted away twice this morning on poor Arthur's trying to suppress a cough.[207]

'[N]othing w^d have been so judicious as Friction': friction, that rubbing against the unpleasant surfaces of life which pervades *The Watsons*, is here remade as absurdist farce, which looks back to *Gulliver* and anticipates the likes of *Molloy*.[208] The enthusiastic relish of Diana Parker's tone sits brilliantly at odds with the painfully excessive numbers and durations it measures ('six Hours', 'three days', 'Six Leaches a day for 10 days together', '3 Teeth'); but, as with Mrs Norris's relationship to the rest of the Bertram household in *Mansfield Park*, it only pushes to one extreme a concern held more diffusely in the world of *Sanditon*. I have described Austen as a poet of domestic pathology, but she has also been the object of pathological speculation herself: in the *British Medical Journal* for 1964, Dr Zachary Cope used the evidence of her late letters to conjecture a diagnosis of Addison's disease as the cause of the novelist's death, concluding his article in a manner that could at best only have been half-intentional. 'If our surmise be correct,' he remarks, 'Jane Austen did something more than write excellent novels – she also described the first recorded case of Addison's disease of the adrenal bodies.'[209] This *gauche* moment of professional zeal, however, does fortuitously touch on some home truths about Austen's last two works of fiction; for, in *Persuasion* and *Sanditon*, life has to share its imaginative and textual space with inescapably inanimate things, and with the sense that one will one day be inanimate oneself – with the likes of furniture, and 'Addison's disease of the adrenal bodies'. Anne Elliot in *Persuasion* is living proof of this uncomfortable truth; for, as the novel opens, she is treated as if her life were over, and as if she were part of the furniture.

Mansfield Park is much concerned with the succession of estates; but the Bertrams (thanks in part to the tainted incomes from Antigua, of course) are not troubled by the kind of gritty financial demands which define the worlds of *Persuasion* and *Sanditon* – issues like Mr Shepherd's financial agency for the Elliots, and the dependence of Sanditon's whole economy on its conversion into "'Lodgings to let'".[210] As well as economics, time seems to make different demands in these works. As I discussed above, *Mansfield Park* stops just as it catches up with Fanny, that closing 'had long been' pointing to that stored inheritance into which she is about to pass; at the beginning of *Persuasion*, however, pluperfect verbs gang up on Anne. Whereas Elizabeth Elliot 'had succeeded [...] to all that was possible, of her mother's rights and consequence', and 'her influence had always been great',[211] the auxiliary 'had' crowds malevolently around her sister with the force of a *fait accompli*:

> A few years earlier, Anne Elliot had been a very pretty girl, but her bloom had vanished early; and as even in its height, her father had found little to admire in her (so totally different were her delicate features and mild dark eyes from his own); there could be nothing in them now that she was faded and thin, to excite his esteem. He had never indulged much hope, he had now none, of ever reading her name in any other page of his favourite work.[212]

Anne is the subject of only one of the verbs in this passage – the uninfluential 'had been a very pretty girl' – and from that point on, the verbs either slip away from her, or judge her harshly. It is hard to live in time when time itself appears to be treating you as a has-been – or, more properly, a had-been; in this light, it is not coincidental that *Persuasion* should open with Anne at the age of twenty-seven. For one thing, twenty-seven would have counted as a representative cut-off point for a woman's matrimonial eligibility in Austen's time; but twenty-seven is also another example of those little private references which occasionally crop up in the novels, like the topaz cross in *Mansfield Park*. Austen was just about to turn twenty-seven herself when, in December 1802, she accepted Harris Bigg-Wither's proposal, only to recant the next morning: a fact which lends an added poignancy to the fact that twenty-seven, as David Nokes has remarked, often marks the grand climacteric of womens' romantic hopes in the novels.[213] Anne is pushed, spatially and temporally, to the side of her own life, and the novel renders this condition both in its accounts of space, and its employments of textual spacing.

Emily Dickinson wrote of 'the undeveloped Freight/ of a delivered syllable';[214] the visual workings of text can go some way towards suggesting that 'undeveloped Freight', since if words on a page are unvoiced, the look of a page can move further *sotto voce*. *Persuasion* opens with the narration of an act of reading, as Sir Walter looks over the Baronetage; the imagined presence of the book is repeatedly suggested as a point of focus ('there he found occupation in an idle hour', 'there any unwelcome sensations [...] changed naturally into pity and contempt'), a hint made more explicit when the text approximates his experience of 'there':

> there, if every other leaf were powerless, he could read his own history with an interest which never failed—this was the place at which the favourite volume always opened:
> ## "ELLIOT OF KELLYNCH-HALL.
> "Walter Elliot, born March 1, 1760, married, July 15, 1784, Elizabeth, daughter of James Stevenson, Esq. of South Park, in the county of Gloucester; by which lady (who died 1800) he has issue Elizabeth, born June 1, 1785; Anne, born August 9, 1787; a still-born son, Nov. 5, 1789; Mary, born Nov. 20, 1791."
> Precisely such had the paragraph originally stood from the printer's hands; but Sir Walter had improved it by adding, for the information of himself and his family, these words, after the date of Mary's birth—"married, Dec. 16, 1810, Charles, son and heir of Charles Musgrove, Esq. of Uppercross, in the county of Somerset,"—and by inserting most accurately the day of the month on which he had lost his wife.[215]

Despite numerous references to the precise details and placements of the physical document ('Precisely such', 'after the date of Mary's birth', 'inserting most accurately'), Austen's approximating a page of Sir Walter's book does not aspire to an accurate reproduction; rather, as at the opening of *Great Expectations*, in which a reader encounters a more typographically regular version of the chiselled gravestones which Pip remembers reading ('*Also Georgiana Wife of the Above*'[216]), the passage works as an alerting device, pointing to the possibility that the textual surfaces of Austen's novel may be at least as rewarding to look at as the Baronetage, that the look of the book may be worthy of scrutiny, as are many of the looks depicted therein.[217] *Persuasion* is especially rich in 'undeveloped Freight', weights with which its surfaces are pregnant, as in that parenthesis – not quite commentary, not quite *style indirect* – describing Sir Walter's reservations about Anne: '(so totally different were her delicate features and mild dark eyes from his own)'. It is a selfish and petty criterion for parental affection, but Austen's grammar also makes it painfully unavoidable – although, in popular convention after Johnson, that should not have been the case. John Lennard has called attention to the *Dictionary*'s definition of 'PARENTHESIS', one which is 'as bizarre as it has been influential' ('it may be taken out, without injuring the sense of that which incloses it'[218]); Austen's parenthesis does something rather different. Without the bracketed aside about Anne's eyes, the rest of the sentence makes no sense, since 'them' no longer has a referent: thus the narrative discourse can no more escape Sir Walter's overbearing presence than can his daughter.

The spaces and spacings of *Persuasion* can also say more about Anne than she fully knows she is saying herself; her first speech in the book, delayed until well into the third chapter, measures her reticence in its monosyllabic announcement 'Here Anne spoke,—',[219] as if the very novel were suddenly surprised by her audacity. The long dash prefaces each of Anne's conversational entrances in this chapter ('Anne, after the little pause which followed, added—',[220] 'After waiting another moment—'[221]): the narrative furnishes an unvocalized catch in the voice as one reads, giving a reader a pause for thought. This is not the first time the visual influence of elliptical marks makes itself felt in Austen; for instance, I mentioned in Chapter 1 the typographical performance which accompanies Mary Bennet's discoursing on elopement in *Pride and Prejudice*. Perhaps the strangest example, though, is the addition Austen made for the second edition of *Mansfield Park*, published by John Murray in 1816 – not least because it is the only instance in the major novels of Austen's employing something like a modern ellipsis.[222] In Volume I, Chapter 16, Fanny finds herself called upon to praise Mary Crawford, and thereby to flatter Edmund's good taste, but cannot quite bring herself to do so, a comic quandary which gains by the added punctuation in the 1816 text:

> "She never appeared more amiable than in her behaviour to you last night. It gave her a very strong claim on my good will."
> "She *was* very kind indeed, and I am glad to have her spared." ....
> She could not finish the generous effusion. Her conscience stopt her in the middle, but Edmund was satisfied.[223]

Neither wholly part of Fanny's speech nor of the external narration, Austen's odd four-point ellipsis performs a kind of Cartesian slapstick, as Fanny's conscience intercedes between her voice and herself. In *Persuasion*, the long dashes are matched well to the atmosphere of a novel so attuned to the multiple pressures behind silences and glances that a reader can almost feel the weight of the air. Those dashes silently mark the 'undeveloped Freight' of emotion, the weights of remembered pain which Sir William's dismissal of naval honour is at once glossing over and raking up. 'Anne,' Tanner has perceptively remarked, 'is, precisely, in between, and she lives in in-betweenness'.[224] Dashes are likewise channels of 'in-betweenness', but they also operate as the conventional markers for the rhetorical figure of *aposiopesis*, 'breaking off a sentence with the sense incomplete',[225] a figure with which Austen would have been familiar from her reading of *Tristram Shandy* ('Make this dash,—'tis an Aposiopesis'[226]). As befits a character who starts the novel living under erasure, as 'nothing', existing almost outside the narrative as someone who 'had been' but whose eyes have 'nothing in them now', Anne becomes identified with the blank dash '—': a notation of absence, of aposiopesis, of being prematurely cut off at twenty-seven.

It is, however, a significant absence. 'Here Anne spoke,—' has, in the light of the novel as a whole, a commemorative function, since it is the first time that Anne governs a verb in the standard aorist tense of fiction; hence the dash before her first speech forms a watershed, Anne's return to active time. Taken on these terms, then, the phrase has the ring of 'Thus spake Anne' or of a plaque on a building; compare Anne's feeling for the precise date on which Kellynch changes hands ('She could not think of much else on the 29th of September'[227]). On the surface, this might lend substance to Marilyn Butler's objection to *Persuasion*, which traces the novel's twentieth-century popularity to 'the subjectivism of later thinking';[228] however, Butler underplays the care with which Austen composes her novel so as to create a co-ordinate double life for its important moments. This derives from the text's ability to provide an external retrospect, an organization and shape which the experience of 'real time' often lacks. But *Persuasion* also recognizes that for a moment to have become a cherished memory, it must even at the time have had a *potential* significance, an 'undeveloped Freight': some quality which may not have been apparent at the time, but which connects it to other times. One of the things verse and narrative can do is to reveal, in the present of reading, continuities between moments both past and future ('in this moment there is life and food/ For future years'[229]). *Persuasion* is willing to comprehend contingency and posterity, without reducing them to each other, trying to make the intimate and immediate cohabit with the larger and less personal flow of time. Austen is 'acutely time-conscious' in this novel, ever aware that neither people nor books can escape it; and it is an awareness focused through her imagination of how people live and move in rooms.

When Anne and Wentworth finally fail to avoid meeting again – an event both desired and feared – the scene flurries by the reader as it 'rushed on Anne':

> Mary, very much gratified by this attention, was delighted to receive him; while a thousand feelings rushed on Anne, of which this was the most consoling, that it would soon be over. And it was soon over. In two minutes after Charles's preparation, the others appeared; they were in the drawing-room. Her eye half met Captain Wentworth's; a bow, a curtsey passed; she heard his voice—he talked to Mary, said all that was right; said something to the Miss Musgroves, enough to mark an easy footing: the room seemed full—full of persons and voices—but a few minutes ended it. Charles shewed himself at the window, all was ready, their visitor had bowed and was gone; the Miss Musgroves were gone too, suddenly resolving to walk to the end of the village with the sportsmen: the room was cleared, and Anne might finish her breakfast as she could.[230]

This passage is typical of *Persuasion* in several ways: the impressionistic flash of events, the precise detailing of time and place ('two minutes', 'at the window'), the activity of social gesture ('a bow, a curtsey passed'), and that final bathetic shift of cadence, letting the sentence's breath out at last to leave Anne suspended over her breakfast. But is it strictly true to say that Anne and Wentworth 'meet' here? Rather, like their eyes, they 'half met', and the awkwardness of that encounter is no small matter. *Mansfield Park*, as I have discussed, is interested in Fanny's bashfully averted eyes; *Persuasion* parallels Anne's reemergence into life by noticing how replete the English language is with active, sociable metaphors for what eyes can do: over the course of the novel, they 'speak', 'wander', 'reach' and even 'devour'.[231] Gilbert Austin noted in *Chironomia* that we 'seem to have the power, as it were, of touching each other by the sense of sight',[232] and more recently, Sartre offered his masterly analysis of what happens when one person, in that sense attributed to Austen, catches another's eye. 'It is not when eyes are looking at you,' he points out, 'that you can find them beautiful or ugly, that you can remark on their colour. The Other's look hides his eyes; he seems to go *in front of them.*'[233] Sartre's point is that if the look operates as a channel of intention, then 'catching the eye' makes its participants recognize themselves as both subjects and objects; and if this is true, noticing can yield more than subjective impressions, as Anne and Wentworth find out.

One way in which Austen invites her readers to imagine such experiences is by calling into play those 'little things – like [...] the arrangement of the furniture', which RW Chapman saw at work in the writer's correspondence. At the very end of her life, it was a brute fact of her physical decline that she was confined to a couple of rooms and a sofa in Winchester; likewise, her niece Caroline's last memory of her is of furniture ('There's a chair for the married lady, and a little stool for you, Caroline.' – It is strange, but those trifling words are the last of her's that I can remember'[234]). But in less troubled times, too, Austen's feelings of familial happiness could become so entwined with her thoughts of the furniture, as to make tables speak:

> The Tables are come, & give general contentment. I had not ex-
> pected that they would so perfectly suit the fancy of us all three, or
> that we should so well agree in the disposition of them; but nothing
> except their own surface could have been smoother;—the two ends
> put together form our constant Table for everything, & the centre
> peice stands exceedingly well under the glass; holds a great deal
> most commodiously, without looking awkwardly.—They are both
> covered with green baize & send their best Love.[235]

Taking the metaphor of 'table-talk' (and singing sofas) in new directions, 'send their best Love' sends its own double-taking chime back through 'covered with green baize'; all at once, furniture comes to life ('the disposition of them'), and a bare physical fact takes on a lively, sociable undertone, as if the 'green baize' were the new tables' 'Sunday best', worn to impress Cassandra. This little moment of sibling comedy involves itself with Austen's surround-ings in a way that is not simply symbolic; furniture has here, as it does in *Persuasion*, more the feeling of an 'objective correlative'.[236] Animistic furniture appears repeatedly in the last two fictions, for example in Lady Denham's worry, in *Sanditon*, that the boarding-school travellers 'may hurt the Furni-ture'.[237] In *Persuasion*, too, one of Mr Shepherd's arguments for letting Kellynch to the Crofts is that 'he did not know, whether furniture might not be in danger of suffering as much where there was no lady, as where there were many children. A lady, without a family, was the very best preserver of furniture in the world.'[238] Typically, though, it is Anne, exiled at Uppercross, who hints at furniture's fullest psychological importance:

> So passed the first three weeks. Michaelmas came; and now
> Anne's heart must be in Kellynch again. A beloved home made
> over to others; all the precious rooms and furniture, groves, and
> prospects, beginning to own other eyes and other limbs![239]

Furniture can become marked, worn, even 'hurt' by use over time, but Anne's perceptions ('all the precious rooms and furniture [...] beginning to own

other eyes and limbs') point to the other part of the truth: that furniture can
own us as much as we own it, not only structuring movements, but providing
a place for mental associations and memories. *Persuasion*, for all its painful displacements, is also full of scenes revisited, as when the party passes back
through Lyme after Louisa's fall, 'treading back with feelings unutterable, the
ground which so lately, so very lately, and so light of heart, they had passed
along'.[240] Memories of places and events may be inescapably painful at times
in the novel, but it is only by accepting that condition, that the rebirth it
describes comes about.

Like Anne, Wentworth also has to make room for others in his manoeuvres
around their furniture. This is especially evident when the two of them have
awkwardly to share a sofa, and listen to Mrs Musgrove's laments over her
feckless late son:

> in another moment he was perfectly collected and serious; and
> almost instantly afterwards coming up to the sofa, on which she and
> Mrs. Musgrove were sitting, took a place by the latter, and entered
> into conversation with her, in a low voice, about her son, doing it
> with so much sympathy and natural grace, as shewed the kindest
> consideration for all that was real and unabsurd in the parent's feel-
> ings.
>
> They were actually on the same sofa, for Mrs. Musgrove had most
> readily made room for him;—they were divided only by Mrs.
> Musgrove. It was no insignificant barrier indeed. [241]

'It', instead of the 'she' one might expect, is particularly catty on Austen's
part, making Mrs Musgrove seem like an inanimate barrier, and her punctuation colludes in its widened pause (';—'); the narrative is less interested in the
body as a symbol than as an irreducible physical mass, as when Charlotte
Heywood, meeting Arthur Parker in *Sanditon*, 'drew back her Chair to have all
the advantage of his Person as a screen, & was very thankful for every inch of
Back & Shoulders beyond her pre-conceived idea'.[242] The whole scene with
the sofa explores how a pair of supposedly former lovers might react to being
close to each other with only someone like Mrs Musgrove in the way; it tells
simple truths about bodies as well as deriving complex effects from them. For
instance, if Mrs Musgrove becomes a kind of dead weight, her own behaviour
moves the other way, coming to life in the anthropomorphic huff and puff of
her 'large fat sighings'.[243] Wentworth must respond to them with delicacy, or
at least 'with so much sympathy and natural grace, as shewed the kindest consideration for all that was real and unabsurd in the parent's feelings'.
'Unabsurd' has a Wordsworthian ring to it; and like Wordsworth, Austen is

open to the possibilities of compounded 'un-' adjectives, especially their ability to include their own opposites. One cannot say an 'un-' word without
summoning up the pressure of the contrary sense against which it stands, and
from which it is only separated by two letters; and given that there are few, if
any, two-letter adjectives in English, the contrary sense will always cast a
longer shadow. A famous instance of this quality in Wordsworth is that
moment in 'Nutting' where the speaker is about to have a violent, uncanny
confrontation with nature:

> I forc'd my way
> Until I came to one dear nook
> Unvisited, where not a broken bough
> Droop'd with its wither'd leaves, ungracious sign
> Of devastation, but the hazels rose
> Tall and erect, with milk-white clusters hung,
> A virgin scene![244]

'Unvisited' becomes the syntactic and emotional pivot in Wordsworth's poem
of lost illusions and snapped twigs, since from that point onwards the sense of
the lines runs in parallel with the destruction which the word compacts ('not a
broken bough/ Droop'd'); however hard the speaker tries to fend off the
narration of his shameful memory, 'Unvisited' contains the 'visit' it sets out to
postpone. Austen's 'unabsurd' is less tragically duplicitous than its Wordsworthian predecessor; the word in *Persuasion* locates itself precisely near its
inescapable relative, much as Anne and Wentworth have to deal with their
own inescapable relatives. 'Unabsurd' balances sympathy with discernment,
and for all its distinction from 'absurd', it remembers its roots; one of only two
recorded uses, it also acts as an accommodating swerve in the language, making room for Mrs Musgrove's excessive grieving, as she makes room for
Wentworth on the sofa.

If the Anne Elliot of the opening chapters of *Persuasion* is disenfranchised,
practically invisible, and literally inaudible (at least until Chapter 3), the
description of Louisa's fall measures how far she has come; indeed, Wentworth later admits that it is this incident which brings home to him 'the
perfect excellence of the mind with which Louisa's could so ill bear a comparison':

> "Is there no one to help me?" were the first words which burst
> from Captain Wentworth, in a tone of despair, and as if all his own
> strength were gone.
> "Go to him, go to him," cried Anne, "for heaven's sake go to him.

> I can support her myself. Leave me, and go to him. Rub her hands, rub her temples; here are salts,—take them, take them."[245]

In this bustle of imperatives, Anne regains the centre stage, keeping her head when all around her are losing theirs; even Wentworth's characteristic glance seems to be lingering:

> "Anne, Anne," cried Charles, "what is to be done next? What, in heaven's name, is to be done next?"
> Captain Wentworth's eyes were also turned towards her.[246]

'[W]ere' is presumably an imperfect here, so the sense is of Wentworth's waiting on Anne's command, or her look; and, in the revised version of the novel's climax, that is exactly what Austen has him do ("'A word, a look will be enough to decide whether I enter your father's house this evening, or never'"[247]). As that rewritten climax approaches the final marriage, Austen's populated language becomes an audience, perhaps even a chorus, for the couple's rediscovery of their love: what in the cancelled chapters is a fortunate circumstance, is remade as one of the most distinctive speeches in nineteenth-century fiction. Anne begins Chapter 10 of the last volume reminding herself that she 'must talk to Lady Russell',[248] and comes out of Chapter 11 having made what may truly be the speech of her life. However, to get to this point, she has had to realize that returning to active time also makes her subject to its attritions. Her first attempt at reasoning out her relationship to Wentworth does not quite work, seemingly because she pitches it wrongly. 'She tried to be calm,' we are told,

> and leave things to take their course, and tried to dwell much on this argument of rational dependance—"Surely, if there be constant attachment on each side, our hearts must understand each other ere long. We are not boy and girl, to be captiously irritable, misled by every moment's inadvertence, and wantonly playing with our own happiness."
> And yet, a few minutes afterwards, she felt as if their being in company with each other, under their present circumstances, could only be exposing them to inadvertencies and misconstructions of the most mischievous kind.[249]

Anne and Wentworth are not 'boy and girl', and the narrative does not attempt to treat them as if they were. Anne knows she is, in all senses, going over old ground, and it is her knowledge of having been there before that animates her great speech about how many have been there before her; an intimate memory of the silent interlocutor on the other side of the room, separated from her and Harville by one of Austen's most extraordinary stage directions: 'The window at which he [Harville] stood, was at the other end of the room from where the two ladies were sitting, and though nearer to Captain Wentworth's table, not very near'.[250] The narrative brings together eyes, voices and furniture, in the image of Anne watching Wentworth listen to her:

> "We shall never agree upon this question"—Captain Harville was beginning to say, when a slight noise called their attention to Captain Wentworth's hitherto perfectly quiet division of the room. It was nothing more than that his pen had fallen down, but Anne was half inclined to suspect that the pen had only fallen, because he had been occupied by them, striving to catch sounds, which yet she did not think he could have caught.[251]

So it is that Wentworth, like Anne, begins 'to feel himself alive again',[252] but the lovers' redemption of time is also inevitably a redemption *into* time, subjecting them to the 'tax of quick alarm'[253] in wartime, and the equally 'quick' possibility of the captain's death. This is still an achievement, though: far from the static, marginalizing pluperfects of the beginning of the novel, the tenses shift lithely around its conclusion, as if to show what 'the power of conversation' might do to 'make the present hour a blessing indeed, and prepare it for all the immortality which the happiest recollections of their future lives could bestow. There they exchanged again those feelings and those promises which had once before seemed to secure every thing, but which had been followed by so many, many years of division and estrangement.'[254] One of mature love's heroisms is that a couple can revive their capacity for wonder and surprise even in the knowledge of what has been and gone; a person cannot plead innocence in a situation like this. Austen's treatment of Anne and Wentworth, too, has its eyes wide open without ever sounding wide-eyed; she gives the couple a version of that insight which animates the novel itself for the reader, an insight into the weight *in* moments rather than the simple aggregate weight *of* moments.

She neither exaggerates nor downplays the importance of such moments and such characters. When, in the final chapter of *Persuasion*, Austen's prose adopts its 'knowing narrator' voice, there is a vulnerable irony at work ('if such parties succeed, how should a Captain Wentworth and an Anne Elliot, with the advantage of maturity of mind, consciousness of right, and one independent fortune between them, fail of bearing down every opposition?'[255]).

For one thing, the indefinite articles chime disquietingly with Emma Woodhouse's acquisitive desire for 'a Harriet Smith'; they also look forward to *Sanditon*, a work of art which has its being, more surely than any of Austen's previous fictions, in an age of mechanical reproduction. The world of *Sanditon* is one where, largely owing to its greater emphasis on production and consumption, names and identities are less stable: there can be more than one place with the same name; the local businesses are named and branded in ways that barely feature in the major novels ('you can get a Parasol at Whitby's for little Mary at any time, or a large Bonnet at Jebb's'[256]); and the houses which should enrich Sanditon themselves bear generic, endlessly reproducible (and nowadays ominously familiar) seaside names: 'A little higher up, the Modern began; & in crossing the Down, a Prospect House, a Bellevue Cottage, & a Denham Place were to be looked at by Charlotte with the calmness of amused Curiosity, & by M[r]. P. with the eager eye which hoped to see scarcely any empty houses'.[257] In some ways, of course, Anne and Wentworth too are just another pair of fictional lovers, and as such, perhaps not even that: little, mechanically reproducible swirls of imagination and printer's ink, strutting and fretting their hour on the page. On that page, though, '*and an An*ne Elliot' (italics mine) may conveniently repeat some of the same bits of type, but the phrase does not sound quite right. A reader needs to exercize some government of the tongue in order to stop the words sounding glib, or becoming unpronounceable: 'she was only Anne'[258] in more ways than one.

As the lovers look back along the path that has led to their unexpected reunion, we are told of the concert: 'That evening seemed to be made up of exquisite moments'.[259] They have been there before, and so have we. '[M]oments' recalls the crisis on the Cobb, 'the steps from which Louisa Musgrove fell':

> "A surgeon!" said Anne.
>
> He caught the word; it seemed to rouse him at once, and saying only "True, true, a surgeon this instant," was darting away, when Anne eagerly suggested,
>
> "Captain Benwick, would it not be better for Captain Benwick? He knows where a surgeon is to be found."
>
> Every one capable of thinking felt the advantage of the idea, and in a moment (it was all done in rapid moments) Captain Benwick had resigned the poor corpse-like figure entirely to the brother's care, and was off to the town with the utmost rapidity.[260]

It is fitting that this should have been the point in *Persuasion* which Tennyson most wished to relive: '(it was all done in rapid moments)' rubs against 'in a moment', coming from another tense, as if from another time; it plants a retrospect in the heart of an immediate event, allowing design to sound alongside clutter. What Eliot said about Tennyson also applies to Austen's narrative, in that her surface is intimate with her depths:[261] *Persuasion* testifies at once to art's ability to compose and explore such moments, and moments' potential for being thus dwelt upon and dwelt in.

The example of the much-travelled Crofts is a reminder that Anne and Wentworth, as a naval couple in a time of war, will themselves become subject to sudden and violent displacements; *Sanditon*, Austen's last fictional work, breaks off with a tableau of displaced furniture in Lady Denham's home, in which the portrait of her un-titled first husband Mr Hollis is usurped by the grander picture of her second:

> Charlotte had leisure to look about, & to be told by Mrs P. that the whole-length Portrait of a stately Gentleman, which placed over the Mantlepeice, caught the eye immediately, was the picture of Sir H. Denham—& that one among many Miniatures in another part of the room, little conspicuous, represented Mr Hollis.—Poor Mr Hollis!—It was impossible not to feel him hardly used; to be obliged to stand back in his own House & see the best place by the fire constantly occupied by Sir H. D.[262]

Indeed, the social and ethical environments which Austen's fiction describes, and on which the morality of polite eighteenth-century conversation had depended, were themselves being displaced by the time she died. The traditional domestic circle still exists in *Sanditon*, in the shape of the Heywoods' home ('Marrying early & having a very numerous Family, their movements had been long limitted to one small circle'[263]); but the circle which really matters now is the vertiginous circle of consumer consumption:

> the Miss Beauforts were soon satisfied with "the Circle in which they moved in Sanditon" to use a proper phrase, for every body must now "move in a Circle", —to the prevalence of which rotatory Motion, is perhaps to be attributed the Giddiness & false steps of many.[264]

All is motion and displacement; but even *Sanditon*, just before it (and Austen's fiction) cuts off for good, finds room for a sudden, irreducible moment of emotional mystery, as Charlotte Heywood 'caught a glimpse over the pales of something White & Womanish in the field on the other side [...] Miss Brereton seated, apparently very composedly—& Sir E. D. by her side'.[265]

And the new forces of mechanical reproduction and circulation afforded Austen opportunities; as witnessed by Henry Austen's concentration on his sister's pen, however consciously she may or may not have written *for* the marketplace, she inevitably wrote *in* it – a circumstance which has had creative consequences.

One notable sentence survived the revisions to the end of *Persuasion*; in both versions of the text, Wentworth looks back to Lyme ('There, he had learnt to distinguish between the steadiness of principle and the obstinacy of self-will, between the darings of heedlessness and the resolution of a collected mind'[266]). Austen, who began her fictional career sending up abuses of Johnsonian style, here allows the purer version to sound in her work, and stand witness to her writing; Johnson was in the air of the language she used, the populated air to which she gave up her own words, as she surrendered her works to time. *Persuasion* has survived in a way which typifies the distinctiveness of Austen's fictional achievement, compared to her influences: neither a didactic tract nor a sentimental prompt, this novel of going over old ground has itself become a populated space, an imaginative meeting place, and the starting point of another narrative – for Tennyson, for Beckett, for its whole history of readership. Such feats of literary time travel will not make us better people, but they may, at least for a while, broaden the mind. TS Eliot wrote:

> To be conscious is not to be in time
> But only in time can the moment in the rose-garden,
> The moment in the arbour where the rain beat,
> The moment in the draughty church at smokefall
> Be remembered; involved with past and future.
> Only through time time is conquered.[267]

As the narrator of *Persuasion* puts it: 'This may be bad morality to conclude with, but I believe it to be truth'.[268]

NOTES

PREFACE

1 I have discussed this elsewhere; see my chapter 'Editing Keats's Hands' in Joe Bray, Miriam Handley, and Anne C Henry (eds), *Ma(r)king the Text: The Presentation of Meaning on the Literary Page* (Aldershot: Ashgate, 2000), pp. 201–16.

2 Hugh Sykes Davies, *Wordsworth and the Worth of Words*, ed. John Kerrigan and Jonathan Wordsworth (Cambridge: Cambridge University Press, 1986), p. 118.

3 'The State of the Art', Pocock's introduction to *Virtue, Commerce, and History: Essays on Political Thought and History, Chiefly in the Eighteenth Century* (Cambridge: Cambridge University Press, 1985), pp. 1–34, offers an invaluable overview of these developments in historiography.

4 'My book's subtitle is wrenched out of Hobbes. "Words, contexture, and other circumstances of Language" I take to signify the relation of word to word and of the body of words to those contingencies and accommodations marginally glossed among the "Lawes of Nature" in *Leviathan*: "covenants of mutuall trust", "covenants exhorted by feare", "justice of manners and justice of actions", "submission to arbitrement", etc.', *The Enemy's Country: Words, Contexture, and other Circumstances of Language* (Stanford, CA: Stanford University Press, 1991), p. xii. See also Hill's remark on Samuel Johnson, that 'one cannot unperplex a philosophy of language from an aesthetic of style, an aesthetic of style from the unhappy circumstances.' ibid., p. 9.

5 Compare Pocock's assertion that the historian 'needs a means of understanding how a speech act is performed within a language context, and in particular how it is performed and innovates upon it.' *Virtue, Commerce, and History*, p. 14.

1: THE MORALITY OF CONVERSATION

1 Rudyard Kipling, *Collected Stories* (London: David Campbell Publishers, 1994), p. 741.

2 Conor Cruise O'Brien, *The Great Melody: A Thematic Biography and Commented Anthology of Edmund Burke* (London: Sinclair-Stevenson, 1992), p. 178.

3 'I perceive by the Date of your Letters that you <are a> great proficient in the Noble Science of Astronomy [...] Let us cast our eyes up to the spangled Canapy of heaven, where innumerable Luminaries at such an immense Distance from us cover the face of the Skies! All Suns as great as that which illumines us, surrounded with earths perhaps no way inferior to the Ball which we inhabit! and no part of the amazing whole unfilld! System running into System! and worlds bordering on worlds!' To Richard Shackleton, c. 14 June 1744, *The Correspondence of Edmund Burke*, ed. Thomas W Copeland, 10 vols

(Cambridge: Cambridge University Press; Chicago: University of Chicago Press, 1958–78), i., p. 18.

4 Edmund Burke, *Reflections on the Revolution in France* [1790], ed. Conor Cruise O'Brien (Harmondsworth: Penguin, 1968), p. 169.

5 Fanny Burney, diary entry for 16 February 1788; *Diary and Letters of Madame D'Arblay*, ed. Charlotte Barrett, pref. Austin Dobson, 6 vols (London: Macmillan and Co., 1904–5), iii., p. 449.

6 William Austen-Leigh and Richard Arthur Austen-Leigh, *Jane Austen, Her Life and Letters: A Family Record* (London: Smith, Elder, 1913), p. 41.

7 Quoted in Stanley Ayling, *Edmund Burke: His Life and Opinions* (London: Cassell, 1988), p. 116.

8 Gerald W Chapman, *Edmund Burke: The Practical Imagination* (Cambridge, MA: Harvard University Press, 1967), p. 216. Frans De Bruyn also devotes an illuminating chapter to 'Theatre and Counter-Theatre in Burke's *Reflections on the Revolution in France*' in his study *The Literary Aesthetics of Edmund Burke: The Political Uses of Literary Form* (Oxford: Clarendon Press, 1996), pp. 165–208.

9 JT Boulton, *The Language of Politics in the Age of Wilkes and Burke* (London: Routledge and Kegan Paul; Toronto: University of Toronto Press, 1963), p. 121.

10 The work itself is now lost, but it was reviewed in the *St James's Chronicle* in June 1791.

11 Mary Wollstonecraft, *A Vindication of the Rights of Men, in a Letter to the Right Honourable Edmund Burke; Occasioned by his Reflections on the Revolution in France* [1790], in *The Vindications*, ed. DL Macdonald and Kathleen Scherf (Peterborough, Ontario: Broadview Press, 1997), p. 92.

12 John Thelwall, *Sober Reflections on the Seditious and Inflammatory Letter of the Right Hon. Edmund Burke, to a Noble Lord: Addressed to the Serious Consideration of his Fellow Citizens* (London: HD Symonds, 1796), p. 3.

13 ibid., p. 37.

14 See Ayling, *op. cit.*, p. 219. The quotation is from *King Lear*, III. vi., 61–2.

15 *The Parliamentary History of England from the Norman Conquest in 1066 to the year 1803*, ed. W Cobbett, 36 vols (London: R Bagshaw; Longmans & Co., 1806–20), xxx, p. 189.

16 See his *Myth and Reality in Late-Eighteenth Century British Politics* (London: Macmillan, 1970).

17 See *In Frankenstein's Shadow: Myth, Monstrosity, and Nineteenth-Century Writing* (Oxford: Clarendon Press, 1987), especially pp. 10–29.

18 Wolfgang Iser offers a suggestive reason for why the foreclosure of direct cinematic visualization may disappoint readers of novels on which films are based. 'The feeling that the film version is not what we had imagined is not the real reason for our disappointment; it is more of an epiphenomenon. The real reason is that we have been excluded, and we resent not being allowed to retain the images which we had produced and which enabled us to be in the presence of our products as if they were real possessions.' *The Act of Reading: A Theory of Aesthetic Response* (Baltimore, MD & London: Johns Hopkins University Press, 1978), p. 139.

19 Marilyn Butler, *Jane Austen and the War of Ideas* (Oxford: Clarendon Press, 1975; 2nd edn, 1987), p. 173.

20 Or indeed, 'he'; it is not always clear whether Austen's narrators are clearly gendered, or are even offered as the same persona all the way through the novels in which they appear.

21 Jane Austen, *Northanger Abbey and Persuasion* [1818], ed. RW Chapman (Oxford: Oxford

University Press, 1923; 3rd edn, 1933), pp. 37–8. All subsequent references to this edition, by the title of the individual novel, unless otherwise indicated.

22 ibid., p. 252.

23 Richard Steele, *The Tatler*, no. 3, Thursday, 14 April to Saturday, 16 April 1709, in *Selections from 'The Tatler' and 'The Spectator'*, ed. Angus Ross (Harmondsworth: Penguin, 1982), p. 70.

24 James Boswell, *The Life of Samuel Johnson* [1791], ed. RW Chapman (Oxford: Oxford University Press, 1904; rev. edn., 1970), p. 509.

25 Edward A and Lillian D Bloom, 'Joseph Addison: The Artist in the Mirror' in Edward A Bloom, Lillian D Bloom and E Leites, *Educating the Audience: Addison, Steele, and Eighteenth-Century Culture* (Los Angeles: William Andrews Clark Memorial Library, 1984), p. 6.

26 *The Spectator*, 125, 24 July 1711; *The Spectator* [1711–1712], ed. DF Bond, 5 vols (Oxford: Clarendon Press, 1965), i. p. 509. All subsequent refences to this edition, cited as *Bond*.

27 *The Spectator*, 2, 2 March 1711; *Bond*, i., p. 8.

28 *The Spectator*, 125; *Bond*, i., pp. 509–10.

29 Lawrence E Klein, 'The Political Significance of "Politeness" in Early Eighteenth-Century Britain' in Gordon J Schochet, Patricia E Tatspaugh and Carol Brobeck, eds, *Politics, Politeness, and Patriotism* (Washington, DC: Folger Institute, 1993), p. 95.

30 Pocock, *Virtue, Commerce, and History*, p. 236.

31 *The Spectator*, 119, 17 July 1711; *Bond*, i., p. 486.

32 ibid., pp. 486–7.

33 For the circumstances of Harley's rise, see David Nokes, *Jonathan Swift: A Hypocrite Reversed* (Oxford: Oxford University Press, 1985), pp. 117–49.

34 Anthony Ashley Cooper, Third Earl of Shaftesbury, *Characteristics of Men, Manners, Opinions, Times* [1711], ed. Lawrence E Klein (Cambridge: Cambridge University Press, 1999), p. 97.

35 ibid., p. 192.

36 ibid., p. 35.

37 Lawrence E Klein, 'Shaftesbury, Politeness, and the Politics of Religion' in Nicholas Phillipson and Quentin Skinner, eds, *Political Discourse in Early Modern Britain* (Cambridge: Cambridge University Press, 1993), p. 301.

38 Samuel Johnson, 'Addison' in *Lives of the English Poets* [1781], intr. LA Hind, 2 vols (London: JM Dent & Sons Ltd, 1925), i., p. 334.

39 *The Spectator*, 10, 12 March 1711; *Bond*, i., p. 44.

40 ibid.

41 ibid., pp. 44–5.

42 Johnson, *Lives of the English Poets*, i., p. 367.

43 *The Spectator*, 125; *Bond*, i., p. 512.

44 Joseph Addison, *The Freeholder* [1715–1716], ed. J Leheny (Oxford: Clarendon Press, 1989), p. 179. All subsequent references to this edition, cited as *Leheny*.

45 See Anthony Giddens, *The Third Way: The Renewal of Social Democracy* (Cambridge: Polity Press, 1998); *The Third Way and its Critics* (Malden, MA: Polity Press, 2000).

46 *The Spectator*, 57, 5 May 1711; *Bond*, i., pp. 243–4.

47 Shaftesbury, *Characteristics*, p. 59.

48 Addison, *The Freeholder*, XLV, 25 May 1716; *Leheny*, p. 235.

49 *The Spectator*, 35, 10 April 1711; *Bond*, i., p. 147.

50 Shaftesbury, *Characteristics*, p. 31.

51 Edward A and Lillian D Bloom, *Joseph Addison's Sociable Animal* (Providence: Brown University Press, 1971), p. 59.

52 *The Spectator*, 106, 2 July 1711; *Bond*, i., p. 439.

53 Addison, *The Freeholder* XXII, 5 March 1716; *Leheny*, p. 133.

54 *The Freeholder* XI, 27 January 1716; ibid., p. 88.

55 *The Freeholder* XXXVIII, April 30 1716; ibid., p. 205.

56 *The Spectator*, 1, 1 March 1711; *Bond*, i., p. 5.

57 *The Conversation of Gentlemen Considered* (London: J Hayles, 1738), p. 2.

58 ibid., p. 18.

59 ibid., p. 37.

60 *The Art of Conversation; or The Polite Entertainer* (London: R Willey & J Ryall, 1757), p. 7.

61 ibid., p. 44.

62 ibid., p. 101.

63 Peter Burke, *The Art of Conversation* (Cambridge: Polity Press, 1993), p. 92.

64 Alasdair MacIntyre, *Against the Self-Images of the Age: Essays on Ideology and Philosophy* (London: Duckworth, 1971), p. 10.

65 *Hints towards an Essay on Conversation* in *The Prose Works of Jonathan Swift*, ed. H Davis et al., 16 vols (Oxford: Basil Blackwell, 1939–1974), iv., p. 92. All subsequent references to this edition, cited as *Prose Works*.

66 Lawrence E Klein, *Shaftesbury and the Culture of Politeness* (Cambridge: Cambridge University Press, 1994), p. 182.

67 Flann O'Brien (Brian O'Nolan), *The Best of Myles*, ed K O'Nolan (London: MacGibbon & Kee, 1968; repr. London: Grafton, 1987), p. 202.

68 Jonathan Swift, *A Complete Collection of Genteel and Ingenious Conversation, according to the Most Polite Mode and Method* [1738], in *Prose Works*, iv., p. 159.

69 *The Spectator*, 10; *Bond*, i., pp. 44–5.

70 Swift, *Prose Works*, iv., p. 105.

71 ibid., p. 103.

72 ibid., p. 117.

73 *The World*, 12 August 1756, quoted in Roger Coxon, *Chesterfield and his Critics* (London: George Routledge & Sons, 1925), p. 257.

74 Boswell, *The Life of Samuel Johnson*, p. 188.

75 ibid.

76 To his son, 19 October 1848; Philip Dormer Stanhope, Fourth Earl of Chesterfield, *Lord Chesterfield's Letters* [1774], ed. David Roberts (Oxford: Oxford University Press, 1992), p. 105.

77 To his son, 8 January 1750; ibid., p. 191.

78 To his son, 20 December 1748; ibid., p. 124.

79 To his son, 9 October 1747; ibid., p. 57.

80 To his son, 22 September 1749; ibid., p. 159.

81 Boswell, *The Life of Samuel Johnson*, p. 754.

82 To his son, 26 November 1749; *Lord Chesterfield's Letters*, p. 185.

83 To his son, 19 October 1748; ibid., p. 106.

84 Shaftesbury, *Characteristics*, p. 177.

85 Francis Hutcheson, *An Enquiry Concerning the Ideas of Our Ideas of Virtue or Moral Good* [1725] in *Philosophical Writings*, ed. RS Downie (London: JM Dent, 1994), p. 71.

86 Quentin Skinner, *The Foundations of Modern Political Thought*, 2 vols (Cambridge: Cambridge University Press, 1978), i., p. 138.

87 Jane Austen, 'The History of England from the reign of Henry the 4th to the death of Charles the 1st' in *Minor Works*, ed. RW Chapman (Oxford: Oxford University Press, 1954; rev. edn, 1963), p. 140. All subsequent references to this edition.

88 Jane Austen, *Emma* [1816], ed. RW Chapman (Oxford: Oxford University Press, 1923; 3rd edn, 1933), p. 396. All subsequent references to this edition, unless otherwise indicated.

89 '[…] He may be very "aimable," have very good manners, and be very agreeable; but he can have no English delicacy towards the feelings of other people: nothing really amiable about him.' ibid., p. 149.

90 David Nokes, amongst others, suggests the Burney source; see his *Jane Austen: A Life* (London: Fourth Estate, 1997), p. 394. However, Chesterfield writes: 'It is extremely engaging, to people of every nation, to meet with a foreigner who hath taken pains enough to speak their language correctly; it flatters that local and national pride and prejudice of which everybody hath some share'. To his son, 2 March 1752; *Lord Chesterfield's Letters*, p. 254.

91 Samuel Taylor Coleridge, *Shakespearian Criticism*, ed. TM Raysor, 2 vols (London: Dent, 1960), ii., p. 74.

92 James Beattie, 'The Theory of Language' in *Dissertations Moral and Critical* (London: W Strahan, 1783), p. 233.

93 ibid., p. 237.

94 ibid., p. 269.

95 See Ferdinand de Saussure, *Course in General Linguistics*, trans. Wade Baskin (London: P Owen, 1960; repr. London: Fontana, 1974), esp. pp. 65–100.

96 Murray Cohen, *Sensible Words: Linguistic Practice in England, 1640–1785* (Baltimore and London: Johns Hopkins University Press, 1977), p. xxiii.

97 Thomas Hobbes, *Leviathan* [1651], ed. R Tuck (Cambridge: Cambridge University Press, 1991), p. 36.

98 ibid., p. 25.

99 ibid., p. 51.

100 John Locke, *An Essay Concerning Human Understanding* [1690], ed. Peter H Nidditch (Oxford: Clarendon Press, 1975), pp. 475–6.

101 George Berkeley, *Berkeley's Commonplace Book* [1705–1708], ed. GA Johnston (London: Faber & Faber, 1930), p. 19.

102 Geoffrey Hill, 'Our Word is Our Bond', in *The Lords of Limit: Essays on Literature and Ideas* (London: Andre Deutsch, 1984), p. 140.

103 William Tyndale, *Doctrinal Treatises* (Cambridge: Parker Society, 1848), p. 263.

104 Cohen, *op. cit.*, p. 51.

105 ibid., p. 27.

106 James Harris, *Hermes or A Philosophical Inquiry Concerning Universal Grammar* (London: J Nourse & P Vaillant, 1751; 2nd edn, 1765), p. 395.

107 ibid., p. 57.

108 Beattie, *op. cit.*, p. 330.

109 Harris, *op. cit.*, p. 336.

110 ibid., p. 268.

111 ibid., p. 269.

112 John A Dussinger, *The Discourse of the Mind in Eighteenth-Century Fiction* (The Hague and Paris: Mouton, 1974), pp. 21–2.

113 James Burnet, Lord Monboddo, *Of The Origin and Progress of Language*, 6 vols

(Edinburgh: A Kincaid & W Creech; London: T Cadell, 1773–92; repr. Menston: Scolar Press, 1967), i., p. 5.

114 Beattie, *op. cit.*, p. 414.

115 Harris, *op. cit.*, p. 11.

116 Stephen K Land, *The Philosophy of Language in Britain: Major Theories from Hobbes to Thomas Reid* (New York: AMS Press, 1986), p. 200.

117 Harris, *op. cit.*, p. 290.

118 JL Austin, *How to Do Things with Words*, ed. JO Urmson (Oxford: Oxford University Press, 1962), pp. 99–100.

119 ibid., p. 76.

120 John Horne Tooke, *ΕΠΕΑ ΠΤΕΡΟΕΝΤΑ, or, The Diversions of Purley* (London: J Johnson, 1786), p. 293.

121 Tyndale, *op. cit.*, p. 157–8.

122 Horne Tooke, *op. cit.*, p. 304.

123 ibid., p. 510.

124 Olivia Smith, *The Politics of Language, 1791–1819* (Oxford: Clarendon Press, 1984), p. 123.

125 Horne Tooke, *op. cit.*, p. 343–4.

126 ibid., pp. 348–9.

127 ibid., p. 384.

128 Thomas Hardy, 'Memories of Church Restoration' [1906], in *The Personal Writings of Thomas Hardy*, ed. H Orel (London and Melbourne: Macmillan, 1967), p. 214.

129 Horne Tooke, MS marginalia in copy of *ΕΠΕΑ ΠΤΕΡΟΕΝΤΑ*, British Library shelf-mark c. 60. i. 15, opp. p. 106.

130 ibid., opp. p. 102.

131 JL Austin, *Sense and Sensibilia*, ed. GJ Warnock (Oxford: Oxford University Press, 1962), p. 73.

132 To James Stanier Clarke, 11 December 1815; *Jane Austen's Letters*, ed. D Le Faye (Oxford and New York, 1995), p. 306. All subsequent reference to this edition, cited as *Letters*.

133 Roland Barthes, 'The Death of the Author' [1968] in *Image Music Text*, trans. Stephen Heath (London: Fontana Press, 1977), p. 148.

134 Alberto Manguel, *A History of Reading* (London: HarperCollins, 1996), pp. 122–3.

135 To Cassandra Austen, 25 April 1811; *Letters*, p. 182.

136 To Cassandra Austen, 29 January 1813; ibid., p. 201.

137 See also Christopher Ricks's essay 'Jane Austen and the Business of Mothering' [1982], in *Essays in Appreciation* (Oxford: Clarendon Press, 1996), pp. 90–113.

138 *Northanger Abbey*, p. 250.

139 Eric Griffiths, *The Printed Voice of Victorian Poetry* (Oxford: Clarendon Press, 1989), pp. 12–13.

140 To George Cheyne, 31 August 1741; *Selected Letters of Samuel Richardson*, ed. John Carroll (Oxford: Clarendon Press, 1964), p. 47.

141 To Lady Echlin, 22 September 1755; ibid., p. 322.

142 Austin, *How to Do Things with Words*, p. 75.

143 See Lennard J Davis, *Factual Fictions: The Origins of the English Novel* (New York: Columbia University Press, 1983); J Paul Hunter, *Before Novels: The Cultural Contexts of Eighteenth Century English Fiction* (New York and London: WW Norton & Co., 1990).

144 To Aaron Hill, ?January–February 1741; Richardson, *Selected Letters*, p. 42.

145 Samuel Richardson, preface to *Pamela; or Virtue Rewarded* [1740; 14th edn, 1801], ed. Margaret Anne Doody (Harmondsworth: Penguin, 1985), p. 31. All subsequent references to this edition.

146 Boswell, *The Life of Samuel Johnson*, p. 480.

147 Richardson, *Pamela*, p. 72.

148 ibid., p. 380.

149 See *A Collection of Moral and Instructive Sentiments, Maxims, Cautions, and Reflexions, Contained in the Histories of Pamela, Clarissa, and Sir Charles Grandison* (London: S Richardson, C Hitch, L Hawes et al., 1755).

150 Richardson, *Selected Letters*, p. 311.

151 John Mullan, *Sentiment and Sociability: The Language of Feeling in The Eighteenth Century* (Oxford: Clarendon Press, 1988), p. 96.

152 Richardson, *Pamela*, p. 221.

153 Henry Fielding, *Joseph Andrews* and *Shamela* [1742 & 1741], ed. A Humphreys et al. (London: JM Dent 1973; rev. edn, 1993), p. 36.

154 ibid., p. 7.

155 Laurence Sterne, *The Life and Opinions of Tristram Shandy, Gentleman* [1759–67], ed. G Petrie (Harmondsworth: Penguin, 1967), pp. 412–13.

156 ibid., p. 369.

157 Mullan, *op. cit.*, p. 146.

158 *Address to a Young Lady, on her Entrance into the World*, 2 vols (London: Hookham & Carpenter, 1796), i., p. 39.

159 ibid., p. 2.

160 Jane West, *Letters to a Young Lady; in which the Duties and Character of Women are Considered, Chiefly with a Reference to Prevailing Opinions*, 3 vols (London: Longman, Hurst, Rees & Orme, 1806; 4th edn, 1811), i., p. 53.

161 ibid., i., pp. 64–5.

162 Hester Lynch Piozzi, *British Synonymy; or, an Attempt at Regulating the Choice of Words in Familiar Conversation*, 2 vols (London: n.p., 1794), i., p. 14.

163 ibid., ii., p. 34.

164 ibid., i., pp. 79–80.

165 ibid., i. p. 69.

166 James Barry, John Opie and Henry Fuseli, *Lectures on Painting, by the Royal Academicians*, ed. Ralph N Wornum (London: Henry G Bohn, 1848), p. 390.

167 Cited in *OED*, p. 1718.

168 William Godwin, *Enquiry Concerning Political Justice* [1793], ed. I Kramnick (Harmondsworth: Penguin, 1976), p. 288.

169 Mary Wollstonecraft, *A Vindication of the Rights of Woman* [1792] in *The Vindications*, p. 111.

170 To Cassandra Austen, 20–21 November 1800; *Letters*, p. 61.

171 Jane Austen, *Mansfield Park* [1814], ed. R W Chapman (Oxford: Oxford University Press, 1923; 3rd edn, 1934), p. 14. All subsequent references to this edition, unless otherwise indicated.

172 Geoffrey Hill, 'Jonathan Swift: The Poetry of "Reaction" ' [1968] in *The Lords of Limit*, p. 67.

173 Jane Austen, *Sense and Sensibility* [1811], ed. RW Chapman (Oxford: Oxford University Press, 1923; 3rd edn, 1933), title page. All subsequent references to this edition.

174 To Thomas Poole, 28 January 1810; *Selected Letters*, ed. HJ Jackson (Oxford: Oxford University Press, 1988), pp. 142–3.

175 'But if the Gentry and *Clerisy* (including all the learned & educated) do this, then the nation does it—*or* a commotion is at hand.' To CA Tulk; ibid., pp. 229–30.

176 Introduction to Martin Nystrand, ed., *What Writers Know: The Language, Process, and Structure of Written Discourse* (New York: Academic Press, 1982), p. 4.

177 Barthes, *Image Music Text*, p. 146.

178 Wolfgang Iser, *The Implied Reader: Patterns of Communication in Prose Fiction from Bunyan to Beckett* (Baltimore and London: Johns Hopkins University Press, 1974), p. 275.

179 William Godwin, *The Enquirer: Reflections on Education, Manners, and Literature in a Series of Essays* (London: GG & J Robinson, 1797; repr. New York: AM Kelley, 1965), p. 135.

180 Gérard Genette, *Narrative Discourse*, trans. JE Lewin (Ithaca: Cornell University Press, 1980), p. 27.

181 To Cassandra Austen, 11–12 October 1813; *Letters*, p. 234.

182 To Cassandra Austen, 29 January 1813; ibid., p. 202.

183 Walter Scott, 'Marmion' [1808] in *Selected Poems*, ed. James Reed (Manchester: Carcanet, 1992), p. 244.

184 Journal entry, 14 March 1826, quoted in BC Southam, ed., *Jane Austen: The Critical Heritage*, 2 vols (London: Routledge & Kegan Paul, 1968–87), i., p. 106. Hereafter *JACH* in notes.

185 Pocock, *Virtue, Commerce, and History*, pp. 21–2. He is referring to Stanley Fish's *Is There a Text in This Class? The Authority of Interpretive Communities* (Cambridge, MA: Harvard University Press, 1980).

186 Kelvin Everest, 'Historical Reading and Editorial Practice' in Bray, Handley and Henry, eds, *Ma(r)king the Text*, pp. 198–9.

187 Barthes, *Image Music Text*, p. 146.

188 Jonathan Bate, *Shakespeare and the English Romantic Imagination* (Oxford: Clarendon Press, 1986), p. 6.

189 See CT Onions, *A Shakespeare Glossary*, rev. R-D Eagleson (Oxford: Clarendon Press, 1911; 3rd edn, 1986), p. 178.

190 *Quarterly Review*, January 1821; quoted in *JACH*, i., p. 98.

191 *Edinburgh Review*, January 1843; ibid., i., p. 122.

192 *Fraser's Magazine*, December 1847; ibid., i., p. 125.

193 Hallam Tennyson, *Alfred Lord Tennyson: A Memoir by his Son*, 2 vols (London: Macmillan & Co., 1897), ii., p. 372.

194 Kipling, *Collected Stories*, p. 738.

195 Henry James, 'The Lesson of Balzac' [1905] in *Literary Criticism: French Writers, Other European Writers, The Prefaces to the New York Edition* (New York and Cambridge: Library of America, 1984), p. 118. Hereafter *Literary Criticism*.

196 James to George Pellew, June 1883 in *The Critical Muse: Selected Literary Criticism* (Harmondsworth: Penguin, 1987), p. 173.

197 James, *Literary Criticism*, p. 118.

198 James, *The Critical Muse*, p. 173.

199 James, *The Portrait of a Lady* [1881], ed. Priscilla L Walton (London, JM Dent, 1995), p. 230.

200 Preface to the New York edition of *The Portrait of a Lady* [1908]; *Literary Criticism*, p. 1083.

201 *Englishwoman's Domestic Magazine*, July 1886; quoted in *JACH*, i., p. 202.

202 Percy Fitzgerald, *Jane Austen: A Criticism and Interpretation* (London: Jarrold & Sons, 1912), p. 7.

203 Fanny Burney, preface to *Evelina, or the History of a Young Lady's Entrance into the World* [1778], ed. Stewart J Cooke (New York and London: WW Norton & Co., 1998), p. 6.

204 To WS Williams, 12 April 1850; quoted in *JACH*, i., p. 128.

205 Gilbert Ryle, *The Concept of Mind* (London: Hutchinson, 1949; repr. Harmondsworth: Penguin, 1990), p. 63.

206 ibid., p. 57.

207 'Eminent Women Series', 1889; quoted in *JACH*, ii., p. 189.

208 *The Spectator*, lxiv, 1890; quoted in *JACH*, ii., p. 196.

209 ibid.

210 Barbara Everett, 'Hard Romance', *London Review of Books*, 8/2/1996, p. 12.

211 FR Leavis, *The Great Tradition* (London: Chatto & Windus, 1948; repr. Harmondsworth, Penguin, 1962), p. 9.

212 William Empson remarks: 'A word may become a sort of solid entity, able to direct opinion, thought of as like a person; also it is often said (whether this is the same idea or not) that a word can become a "compacted doctrine", or even that all words are compacted doctrines inherently'. *The Structure of Complex Words* (London: Chatto & Windus, 1951; repr. London: Hogarth Press, 1985), p. 39.

213 'The kind of vacuity isn't peculiarly American; it is a vacuity that technologico-Benthamite civilization is creating and establishing in this country.' FR Leavis, *English Literature in Our Time and the University* (London: Chatto & Windus, 1969; repr. Cambridge: Cambridge University Press, 1979), p. 24.

214 FR Leavis, *Revaluation: Tradition and Development in English Poetry* (London: Chatto & Windus, 1936; repr. Harmondsworth: Penguin, 1964), p. 50.

215 ibid., p. 52.

216 ibid., p. 53.

217 ibid., p. 56.

218 ibid., p. 209.

219 '"Lawrence Scholarship" and Lawrence' [1963] in *'Anna Karenina' and Other Essays* (London: Chatto & Windus, 1967), p. 174.

220 John Casey, *The Language of Criticism* (London: Methuen & Co., 1966), p. 170.

221 ibid., p. 171.

222 Immanuel Kant, *Critique of Pure Reason* [1781], trans. JMD Meiklejohn (London: JM Dent & Sons, 1934; repr. 1991), p. 30.

223 Leavis, *The Great Tradition*, p. 52.

224 *The Oxford Authors: Gerard Manley Hopkins*, ed. Catherine Phillips (Oxford: Oxford University Press, 1986), p. 119. There is a good discussion of this in Geoffrey Hill's '"Perplexed Persistence": the Exemplary Failure of TH Green' [1975] in *The Lords of Limit*, pp. 104–20.

225 Leavis, *The Great Tradition*, p. 18.

226 William Shakespeare, *Hamlet*, III. i., 62–3, in *The Norton Facsimile: The First Folio of Shakespeare*, ed. Charlton Hinman (New York: Garland, 1968), p. 773.

227 William Shakespeare, *Troylus and Cressida*, III. ii., 79–82; ibid., p. 601.

228 'Rereading, an operation contrary to the commercial and ideological habits of our society, which would have us "throw away" the story once it has been consumed ("devoured"), so that we can then move on to another story, buy another book, and which is tolerated only in certain marginal categories of readers (children, old people,

and professors), rereading is here suggested at the outset […] rereading is no longer consumption but play (that play which is the return of the different).' *S/Z*, trans. R Miller (New York: Farrar, Strauss and Giroux, 1974; repr. Oxford: Blackwell, 1990), pp. 15–16.

229 FR Leavis, *New Bearings in English Poetry* (1932; 2nd edn 1950; repr. Harmondsworth 1963), p. 16.

230 TS Eliot, 'Arnold and Pater' [1930] in *Selected Essays* (London: Faber and Faber, 1932; 5th edn, 1951), p. 434.

231 Leavis, *English Literature in Our Time and the University*, p. 59.

232 Leavis, *The Great Tradition*, p. 16.

233 Leavis, *English Literature in Our Time and the University*, p. 170.

234 Martha C Nussbaum, *Love's Knowledge: Essays on Philosophy and Literature* (New York and Oxford: Oxford University Press, 1990), p. 95.

235 ibid., p. 350.

236 Charles Dickens, 'Where We Stopped Growing' [1853] in *'Gone Astray' and Other Papers from Household Words, 1851–59*, ed. Michael Slater (London: JM Dent, 1998), p. 110.

237 Nussbaum, *Love's Knowledge*, p. 148.

238 James, preface to the New York edition of *The Princess Casamassima* [1908]; *Literary Criticism*, p. 1096.

239 Nussbaum, *Love's Knowledge*, p. 152.

240 ibid., p. 164.

241 James, *The Critical Muse*, p. 195.

242 Charles Dickens, *Christmas Books* [1852], intr. E Farjeon (Oxford: Oxford University Press, 1954), pp. 314–98.

243 George Gordon, Lord Byron, 'Remembrance' [1806]; *The Complete Poetical Works*, ed. JJ McGann, 7 vols (Oxford: Clarendon Press, 1980–93), i., p. 6.

244 Samuel Beckett, 'Stirrings Still' [1988] in *As the Story Was Told: Uncollected and Late Prose* (London: John Calder, 1990), p. 128.

245 Nussbaum, *Love's Knowledge*, p. 162.

246 ibid., p. 236.

247 Charles Dickens, *David Copperfield* [1849–1850], ed. Jeremy Tambling (London: Penguin, 1996), pp. 59–60.

248 See, for example, his defence of fairy tales against moralistic rewriting: 'Frauds on the Fairies'[1853]; *'Gone Astray' and Other Papers*, pp. 166–74.

249 See the discussion of Nussbaum in Peter Lamarque and Stein Hagstrum Olsen, *Truth, Fiction and Literature* (Oxford: Clarendon Press, 1994), pp. 386–94.

250 Martha C Nussbaum, *Poetic Justice: The Literary Imagination and Public Life* (Boston: Beacon Press, 1995), p. 12.

251 Nussbaum, *Love's Knowledge*, p. 171.

252 Kipling, *Collected Stories*, pp. 742–3.

253 ibid., p. 745.

254 Brian Southam, 'Jane Austen and her Readers' in *Collected Reports of the Jane Austen Society, 1966–75*, intr. Elizabeth Jenkins (Folkestone: n. p., 1977), p. 86.

255 Marcel Proust, 'Days of Reading (1)' in *Against Sainte-Beuve and Other Essays*, trans. John Sturrock (Harmondsworth: Penguin, 1988; repr. 1994), p. 210.

256 ibid., pp. 213–14.

257 George Craig writes suggestively of reading practice: 'Unable to reach any reader

direct, the writer works in the area between the subject (his whole self, forever unknowable) and the "I" that he knows (writer, reader, comparer, aspirer); the work is a dialogue across the space between; the result is his language – provisional, opaque, other.' 'So Little Do We Know of What Goes on When We Read', in Philip Davis, ed., *Real Voices: On Reading* (Basingstoke and London: Macmillan, 1997), p. 57. Compare DW Harding: 'the process of looking on at and entering into other people's activity, or representations of it, does enlarge the range, not of the onlooker's experience but of his quasi-experience and partial understanding. For it has to be remembered that the subtlest and most intense empathetic insight into the experience of another person is something far different from having the experience oneself'. 'Psychological Processes in the Reading of Fiction', *British Journal of Aesthetics*, 2 (1962), p. 145.

258 Capel Lofft, *Remarks on the Letter of the Rt. Hon. Edmund Burke, concerning the Revolution in France* (London: J Johnson, 1790), pp. 77–8.

259 To Anna Austen, 28 September 1814; *Letters*, p. 277.

INTERLUDE: AUSTEN'S EARLY FICTION

1 Jane Austen, *Minor Works*, p. 430.

2 Hugh Blair, *Lectures on Rhetoric and Belles Lettres*, 2 vols (London: W Strahan; Edinburgh: T Cadell & W Creech, 1783), i., pp. 250–1.

3 *Love and Freindship* [1790]; *Minor Works*, pp. 78–9.

4 'Amongst her favourite writers, Johnson in prose, Crabbe in verse, and Cowper in both, stood high.' James Edward Austen-Leigh, *A Memoir of Jane Austen* [1870] in Austen-Leigh, et al., *A Memoir of Jane Austen and Other Family Recollections*, ed. Kathryn Sutherland (Oxford: Oxford University Press, 2002), p. 71. All subsequent references to this edition, cited as *Memoir*.

5 Samuel Johnson, preface to *The Plays of William Shakespeare* [1765], in *Samuel Johnson on Shakespeare*, ed. HR Woudhuysen (Harmondsworth, 1989), pp. 121–2.

6 ibid., p. 122.

7 Archibald Campbell, *Lexiphanes, a Dialogue*, 2nd edn (London: J Knox, 1767), p. xvii.

8 ibid., p. 2.

9 Jane Austen, 'Henry and Eliza' [1787–1790]; *Minor Works*, p. 37.

10 *Northanger Abbey*, p. 108.

11 Blair, *op. cit.*, i., p. 303.

12 Geoffrey Hill, 'An Apology for the Revival of Christian Architecture in England' [1978] in *Collected Poems* (Harmondsworth: Penguin, 1985), pp. 152–64.

13 Ian Watt, *The Rise of the Novel: Studies in Defoe, Richardson and Fielding* (Berkeley and Los Angeles: University of California Press, 1957), p. 13.

14 Margaret Anne Doody, 'The Short Fiction', in Edward Copeland and Juliet McMaster, eds, *The Cambridge Companion to Jane Austen* (Cambridge: Cambridge University Press, 1997), p. 93.

15 Samuel Richardson, *Clarissa; or The History of a Young Lady* [1747–1748], ed. Angus Ross (Harmondsworth: Penguin, 1985), p. 893. All subsequent references to this edition, unless otherwise indicated.

16 Philip Stevick, 'The Theory of Fictional Chapters' in Philip Stevick, ed., *The Theory of the Novel* (New York: Free Press, 1967), p. 183.

17 Henry Fielding, *The History of Tom Jones* [1749], ed. RPC Mutter (Harmondsworth: Penguin, 1966), pp. 151, 121.

18 Sterne, *Tristram Shandy*, p. 454.

19 *Minor Works*, p. 45.

20 ibid.

21 ibid., p. 55.

22 ibid., p. 56.

23 ibid., p. 55.

24 ibid., p. 42.

25 ibid., p. 139.

26 ibid., p. 102.

27 Susan Sontag, 'Notes on "Camp"' [1964] in *A Susan Sontag Reader* (Harmondsworth: Penguin, 1982), p. 105.

28 Genette, *Narrative Discourse*, pp. 263–4.

29 Doody, *op. cit.*, p. 92.

30 William Wordsworth, 'Resolution and Independence' [1807] in *The Poems*, ed. John O Hayden, 2 vols (Harmondsworth: Penguin, 1977), i., p. 555. All subsequent references to this edition, unless otherwise indicated.

31 Lewis Carroll [CL Dodgson], *Through the Looking-Glass, and What Alice Found There* [1871] in *The Annotated Alice*, ed. M Gardner (London: Anthony Blond Ltd, 1964; repr. Harmondsworth: Penguin, 1965; rev. edn, 1970), p. 311.

32 Wordsworth, *The Poems*, i., p. 556.

33 Carroll, *The Annotated Alice*, p. 313.

34 Kipling, *Collected Stories*, p. 743.

35 *Minor Works*, p. 14.

36 ibid., p. 18.

37 ibid., p. 22.

38 ibid., p. 31.

39 'The Generous Curate' [1793]; ibid., p. 73.

40 Vladimir Propp, *Morphology of the Folktale*, trans. L Scott (Austin, TX and London: University of Texas Press, 1958; 2nd edn, 1968), p. 96.

41 Everett, 'Hard Romance', p. 12.

42 *Northanger Abbey*, p. 158.

43 ibid., pp. 158–9.

44 ibid., p. 159.

45 ibid., pp. 25–6.

46 ibid., p. 15.

47 Vicesimus Knox, *Elegant Extracts: or Useful and Entertaining Pieces of Poetry Selected for the Improvement of Youth, etc.* (London: Charles Dilly, 1784).

48 *Northanger Abbey*, p. 15.

49 ibid., p. 164.

50 ibid.

51 William Godwin, *Things as They Are, or The Adventures of Caleb Williams* [1794], ed. David McCracken (Oxford: Oxford University Press, 1970), p. 132.

52 George Colman the Younger, *The Iron Chest* (London: Cadell & Davies, 1796; repr. Oxford: Woodstock, 1989).

53 Peter Teuthold, *The Necromancer; or The Tale of the Black Forest* [1794] (London: Folio Press, 1968), pp. 92–3.

54 *Northanger Abbey*, p. 48.

55 Matthew Lewis, *The Monk* [1796], ed. Howard Anderson (Oxford: Oxford University Press, 1973), p. 107.

56 *Northanger Abbey*, p. 200.

57 ibid., p. 199.

58 'Lady Harriet Marlow' [William Beckford], *Modern Novel Writing, or The Elegant Enthusiast*, 2 vols (London: GG & J Robinson, 1796; repr. New York and London: Garland, 1974), title pages.

59 ibid., ii., p. 48.

60 ibid., ii., p. 50.

61 Charlotte Lennox, *The Female Quixote, or The Adventures of Arabella* [1752], ed. Margaret Dalziel (Oxford: Oxford University Press, 1989), p. 7.

62 ibid., p. 381.

63 Mary Brunton, *Self-Control: A Novel*, 4th edn (Edinburgh: George Ramsay & Co.; London: Longman, Hurst, Reese, Orme & Brown, 1811; repr. London: H Colburn & R Bentley, 1832), p. 70.

64 *Northanger Abbey*, p. 201.

65 Sigmund Freud, 'The "Uncanny"' [1919] in *Art and Literature*, trans. J Strachey et al. (Harmondsworth: Penguin, 1985), p. 367.

66 *Northanger Abbey*, p. 108.

67 ibid., pp. 112–13.

68 ibid., pp. 20–1.

69 ibid., p. 200.

70 Kipling, *Collected Stories*, p. 743.

71 *Northanger Abbey*, p. 244.

72 Boswell, *The Life of Samuel Johnson*, p. 696.

73 *Tristram Shandy*, p. 535.

74 Kipling, *Collected Stories*, p. 743.

75 ibid., p. 752.

76 Gabriel Josipovici, *On Trust: Art and the Temptations of Suspicion* (New Haven and London: Yale University Press, 1999), p. 249.

77 James, preface to the New York edition of *Roderick Hudson* [1907]; *Literary Criticism*, p. 1041.

78 *Minor Works*, p. 74.

2: FLIRTING

1 *Letters*, p. 6.

2 Jane Austen, *Pride and Prejudice* [1813], ed. RW Chapman (Oxford: Oxford University Press, 1923; 3rd edn, 1932), p. 221. All subsequent references to this edition.

3 *Memoir*, p. 70.

4 Proverbs 31:26, in the translation of the Authorized Version. This is the spelling which appears on the plaque.

5 Proverbs 31:10, Authorized Version.

6 *North British Review*, April 1870; *JACH*, i, p. 253.

7 See his introduction to *JACH*, ii, pp. 1–158.

8 James, *Literary Criticism*, p. 118.

9 *JACH*, i, p. 243.

10 ibid., i. p. 253.

11 ibid., i. p. 251.

12 Alexander Pope, 'An Essay on Man', Epistle II [1733], ll. 23–6; *The Poems of Alexander Pope*, ed. John Butt (London: Methuen, 1963; rev. edn, 1968), p. 517.

13 Cassandra Austen to Fanny Knight, [?] July 1817; *Letters*, p. 514.

14 Christopher Ricks discusses this aspect of the remark in *Beckett's Dying Words* (Oxford: Clarendon Press, 1993), p. 69.

15 In Plato's *Phaedo*, Socrates characterizes the philosopher's life thus: 'those who practice philosophy aright are cultivating dying, and for them, least of all men, does being dead hold any terror'; *Phaedo*, trans. David Gallup (Oxford: Oxford University Press, 1993), p. 14.

16 RF Brissenden, *Virtue in Distress: Studies in the Novel of Sentiment from Richardson to Sade* (London: Macmillan, 1974), p. 98.

17 Gilbert Ryle might well have claimed, with reason, that the metaphor of minds' inhabiting bodies is itself logically misguided and misleading; see *The Concept of Mind*, especially ch. 1. Nevertheless, despite its logically fantastic status, the metaphor has a great tenacity in the history of poetry, from Lucretius, through Donne, to Larkin.

18 *JACH*, i, p. 265.

19 *OED*, p. 211.

20 As a Catholic writer, and the biographer of the recusant Edmund Campion, Simpson lived in the ambience of JH Newman's ideas on 'development'. Of particular relevance to Austen's case is Newman's account of the third test of development, the power of assimilation: 'doctrine and views which relate to man are not placed in a void, but in the crowded world, and make way for themselves by interpenetration, and develop by absorption.' *An Essay on the Development of Christian Doctrine* [1845], ed. JM Cameron (Harmondsworth: Penguin, 1974), p. 131.

21 *Minor Works*, p. 13.

22 ibid., p. 398.

23 *Memoir*, pp. 133–4.

24 ibid., p. 133. Austen-Leigh was referring to William Harness's *The Life of Mary Russell Mitford, Authoress of 'Our Village', etc., related in a selection from her Letters to her Friends*, ed. AE L'Estrange (London: Richard Bentley, 1870).

25 ibid.

26 *Evelina*, pp. 196–7.

27 Juliet McMaster suggests that '[t]he lover becomes particularly sensitive to the name of his beloved [...] On the other hand the lover may become reticent about the name, and be unable to pronounce it, though he thinks it all the time (Jane Austen's heroines usually belong in the latter category).' *Jane Austen on Love* (Victoria, BC: English Literary Studies Monographs, 13, 1978), p. 13.

28 July 1779; quoted in *Dr Johnson and Fanny Burney: Extracts from Fanny Burney's Prose, 1777–84*, ed. Nigel Wood (Bristol: Bristol Classical Press, 1989), p. 59.

29 'There are two Traits in her character which are pleasing; namely, she admires Camilla, & drinks no cream in her Tea.' To Cassandra Austen, 15 September 1796; *Letters*, p. 14.

30 Fanny Burney, *Camilla: or a Picture of Youth* [1796], ed. Edward A and Lillian D Bloom (Oxford: Oxford University Press, 1972), p. 900.

31 Christopher Ricks, 'Thomas Lovell Beddoes: "A Dying Start"' in *The Force of Poetry* (Oxford: Oxford University Press, 1984), p. 154.

32 *Northanger Abbey*, p. 163.
33 *Mansfield Park*, p. 85.
34 To Cassandra Austen, 9–10 January 1796; *Letters*, p. 1.
35 ibid., p. 2.
36 *Memoir*, p. 10.
37 To Cassandra Austen, 15 January 1796; *Letters*, p. 4.
38 *JACH*, i, p. 264.
39 To Cassandra Austen, 17 November 1798; *Letters*, p. 19.
40 Juliet McMaster describes this well: 'Jane Austen's fine sense of the rub of intimacy, of the way the constant contact in a close union produces sparks or smoothness, soreness or consonant grooves, is spelled out morally, but is also physically suggestive.' *Jane Austen on Love*, p. 79.
41 *JACH*, i, p. 42.
42 ibid., p. 46.
43 ibid., p. 47.
44 Geoffrey Hill, 'Poetry as "Menace" and "Atonement"' [1978] in *The Lords of Limit*, p. 2.
45 Samuel Taylor Coleridge, *Biographia Literaria* [1817], ed. James Engell and Walter Jackson Bate, 2 vols in 1 (Princeton: Princeton University Press, 1983), ii., p. 143.
46 Thomas Gisborne, *An Enquiry into the Duties of the Female Sex* (London: n. p., 1797), pp. 174–5.
47 To Cassandra Austen, 4 February 1813; *Letters*, p. 203.
48 Butler, *Jane Austen and the War of Ideas*, p. 197.
49 *Pride and Prejudice*, p. 231.
50 ibid., pp. 283–4.
51 ibid., pp. 232.
52 Maynard Mack remarks of *The Dunciad*: 'Plainly, something in Pope responds to the secret resources of dulness, elaborates them with visible delight, even educes from them a strange beauty – for the ear as well as the eye'; *Alexander Pope: A Biography* (New Haven & London: Yale University Press, 1985), p. 461. Compare Geoffrey Hill on Swift's satire: 'However deliberately the retrenching moralist may stand at guard [...] the poetic imagination still cherishes the creatures of its invention'; 'Jonathan Swift: the Poetry of "Reaction"', in *The Lords of Limit*, p. 79.
53 John Bayley, 'The "Irresponsibility" of Jane Austen' in BC Southam, ed., *Critical Essays on Jane Austen* (London: Routledge & Kegan Paul, 1968), p. 8.
54 ibid., p. 6.
55 *Much Ado About Nothing*, III. i, 51–2; *The Norton Facsimile*, p. 128.
56 *JACH*, i, p. 244.
57 *Mansfield Park*, p. 63.
58 ibid., p. 265.
59 *Pride and Prejudice*, p. 279.
60 Boswell, *The Life of Samuel Johnson*, p. 705.
61 Johnson, 'Waller', in *Lives of the English Poets*, i., p. 148.
62 William Empson, *Some Versions of Pastoral* (London: Chatto & Windus, 1935; repr. London: Hogarth Press, 1986), p. 64.
63 *Letters*, p. 1.
64 *Tristram Shandy*, p. 120.
65 MacIntyre, *After Virtue: A Study in Moral Theory* (London: Duckworth, 1981), p. 243.
66 *Pride and Prejudice*, pp. 11–12.

67 ibid., p. 6.

68 ibid., p. 11.

69 R Allen Harris, 'Social Definition in *Pride and Prejudice*: An Exercise in Extensional Semantics', *English Studies in Canada* 17:2 (1991), p. 164.

70 ibid., p. 174.

71 Joe Bray notes: 'Richardson's "last correction" of *Pamela* gave him the opportunity to respond to those who had imputed the character of his heroine, and to reassert both her innocence and the sincerity of her opposition to Mr B. [...] Part of the means by which Richardson created this new, tougher, more satirical Pamela was through the addition of italics.' '"Attending to the *minute*": Richardson's revisions of italics in *Pamela*' in Bray, Handley and Henry, eds, *Ma(r)king the Text*, p. 117.

72 Barbara Hardy, *A Reading of Jane Austen* (London: Athlone Press, 1975; 2nd edn, 1979), p. 49. Juliet McMaster also suggests: 'The similarity between these two gayest of their authors' works sometimes tempts me to speculate whether Jane Austen was consciously following Shakespeare's play'; *Jane Austen on Love*, p. 48.

73 *Much Ado About Nothing*, I. i., 123; *The Norton Facsimile*, p. 120.

74 *OED*, p. 747.

75 *Much Ado About Nothing*, III. i., 34; *The Norton Facsimile*, p. 127.

76 *OED*, p. 2452.

77 'A quibble is to Shakespeare what luminous vapours are to the traveller; he follows it at all adventures, it is sure to lead him out of his way, and sure to engulf him in the mire.' *Johnson on Shakespeare*, p. 132. At the beginning of the century, it had also been a distinctive trait in polite Whig aesthetics to associate wordplay negatively with the superseded manners of the seventeenth century. Shaftesbury welcomed 'the decline and ruin of a false sort of wit, which so much delighted our ancestors that their poems and plays as well as sermons were full of it. All humour had something of the quibble. The very language of the Court was punning.' 'Sensus Communis', in *Characteristics*, p. 31. In *Spectator* 61, 10 May 1711, Addison declared: 'There is no kind of false Wit which has been so recommended by the Practice of all Ages, as that which consists in a Jingle of Words, and is comprehended under the general name of *Punning*.' *Bond*, i., p. 259.

78 MM Mahood, *Shakespeare's Wordplay* (London: Methuen, 1957), p. 9.

79 TS Eliot, 'Shakespeare and the Stoicism of Seneca' [1927], in *Selected Essays*, p. 135.

80 See his preface to the 1964 edition of *The Use of Poetry and the Use of Criticism* (London: Faber and Faber, 1933; 2nd edn, 1964), pp. 9–10.

81 *Much Ado About Nothing*, V. iv. 98; *The Norton Facsimile*, p. 139.

82 *JACH*, i., p. 125.

83 *Pride and Prejudice*, p. 10.

84 Jane Austen, *Emma* [1816] ed. RW Chapman (Oxford 1923; 3rd edn 1933), p. 5. All subsequent references are to this edition. This particular joke in *Emma* was brought to my attention by Barney Harkins.

85 Southam, 'Jane Austen and her Readers'; *Collected Reports of the Jane Austen Society 1966–75*, p. 79.

86 *Characteristics*, p. 31.

87 *Pride and Prejudice*, p. 94.

88 ibid., p. 3.

89 ibid., p. 19.

90 ibid., p. 35.

91 Paul Grice, 'Logic and Conversation' [1967] in *Studies in the Way of Words* (Cambridge, MA: Harvard University Press, 1989), pp. 24–5.

92 ibid., p. 28.

93 *Pride and Prejudice*, p. 180.

94 ibid., p. 49.

95 Paul Langford, *A Polite and Commercial People: England 1727–1783* (Oxford: Oxford University Press, 1989), p. 115.

96 Fitzgerald, *Jane Austen: A Criticism and Interpretation*, p. 102.

97 ibid., p. 21–2.

98 ibid., p. 53.

99 Goffman notes: 'Queen Victoria enforced the rule that anyone seeing her approach when she was driving in her pony-cart on the palace grounds should turn his head or walk in another direction; therefore great statesmen sometimes were required to sacrifice their own dignity and jump behind the shrubbery when the queen unexpectedly approached.' *The Presentation of Self in Everyday Life* (Garden City, NY: Doubleday, 1959; repr. London: Allen Lane, 1969), p. 122. See also Edward T Hall, *The Hidden Dimension* (Garden City, NY: Doubleday, 1966), pp. 101–12.

100 Compare Charlotte Smith's *The Emigrants* [1793], Book the First, 94–101:

> Behold, in witness of this mournful truth,
> A group approach me, whose dejected looks,
> Sad Heralds of distress! proclaim them Men
> Banish'd for ever and for conscience sake
> From their distracted Country, whence the name
> Of Freedom misapplied, and much abus'd
> By lawless Anarchy, has driven them far
> To wander;

The Poems of Charlotte Smith, ed. Stuart Curran (New York and Oxford: Oxford University Press, 1993), p. 138.

101 Fanny Burney, journal entry of 9 April 1793, in *Selected Letters and Journals*, ed. Joyce Hemlow (Oxford: Oxford University Press, 1986), p. 6.

102 To Cassandra Austen, 29 January 1813; *Letters*, p. 202.

103 *Pride and Prejudice*, p. 51.

104 *OED*, p. 1909.

105 See Peter Sabor, ' "Staring in Astonishment": Portraits and Pictures in *Persuasion*' in Juliet McMaster and Bruce Stovel, eds, *Jane Austen's Business: Her World and Her Profession* (Basingstoke and London: Macmillan, 1996), pp. 17–29.

106 Richardson, *Clarissa*, p. 400.

107 Samuel Richardson, *Sir Charles Grandison* [1753–1754], ed. Jocelyn Harris, 3 vols in 1 (Oxford: Oxford University Press, 1972), i, p. 183.

108 Anne Radcliffe, *The Mysteries of Udolpho* [1794], ed. Bonamy Dobrée (Oxford: Oxford University Press, 1966), p. 1.

109 *Minor Works*, p. 383.

110 *Pride and Prejudice*, p. 7.

111 ibid., p. 60.

112 To Cassandra Austen, 26 May 1801; *Letters*, p. 135.

113 *Pride and Prejudice*, p. 289. I borrow here from my 'Editing Keats's Hands'; Bray, Handley and Henry (eds), *Ma(r)king the Text*, p. 210.

114 ibid., p. 97.

115 DW Harding, 'Character and Caricature in Jane Austen', in *Critical Essays on Jane Austen*, ed. BC Southam (London: Routledge & Kegan Paul, 1968), p. 84.

116 *Pride and Prejudice*, p. 98.

117 ibid.

118 Clarissa writes to her brother: 'Nor will I, but by distant civilities, return the compliments of any of my acquaintance.' *Clarissa*, p. 118.

119 *Pride and Prejudice*, p. 106.

120 ibid., p. 108.

121 Alasdair MacIntyre remarks on Edward Glover's defence of psychoanalysis: 'The difficulty with this argument lies in its covert circularity. We cannot trust present experimental techniques because their use neglects the operation of unconscious factors; the only factors which would be reliable would therefore be those which took account of the operation of such factors. But to admit the existence of the kind of unconscious factors of which Dr Glover speaks is already to concede substantial truth to the very body of theory which we require to be tested.' 'Psychoanalysis: the future of an illusion' in *Against the Self-Images of the Age*, p. 33.

122 *Pride and Prejudice*, p. 108.

123 ibid., p. 265.

124 ibid., p. 263.

125 ibid., p. 91.

126 Reuben A Brower, 'Light and Bright and Sparkling: Irony and Fiction in *Pride and Prejudice*' [1951] in Ian Watt, ed., *Jane Austen: A Collection of Critical Essays* (Englewood Cliffs, NJ: Prentice-Hall, 1963), p. 67.

127 *Pride and Prejudice*, p.175.

128 St Augustine remarks: 'Infancy did not "depart", for it has nowhere to go. Yet I was no longer a baby incapable of speech but already a boy with power to talk. This I remember. But how I learned to talk I discovered only later.' *Confessions*, trans. Henry Chadwick (Oxford: Oxford University Press, 1991), p. 10. Wittgenstein also comments: 'When we first begin to *believe* anything, what we believe is not a single proposition, it is a whole system of propositions. (Light dawns gradually over the whole.)' *On Certainty*, trans. D Paul and GEM Anscombe (Oxford: Blackwell, 1979), p. 21e.

129 *Pride and Prejudice*, p. 380.

130 *Emma*, p. 431.

131 Paul Ricoeur comments: 'The necessity of disconnecting the system of tenses from our lived experience of time and the impossibility of separating them completely seem to me marvelously to illustrate the status of narrative configurations as at one and the same time being autonomous in relation to everyday experience and mediating between what precedes and what follows a narrative.' *Time and Narrative*, trans. Kathleen McLaughlin and David Pellauer, 3 vols (Chicago and London: University of Chicago Press, 1984–1988), ii., p. 62. See also Stephen Jay Gould, *Time's Arrow, Time's Cycle: Myth and Metaphor in the Discovery of Geological Time* (Cambridge, MA and London: Harvard University Press, 1987), esp. pp. 1–19.

132 Philip Larkin, *Collected Poems*, ed. A Thwaite (London: Faber and Faber, 1988), p. 167.

133 See Monika Fludernik, *The Fictions of Language and the Languages of Fiction* (London: Routledge, 1993), pp. 319–59; and Geoffrey Leech and Michael Short, *Style in Fiction* (London: Longman, 1981), pp. 318–51.

134 *Pride and Prejudice*, p. 98–9.

135 Most influential in this regard is Michel Foucault's account of Bentham's design for

the 'Panopticon': 'Il suffit alors de placer un surveillant dans la tour centrale, et dans chaque cellule d'enfermer un fou, un malade, un condamné, un ouvrier ou un écolier [...] Autant de cages, autant de petits théâtres, où chaque acteur est seul, parfaitement individualisé et constamment visible. Le dispositif panoptique aménage des unités spatiales qui permettent de voir sans arrêt et de reconnaître aussitot [...] La visibilité est un piège.' [All one needs to do is to place a watchman in the central tower, and then lock up in each cell a madman, a sick man, a condemned man, a workman, a scholar [...] The cages become so many little theatres, in which each actor is alone, perfectly isolated and constantly visible. The panoptic system creates a spatial unity which provides uninterrupted views and instant recognition [...] Visibility is a trap.] *Surveiller et punir: Naissance de la prison* (Paris: Gallimard, 1975), p. 201–2.

136 Nicola J Watson, *Revolution and the Form of the British Novel, 1790–1825* (Oxford: Clarendon Press, 1994), p. 136.

137 Käte Hamburger, *The Logic of Literature*, trans. Marilynn J Rose (Bloomington and London: Indiana University Press, 1973), p. 139. Ricoeur explicates Hamburger's thesis illuminatingly: 'Contrary to the prejudice that the power to describe the subjects of action, thought, and feeling from inside is derived from a subject's self-confession and examination of conscience, she goes so far as to suggest that it is the third-person novel, that is, the novel that recounts the thoughts, feelings, and words of a fictive other, that has gone furthest in the inspection of what goes on inside minds.' *Time and Narrative*, ii., p. 89.

138 Dorrit Cohn, *Transparent Minds: Narrative Modes for Presenting Consciousness in Fiction* (Princeton, NJ: Princeton University Press, 1978), p. 115.

139 William Wordsworth, Preface to *Lyrical Ballads, with Pastoral and Other Poems* [1802], in *Poems*, i., p. 883.

140 ibid., p. 885.

141 ibid.

142 Sir Joshua Reynolds, 'Discourse XI' [December 10, 1782], in *Discourses on Art*, ed. RR Wark (San Marino, CA 1959; repr. New Haven and London 1997), p. 200.

143 Michael Rosenthal, *The Art of Thomas Gainsborough: 'a little business for the eye'* (New Haven and London: Yale University Press, 1999), p. 149.

144 Georges Vigne comments of the de Senonnes portrait: 'The celebrated mirror reflection, in addition to innocently heightening the impression of a chance encounter, certainly figures in this curious meditation, for it suggests that everything in painting is both illusion and reality, that image and its double have the same status, both of them being fabrications.' *Ingres*, trans. J Goodman (New York: Abbeville Press, 1995), p. 100.

145 Leech and Short, are also drawn towards the mirror-metaphor: 'Like a hall of mirrors, each mirror capable of replicating the image in another, a discourse can embody narrators within narrations, reflectors within reflections, and so on *ad infinitum*.' *Style in Fiction*, p. 348.

146 Wayne C Booth notes: '[S]ince the Enlightenment people have increasingly thought of their own essential natures not as something to be built, or built up, through experience with other characters but rather as something – a 'true self' – to be found by probing within [...] In that search, one tends to peel off the inauthentic, insincere, alien influences that might deflect the self from its unique, individual destiny.' *The Company We Keep: An Ethics of Fiction* (Berkeley: University of California Press, 1988), p. 237.

147 'While other literary forms induced the reader to contemplate the exemplariness they embodied, the novel confronted him with problems arising from his own surroundings, at the same time holding out various potential solutions which the reader himself had, at least partially, to formulate. What was presented in the novel led to a specific effect: namely, to involve the reader in the world of the novel and so help him to understand it – and ultimately his own world – more clearly.' Iser, *The Implied Reader*, p. xi.

148 MacIntyre, *After Virtue*, p. 221.

149 To Cassandra Austen, 4 February 1813; *Letters*, p. 203.

150 DW Harding, 'Regulated Hatred: An Aspect of the Work of Jane Austen' [1940] in *Regulated Hatred and Other Essays*, ed. Monica Lawlor (London and Atlantic Highlands: Athlone Press, 1998), p. 22.

151 *Persuasion*, p. 5.

152 *Pride and Prejudice*, p. 232.

153 Proverbs 31:1, in the translation of the Authorized Version.

3: THROWING THE VOICE

1 Oliver Goldsmith, 'Retaliation' [1774]; *Collected Works of Oliver Goldsmith*, ed. Arthur Friedman, 5 vols (Oxford: Clarendon Press, 1966), iv., p. 357.

2 To Cassandra Austen, 3–5 January 1801; *Letters*, p. 68.

3 Norman Page, *The Language of Jane Austen* (Oxford: Oxford University Press, 1972), p. 169.

4 Janet Gurkin Altman, *Epistolarity: Approaches to a Form* (Columbus: Ohio State University Press, 1982), p. 13.

5 Angel Day, *The English Secretary; or Methods of Writing Epistles and Letters, with a Declaration of such Tropes, Figures, and Schemes, as either usually or for ornament sake are therein required* [1586; 2nd edn, 1599], ed. RO Evans, 2 vols in 1 (Gainesville, Fl.: Scholars' Facsimiles and Reprints, 1967), p. 1.

6 Sigmund Freud, *Civilisation and Its Discontents* [1930], trans. J Rivière, rev. & ed. J Strachey (Harmondsworth: Penguin, 1963), p. 28.

7 *Tristram Shandy*, p. 286.

8 Hegel remarks of the word 'now' written down the previous night: 'The Now that is night is *preserved*, i.e., it is treated as it professes to be, as something that *is*; but it proves to be, on the contrary, something that is *not*. The Now does indeed preserve itself, but as something that is *not* night; equally, it preserves itself in face of the Day that it now is, as something that also is not Day [...] This self-preserving Now is, therefore, not immediate but mediated [...]'. *Phenomenology of Spirit*, trans. AV Miller (Oxford: Oxford University Press, 1977), p. 60.

9 To Cassandra Austen, 1 November 1800; *Letters*, p. 52.

10 ibid.

11 *Minor Works*, p. 175.

12 To Cassandra Austen, 7–8 January 1807; *Letters*, p. 117.

13 To Cassandra Austen, 8–9 February 1807; *Letters*, p. 118.

14 To George and Georgiana Keats, 17–27 September 1819; *The Letters of John Keats*, ed. M Buxton Forman (Oxford: Oxford University Press, 1931; 4th edn, 1952), pp. 417–18.

15 Eric Griffiths illuminatingly discusses these aspects of Keats's letter in *The Printed Voice of Victorian Poetry*, pp. 36–7.

16 'In American society there is what is called a telephone voice', a cultivated form of speech not employed in face-to-face talk because of the danger of doing so.' Goffman, *The Presentation of Self in Everyday Life*, p. 215.

17 To Publius Nigidius Figulus, August/ September 46 BC; Cicero, *The Letters to His Friends I* (Cambridge, MA & London: Harvard University Press & William Heinemann, 1979), p. 304. The events to which Cicero refers involve Caesar's ascendancy over Pompey's faction.

18 *The English Secretary*, pp. 2, 4.

19 David Marshall, *The Figure of Theater: Shaftesbury, Defoe, Adam Smith, and George Eliot* (New York: Columbia University Press, 1986), p. 41.

20 Blair, *Lectures on Rhetoric and Belles Lettres*, ii., p. 297.

21 ibid., ii., p. 301.

22 ibid., ii. p. 298.

23 To Marcus Caelius Rufus, 14 November 51 BC; Cicero, op. cit., p. 122.

24 GF Singer, *The Epistolary Novel: Its Origin, Development, Decline and Residuary Influence* (Philadelphia: University of Pennsylvania Press, 1933), p. 34.

25 ibid., pp. 4–5.

26 *The Rambler*, 43 (14 August 1750); *The Yale Edition of the Works of Samuel Johnson*, ed. EL McAdam, *et al.*, 16 vols (New Haven and London: Yale University Press, 1958–), iii., p. 232.

27 Review of Soame Jenyns, *A Free Enquiry into the Nature and Origin of Evil*; *The Oxford Authors: Samuel Johnson*, ed. Donald Greene (Oxford: Oxford University Press, 1984), p. 522.

28 'Pope', in *Lives of the English Poets*, ii., p. 206.

29 Boswell relates the conversation of 19 September 1777: 'I mentioned to him that Dr. Hugh Blair, in his lectures on Rhetorick and Belles Lettres, which I heard him deliver at Edinburgh, had animadverted on the Johnsonian style as too pompous; and attempted to imitate it, by giving a sentence of Addison in *The Spectator*, No. 411, in the manner of Johnson.' *The Life of Samuel Johnson*, p. 853.

30 Bruce Redford, *The Converse of the Pen: Acts of Intimacy in the Eighteenth-Century Familiar Letter* (Chicago & London: University of Chicago Press, 1986), p. 206.

31 Coleridge, *Biographia Literaria*, i., 124.

32 MacIntyre, *After Virtue*, p. 129.

33 To Cassandra Austen, 10–11 January 1809; *Letters*, p. 162.

34 ibid., p. 163.

35 ibid., p. 164.

36 *Mansfield Park*, p. 152.

37 Introduction to *Jane Austen's Letters* (London: Oxford University Press, 1932), repr. in *Letters*, p. xii.

38 Mary A Favret, *Romantic Correspondence: Women, Politics and the Fiction of Letters* (Cambridge: Cambridge University Press, 1993), p. 12.

39 Redford, *op. cit.*, p. 221.

40 To Cassandra Austen, 24 January 1809; *Letters*, p. 169.

41 Carol Houlihan Flynn, 'The Letters' in Copeland & McMaster, eds, *The Cambridge Companion to Jane Austen*, p. 102.

42 To Cassandra Austen, 24 January 1809; *Letters*, pp. 169–70.

43 To Cassandra Austen, 30 January 1809; *Letters*, p. 172.

44 To Cassandra Austen, 12–13 May 1801; *Letters*, p. 84.

45 ibid., p. 85.

46 Otto Jespersen, *Language; its Nature, Development and Origin* (London: George Allen & Unwin, 1922), p. 250.

47 Singer, *op. cit.*, p. 86.

48 Virginia Woolf, *A Room of One's Own* [1929], in *A Room of One's Own and Three Guineas*, intr. Hermione Lee (London: Chatto & Windus/ Hogarth Press, 1984), p. 71.

49 Gabriel Josipovici, 'Text and Voice' [1980] in *Text and Voice: Essays 1981–1991* (Manchester: Carcanet; New York: St Martin's Press, 1992), p. 136.

50 To Cassandra Austen, 15 September 1813; *Letters*, p. 217.

51 'Odsbobs! I hear him just coming in at the door. You see I write in the present tense, as Parson Williams says. Well, he is in bed between us, we both shamming a sleep; he steals his hand into my bosom, which I, as if in my sleep, press close to me with mine, and then pretend to awake.' *Joseph Andrews and Shamela*, p. 15.

52 *Letters*, p. 218–19.

53 Flynn, *op. cit.*, p. 104.

54 *Memoir*, pp. 73–4.

55 Mark 12:31, in the translation of the Authorized Version.

56 DW Harding, introduction to *Persuasion and A Memoir of Jane Austen* (Harmondsworth: Penguin, 1965), p. 268.

57 James Stanier Clarke to Jane Austen, 16 November 1815; *Letters*, p. 296.

58 To James Stanier Clarke, 11 December 1815; *Letters*, p. 306.

59 To Fanny Knight, 30 November 1814; *Letters*, p. 286.

60 William Milns, *The Well-Bred Scholar, or Practical Essays on the Best Methods of Improving the Taste, and Assisting the Exertions of Youth in their Literary Pursuits* (London: S Gosnell, Messrs Rivington, T Boosey, 1794), p. 47–8.

61 To Cassandra Austen, 23–4 September 1813; *Letters*, p. 225.

62 *Hamlet*, II. ii., 374–5; *The Norton Facsimile*, p. 771.

63 To Cassandra Austen, 12–13 May 1801; *Letters*, p. 86.

64 To Cassandra Austen, 27–8 October 1798; ibid., p. 17.

65 *Emma*, p. 431.

66 Josipovici, *On Trust*, p. 3.

67 Steven Connor, *Dumbstruck: A Cultural History of Ventriloquism* (New York: Oxford University Press, 2000), p. 7.

68 Gisborne, *op. cit.*, p. 112.

69 To Fanny Knight, 23–5 March 1817; *Letters*, p. 335.

70 To James Edward Austen, 16–17 December 1816; *Letters*, p. 323.

71 *Minor Works*, p. 251.

72 Mary Augusta Austen-Leigh, *Personal Aspects of Jane Austen* (London: John Murray, 1920), p. 104.

73 Margaret Drabble, introduction to *Lady Susan, The Watsons, Sanditon* (Harmondsworth: Penguin, 1974), p. 15.

74 See his *Jane Austen's Literary Manuscripts: A Study of the Novelist's Development through the Surviving Papers* (Oxford: Oxford University Press, 1964), pp. 45–62.

75 See '*Lady Susan* and the Single Effect', ch. 2. of *Jane Austen's Novels: The Art of Clarity* (New Haven and London: Yale University Press, 1992), pp. 25–44.

76 *Minor Works*, p. 86.

77 ibid., p. 88.

78 Norman Holland, *Laughing: A Psychology of Humor* (Ithaca & London: Cornell University Press, 1982), p. 47.

79 Introduction to *Jane Austen's 'Sir Charles Grandison'* (Oxford: Clarendon Press, 1980), p. 21.

80 Mullan, *op. cit.*, p. 113.

81 Choderlos de Laclos, *Les Liaisons dangereuses* [1782] (Paris: Gallimard, 1972), 319–20. All subsequent references to this edition (more out of concern for historical accuracy than appreciation of its style) I reproduce the translations of *Dangerous Connections* [1784], 2ⁿᵈ edn, 4 vols in 2 (London: J Ebers, 1812); iii, p. 152.

82 *Minor Works*, p. 250.

83 To his son, 24 November 1749; Chesterfield, *Letters*, p. 179. David Nokes (*Jane Austen: A Life*, p. 377), notes the Chesterfieldian echo in Austen's borrowing of the phrase 'mais le moyen' in her letter to Cassandra of 18–20 April 1811; *Letters*, p. 181.

84 Shaftesbury, *Characteristics*, p. 205.

85 *Minor Works*, p. 274.

86 *Persuasion*, p. 204.

87 Janet Gurkin Altman remarks: 'For the external reader, reading an epistolary novel is very much like reading over the shoulder of another character whose own readings – and misreadings – must enter into our experience of the work'. *Epistolarity*, p. 111.

88 *Minor Works*, p. 247.

89 ibid., p. 248–9.

90 ibid., p. 254.

91 See Shirley Van Marter, 'Richardson's Revisions of *Clarissa* in the Second Edition', *Studies in Bibliography*, 26 (1973), pp. 107–32; 'Richardson's Revisions of *Clarissa* in the Third and Fourth Editions', *Studies in Bibliography*, 28 (1975), pp. 119–52.

92 Mullan, *op. cit.*, p. 107.

93 *Clarissa*, p. 36.

94 ibid., p. 66.

95 ibid., p. 114.

96 ibid., p. 79.

97 John Preston, *The Created Self: The Reader's Role in Eighteenth-Century Fiction* (London: Heinemann, 1970), p. 91.

98 See, for example, William Beatty Warner, *Reading 'Clarissa': The Struggles of Interpretation* (New Haven & London: Yale University Press, 1979); Terry Castle, *Clarissa's Ciphers: Meaning and Disruption in Richardson's 'Clarissa'* (Ithaca & London: Cornell University Press, 1982); John Allen Stevenson, '"Alien Spirits": The Unity of Lovelace and Clarissa', in Albert J Rivero, ed., *New Essays on Samuel Richardson* (Basingstoke & London: Macmillan, 1996).

99 Castle, *op. cit.*, p. 57.

100 *Clarissa*, pp. 102–3.

101 ibid., p. 234.

102 ibid., p. 378.

103 ibid., pp. 379–80.

104 ibid., p. 383.

105 Castle, *op. cit.*, p. 106.

106 *Clarissa*, p. 967.

107 Tony Tanner, *Jane Austen* (Basingstoke and London: Macmillan, 1986), p. 19.

108 See Simon Davies, 'Laclos dans la littérature anglaise du XIXe siècle' in René Pomeau, intr., *Laclos et le libertinage* (Paris: Presses Universitaires de France, 1983), pp. 255–64.

109 Gard, *Jane Austen's Novels*, p. 41.

110 Christine Roulston, *Virtue, Gender, and the Authentic Self in Eighteenth-Century Fiction* (Gainesville: University Press of Florida, 1998), p. 186.

111 *Les Liaisons dangereuses*, p. 40; *Dangerous Connections*, i., p. 16.

112 *Les Liaisons dangereuses*, p. 137–8; *Dangerous Connections*, i., p. 244.

113 *Les Liaisons dangereuses*, p. 136; *Dangerous Connections*, pp. 240–1.

114 *Minor Works*, p. 257.

115 Roulston, op. cit. p. 175. See also James Grantham Turner, 'Lovelace and the Paradoxes of Libertinism' in Margaret Anne Doody and Peter Sabor, eds, *Samuel Richardson: Tercentenary Essays* (Cambridge: Cambridge University Press, 1989), pp. 70–88.

116 *Clarissa*, p. 558.

117 ibid., p. 520.

118 Thomas Hardy, *The Mayor of Casterbridge* [1886], ed. Martin Seymour-Smith (Harmondsworth: Penguin, 1978), p. 411.

119 *Minor Works*, p. 243.

120 ibid., pp. 243–4.

121 ibid., p. 251.

122 *OED*, p. 136.

123 Tom Keymer, *Richardson's 'Clarissa' and the Eighteenth-Century Reader* (Cambridge: Cambridge University Press, 1992), p. 244.

124 *Northanger Abbey*, p. 169.

125 *Minor Works*, pp. 302–3.

126 ibid., p. 267.

127 ibid., p. 311.

128 ibid., pp. 251–2.

129 ibid., p. 302.

130 ibid., p. 269.

131 ibid., p. 305.

132 Joseph Butler, 'Sermon XII: Upon the Love of Our Neighbour' in *The Works of Joseph Butler, D.C.L., Sometime Lord Bishop of Durham*, ed. WE Gladstone, 2 vols (Oxford: Clarendon Press, 1897), ii., p. 180. For Austen's possible debts to Butler, see Philip Drew, 'Jane Austen and Bishop Butler', *Nineteenth-Century Fiction*, 35:2 (1980), pp. 127–49.

133 Butler, *op. cit.*, i., p. 181.

134 Samuel Beckett, *Endgame* (London: Faber and Faber, 1958), p. 32.

135 Connor, *op. cit.*, p. 307.

136 See Patrick Piggott, *The Innocent Diversion: A Study of Music in the Life and Writings of Jane Austen* (London: Douglas Cleverdon, 1979).

137 *Emma*, p. 276.

138 *Sense and Sensibility*, p. 348.

139 *Emma*, pp. 273–4.

140 MacIntyre, *After Virtue*, p. 199.

141 *Emma*, p. 43.

142 ibid., p. 71.

143 ibid., p. 129.

144 ibid., p. 371.

145 ibid., p. 376.

146 ibid., p. 5.

147 ibid., p. 376.

148 Adam Piette, *Remembering and the Sound of Words: Mallarmé, Proust, Joyce, Beckett* (Oxford: Clarendon Press, 1996), p. 45.

149 ibid., p. 43 and *passim*.

150 Sigmund Freud, *The Psychopathology of Everyday Life* [1901], trans. A Tyson, ed. J Strachey, A Richards, A Tyson (Harmondsworth: Penguin, 1975), p. 131.

151 ibid., p. 344.

152 *Emma*, pp. 23–4.

153 ibid., pp. 118.

154 ibid., pp. 52.

155 *OED*, p. 2248. Susan Eilenberg discusses the overlap of 'propriety', 'property' and 'possession' in *Strange Power of Speech: Wordsworth, Coleridge, and Literary Possession* (New York & London: Oxford University Press, 1992).

156 Connor, *op. cit.*, pp. 42–3.

157 *Emma*, p. 5.

158 ibid., p. 181.

159 Everett, 'Hard Romance', p. 14.

160 To Cassandra Austen, 24–5 October 1808; *Letters*, p. 151.

161 *Emma*, p. 26.

162 ibid., p. 36.

163 ibid., p. 135.

164 ibid., p. 181.

165 ibid., pp. 412–13.

166 ibid., p. 22.

167 ibid., p. 20.

168 ibid., p. 24.

169 ibid., p. 87.

170 ibid., pp. 51–2.

171 *Pride and Prejudice*, p. 208.

172 *Emma*, p. 408.

173 Nancy S Struever, 'The Conversable World: Eighteenth-Century Transformations of the Relation of Rhetoric and Truth', in B Vickers & NS Struever, eds, *Rhetoric and the Pursuit of Truth: Language Change in the Seventeenth and Eighteenth Centuries* (Los Angeles: William Andrews Clark Memorial Library, 1985), p. 99.

174 *Emma*, pp. 42–3.

175 Katie Roiphe relates the story of a 'male feminist' on an American campus: 'He tells me that someone he knew joined a feminist group because he wanted to sleep with a really sexy feminist and figured that politics was the fastest way to her heart. Peter does not say he himself became interested in feminism to pick up women. He does say "We have to ask to what extent is a commitment to feminism on the part of a man an attempt to get a woman into bed. To deny that's true at all would be preposterous. I think a commitment to antisexism *should* be attractive."' *The Morning After: Sex, Fear, and Feminism* (London: Hamish Hamilton, 1994), pp. 134–5.

176 *Emma*, p. 42.

177 ibid., p. 130.

178 See Janine Barchas, *The Annotations in Lady Bradshaigh's Copy of 'Clarissa'* (Victoria, BC: English Literary Studies Monographs 76, 1998).

179 ibid., p. 370.

180 *2 Henry IV*, I. ii., 8–9; *The Norton Fascimile*, p. 396.

181 Struever, *op. cit.*, p. 99.

182 Tanner, *Jane Austen*, p. 203.

183 Austen-Leigh, *Personal Aspects of Jane Austen*, p. 68.

184 *Emma*, p. 69.

185 *OED*, pp. 2925, 2494.

186 Johnson, *A Dictionary of the English Language*, ii., 24P & 21P.

187 *Emma*, p. 398.

188 Butler, *Jane Austen and the War of Ideas*, p. 176.

189 *Emma*, p. 408.

190 ibid., p. 335.

191 ibid., pp. 422–3.

192 'We are not isolated free choosers, monarchs of all we survey, but benighted creatures sunk in a reality whose nature we are constantly and overwhelmingly tempted to deform by fantasy. Our current picture of freedom encourages a dream-like facility; whereas what we require is a renewed sense of the difficulty and complexity of the moral life and the opacity of persons.' Iris Murdoch, 'Against Dryness', *Encounter* 16:1 (1961), p. 20.

193 'If the fixture of Momus's glass in the human breast, according to the proposed emendation of that arch-critic, had taken place [...] nothing more would have been wanting, in order to have taken a man's character, but to have taken a chair and gone softly, as you would to a dioptrical bee-hive, and looked in [...]'. *Tristram Shandy*, p. 96.

194 *Emma*, p. 391.

195 ibid., p. 404.

196 ibid., p. 434.

197 Tristram remarks that 'our minds shine not through the body, but are wrapt up here in a dark covering of uncrystallized flesh and blood; so that, if we would come to the specific characters of them, we must go some other way to work', *Tristram Shandy*, p. 97.

198 *Emma*, p. 431.

199 See Propp, *Morphology of the Folktale*, p. 97 and *passim*.

200 GK Chesterton, *Criticisms and Appreciations of the Works of Charles Dickens* [1911], intr. M Slater (London:, JM Dent & Co., 1992), p. 136.

201 *Emma*, p. 426. See also Janis P Stout, 'Jane Austen's Proposal Scenes and the Limitations of Language', *Studies in the Novel*, 144 (1982), pp. 316–26.

202 *Emma*, p. 425.

203 'Since Knightley is established early as completely reliable, we need no views of his secret thoughts. He has no secret thoughts, except for the unacknowledged depths of his love for Emma and his jealousy of Frank Churchill.' Wayne C Booth, *The Rhetoric of Fiction* (Chicago and London: University of Chicago Press, 1961), p. 254.

204 *Emma*, p. 430.

205 ibid., p. 431.

206 ibid., p. 474.

207 ibid., p. 444.

208 ibid., p. 445.

209 *Sense and Sensibility*, pp. 363–4.

210 John Updike, foreword to *Your Lover Just Called: Stories of Joan and Richard Maple* (Harmondsworth: Penguin, 1980), p. 9.

211 *Emma*, p. 371. The charade doesn't quite work, since, whether pronounced alphabetically or 'phonically', the letters M and A are not identical with the phonemes of 'Emma'. Mark Loveridge traces the source of the pun to a moral formula in Francis Hutcheson; 'Francis Hutcheson and Mr. Weston's Conundrum in Emma', *Notes and Queries*, 30:3, n.s. (1983), pp. 214–16.

212 *Emma*, p. 371.

213 ibid., p. 432.

214 ibid., p. 484.

215 To Cassandra Austen, 24 January 1809; *Letters*, p. 170.

216 *OED*, p. 2130.

217 Wittgenstein, *Tractatus Logico-Philosophicus* [1921], trans. DF Pears and B McGuinness (London: Routledge & Kegan Paul, 1961), p. 147.

218 Frank Kermode, *The Sense of An Ending* (New York: Oxford University Press, 1967), p. 133.

219 Everett, 'Hard Romance', p. 14.

220 Lionel Trilling '*Emma* and the Legend of Jane Austen' [1957] in *Beyond Culture* (Oxford: Oxford University Press, 1980), p. 49.

221 Martin C Battestin argues: 'With its genial and omniscient author, its intricate yet symmetrical design, its inevitable comic denouement, *Tom Jones* offers itself as the paradigm in art of cosmic Justice and Order, at once the mirror and the embodiment of its author's Christian view of life.' *The Providence of Wit: Aspects of Form in Augustan Literature and the Arts* (Oxford: Clarendon Press, 1974), p. 143.

222 *Emma*, p. 181.

223 ibid., pp. 84–5.

224 ibid., p. 85.

225 To Cassandra Austen, 21–3 April 1805; *Letters*, p. 103.

226 *Emma*, p. 156–7.

227 Booth, *The Rhetoric of Fiction*, p. 247.

228 'Her custom of following her creations outside the printed pages enables us to say that the word swept aside unread by Jane Fairfax was "pardon"; and that the Knightleys' exclusion from Donwell was ended by the death of Mr. Woodhouse in two years' time. According to a less well-known tradition, Jane Fairfax survived her elevation only nine or ten years.' Austen-Leigh and Austen-Leigh, *Jane Austen: Her Life and Letters*, p. 307.

229 *Emma*, 164.

230 ibid., p. 165.

231 '"[…] I dare say you have heard those charming lines of the poet,
  'Full many a flower is born to blush unseen,
  'And waste its sweetness on the desert air.'
We must not allow them to be verified in sweet Jane Fairfax."' ibid., pp. 282–3.

232 ibid., p. 521.

233 Everett, 'Hard Romance', p. 14.

234 ibid., p. 10.

235 Bate, *op. cit.*, p. 19.

236 Coleridge, 'Notes on the Tempest', in *Essays and Lectures on Shakspeare* (London: JM Dent, 1907), p. 67.

237 ibid., pp. 64–5.

238 William Hazlitt, *Characters of Shakespear's Plays* [1817–18] (London: JM Dent, 1906), p. 88.

239 Eric Griffiths writes of 'real' and 'ideal': 'Both words, and their cognates, put out many offshoots in the nineteenth century, new senses which branched with irregular luxuriance in many directions. To draw all the relevant Empsonian equations for the interpenetrating structure of these two complex words would be as big a job as charting the double helix of DNA.' *The Printed Voice of Victorian Poetry*, p. 182.

240 *The Tempest*, V. i., 174–84; *The Norton Facsimile*, pp. 35–6.

241 Josipovici, *On Trust*, p. 142.

242 *The Tempest*, V. i., 307–11; *The Norton Facsimile*, p. 37.

243 Although the Johnson/ Steevens text of 1778 retains the original Shakespearean attributions of speeches, the performance text was Kemble's version, *The Tempest; or The Enchanted Island, Written by Shakespeare* (London: J Debrett, 1789). This follows Davenant and Dryden's 1670 version, *The Tempest, or The Enchanted Island*, which splits the speech between their interpolated characters, Dorinda and Hippolito, and omits ''Tis new to thee' completely:

> *Dor.*   O wonder!
> How many goodly Creatures are there here!
> How beauteous mankind is!
> *Hip.*   O brave new world that has such people in't!
>
> > *The Works of John Dryden*, ed. Edward Niles Hooker,
> > HT Swedenberg, Jr., Vinton A Dearing et al.,
> > 20 vols (Berkeley: University of California
> > Press, 1956–2000), x., p. 98.

244 Genette, *Narrative Discourse*, pp. 68–70.

245 Radcliffe, *The Mysteries of Udolpho*, p. 672.

246 Burney, *Camilla*, p. 908.

247 Charles Dickens, *Little Dorrit* [1857], ed. John Holloway (Penguin: Harmondsworth, 1967), p. 895.

248 George Eliot, *Middlemarch* [1871–2], ed. WJ Harvey (Penguin: Harmondsworth, 1965), p. 896.

249 *Minor Works*, p. 191.

250 *Sense and Sensibility*, p. 380.

251 ibid., p. 379.

252 *Pride and Prejudice*, p. 387.

253 *Mansfield Park*, p. 468. In *Persuasion*, the only characters who are demarcated off in the external prolepsis are, disturbingly, Mr Elliot and Mrs Clay, who are narrated, unlike the others, as still existing in the present of narration: 'She has abilities, however, as well as affections; and it is now a doubtful point whether his cunning, or hers, may finally carry the day […].' *Persuasion*, p. 250.

254 Proust, 'Days of Reading (1)'; *Against Sainte-Beuve*, p. 210.

255 Kipling, *Collected Stories*, p. 754.

256 Sheila Kaye-Smith and GB Stern, *Talking of Jane Austen* (London and Toronto: Cassell and Company, 1943); Marvin Mudrick, *Jane Austen: Irony as Defence and Discovery* (Princeton and London: Princeton University Press, 1952); Edmund Wilson, 'A Long

Talk about Jane Austen' [1945], in Watt, ed., *Jane Austen: A Collection of Critical Essays*, pp. 35–40.

257 Booth, *The Company We Keep*, pp. 434–5.

258 Emma Tennant, *Emma in Love: Jane Austen's 'Emma' Continued* (London: Fourth Estate, 1996).

259 *Minor Works*, p. 313.

260 *Northanger Abbey*, p. 252.

261 DA Miller, *Narrative and Its Discontents: Problems of Closure in the Traditional Novel* (Princeton: Princeton University Press, 1981), p. 54.

262 'HONEY-MOON. n.s. [honey *and* moon] The first month after marriage, when there is nothing but tenderness and pleasure.' Johnson, *A Dictionary of the English Language*, i., opp. 11M.

4: HABIT AND HABITATION

1 William Wordsworth, *The Prelude: 1799, 1805, 1850*, ed. Jonathan Wordsworth, MH Abrams and Stephen Gill (New York and London: WW Norton & Company, 1979), l. 424.

2 Henry Wotton, *The Elements of Architectvre* (London: John Bill, 1624; repr. London & New York: Da Capo Press and Theatrum Orbis Terrarum, 1970), p. 119.

3 Henry Austen, 'Biographical Notice of the Author' [1818] in *Northanger Abbey and Persuasion*, p. 3.

4 *Mansfield Park*, p. 468.

5 Samuel Johnson, 'An Essay on Epitaphs' [1740] in *The Oxford Authors: Samuel Johnson*, ed. Donald Greene (Oxford: Oxford University Press, 1984), p. 101.

6 Samuel Johnson, *An Account of the Life of Mr Richard Savage* [1744], ed. C Tracy (Oxford: Oxford University Press, 1971), p. 15.

7 William Wordsworth, 'Essays upon Epitaphs', I [1809–10] in *Selected Prose*, ed. John O Hayden (London: Penguin, 1988), p. 333.

8 *Mansfield Park*, p. 461.

9 Hallam, Lord Tennyson, *Alfred Lord Tennyson: A Memoir by his Son*, 2 vols (London: Macmillan and Co., 1897), p. 47.

10 *Persuasion*, p. 25.

11 Gérard Genette, 'Espace et Langage' in *Figures, I* (Paris: Editions de Seuil, 1966), p. 106.

12 ibid., p. 108.

13 See Joseph Frank, 'Spatial Form in Modern Literature' in *The Widening Gyre* (New Brunswick, NJ: Rutgers University Press, 1963.

14 William Gilpin, *Observations on Cumberland and Westmorland* [1786], 2 vols (Poole & New York: Woodstock Books, 1996), i, p. xxii.

15 ibid., i., pp. xxvi–xxvii.

16 Charles Lamb to Thomas Manning, 24 September 1802, in *Selected Prose*, ed. Adam Phillips (Harmondsworth: Penguin, 1985), p. 320. Compare Wordsworth's 'Description of the Scenery of the Lakes' [1810]: 'The lakes had now become celebrated; visitors flocked hither from all parts of England; the fancies of some were smitten so deeply, that they became settlers; and the islands of Derwentwater and Windermere, as they offered the strongest temptation, were the first places seized upon, and were instantly defaced by the intrusion.' Wordsworth, *Selected Prose*, p. 45.

17 ibid., p. 321.

18 Malcolm Andrews, *The Search for the Picturesque: Landscape Aesthetics and Tourism in Britain, 1760–1800* (Aldershot: Scolar Press, 1989), p. 67.

19 'I have see nobody in London yet with such a long chin as Dr Syntax'; To Cassandra Austen, 2–3 March 1814; *Letters*, p. 254.

20 William Combe, *The Tour of Doctor Syntax, In Search of the Picturesque*, 5th edn. (London: n.p., 1812), p. 108.

21 ibid., p. 5.

22 ibid., p. 38.

23 *Minor Works*, p. 380.

24 Swift, *Prose Works*, iv., p. 103.

25 *Tristram Shandy*, pp. 195–6.

26 ibid., p. 138.

27 Gilbert Austin, *Chironomia; or a Treatise on Rhetorical Delivery: Comprehending Many Precepts, both Ancient and Modern, for the Proper Regulation of the Voice, the Countenance and Gesture. Together with an Investigation of the Elements of Gesture, and a New Method for the Notation Thereof; Illustrated by Many Figures* (London: 1806), p. 1.

28 ibid., p. 497.

29 ibid., p. 489.

30 ibid., p. 377.

31 William Hazlitt, 'My First Acquaintance with Poets' [1823] in *Selected Writings*, ed. Ronald Blythe (Harmondsworth: Penguin, 1970), p. 60.

32 Davies, *Wordsworth and the Worth of Words*, p. 247.

33 *The Prelude*, pp. 48–50.

34 ibid., p. 424.

35 ibid., p. 84.

36 ibid., p. 402.

37 To Cassandra Austen, 21–2 May 1801; *Letters*, p. 89.

38 Oliver Sacks, *Seeing Voices: A Journey into the World of the Deaf* (Berkeley: 1989), p. 87.

39 To Cassandra Austen, 28 December 1808; *Letters*, pp. 160–1.

40 *Memoir*, p. 50.

41 Austen-Leigh and Austen-Leigh, *Jane Austen: Her Life and Letters*, pp. 155–6.

42 Nokes, *Jane Austen*, p. 221.

43 'Burnt Norton' [1935], in *The Complete Poems and Plays of T. S. Eliot* (London: Faber and Faber, 1969), p. 171.

44 Nikolaus Pevsner, 'The Architectural Setting of Jane Austen's Novels', *Journal of the Warburg and Courtauld Institutes*, 31 (1968), p. 404.

45 *Minor Works*, p. 315.

46 ibid., p. 322.

47 Nokes, *Jane Austen*, p. 253.

48 *Minor Works*, p. 328.

49 ibid.

50 ibid., p. 332.

51 Joseph A Kestner, *The Spatiality of the Novel* (Detroit: Wayne State University Press, 1978), p. 57.

52 Adam Phillips, 'Clutter: A Case History' in *Promises, Promises: Essays on Literature and Psychoanalysis* (London: Faber and Faber, 2000), pp. 70–1. For further discussion of the uses of mess, see also David Trotter, *Cooking with Mud: The Idea of Mess in Nineteenth-Century Art and Fiction* (Oxford: Oxford University Press, 2000).

53 ibid., p. 71.

54 Hegel, *Elements of the Philosophy of Right* [1821], trans. H Nisbet (Cambridge: Cambridge University Press, 1991), p. 199.

55 Peter Brooks, *Reading for the Plot: Design and Intention in Narrative* (Cambridge, MA: Harvard University Press, 1984), p. 12.

56 *Letters*, p. 343.

57 '*Mansfield Park* by the author of S & S.—P. & P.' To ? Francis Austen, 21 March 1814; *Letters*, p. 262.

58 'Opinions of *Mansfield Park*' [1815–16]; *Minor Works*, pp. 431–2.

59 Lionel Trilling, '*Mansfield Park*' [1954] in *The Opposing Self: Nine Essays in Criticism* (Oxford: Oxford University Press, 1980), pp. 184–5.

60 'I return you the Quarterly Review with many Thanks. The Authoress of *Emma* has no reason I think to complain of her treatment in it—except in the total omission of Mansfield Park.—I cannot but be sorry that so clever a Man as the Reviewer of *Emma*, should consider it as unworthy of being noticed.' To John Murray, 1 April 1816; *Letters*, p. 313.

61 Kipling, *Collected Stories*, p. 741.

62 Trilling, op. cit., p. 185.

63 Edward W Said, *Culture and Imperialism* (London: Chatto & Windus, 1993), pp. 100–1.

64 *Mansfield Park*, pp. 14–15.

65 ibid., p. 382.

66 ibid., p. 473.

67 ibid., p. 465.

68 ibid., p. 141.

69 ibid., p. 12.

70 ibid., p. 13.

71 ibid., p. 151.

72 ibid., pp. 27–8.

73 See Joan Klingel Ray, 'Jane Austen's Case Study of Child Abuse', *Persuasions*, 13 (1991), pp. 16–26.

74 Christopher Ricks, 'William Wordsworth 2: "A Sinking Inward into Ourselves from Thought to Thought"' in *The Force of Poetry*, p. 134.

75 *Mansfield Park*, pp. 29–30.

76 ibid., pp. 28–9.

77 ibid., p. 6.

78 Mark 12:42, in the translation of the Authorized Version.

79 Harding, *Regulated Hatred and Other Essays on Jane Austen*, p. 87.

80 ibid., p. 89.

81 To Cassandra Austen, 29 January 1813; *Letters*, p. 202.

82 *Mansfield Park*, p. 49.

83 ibid.

84 ibid., p. 51.

85 Johnson, *A Dictionary of the English Language*, 7E.

86 *Pride and Prejudice*, p. 246.

87 *Persuasion*, p. 100.

88 *Minor Works*, pp. 396–7.

89 Donald Davie, 'Homage to William Cowper', *Collected Poems* (Chicago: University of Chicago Press, 1991), p. 17.

90 *Northanger Abbey*, p. 7.

91 *Memoir*, p. 71.

92 *Northanger Abbey*, p. 7.

93 *Memoir*, p. 71.

94 ibid.

95 ibid., p. 48.

96 To Cassandra Austen, 18 December 1798; *Letters*, p. 27.

97 To Cassandra Austen, 24 September 1813; *Letters*, p. 228.

98 'He has more of Cowper than of Johnson in him, fonder of Tame Hares & Blank verse than of the full tide of human Existence at Charing Cross.' To Cassandra Austen, 3 November 1813; *Letters*, p. 250.

99 William Cowper, *The Task* [1785], Book I, 721–2, in *The Poems of William Cowper*, ed. JD Baird and C Ryskamp, 3 vols (Oxford: Oxford University Press, 1980–95), ii., p. 135. All future references to this edition.

100 Book III, 40–1; ii., p. 164.

101 In fact, the majority of senses of 'domestic' and 'domesticate' available to Cowper would have had no directly judgmental application. The main senses of 'domestic' listed in the *OED* include 'Of or belonging to the home, house, or household; pertaining to one's place of residence or family affairs; household, home, "family"'; 'Of or pertaining to one's own country or nation; not foreign, internal, inland, "home"'; likewise, the dictionary only lists one sense of 'domesticated' as meaning 'Made domestic or familiar; tamed, naturalized,' which can be applied to humans. Johnson's senses of 'DOMESTICK' are 'Belonging to the house; not relating to things publick'; 'Private; done at home; not open'; 'Inhabiting the house; not wild'; 'Not foreign, intestine', and his definition of 'DOMESTICATE' is 'To make domestick, to withdraw from the publick'. See *A Dictionary of the English Language*, 7K.

102 *The Task*, Book I, 1–5; ii., p. 117.

103 ibid., Book I, 7; ii., p. 117.

104 Martin Priestman, *Cowper's 'Task': Structure and Influence* (Cambridge: Cambridge University Press, 1983), p. 31.

105 *The Poems of William Cowper*, iii., pp. 30–1.

106 ibid., p. 31.

107 William Cowper, *Adelphi* [1772] in *The Letters and Prose Writings of William Cowper*, ed. J King and C Ryskamp, 5 vols (Oxford: Oxford University Press, 1979–86), i, pp. 23–4. Hereafter cited as *Letters and Prose Writings*.

108 ibid., p. 59.

109 *The Poems of William Cowper*, i, 174.

110 Alexander Pope, *Peri Bathous: or, Martinus Scriblerus, His Treatise of the Art of Sinking in Poetry* [1728] in *The Prose Works of Alexander Pope* ed. N Ault and R Cowler, 2 vols (Oxford: Oxford University Press, 1936 and 1986), ii, p. 208.

111 To John Newton, 10 December 1785; *Letters and Prose Writings*, ii, p. 420.

112 To John Thelwall, 17 December 1796; *Selected Letters*, p. 38.

113 To Lady Hesketh, 28 July 1788; *Letters and Prose Writings*, vol. iii., p. 195.

114 *The Task*, I, 749; ii., p. 136.

115 See Priestman, *op. cit.*, and TE Blom, 'Eighteenth-Century Reflexive Process Poetry', *Eighteenth-Century Studies*, x (1976), pp. 52–72.

116 To William Unwin, 10 October 1784; *Letters and Prose Writings*, ii, p. 285.

117 *The Task*, I, 103–9; ii, p. 119.

118 ibid., IV, 36–7; ii, p. 188.

119 Priestman, *op. cit.*, p. 48.

120 Tanner, *Jane Austen*, p. 162.

121 *Mansfield Park*, pp. 146–7.

122 ibid., p. 145.

123 'No person seems better to have understood the secret of heightening, or of setting terrible things, if I may use the expression, in their strongest light by the force of a judicious obscurity, than Milton.' *A Philosophical Enquiry into the Origin of Our Ideas of the Sublime and Beautiful* [1757], ed. Adam Phillips (Oxford: Oxford University Press, 1990), p. 55.

124 'Lines Composed a Few Miles Above Tintern Abbey…'; *Poems*, i, p. 360.

125 *Mansfield Park*, p. 107.

126 ibid., p. 108.

127 ibid., p. 111.

128 ibid., p. 112.

129 ibid., pp. 112–13.

130 ibid., p. 113.

131 David Selwyn, *Jane Austen and Leisure* (London: The Hambledon Press, 1999), p. 126.

132 *Mansfield Park*, p. 470.

133 ibid., p. 313.

134 ibid., p. 314.

135 ibid., p. 317. Gilbert Austin also notes: 'To look fairly in the face or rather in the eyes of those who are objects of respect, bespeaks, in youth especially, a candid and ingenuous mind: as on the contrary an habitual down look, as it is vulgarly called, and averted and unsteady eyes, are universally understood to indicate the opposite character'; *Chironomia*, p. 107.

136 *Mansfield Park*, pp. 445–6.

137 Gaston Bachelard, *The Poetics of Space* [1958] trans. M Jolas (Boston, 1969), p. 8.

138 *Mansfield Park*, p. 113. John A Dussinger offers a useful insight into this flexibility: 'Since any encounter is a kinetic arrangement of intentions lasting only for the moment, its historical existence is subject to doubt even for those who had directly experienced it.' *In The Pride of the Moment: Encounters in Jane Austen's World* (Columbus: Ohio State University Press, 1990), p. 39.

139 ibid., p. 56.

140 ibid., pp. 151–2.

141 DW Harding, *Experience into Words* (London: 1963; repr. Harmondsworth: Penguin, 1974), p. 73.

142 To John Hamilton Reynolds, 3 February 1818; *The Letters of John Keats*, p. 95.

143 *Mansfield Park*, p. 88.

144 ibid., p. 99.

145 *OED*, p. 1240.

146 Simon Varey, *Space and the Eighteenth-Century English Novel* (Cambridge: Cambridge University Press, 1990), p. 7.

147 Said, *Culture and Imperialism*, p. 107.

148 *The Task*, I, 96–102; ii., p. 119.

149 ibid., IV, 135; ii., p. 190.

150 ibid., II, 285–6; ii., p. 146.

151 *Mansfield Park*, p. 71.

152 ibid., p. 447.

153 See Everett, 'Hard Romance', p. 12.

154 John Sutherland has some illuminating hypotheses on Pug's gender; see his 'Pug: Dog or Bitch?' in *Can Jane Eyre Be Happy?* (Oxford: Oxford University Press, 1997), pp. 31–6.

155 Brooks, *Reading for the Plot*, p. xi.

156 *Mansfield Park*, p. 3.

157 Tanner, *Jane Austen*, p. 173.

158 *Mansfield Park*, p. 203.

159 Samuel Beckett to Thomas McGreevy, 14 February 1935; quoted in James Knowlson, *Damned to Fame: The Life of Samuel Beckett* (London: Bloomsbury, 1996), p. 203.

160 *Mansfield Park*, p. 438.

161 *The Task*, IV, 5–7; ii, p. 187.

162 ibid., IV, 36–41 and 50–6; ii. p. 188.

163 *Mansfield Park*, p. 439.

164 ibid., pp. 439–40.

165 Davies, op. cit., p. 87.

166 Many thanks to Kendal Gaw for pointing this out to me.

167 JF Burrows, *Computation into Criticism: A Study of Jane Austen's Novels and an Experiment in Method* (Oxford: Clarendon Press, 1987), p. 2.

168 Wordsworth, *Poems*, i. p. 602.

169 Paul De Man, *The Rhetoric of Romanticism* (New York: Columbia University Press, 1984), p. 57.

170 *The Prelude*, l. 216.

171 Kestner, op. cit., p. 121.

172 *Mansfield Park*, p. 172.

173 ibid., p. 311.

174 ibid., p. 359.

175 ibid., p. 386.

176 Kestner, op. cit., p. 58.

177 Brooks, *Reading for the Plot*, p. 215.

178 Gustave Flaubert, *L'Éducation sentimentale* [1869] (Paris: Gallimard, 1965), p. 459.

179 Gard, *Jane Austen's Novels*, p. 150.

180 George Levine, *Darwin and the Novelists: Patterns of Science in Victorian Fiction* (Cambridge MA: Harvard University Press, 1988), p. 82.

181 *Mansfield Park*, p. 26.

182 ibid., p. 444.

183 ibid., p. 461.

184 ibid., p. 469.

185 Dante Alighieri, *Inferno*, Canto V, 121–3. 'No greater grief than to remember days/ Of joy, when mis'ry is at hand.' HF Cary, *The Vision: or Hell, Purgatory, and Paradise of Dante Alighieri* (2nd edn; 3 vols, 1819), i, p. 47.

186 *Mansfield Park*, p. 467.

187 ibid., p. 470.

188 'Is there not something a little odd, to say the least, about making an admirable public object out of one's feeling of guilt and penitence before God?'; 'Postscript: Christianity and Art' in *The Dyer's Hand and Other Essays* (New York: Random House, 1962), p. 458. Thanks to Sophie Ratcliffe for bringing this to my attention.

189 Gisborne, op. cit., p. 158.

190 *Minor Works*, p. 380.

191 To Thomas McGreevy, 25 July 1935; quoted in Knowlson, op. cit., p. 203.

192 TS Eliot, '*In Memoriam*', in *Selected Essays* (London: Faber and Faber, 1932; 3rd edn, 1950), p. 337.

193 *Persuasion*, pp. 21–2.

194 Based on the evidence of the De Rose/ McGuire *Concordance to the Works of Jane Austen*, 3 vols (New York: Garland, 1982), the citation-statistics for certain colour words in Austen's full-length novels are as follows: 'red' (18); 'green' (24); 'grey' (17); 'blue' (17); 'black' (30); 'white' (39); 'pink' (5); 'purple' (4).

195 Hardy, *A Reading of Jane Austen*, p. 149.

196 *Persuasion*, p. 34.

197 *The Task*, III, 463; ii., p. 174.

198 *Persuasion*, p. 92.

199 *Minor Works*, p. 380. David Trotter offers a brilliant analysis of the role of cabbages in Turner's Art in *Cooking with Mud*, pp. 33–59.

200 To Cassandra Austen, 24 May 1813; *Letters*, p. 212.

201 To Fanny Knight, 23–5 March 1817; *Letters*, p. 335.

202 ibid., pp. 335–6.

203 *Minor Works*, p. 373.

204 Christopher Ricks suggests that 'Keats's mis-spellings are often indications of how his imagination was working, and are sometimes indications of an achieved suggestiveness which works within the poem itself'. *Keats and Embarrassment* (Oxford: Oxford University Press, 1974), p. 72.

205 *Minor Works*, p. 412.

206 ibid., p. 386.

207 ibid., pp. 386–7.

208 At the Grand Academy of Lagado, the Projector who has been trying for eight years to extract sunbeams from cucumbers 'did not doubt in eight years more, that he should be able to supply the Governor's gardens with sunshine at a reasonable rate'; *Gulliver's Travels*, pp. 223–4. In Beckett, Father Ambrose recommends bicarbonate of soda for Moran's hen: 'have her swallow a few dessertspoonfuls, several times a day, for a few months. You'll see, you won't know her.' *Molloy* [1955] in *The Beckett Trilogy* (London: Picador, 1979), p. 93.

209 Zachary Cope, 'Jane Austen's Last Illness', *British Medical Journal* (1964), 2:183.

210 *Minor Works*, p. 383.

211 *Persuasion*, p. 5.

212 ibid., p. 6.

213 Nokes, *Jane Austen*, pp. 251–2.

214 T Hughes (ed.), *A Choice of Emily Dickinson's Verse* (London: Faber and Faber, 1968), p. 58.

215 *Persuasion*, p. 3.

216 Charles Dickens, *Great Expectations* [1860–1], ed. A Calder (Harmondsworth: Penguin, 1965), p. 35.

217 Michael Butor points out: 'Reproducing a page, or even a line, within another page affords an optical partitioning whose properties are quite different from those of the usual partitioning of a quotation. It serves to introduce new tensions into the text, the very tensions we so often feel today in our cities covered with slogans, titles and signs,

noisy with broadcast songs and speeches, those shocks and jolts which occur when what we are reading or listening to is brutally occulted.' 'The Book as Object' in *Inventory*, ed. Richard Howard (London: Jonathan Cape, 1970), p. 55.

218 John Lennard, *But I Digress: The Exploitation of Parenthesis in English Printed Verse* (Oxford: Clarendon Press, 1991), p. 91.

219 *Persuasion*, p. 19.

220 ibid., p. 21.

221 ibid., p. 23.

222 It may not have been precisely the mark Austen herself wrote, since, as Anne Henry has noted, the three-dot ellipsis was only common practice '[f]rom about 1850' ('The re-mark-able rise of "…": reading ellipsis marks in literary texts' in Bray, Handley and Henry (eds), op. cit., p. 137); but Austen did revise *Mansfield Park* herself, so the mark must at least translate something which she had indicated. She does employ ellipsis points of numerous lengths (including four dots) in Sophia's death in *Love and Friendship* (see above, p. 63).

223 *Mansfield Park*, p. 156. The authority of the 1816 version as copy-text has recently been challenged by Kathryn Sutherland: see the introduction to her edition of the novel (London: Penguin, 1996), pp. vii–xxxiii, and her 'Speaking commas \ reading commas: punctuating *Mansfield Park*' in Bray, Handley and Henry (eds), op. cit., pp. 217–34.

224 Tanner, *Jane Austen*, p. 209. See also JL Kastely, '*Persuasion*: Jane Austen's Philosophical Rhetoric', *Philosophy and Literature*, 15:1 (1991), pp. 74–88.

225 Brian Vickers, *In Defence of Rhetoric* (Oxford: Clarendon Press, 1998), p. 492.

226 *Tristram Shandy*, p. 120.

227 *Persuasion*, p. 48.

228 Butler, *Jane Austen and the War of Ideas*, p. 279.

229 Wordsworth, 'Lines Composed a Few Miles above Tintern Abbey'; *Poems*, i., p. 359.

230 *Persuasion*, pp. 59–60.

231 'His bright, proud eye spoke' (p. 62); 'she had no reason to suppose his eye wandering towards her while she spoke' (p. 63); 'her eye could not reach him' (p. 186); 'her eyes devoured the following words' (p. 237).

232 Austin, *Chironomia*, p. 102.

233 Jean-Paul Sartre, *L'être et le néant* [1943], trans. HE Barnes as *Being and Nothingness* (London: Routledge and Kegan Paul, 1958), p. 258.

234 Caroline Austen, *My Aunt Jane Austen* (Chawton: The Jane Austen Society, 1952; 2nd edn, 1991), pp. 14–15.

235 To Cassandra Austen, 8–9 November 1800; *Letters*, p. 55.

236 'The only way of expressing emotion in the form of art is by finding an "objective correlative"; in other words, a set of objects, a situation, a chain of events which shall be the form of that *particular* emotion; such that when the external facts, which must terminate in sensory experience, are given, the emotion is immediately evoked.' TS Eliot, 'Hamlet' [1919], in *Selected Essays*, p. 145.

237 *Minor Works*, p. 393.

238 *Persuasion*, p. 22.

239 ibid., pp. 47–8.

240 ibid., p. 111.

241 ibid., pp. 67–8.

242 *Minor Works*, p. 415.

243 *Persuasion*, p. 68.

244 'Nutting' [pub. 1800] in *Lyrical Ballads*, ed. RL Brett and AR Jones, 2nd edn (London: Methuen, 1963; repr. London: Routledge, 1991), p. 197.

245 *Persuasion*, p. 110.

246 ibid., p. 111.

247 ibid., p. 238.

248 ibid., p. 212.

249 ibid., p. 221.

250 ibid., pp. 231–2.

251 ibid., pp. 233–4.

252 ibid., p. 242.

253 ibid., p. 252.

254 This is the original reading, which Chapman, following a conjecture by AC Bradley , changes to 'prepare for it'. Harding, who retains the original wording in his edition, argues: 'this is more like Bradley's elegance than Jane Austen's. It would imply that the lovers were preparing for the future recall of the moment; and this would be too much deliberated. Jane Austen's phrase means that they spontaneously made it so perfect as to be worthy of the long remembrance which she knows it was destined to have.' Another, less interpretatively based reason might be the desire to avoid conjectural or virtual copy-texts, a desire famously espoused by Jack Stillinger in his *The Texts of Keats's Poems* (Cambridge, Mass.: Harvard University Press, 1974).

255 *Persuasion*, p. 248.

256 *Minor Works*, p. 381.

257 ibid., p. 384.

258 *Persuasion*, p. 5.

259 ibid., p. 244.

260 ibid., p. 110. I am grateful to Barney Harkins for pointing this out to me.

261 'Tennyson's surface, his technical accomplishment, is intimate with his depths'; '*In Memoriam*' in *Selected Essays*, p. 337.

262 *Minor Works*, p. 427. Compare the description of Uppercross in *Persuasion*, which is caught between old and new ideas of space and *décor*: 'Oh! could the originals of the portraits against the wainscot, could the gentlemen in brown velvet and the ladies in blue satin have seen what was going on, have been conscious of such an overthrow of all order and neatness! The portraits themselves seemed to be staring in astonishment.' *Persuasion*, p. 40.

263 *Minor Works*, p. 373.

264 ibid., p. 422.

265 ibid., p. 426.

266 *Persuasion*, p. 242.

267 'Burnt Norton'; *Complete Poems*, p. 173.

268 *Persuasion*, p. 248.

BIBLIOGRAPHY

Addison, J, *The Freeholder* [1715–16], ed. J Leheny (Oxford: Clarendon Press, 1979).

Altman, JG, *Epistolarity: Approaches to a Form* (Columbus: Ohio State University Press, 1982).

Andrews, M, *The Search for the Picturesque: Landscape Aesthetics and Tourism in Britain, 1760–1800* (Aldershot: Scolar Press, 1989)

Anon., *The Conversation of Gentlemen Considered* (London: J Hayles, 1738).

——, *The Art of Conversation; or, The Polite Entertainer* (London: R Willey and J Ryall, 1757).

——, *Dangerous Connections: A Series of Letters, Selected from the Correspondence of a Private Circle* [1784], 2nd edn, 4 vols in 2 (London: J Ebers, 1812).

——, *Address to a Young Lady, on her Entrance into the World,* 2 vols. (London: Hookham & Carpenter, 1796).

Aristotle, *Nicomachean Ethics*, trans. JAK Thomson (London: Allen & Unwin, 1953; repr. Harmondsworth: Penguin, 1955; rev. edn., 1976).

Auden, WH, *The Dyer's Hand and Other Essays* (New York: Random House, 1962).

Augustine, St, *Confessions*, trans. H Chadwick (Oxford: Oxford University Press, 1991).

Austen, C, *My Aunt Jane Austen* (Chawton: The Jane Austen Society, 1952; 2nd edn, 1991).

Austen, J, *Pride and Prejudice* [1813], ed. RW Chapman (Oxford: Oxford University Press, 1923; 3rd edn, 1932).

——, *Sense and Sensibility* [1811], ed. RW Chapman (Oxford: Oxford University Press, 1923; 3rd edn, 1933).

——, *Emma* [1816], ed. RW Chapman (Oxford: Oxford University Press, 1923; 3rd edn, 1933).

——, *Northanger Abbey and Persuasion* [1818], ed. RW Chapman (Oxford: Oxford University Press, 1923; 3rd edn, 1933).

——, *Mansfield Park* [1814], ed. RW Chapman (Oxford: Oxford University Press, 1923; 3rd edn, 1934).

——, *Minor Works*, ed. RW Chapman (Oxford: Oxford University Press, 1954; rev. edn, 1963).

——, *Persuasion and A Memoir of Jane Austen*, ed. DW Harding (Harmondsworth: Penguin, 1965).

——, *Lady Susan, The Watsons, Sanditon*, ed. M Drabble (Harmondsworth: Penguin, 1974).

——, *Jane Austen's 'Sir Charles Grandison'*, ed. BC Southam (Oxford: Clarendon Press, 1980).

——, *The Manuscript Chapters of Persuasion*, ed. RW Chapman (London: Athlone Press, 1985).

——, *Jane Austen's Letters*, ed. D Le Faye (Oxford: Oxford University Press, 1995).

——, *Mansfield Park*, ed. K Sutherland (London: Penguin, 1996).

Austen-Leigh, JE et al., *A Memoir of Jane Austen and Other Family Recollections*, ed. K Sutherland (Oxford: Oxford University Press, 2002).

Austen-Leigh, MA, *Personal Aspects of Jane Austen* (London: John Murray, 1920).

Austen-Leigh, W and Austen-Leigh, RA, *Jane Austen: Her Life and Letters, A Family Record* (London: Smith, Elder, 1913).

Austin, G, *Chironomia; or a Treatise on Rhetorical Delivery: Comprehending Many Precepts, both Ancient and Modern, for the Proper Regulation of the Voice, the Countenance and Gesture. Together with an Investigation of the Elements of Gesture, and a New Method for the Notation Thereof; Illustrated by Many Figures* (London: T Cadell & W Davies, 1806).

Austin, JL, *Philosophical Papers*, ed. JO Urmson and GJ Warnock (Oxford: Clarendon Press, 1961; 2nd edn, 1970).

——, *How to Do Things with Words*, ed. JO Urmson (Oxford: Oxford University Press, 1962).

——, *Sense and Sensibilia*, ed. GJ Warnock (Oxford: Oxford University Press, 1962).

Ayling, S, *Edmund Burke: His Life and Opinions* (London: Cassell, 1988).

Bachelard, G, *The Poetics of Space*, trans. M Jolas (Boston: Beacon Press, 1969).

Bal, M, *Narratology: Introduction to the Study of Narrative*, trans. C Van Boheemen (Toronto: University of Toronto Press, 1985; 2nd edn, 1997).

Barchas, J, *The Annotations in Lady Bradshaigh's Copy of 'Clarissa'* (Victoria, BC: English Literary Studies Monographs 76, 1998).

Baldick, C, *In Frankenstein's Shadow: Myth, Monstrosity and Nineteenth-Century Writing* (Oxford: Clarendon Press, 1987).

Barry, J, Opie, J and Fuseli, H, *Lectures on Painting, by the Royal Academicians*, ed. RN Wornum (London: Henry G Bohn, 1848).

Barthes, R, *S/Z*, trans. R Miller (New York: Farrar, Strauss and Giroux, 1974; repr. Oxford: Blackwell, 1990).

——, *Image Music Text*, trans. S Heath (London: Fontana Press, 1977).

Bate, J, *Shakespeare and the English Romantic Imagination* (Oxford: Clarendon Press, 1989).

——, (ed.), *The Romantics on Shakespeare* (London: Penguin, 1992).

Bate, WJ, *Samuel Johnson* (London: Chatto & Windus, 1978; repr. London: Hogarth Press, 1984).

Battestin, MC, *The Providence of Wit: Aspects of Form in Augustan Literature and the Arts* (Oxford: Clarendon Press, 1974).

Beattie, J, *Dissertations Moral and Critical* (London: W Strahan, 1783).

Beckett, S, *Endgame* (London: Faber and Faber, 1958).

——, *The Beckett Trilogy* (London: Picador, 1979).

——, *As the Story Was Told: Uncollected and Late Prose* (London: John Calder, 1990).

Berkeley, G, *Berkeley's Commonplace Book*, ed. GA Johnston (London: Faber and Faber, 1930).

Blair, H, *Lectures on Rhetoric and Belles Lettres*, 2 vols (London: W Strahan; Edinburgh: T Cadell & W Creech, 1783).

Blom, TE, 'Eighteenth-Century Reflexive Process Poetry', *Eighteenth-Century Studies*, 10 (1976), pp. 52–72.

Bloom, EA and Bloom, LD, *Joseph Addison's Sociable Animal* (Providence: Brown University Press, 1971).

——, (eds), *Addison and Steele: The Critical Heritage* (London: Routledge & Kegan Paul, 1980).

—— and E Leites (eds), *Educating the Audience: Addison, Steele, and Eighteenth-Century Culture* (Los Angeles: William Andrews Clark Memorial Library, 1984)

Booth, WC, *The Rhetoric of Fiction* (Chicago and London: University of Chicago Press, 1961).

——, *The Company We Keep: An Ethics of Fiction* (Berkeley: University of California Press, 1988).

Boswell, J, *The Life of Samuel Johnson* [1790], ed. RW Chapman (Oxford: Oxford University Press, 1904; rev. edn., 1970).

Boulton, JT, *The Language of Politics in the Age of Wilkes and Burke* (London: Routledge & Kegan Paul; Toronto: University of Toronto Press, 1963).

Bray, J, Handley, M and Henry, AC (eds), *Ma(r)king the Text: The Presentation of Meaning on the Literary Page* (Aldershot: Ashgate, 2000).

Brewer, J, *The Pleasures of The Imagination: English Culture in the Eighteenth Century* (London: HarperCollins, 1997).

Brissenden, RF, *Virtue in Distress: Studies in the Novel of Sentiment from Richardson to Sade* (London: Macmillan, 1974).

Brooks, P, *Reading for the Plot: Design and Intention in Narrative* (Cambridge, MA: Harvard University Press, 1984).

Brunton, M, *Self-Control: A Novel* (Edinburgh: George Ramsay & Co.; London: Longman, Hurst, Reese, Orme & Brown, 1811; 4th edn, repr. London: H Colburn & R Bentley, 1832).

Burke, E, *The Correspondence of Edmund Burke*, ed. TW Copeland et al., 10 vols (Cambridge: Cambridge University Press; Chicago: University of Chicago Press, 1958–78).

——, *Reflections on the Revolution in France* [1790], ed. CC O'Brien (Harmondsworth: Penguin, 1968).

——, *A Philosophical Enquiry into the Origin of Our Ideas of the Sublime and Beautiful* [1757], ed. A Phillips (Oxford: Oxford University Press, 1990).

——, *Pre-Revolutionary Writings*, ed. I Harris (Cambridge: Cambridge University Press, 1993).

Burke, K, *Counter-Statement* (Los Altos, CA: Hermes, 1931; 2nd edn, 1953).

Burke, P, *The Art of Conversation* (Cambridge: Polity Press, 1993).

Burnet, J, Lord Monboddo, *Of The Origin and Progress of Language*, 6 vols (Edinburgh: A Kincaid & W Creech; London: T Cadell, 1773–92; repr. Menston, Scolar Press, 1967).

Burney, F, *Diary and Letters of Madame D'Arblay*, ed. C Barrett, intr. A Dobson, 6 vols (London: Macmillan and Co., 1904–5).

——, *Camilla: or a Picture of Youth* [1796], ed. EA Bloom and LD Bloom (Oxford: Oxford University Press, 1972).

——, *Selected Letters and Journals*, ed. J Hemlow (Oxford: Oxford University Press, 1986).

——, *Cecilia, or, Memoirs of an Heiress*, ed. P Sabor and MA Doody (Oxford: Oxford University Press, 1988).

——, *Dr Johnson and Fanny Burney: Extracts from Fanny Burney's Prose, 1777–84*, ed. N Wood (Bristol: Bristol Classical Press, 1989).

——, *Evelina, or the History of a Young Lady's Entrance into the World* [1778], ed. SJ Cooke (New York and London: WW Norton & Co., 1998).

Burrows, JF, *Jane Austen's 'Emma'* (Sydney: Sydney University Press, 1968).

——, *Computation into Criticism: A Study of Jane Austen's Novels and an Experiment in Method* (Oxford: Clarendon Press, 1987).

Bush, D, *Jane Austen* (London: Macmillan, 1975).

Butler, J, *The Works of Joseph Butler, D.C.L., Sometime Lord Bishop of Durham*, ed. WE Gladstone, 2 vols (Oxford: Clarendon Press, 1897).

Butler, M, *Jane Austen and the War of Ideas* (Oxford: Clarendon Press, 1975; 2nd edn, 1987).

——, *Romantics, Rebels and Reactionaries* (Oxford: Oxford University Press, 1981).

——, 'Godwin, Burke, and Caleb Williams', *Essays in Criticism*, 32 (1982), pp. 237–57.

——, (ed.), *Burke, Paine, Godwin and the Revolution Controversy* (Cambridge: Cambridge University Press, 1984).

Butor, M, *Inventory*, ed. R Howard (London: Jonathan Cape, 1970).

Byrne, P, *Jane Austen and the Theatre* (London and New York: Hambledon and London, 2002).

Calderwood, JL and Toliver, HE (eds), *Perspectives on Fiction* (New York: Oxford University Press, 1968).

Campbell, A, *Lexiphanes, a Dialogue*, 2nd edn (London: J Knox, 1767).

Carroll, L [Dodgson, CL], *The Annotated Alice*, ed. M Gardner (London: Anthony Blond Ltd, 1964; repr. Harmondsworth: Penguin, 1965; rev. edn, 1970).

Cary, HF, *The Vision: or Hell, Purgatory, and Paradise of Dante Alighieri*, 3 vols (London: J Barfield, 1814; 2nd edn, 1819).

Casey, J, *The Language of Criticism* (London: Methuen & Co., 1966).

Castle, T, *Clarissa's Ciphers: Meaning and Disruption in Richardson's 'Clarissa'* (Ithaca and London: Cornell University Press, 1982).

Chapman, GW, *Edmund Burke: The Practical Imagination* (Cambridge, MA: Harvard University Press, 1967).

Chapman, RW, *Jane Austen: Facts and Problems* (Oxford: Clarendon Press, 1948).

Chesterton, GK, *Criticisms and Appreciations of the Works of Charles Dickens* [1911], intr. M Slater (London: JM Dent & Co., 1992).

Christie, IR, *Myth and Reality in Late Eighteenth-Century British Politics* (London: Macmillan, 1970).

Cicero, MT, *The Letters to His Friends*, I (Cambridge, MA and London: Harvard University Press and William Heinemann, 1979).

Cobbett, W, ed., *The Parliamentary History of England from the Norman Conquest in 1066 to the year 1803*, ed. W Cobbett, 36 vols (London: R Bagshaw; Longmans & Co., 1806–20).

Cohen, M, *Sensible Words: Linguistic Practice in England, 1640–1785* (Baltimore and London: Johns Hopkins University Press, 1977).

Cohn, D, *Transparent Minds: Narrative Modes for Presenting Consciousness in Fiction* (Princeton: Princeton University Press, 1978).

Coleridge, ST, *Essays and Lectures on Shakspeare* (London: JM Dent, 1907).

——, *Shakespearean Criticism*, ed. TM Raysor, 2 vols (London: JM Dent, 1960).

——, *Biographia Literaria* [1817], ed. J Engell and WJ Bate, 2 vols in 1 (Princeton: Princeton University Press, 1983).

——, *Selected Letters*, ed. HJ Jackson (Oxford: Oxford University Press, 1988).

Collected Reports of the Jane Austen Society, 1966–1975, intr. Elizabeth Jenkins (Folkestone: n. p., 1977).

Collected reports of the Jane Austen Society, 1976–1985 (Overton: Jane Austen Society, 1989).

Collected Reports of the Jane Austen Society, 1986–1995 (Alton: Jane Austen Society, 1997).

Colley, L, *Britons: Forging the Nation, 1707–1837* (New Haven and London: Yale University Press, 1992; rev. edn., London: Vintage, 1996).

Colman, G, the Younger, *The Iron Chest* (London: Cadell & Davies, 1796; repr. Oxford: Woodstock, 1989).

Combe, W, *The Tour of Doctor Syntax, In Search of the Picturesque*, 5th edn. (London: n.p., 1812).

Connor, S, *Dumbstruck: A Cultural History of Ventriloquism* (New York: Oxford University Press, 2000).

Cooper, AA, Third Earl of Shaftesbury, *Characteristics of Men, Manners, Opinions, Times* [1711], ed. LE Klein (Cambridge: Cambridge University Press, 1999).

Cope, Z, 'Jane Austen's Last Illness', *British Medical Journal* (1964), pp. 182–3.

Copeland, E and McMaster, J (eds), *The Cambridge Companion to Jane Austen* (Cambridge: Cambridge University Press, 1997).

Cowper, W, *The Letters and Prose Writings of William Cowper*, ed. J King and C Ryskamp, 5 vols (Oxford: Clarendon Press, 1976–86).

——, *The Poems of William Cowper*, ed. JD Baird and C Ryskamp, 3 vols (Oxford: Clarendon Press, 1980–95).

Coxon, R, *Chesterfield and his Critics* (London: George Routledge & Sons, 1925).

Cunningham, V, *Reading After Theory* (Oxford: Blackwell, 2002).

Culler, J, *Structuralist Poetics: Structuralism, Linguistics and the Study of Literature* (London: Routledge and Kegan Paul, 1975).

Davie, D, *Collected Poems* (Chicago: University of Chicago Press, 1991).

—— *Older Masters: Essays and Reflections on English and American Literature* (Manchester: Carcanet, 1992).

Davies, HS, *Wordsworth and the Worth of Words*, ed. J Kerrigan and J Wordsworth Cambridge: Cambridge University Press, 1986).

Davis, LJ, *Factual Fictions: The Origins of the English Novel* (New York: Columbia University Press, 1983).

Davis, P, *Memory and Writing from Wordsworth to Lawrence* (Liverpool: Liverpool University Press, 1983).

—— *In Mind of Johnson: A Study of Johnson the Rambler* (Athens, GA: University of Georgia Press, 1989).

——, (ed.), *Real Voices: On Reading* (Basingstoke and London: Macmillan, 1997).

Day, A, *The English Secretary; or Methods of Writing Epistles and Letters, with a Declaration of such Tropes, Figures, and Schemes, as either usually or for ornament sake are therein required* [1586; 2nd edn, 1599], ed. RO Evans, 2 vols in 1 (Gainesville, Fl.: Scholars' Facsimiles and Reprints, 1967).

De Bruyn, F, *The Literary Genres of Edmund Burke: The Political Uses of Literary Form* (Oxford: Clarendon Press, 1996).

De Man, P, *The Rhetoric of Romanticism* (New York: Columbia University Press, 1984).

De Rose, PL and McGuire, SW, *A Concordance to the Works of Jane Austen*, 3 vols (New York: Garland, 1982).

Dickens, C, *Christmas Books* [1852], intr. E Farjeon (Oxford: Oxford University Press, 1954).

——, *Little Dorrit* [1857], ed. J Holloway (Penguin: Harmondsworth, 1967).

——, *David Copperfield* [1849–50], ed. J Tambling (London: Penguin, 1996).

——, *'Gone Astray' and Other Papers from Household Words, 1851–59*, ed. M Slater (London: JM Dent, 1998).

Dickinson, E, *A Choice of Emily Dickinson's Verse*, ed. T Hughes (London: Faber and Faber, 1968).

Dickinson, HT, *British Radicalism and the French Revolution, 1789–1815* (Oxford: Blackwell, 1985).

Doody, MA, *A Natural Passion: A Study of the Novels of Samuel Richardson* (Oxford: Clarendon Press, 1974).

—— and Sabor, P (eds), *Samuel Richardson: Tercentenary Essays* (Cambridge: Cambridge University Press, 1989).

Drew, P, 'Jane Austen and Bishop Butler', *Nineteenth-Century Fiction*, 35:2 (1980), pp. 127–49.

Dryden, J, *The Works of John Dryden*, ed. EN Hooker, HT Swedenberg, Jr., VA Dearing et al., 20 vols (Berkeley: University of California Press, 1956–2000).

Duckworth, AM, *The Improvement of the Estate* (Baltimore: Johns Hopkins University Press, 1971).

Dussinger, JA, *The Discourse of the Mind in Eighteenth-Century Fiction* (The Hague and Paris: Mouton, 1974).

——, *In the Pride of the Moment: Encounters in Jane Austen's World* (Columbus: Ohio State University Press, 1990).

Ehrenpreis, I, *Acts of Implication: Suggestion and Covert Meaning in the Works of Dryden, Swift, Pope, and Austen* (Berkeley and London: University of California Press, 1980).

Eilenberg, S, *Strange Power of Speech: Wordsworth, Coleridge, and Literary Possession* (New York and London: Oxford University Press, 1992).

Eliot, G, *Middlemarch* [1871–2], ed. WJ Harvey (Penguin: Harmondsworth, 1965).

Eliot. TS, *Selected Essays* (London: Faber and Faber, 1932; 3rd edn, 1951).

——, *The Use of Poetry and the Use of Criticism* (London: Faber and Faber, 1933; 2nd edn, 1964).

——, *The Complete Poems and Plays of T. S. Eliot* (London: Faber and Faber, 1969).

Empson, W, *The Structure of Complex Words* (London: Chatto & Windus, 1951; repr. London: Hogarth Press, 1985).

——, *Some Versions of Pastoral* (London: Chatto & Windus, 1935; repr. London: Hogarth Press, 1986).

Everett, B, *Poets in Their Time: Essays on English Poetry from Donne to Larkin* (London: Faber and Faber, 1986; repr. Oxford: Clarendon Press, 1991).

——, 'Hard Romance', *London Review of Books*, 8/2/1996, pp. 12–14.

Favret, MA, *Romantic Correspondence: Women, Politics and the Fiction of Letters* (Cambridge: Cambridge University Press, 1993).

Fielding, H, *The History of Tom Jones* [1749], ed. RPC Mutter (Harmondsworth: Penguin, 1966).

——, *The Life of Mr Jonathan Wild the Great* [1743], ed. D Nokes (Harmondsworth: Penguin, 1982).

——, *Amelia* [1751], ed . D Blewett (Harmondsworth: Penguin, 1987).

——, *Joseph Andrews* and *Shamela* [1742 and 1741], ed. A Humphreys et al. (London: JM Dent 1973; rev. edn, 1993).

Fish, S, *Is There a Text in This Class? The Authority of Interpretive Communities* (Cambridge, MA: Harvard University Press, 1980).

Fitzgerald, P, *Jane Austen: A Criticism and Interpretation* (London: Jarrold and Sons, 1912).

Flahiff, FT, 'Place and Replacement in *Mansfield Park*', *University of Toronto Quarterly*, 54:3 (1985), pp. 221–33.

Flaubert, G, *L'Éducation sentimentale* [1869] (Paris: Gallimard, 1965).

Fleishman, A, *A Reading of 'Mansfield Park': An Essay in Critical Synthesis* (Baltimore and London: Johns Hopkins University Press, 1967).

Fludernik, M, *The Fictions of Language and the Languages of Fiction* (London: Routledge, 1993).

Foucault, M, *Surveiller et punir: Naissance de la prison* (Paris: Gallimard, 1975).

Frank, J, *The Widening Gyre* (New Brunswick, NJ: Rutgers University Press, 1963).

Freud, S, *Civilisation and Its Discontents* [1930], trans. J Rivière, rev. and ed. J Strachey (Harmondsworth: Penguin, 1963).

——, *The Psychopathology of Everyday Life* [1901], trans. A Tyson, ed. J Strachey, A Richards, A Tyson (Harmondsworth: Penguin, 1975).

Freud, S, *Art and Literature*, trans. J Strachey, et al. (Harmondsworth: Penguin, 1985).

Gard, R, *Jane Austen's Novels: The Art of Clarity* (New Haven and London: Yale University Press, 1992).

Genette, G, *Figures I* (Paris: Éditions du Seuil, 1966).

——, *Narrative Discourse*, trans. JE Lewin (Ithaca: Cornell University Press, 1980).

——, *Figures of Literary Discourse*, trans. A Sheridan (Oxford: Basil Blackwell, 1982).

——, *Narrative Discourse Revisited*, trans. JE Lewin (Ithaca: Cornell University Press, 1988).

——, *Palimpsests: Literature in the Second Degree* (Lincoln and London: University of Nebraska Press, 1997).

Giddens, A, *The Third Way: The Transformation of Social Democracy* (Cambridge: Polity Press, 1998).

——, *The Third Way and its Critics* (Malden, MA: Polity Press, 2000).

Gilpin, W, *Observations on Cumberland and Westmorland* [1786], 2 vols (Poole & New York: Woodstock Books, 1996).

Gisborne, T, *An Enquiry into the Duties of the Female Sex* (London: n. p., 1797).

Godwin, W, *The Enquirer: Reflections on Education, Manners, and Literature in a Series of Essays* (London: GG & J Robinson, 1797; repr. New York: AM Kelley, 1965).

——, *Things as They Are, or The Adventures of Caleb Williams* [1794], ed. D McCracken (Oxford: Oxford University Press, 1970).

——, *Enquiry Concerning Political Justice* [1793], ed. I Kramnick (Harmondsworth: Penguin, 1976).

Goffman, E, *The Presentation of Self in Everyday Life* (Garden City, NY: Doubleday, 1959; repr. London: Allen Lane, 1969).

Goldsmith, O, *Collected Works of Oliver Goldsmith*, ed. A Friedman, 5 vols (Oxford: Clarendon Press, 1966).

Gordon, G, Lord Byron, *The Complete Poetical Works*, ed. JJ McGann, 7 vols (Oxford: Clarendon Press, 1980–93).

Gould, SJ, *Time's Arrow, Time's Cycle: Myth and Metaphor in the Discovery of Geological Time* (Cambridge, MA and London: Harvard University Press, 1987).

Grice, HP, *Studies in the Way of Words* (Cambridge, MA: Harvard University Press, 1989).

Griffiths, E, *The Printed Voice of Victorian Poetry* (Oxford: Clarendon Press, 1989).

Hall, ET, *The Silent Language* (Garden City, NY: Doubleday, 1959).

——, *The Hidden Dimension* (Garden City, NY: Doubleday, 1966).

Halperin, J, *The Life of Jane Austen* (Brighton: Harvester, 1984).

——, 'The Novelist as Heroine in *Mansfield Park*: A Study in Autobiography', *Modern Language Quarterly*, 44:2 (1983), pp. 136–56.

Hamburger, K, *The Logic of Literature*, trans. MJ Rose (Bloomington and London: Indiana University Press, 1973).

Harding, DW, 'Psychological Processes in the Reading of Fiction', *British Journal of Aesthetics*, 2 (1962), pp. 133–47.

——, *Experience into Words* (London: Chatto and Windus, 1963; repr. Harmondsworth: Penguin, 1974).

——, *Regulated Hatred and Other Essays on Jane Austen*, ed. M Lawlor (London and Atlantic Highlands: Athlone Press, 1998).

Hardy, B, *A Reading of Jane Austen* (London: Athlone Press, 1975; 2nd edn, 1979).

Hardy, T, *The Personal Writings of Thomas Hardy*, ed. H Orel (London and Melbourne: Macmillan, 1967).

——, *The Mayor of Casterbridge* [1886], ed. M Seymour-Smith (Harmondsworth: Penguin, 1978).

[Harness, W.], *The Life of Mary Russell Mitford, Authoress of 'Our Village', etc., related in a selection from her Letters to her Friends*, ed. AE L'Estrange, 3 vols (London: Richard Bentley, 1870).

Harris, J, *Hermes or A Philosophical Inquiry Concerning Universal Grammar* (London: J Nourse & P Vaillant, 1751; 2ⁿᵈ edn, 1765).

Harris, J, *Jane Austen's Art of Memory* (Cambridge: Cambridge University Press, 1989).

Harris, RA, 'Social Definition in *Pride and Prejudice*: An Exercise in Extensional Semantics', *English Studies in Canada*, 17:2 (1991), pp. 163–76.

Hazlitt, W, *Characters of Shakespear's Plays* [1817–18] (London: JM Dent, 1906).

——, *Selected Writings*, ed. R Blythe (Harmondsworth: Penguin, 1970).

Hegel, GWF, *Phenomenology of Spirit*, trans. AV Miller (Oxford: Oxford University Press, 1977).

——, *Elements of the Philosophy of Right* [1821], trans. H Nisbet (Cambridge: Cambridge University Press, 1991).

Hill, G, *The Lords of Limit: Essays on Literature and Ideas* (London: Andre Deutsch, 1984).

——, *Collected Poems* (Harmondsworth: Penguin, 1985).

——, *The Enemy's Country: Words, Contexture, and Other Circumstances of Language* (Stanford: Stanford University Press, 1991).

Hobbes, T, *Leviathan* [1651], ed. R Tuck (Cambridge: Cambridge University Press, 1991).

Holland, N, *Laughing: A Psychology of Humor* (Ithaca & London: Cornell University Press, 1982).

Honan, P, *Jane Austen: Her Life* (New York: Fawcett Columbine, 1987).

Hudson, N, *Samuel Johnson and Eighteenth-Century Thought* (Oxford: Clarendon Press, 1988).

Hume, D, *A Treatise of Human Nature*, ed. EC Mossner (Harmondsworth: Penguin, 1969).

——, *Enquiries: Concerning Human Understanding and the Principles of Morals* [1777], ed. LA Selby-Bigge, rev. PH Nidditch (Oxford: Clarendon Press, 1975).

——, *Dialogues Concerning Natural Religion* [1779], ed. S Tweyman (London: Routledge, 1991).

Hunter, JP, *Before Novels: The Cultural Contexts of Eighteenth Century English Fiction* (New York and London: WW Norton & Co., 1990).

Hutcheson, F, *Philosophical Writings*, ed. RS Downie (London: JM Dent, 1994).

Hutchinson, GO, *Cicero's Correspondence: A Literary Study* (Oxford: Clarendon Press, 1998).

Ihde, D, *Listening and Voice: A Phenomenology of Sound* (Athens, OH; Ohio University Press, 1976).

Iser, W, *The Implied Reader: Patterns of Communication in Prose Fiction from Bunyan to Beckett* (Baltimore and London: Johns Hopkins University Press, 1974).

——, *The Act of Reading: A Theory of Aesthetic Response* (Baltimore and London: Johns Hopkins University Press, 1978).

James, H, *Literary Criticism: French Writers, Other European Writers, The Prefaces to the New York Edition* (New York and Cambridge: Library of America, 1984).

——, *The Critical Muse: Selected Literary Criticism*, ed. R Gard (Harmondsworth: Penguin, 1987).

——, *The Portrait of a Lady* [1881], ed. Priscilla L Walton (London, JM Dent, 1995).

Jespersen, O, *Language; its Nature, Development and Origin* (London: George Allen & Unwin, 1922)

Johnson, S, *Lives of the English Poets* [1781], intr. LA Hind, 2 vols (London: JM Dent & Sons Ltd, 1925).

Johnson, S, *The Yale Edition of the Works of Samuel Johnson*, ed. EL McAdam et al., 16 vols (New Haven and London: Yale University Press, 1958–).

——, *An Account of the Life of Mr Richard Savage* [1744], ed. C Tracy (Oxford: Oxford University Press, 1971).

——, *A Dictionary of the English Language* , 2 vols (London: J & P Knapton, et al., 1755; repr. Harlow: Longman, 1990).

——, *The Oxford Authors: Samuel Johnson*, ed. D Greene (Oxford: Oxford University Press, 1984).

Josipovici, G, *Text and Voice: Essays 1981–1991* (Manchester: Carcanet; New York: St Martin's Press, 1992).

——, *On Trust: Art and the Temptations of Suspicion* (New Haven and London: Yale University Press, 1999).

Kant, I, *Critique of Pure Reason* [1781], trans. JMD Meiklejohn (London: JM Dent & Sons, 1934; repr. 1991).

Kastely, JL, 'Persuasion: Jane Austen's Philosophical Rhetoric', *Philosophy and Literature*, 15:1 (1991), pp. 74–88.

Kaye-Smith, S and Stern, GB, *Talking of Jane Austen* (London and Toronto: Cassell and Company, 1943).

Keats, J, *The Letters of John Keats*, ed. M Buxton Forman (Oxford: Oxford University Press, 1931; 4th edn, 1952).

Kermode, F, *The Sense of an Ending: Studies in the Theory of Fiction* (New York: Oxford University Press, 1967).

Kestner, JA, *Jane Austen: Spatial Structure of Thematic Variations* (Salzburg: Institut für Englische Sprache und Literatur, 1974).

——, *The Spatiality of the Novel* (Detroit: Wayne State University Press, 1978).

Keymer, T, *Richardson's 'Clarissa' and the Eighteenth-Century Reader* (Cambridge: Cambridge University Press, 1992).

Kipling, R, *Collected Stories* (London: David Campbell Publishers, 1994).

Klein. LE, *Shaftesbury and the Culture of Politeness* (Cambridge: Cambridge University Press, 1994).

Knowlson, J, *Damned to Fame: The Life of Samuel Beckett* (London: Bloomsbury, 1996).

Knox, V, *Elegant Extracts: or Useful and Entertaining Pieces of Poetry Selected for the Improvement of Youth, etc.* (London: Charles Dilly, 1784).

Laclos, PC de, *Les Liaisons dangereuses* [1782] (Paris: Gallimard, 1972).

Lamarque, P and Olsen, SH, *Truth, Fiction, and Literature* (Oxford: Clarendon Press, 1994).

Lamb, C, *Selected Prose*, ed. A Phillips (Harmondsworth: Penguin, 1985), p. 320.

Land, SK, *The Study of Language in Britain: Major Theories from Hobbes to Thomas Reid* (New York: AMS Press, 1986).

Lane, H (ed.), *The Deaf Experience: Classics in Language and Education*, trans. F Philip (Cambridge, MA: Harvard University Press, 1984).

Langford, P, *A Polite and Commercial People: England 1727–1783* (Oxford: Oxford University Press, 1989).

Larkin, P, *Collected Poems*, ed. A Thwaite (London: Faber and Faber, 1988).

Lascelles, M, *Jane Austen and her Art* (Oxford: Clarendon Press, 1939).

Leavis, FR, *The Great Tradition* (London: Chatto and Windus, 1948; repr. Harmondsworth, Penguin, 1962).

——, *New Bearings in English Poetry* (London: Chatto & Windus, 1932; 2nd edn, 1950; repr. Harmondsworth: Penguin, 1963).

——, *Revaluation: Tradition and Development in English Poetry* (London: Chatto & Windus, 1936; repr. Harmondsworth: Penguin, 1964).

——, *'Anna Karenina' and Other Essays* (London: Chatto & Windus, 1967).

——, *English Literature in Our Time and the University* (London: Chatto & Windus, 1969; repr. Cambridge: Cambridge University Press, 1979).

——, *The Common Pursuit* (London: Chatto and Windus, 1952; repr. London: Hogarth Press, 1984).

Lee, DA, 'Modality, Perspective and the Concept of Objective Narrative', *Journal of Literary Semantics*, 11:2 (1982), pp. 104–11.

Leech, GN and Short, MH, *Style in Fiction: A Linguistic Guide to English Fictional Prose* (London: Longman, 1981).

Lennard, J, *But I Digress: The Exploitation of Parentheses in English Printed Verse* (Oxford: Clarendon Press, 1991).

Lennox, C, *The Female Quixote, or the Adventures of Arabella* [1752], ed. M Dalziel (Oxford: Oxford University Press, 1989).

Levine, G, *Darwin and the Novelists: Patterns of Science in Victorian Fiction* (Cambridge, MA: Harvard University Press, 1988).

Levinson, SC, *Pragmatics* (Cambridge: Cambridge University Press, 1983).

Lewis, MG, *The Monk* [1796], ed. H Anderson (Oxford: Oxford University Press, 1973).

Locke, D, *A Fantasy of Reason: The Life and Thought of William Godwin* (London: Routledge and Kegan Paul, 1980).

Locke, J, *An Essay Concerning Human Understanding* [1690], ed. PH Nidditch (Oxford: Clarendon Press, 1975).

Lofft, C, *Remarks on the Letter of the Rt Hon. Edmund Burke, concerning the Revolution in France* (London: J Johnson, 1790).

Loveridge, M, *Laurence Sterne and the Argument about Design* (Totowa, NJ: Barnes & Noble, 1982).

——, 'Francis Hutcheson and Mr. Weston's Conundrum in *Emma*', *Notes and Queries*, 30:3, n.s. (1983), pp. 214–16.

MacDonagh, O, *Jane Austen: Real and Imagined Worlds* (New Haven and London: Yale University Press, 1991).

Mack, M, *Alexander Pope: A Biography* (New Haven & London: Yale University Press, 1985).

Mackenzie, H, *The Man of Feeling* [1771], ed. B Vickers (Oxford: Oxford University Press, 1987).

Mackintosh, J, *Vindiciae Gallicae: Defence of the French Revolution and its English Admirers against the Accusations of the Right Hon. Edmund Burke* (London: GGJ & J Robinson, 1791).

MacIntyre, A, *A Short History of Ethics* (London: Routledge and Kegan Paul, 1967).

——, *Against the Self-Images of the Age: Essays on Ideology and Philosophy* (London: Duckworth, 1971).

——, *After Virtue: A Study in Moral Theory* (London: Duckworth, 1981).

——, *Three Rival Versions of Moral Enquiry* (London: Duckworth, 1990).

Macpherson, CB, *Burke* (Oxford: Oxford University Press, 1980).

Mahood, MM, *Shakespeare's Wordplay* (London: Methuen, 1957).

Manguel, A, *A History of Reading* (London: HarperCollins, 1996).

'Marlow, Lady H' [Beckford, W], *Modern Novel Writing, or The Elegant Enthusiast*, 2 vols (London: GG and J Robinson, 1796; repr. New York and London: Garland, 1974).

Marshall, D, *The Figure of Theater: Shaftesbury, Defoe, Adam Smith, and George Eliot* (New York: Columbia University Press, 1986).

Marshall, D, 'True Language and the Acting of Real Feeling: *Mansfield Park*', *Yale Journal of Criticism*, 3:1 (1989), pp. 87–106.

McLuhan, M, *The Gutenberg Galaxy: The Making of Typographical Man* (Toronto: University of Toronto Press, 1962).

McMaster, J, *Jane Austen on Love* (Victoria, BC: English Literary Studies Monographs 13, 1978).

—— and Stovel, B (eds), *Jane Austen's Business: Her World and Her Profession* (Basingstoke and London; New York: Macmillan, St Martin's Press, 1996).

Merleau-Ponty, M, *Phenomenology of Perception*, trans. C Smith (London & New York: Routledge & Kegan Paul, 1962).

Meyersohn, M, 'What Fanny Knew: A Quiet Auditor of the Whole', *Women and Literature*, n.s. 3, ed. J Todd (1983), pp. 224–30.

Miller, DA, *Narrative and Its Discontents: Problems of Closure in the Traditional Novel* (Princeton: Princeton University Press, 1981).

Milns, W, *The Well-Bred Scholar, or Practical Essays on the Best Methods of Improving the Taste, and Assisting the Exertions of Youth in their Literary Pursuits* (London: S Gosnell, Messrs Rivington, T Boosey, 1794).

Monaghan, D (ed.), *Jane Austen in A Social Context* (London: Macmillan, 1981).

Mooneyham, LG, *Romance, Language, and Education in Jane Austen's Novels* (Basingstoke: Macmillan, 1988).

Morgan, S, *In the Meantime: Character and Perception in Jane Austen's Fiction* (Chicago and London: University of Chicago Press, 1980).

Mossner, EC, *Bishop Butler and the Age of Reason* (New York: Macmillan, 1936; repr. Bristol: Thoemmes, 1990).

Mudrick, M, *Jane Austen: Irony as Defence and Discovery* (Princeton and London: Princeton University Press, 1952).

Mullan, J, *Sentiment and Sociability: The Language of Feeling in the Eighteenth Century* (Oxford: Clarendon Press, 1988).

Murdoch, I, 'Against Dryness', *Encounter*, 16:1 (1961), pp. 16–20.

Nagel, T, *Mortal Questions* (Cambridge: Cambridge University Press, 1979).

Newman, JH, *An Essay on the Development of Christian Doctrine* [1845], ed. JM Cameron (Harmondsworth: Penguin, 1974).

Nokes, D, *Jonathan Swift: A Hypocrite Reversed* (Oxford: Oxford University Press, 1985).

——, *Raillery and Rage: A Study of Eighteenth Century Satire* (Brighton: Harvester, 1987).

——, *Jane Austen: A Life* (London: Fourth Estate, 1997).

Nussbaum, MC, *The Fragility of Goodness: Luck and Ethics in Greek Tragedy and Philosophy* (Cambridge: Cambridge University Press, 1986).

——, *Love's Knowledge: Essays on Philosophy and Literature* (New York and Oxford: Oxford University Press, 1990).

——, *Poetic Justice: The Literary Imagination and Public Life* (Boston: Beacon Press, 1995).

Nystrand, M., ed., *What Writers Know: The Language, Process, and Structure of Written Discourse* (New York and London: Academic Press, 1982).

O'Brien, CC, *The Suspecting Glance* (London: Faber and Faber, 1972).

——, *The Great Melody: A Thematic Biography and Commented Anthology of Edmund Burke* (London: Sinclair-Stevenson, 1992).

O'Brien, F [O'Nolan, B], *The Best of Myles*, ed. K O'Nolan (London: MacGibbon & Kee, 1968; repr. London: Grafton, 1987).

Onega, S and Landa, JAG (eds), *Narratology: A Reader* (London: Longman, 1996).

Onions, CT, *A Shakespeare Glossary*, rev. RD Eagleson (Oxford: Clarendon Press, 1911; 3rd edn, 1986).

Page, N, *The Language of Jane Austen* (Oxford: Oxford University Press, 1972).

Paine, T, *Political Writings*, ed. B Kuklick (Cambridge: Cambridge University Press, 1989).

Palmer, FR, *Mood and Modality* (Cambridge: Cambridge University Press, 1986).

Parkes, MB, *Pause and Effect: Punctuation in the West* (Berkeley and Los Angeles: University of California Press, 1993).

Patteson, RF, 'Truth, Certitude, and Stability in Jane Austen's Fiction', *Philological Quarterly*, 60 (1981), pp. 455–69.

Penelhum, T, *Butler* (London: Routledge & Kegan Paul, 1985).

Pevsner, N, 'The Architectural Setting of Jane Austen's Novels', *Journal of the Warburg and Courtauld Institutes*, 31 (1968), pp. 404–22.

Phillips, A, *On Flirtation* (London: Faber and Faber, 1994).

——, *Promises, Promises: Essays on Literature and Psychoanalysis* (London: Faber and Faber, 2000).

Phillipps, KC, *Jane Austen's English* (London: Deutsch, 1970).

Phillipson, N, *Hume* (London: Weidenfeld and Nicolson, 1989).

—— and Skinner, Q (eds), *Political Discourse in Early Modern Britain* (Cambridge: Cambridge University Press, 1993).

Piette, A, *Remembering and the Sound of Words: Mallarmé, Proust, Joyce, Beckett* (Oxford: Clarendon Press, 1996).

Piggott, P, *The Innocent Diversion: A Study of Music in the Life and Writings of Jane Austen* (London: Douglas Cleverdon, 1979).

Piozzi, HL, *British Synonymy; or, an Attempt at Regulating the Choice of Words in Familiar Conversation*, 2 vols (London: n.p., 1794).

Plato, *The Symposium*, trans. W Hamilton (Harmondsworth: Penguin, 1951).

——, *Phaedo*, trans. D Gallup (Oxford: Oxford University Press, 1993).

Pocock. JGA, *Politics, Language, and Time: Essays on Political Thought and History* (New York: Atheneum, 1971; repr. Chicago and London: University of Chicago Press, 1989).

——, *Virtue, Commerce, and History* (Cambridge: Cambridge University Press, 1985).

Pollock, WH, *Jane Austen: Her Contemporaries and Herself, An Essay in Criticism* (London: n.p., 1899).

Pomeau, R (intr.), *Laclos et le libertinage* (Paris: Presses Universitaires de France, 1983).

Poovey, M, *The Proper Lady and the Woman Writer* (Chicago and London: University of Chicago Press, 1984).

Pope, A, *The Prose Works of Alexander Pope*, ed. N Ault and R Cowler, 2 vols (Oxford: Oxford University Press, 1936–86).

——, *The Poems of Alexander Pope*, ed. J Butt (London: Methuen, 1963).

Pratt, ML, *Toward a Speech Act Theory of Literary Discourse* (Bloomington and London: Indiana University Press, 1977).

Preston, J, *The Created Self: The Reader's Role in Eighteenth-Century Fiction* (London: Heinemann, 1970).

Priestley, J, *A Course of Lectures on Oratory and Criticism* [1777], ed. VM Bevilacqua and R Murphy (Carbondale: Southern Illinois University Press, 1965).

Priestman, M, *Cowper's 'Task': Structure and Influence* (Cambridge: Cambridge University Press, 1983).

Propp, V, *Morphology of the Folktale*, trans. L Scott (Austin, TX and London: University of Texas Press, 1958; 2nd edn, 1968).

Prostko, J, '"Natural Conversation Set in View": Shaftesbury and Moral Speech', *Eighteenth-Century Studies*, 23 (1989), pp. 42–61.

Proust, M, *Against Sainte-Beuve and Other Essays*, trans. J Sturrock (London: Penguin, 1988).

Radcliffe, A, *The Mysteries of Udolpho* [1794], ed. B Dobrée (Oxford: Oxford University Press, 1966).

Ray, JK, 'Jane Austen's Case Study of Child Abuse', *Persuasions*, 13 (1991), pp. 16–26.

Redford, B, *The Converse of the Pen: Acts of Intimacy in the Eighteenth-Century Familiar Letter* (Chicago and London: University of Chicago Press, 1986).

Reynolds, J, *Discourses on Art*, ed. RR Wark (San Marino, CA: Henry E Huntington Library, 1959; repr. New Haven and London: Yale University Press, 1997)

Richardson, S, *A Collection of Moral and Instructive Sentiments, Maxims, Cautions, and Reflexions, Contained in the Histories of Pamela, Clarissa, and Sir Charles Grandison* (London: S Richardson, C Hitch, L Hawes et al., 1755).

——, *Selected Letters of Samuel Richardson*, ed. J Carroll (Oxford: Clarendon Press, 1964).

——, *Sir Charles Grandison* [1753–4], ed. Jocelyn Harris, 3 vols in 1 (Oxford: Oxford University Press, 1972).

——, *Clarissa; or The History of a Young Lady* [1747–8], ed. A Ross (Harmondsworth: Penguin, 1985).

——, *Pamela; or Virtue Rewarded* [1740; 14th edn, 1801], ed. MA Doody (Harmondsworth: Penguin, 1985).

Ricks, C, *Keats and Embarrassment* (Oxford: Oxford University Press, 1974).

——, *The Force of Poetry* (Oxford: Oxford University Press, 1984).

——, *Beckett's Dying Words* (Oxford: Clarendon Press, 1993).

——, *Essays in Appreciation* (Oxford: Clarendon Press, 1996).

Ricoeur, P, *Time and Narrative*, trans. K McLaughlin and D Pellauer, 3 vols (Chicago and London: University of Chicago Press, 1984–8).

Rivero, AJ (ed.), *New Essays on Samuel Richardson* (Basingstoke and London: Macmillan, 1996).

Roberts, JM, *The Mythology of the Secret Societies* (London: Secker & Warburg, 1972).

Roiphe, K, *The Morning After: Sex, Fear, and Feminism* (London: Hamish Hamilton, 1994).

Rosenthal, M, *The Art of Thomas Gainsborough: 'a little business for the eye'* (New Haven and London: Yale University Press, 1999).

Roulston, C, *Virtue, Gender, and the Authentic Self in Eighteenth-Century Fiction* (Gainesville: University Press of Florida, 1998).

Ryle, G, *The Concept of Mind* (London: Hutchinson, 1949; repr. Harmondsworth: Penguin, 1990).

——, *Dilemmas* (Cambridge: Cambridge University Press, 1954).

Sacks, O, *Seeing Voices: A Journey into the World of the Deaf* (Berkeley: University of California Press, 1989).

Sadleir, M, *The Northanger Novels: A Footnote to Jane Austen* (Oxford: English Association, 1927).

St Clair, W, *The Godwins and the Shelley: The Biography of a Family* (London: Faber and Faber, 1989).

Said, EW, *Culture and Imperialism* (London: Chatto and Windus, 1993).

——, *Beginnings: Intention and Method* (New York: Basic Books, 1975; repr. London: Granta Books, 1997).

Sartre, J-P, *Being and Nothingness*, trans. HE Barnes (London: Routledge and Kegan Paul, 1958).

Saussure, F de, *Course in General Linguistics*, trans. W Baskin (London: P Owen, 1960; repr. London: Fontana, 1974).

Schochet, GJ, Tatspaugh, PE and Brobeck, C (eds), *Politics, Politeness and Patriotism* (Washington, DC: Folger Institute, 1993).

Scott, W, *Selected Poems*, ed. J Reed (Manchester: Carcanet, 1992).

Searle, JR, *Speech Acts: An Essay in the Philosophy of Language* (Cambridge: Cambridge University Press, 1969).

——, *Expression and Meaning: Studies in the Theory of Speech Acts* (Cambridge: Cambridge University Press, 1979).

Selwyn, D, *Jane Austen and Leisure* (London: The Hambledon Press, 1999).

Shakespeare, W, *The Tempest; or The Enchanted Island, Written by Shakespeare; with Additions from Dryden: As Compiled by J. P. Kemble, and First Acted at the Theatre Royal, Drury Lane, October 13th, 1789* (London: J Debrett, 1789).

——, *The Norton Facsimile: The First Folio of Shakespeare* [1623], ed. C Hinman (New York: WW Norton & Co., 1968).

——, *The Works of William Shakespeare in Ten Volumes*, ed. S Johnson and G Steevens, 10 vols (London: n.p., 1778; repr. London: Routledge/ Thoemmes Press, 1995).

Singer, *The Epistolary Novel: Its Origin, Development, Decline and Residuary Influence* (Philadelphia: University of Pennsylvania Press, 1933).

Skinner, Q, *The Foundations of Modern Political Thought*, 2 vols (Cambridge: Cambridge University Press, 1978).

Smith, C, *The Old Manor House* [1793], ed. AH Ehrenpreis (Oxford: Oxford University Press, 1969).

——, *The Poems of Charlotte Smith*, ed. S Curran (New York and Oxford: Oxford University Press, 1993).

Smith, O, *The Politics of Language, 1791–1819* (Oxford: Clarendon Press, 1984).

Smithers, P, *The Life of Joseph Addison* (Oxford: Clarendon Press, 1954).

Sontag, S, *A Susan Sontag Reader* (Harmondsworth: Penguin, 1982).

Southam, BC, *Jane Austen's Literary Manuscripts: A Study of the Novelist's Development through the Surviving Papers* (Oxford: Oxford University Press, 1964).

—— (ed.), *Jane Austen: A Collection of Critical Essays* (London: Routledge & Kegan Paul, 1968).

—— (ed.), *Jane Austen: The Critical Heritage*, 2 vols (London: Routledge & Kegan Paul, 1968–87).

Spacks, PM, *The Poetry of Vision: Five Eighteenth-Century Poets* (Cambridge, MA: Harvard University Press, 1967).

The Spectator [1711–12], ed. DF Bond, 5 vols (Oxford: Clarendon Press, 1965).

Sperber, D and Wilson, D, *Relevance: Communication and Cognition* (Oxford: Blackwell, 1986).

Stanhope, PD, Fourth Earl of Chesterfield, *Lord Chesterfield's Letters* [1774], ed. D Roberts (Oxford: Oxford University Press, 1992)

Steele, R et al., *The Guardian* [1713], ed. JC Stephens (Lexington: University Press of Kentucky, 1982).

—— and Addison, J., *Selections from The Tatler and The Spectator*, ed. A Ross (Harmondsworth: Penguin, 1982).

Steeves, HR, *Before Jane Austen: The Shaping of the English Novel in the Eighteenth Century* (London: George Allen & Unwin, 1966).

Sterne, L, *The Life and Opinions of Tristram Shandy, Gentleman* [1759–67], ed. G Petrie (Harmondsworth: Penguin, 1967).

Sterne, L, *A Sentimental Journey, The Journal to Eliza, A Political Romance*, ed. I Jack (Oxford: Oxford University Press, 1968).

Stevick, P (ed.), *The Theory of the Novel* (New York: Free Press, 1967).

Stillinger, J, *The Texts of Keats's Poems* (Cambridge, Mass.: Harvard University Press, 1974).

Stokes, M, *The Language of Jane Austen* (Basingstoke: Macmillan, 1991).

Stout, JP, 'Jane Austen's Proposal Scenes and the Limitations of Language', *Studies in the Novel*, 144 (1982), pp. 316–26.

Sturrock, J, *Structuralism and Since: From Lévi-Strauss to Derrida* (Oxford: Oxford University Press, 1979).

Sutherland, J, *Can Jane Eyre Be Happy?* (Oxford: Oxford University Press, 1997).

Swift, J, *The Prose Works of Jonathan Swift*, ed. H Davis et al., 16 vols (Oxford: Basil Blackwell, 1939–74).

——, *Gulliver's Travels* [1726], ed. P Dixon and J Chalker (Harmondsworth: Penguin, 1967).

Tanner, T, *Jane Austen* (Basingstoke and London: Macmillan, 1986).

Tennant, E, *Emma in Love: Jane Austen's 'Emma' Continued* (London: Fourth Estate, 1996).

Tennyson, *Alfred Lord Tennyson: A Memoir by his Son*, 2 vols (London: Macmillan & Co., 1897).

Teuthold, P, *The Necromancer; or The Tale of the Black Forest* [1794] (London: Folio Press, 1968).

Thelwall, J, *Sober Reflections on the Seditious and Inflammatory Letter of the Right Hon. Edmund Burke, to a Noble Lord: Addressed to the Serious Consideration of his Fellow Citizens* (London: HD Symonds, 1796).

Thomas, KG, 'Jane Austen and the Romantic Lyric: *Persuasion* and Coleridge's Conversation Poems', *ELH*, 54:4 (1987), pp. 893–924.

Thompson, E, *Sense and Sensibility: The Diaries* (London: Bloomsbury, 1995).

——, *Sense and Sensibility: The Screenplay* (London: Bloomsbury, 1996).

Tomalin, C, *Jane Austen: A Life* (London: Viking, 1997).

Tooke, JH, *ΕΠΕΑ ΠΤΕΡΟΕΝΤΑ or, The Diversions of Purley* (London: J Johnson, 1786).

——, MS marginalia in copy of *ΕΠΕΑ ΠΤΕΡΟΕΝΤΑ*, British Library shelf-mark C60. i. 15.

Trilling, L, *Beyond Culture: Essays on Literature and Learning* (London: Secker & Warburg, 1966; repr. Oxford: Oxford University Press, 1980).

——, *The Opposing Self: Nine Essays in Criticism* (London: Secker & Warburg, 1955; repr. Oxford: Oxford University Press, 1980).

Trotter, D, *Cooking with Mud: The Idea of Mess in Nineteenth-Century Art and Fiction* (Oxford: Oxford University Press, 2000).

Tyndale, W, *Doctrinal Treatises* (Cambridge: Parker Society, 1848).

Updike, J, *Your Lover Just Called: Stories of Joan and Richard Maple* (Harmondsworth: Penguin, 1980).

Van Marter, S, 'Richardson's Revisions of *Clarissa* in the Second Edition', *Studies in Bibliography*, 26 (1973), 107–32.

——, 'Richardson's Revisions of *Clarissa* in the Third and Fourth Editions', *Studies in Bibliography*, 28 (1975), pp. 119–52.

Varey, S, *Space and the Eighteenth-Century English Novel* (Cambridge: Cambridge University Press, 1990).

Vickers, B, *In Defence of Rhetoric* (Oxford: Clarendon Press, 1998).

——, and Struever, NS, *Rhetoric and the Pursuit of Truth: Language Change in the Seventeenth and Eighteenth Centuries* (Los Angeles: William Andrews Clark Memorial Library, 1985).

Vigne, G, *Ingres*, trans. J Goodman (New York: Abbeville Press, 1995).

Warner, WB, *Reading 'Clarissa': The Struggles of Interpretation* (New Haven and London: Yale University Press, 1979).

Watson, NJ, *Revolution and the Form of the British Novel, 1790–1825* (Oxford: Clarendon Press, 1994).

Watt, I, *The Rise of the Novel: Studies in Defoe, Richardson and Fielding* (Berkeley and Los Angeles: University of California Press, 1957)

—— (ed.), *Jane Austen: A Collection of Critical Essays* (Englewood Cliffs, NJ: Prentice-Hall, 1963).

Weil, S, *Gravity and Grace* , trans E. Craufurd (London: Routledge, 1952; repr. 1992).

West, J, *Letters to a Young Lady; in which the Duties and Character of Women are Considered, Chiefly with a Reference to Prevailing Opinions*, 3 vols (London: Longman, Hurst, Rees & Orme, 1806; 4th edn, 1811).

Wittgenstein, L, *Tractatus Logico-Philosophicus* [1921], trans. DF Pears and B McGuinness (London: Routledge & Kegan Paul, 1961).

——, *On Certainty*, trans. D Paul & GEM Anscombe (Oxford: Blackwell, 1979).

Woolf, V, *A Room of One's Own* and *Three Guineas*, intr. H Lee (London: Chatto & Windus/ Hogarth Press, 1984).

Wordsworth, W, *The Poems*, ed. JO Hayden, 2 vols (Harmondsworth: Penguin, 1977).

——, *The Prelude: 1799, 1805, 1850*, ed. J Wordsworth, MH Abrams and S Gill (New York and London: WW Norton & Company, 1979).

——, *Selected Prose*, ed. John O Hayden (London: Penguin, 1988).

——, *Lyrical Ballads*, ed. RL Brett and AR Jones (London: Methuen, 1963; repr. London: Routledge, 1991).

Wotton, H, *The Elements of Architecture* (London: John Bill, 1624; repr. Amsterdam and New York: Da Capo Press and Theatrum Orbis Terrarum, 1970).

INDEX